THE DEVELOPMENT OF THE ART MARKET IN ENGLAND: MONEY AS MUSE, 1730–1900

FINANCIAL HISTORY

Series Editor: Robert E. Wright

TITLES IN THIS SERIES

1 Slave Agriculture and Financial Markets in Antebellum America: The Bank of the United States in Mississippi, 1831–1852
Richard Holcombe Kilbourne, Jr

2 The Political Economy of Sentiment: Paper Credit and the Scottish Enlightenment in Early Republic Boston, 1780–1820
Jose R. Torre

3 Baring Brothers and the Birth of Modern Finance
Peter E. Austin

4 Gambling on the American Dream: Atlantic City and the Casino Era
James R. Karmel

5 Government Debts and Financial Markets in Europe
Fausto Piola Caselli (ed.)

6 Virginia and the Panic of 1819: The First Great Depression and the Commonwealth
Clyde A. Haulman

7 Towards Modern Public Finance: The American War with Mexico, 1846–1848
James W. Cummings

8 The Revenue Imperative: The Union's Financial Policies during the American Civil War
Jane Flaherty

9 Guilty Money: The City of London in Victorian and Edwardian Culture, 1815–1914
Ranald C. Michie

10 Financial Markets and the Banking Sector: Roles and Responsibilities in a Global World
Elisabeth Paulet (ed.)

11 Argentina's Parallel Currency: The Economy of the Poor
Georgina M. Gómez

12 The Rise and Fall of the American System: Nationalism and the Development of the American Economy, 1790–1837
Songho Ha

13 Convergence and Divergence of National Financial Systems: Evidence from the Gold Standards, 1871–1971
Patrice Baubeau and Anders Ögren (eds)

14 Benjamin Franklin and the Invention of Microfinance
Bruce H. Yenawine, ed. Michele R. Costello

15 The Development of International Insurance
Robin Pearson (ed.)

16 Federal Banking in Brazil: Policies and Competitive Advantages
Kurt E. von Mettenheim

Forthcoming Titles

Camille Gutt and Postwar International Finance
Jean F. Crombois

THE DEVELOPMENT OF THE ART MARKET IN ENGLAND: MONEY AS MUSE, 1730–1900

BY
Thomas M. Bayer and John R. Page

Routledge
Taylor & Francis Group
LONDON AND NEW YORK

First published 2011 by Pickering & Chatto (Publishers) Limited

Published 2016 by Routledge
2 Park Square, Milton Park, Abingdon, Oxfordshire OX14 4RN
711 Third Avenue, New York, NY 10017, USA

First issued in paperback 2015

Routledge is an imprint of the Taylor & Francis Group, an informa business

BRITISH LIBRARY CATALOGUING IN PUBLICATION DATA

Bayer, Thomas M. (Thomas Michael), 1953–
The development of the art market in England: money as muse, 1730–1900. – (Financial history) 1. Art – Economic aspects – Great Britain – History – 18th century. 2. Art – Economic aspects – Great Britain – History – 19th century. 3. Art dealers – Great Britain – History – 18th century. 4. Art dealers – Great Britain – History – 19th century.
I. Title II. Series III. Page, John R.
709.4'1'09033-dc22

ISBN-13: 978-1-138-66130-1 (pbk)
ISBN-13: 978-1-8489-3043-8 (hbk)

Typeset by Pickering & Chatto (Publishers) Limited

CONTENTS

ACKNOWLEDGEMENTS

Our interest in the historical development of the art market dates back to the late 1970s when Thomas Bayer created a legal structure that permitted H.R. 10 (Keough) pension plans for the self-employed to acquire works of art for long-term capital gain. To receive approval by the United States Department of Labor for this concept, he analyzed three decades of auction sales. Several years later, in the early 1980s, James Clifton, then a young professor with the art department of Tulane University in New Orleans, encouraged Thomas to examine the art market and art dealers in a historical context. Since then many individuals have contributed to our investigation: artists, fellow academics, art dealers, auction house specialists, archivists, curators, museum directors, art critics and collectors. We are greatly indebted to all of them.

Special thanks go to Marilyn Brown, friend and mentor. Her encouragement and critical guidance were essential to directing and sustaining our research. Christopher Wood's expert help through the Victorian painters' world and his superb British humour made our work easier and more pleasurable. His untimely death casts the only shadow over an otherwise thoroughly enjoyable project. Jeremy Maas also is no longer with us to receive our heartfelt thanks. But his son, Rupert Maas, has continued his father's interest in and support of scholarly endeavors and deserves our acknowledgement. We would also like to thank Robert Wright for his perceptivity and Daire Carr for his supervision; both were critical in making this book possible. The suggestions of Walter Liedtke, Robert McHarg, Maria Page and Judith Wallick Page proved very constructive. Jeremy Rex-Parkes's and Lynda Mcleod's help with Christie's archives was invaluable, as was the hospitality and friendship of Rob Gray. Please accept our thanks.

We also want to thank Tulane University for two separate grants, the Research Enhancement Fund that supported our collection of the Arthur Tooth data at the Getty Research Center, and the Provost's Fund for Faculty/Student Scholarly Engagement that supported the development of our website accompanying this publication. Jessie Lingenfelter deserves special mention for her undying dedication to the creation of this website.

LIST OF FIGURES AND TABLES

Margarete, Ulrike, Dorothee, Laura, Kristen, Carys, Avery and Reily.
You are the best.
Maria. Quanto è bella, quanto è cara!
Più la vedo, e più mi piace.

INTRODUCTION

> Art follows wealth for its rich rewards.
>
> Karel van Mander (1548-1606), *Schilderboek*

> The simple truth is that capital is the nurse and governess of the arts; not always a very wise or judicious one, but an exceedingly powerful one.
>
> P. G. Hamerton, *Thoughts about Art* (1871)

These two astute remarks, though separated by nearly three hundred years, both tie the flourishing of the arts to money. Perhaps these seem rather obvious statements, because most artists need to exchange their products for either cash or goods in order to sustain their existence. However, both Karel van Mander and P. G. Hamerton assign to the arts a subordinate role. In one observation art *follows* wealth, in the other capital is the art's *nurse* and *governess*. Thus, to reap some of wealth's rich rewards art must follow the path wealth takes. However, art does not just simply follow money. Rather, the relationship between the two is reciprocal. The role of nurse implies caring and nurturing, while the role of governess suggests a formative influence. We note, too, the dates of these statements: both were made when profound changes in patronage were taking place or had already occurred in the Netherlands and England, the countries of these commentators. The traditional support of church, state and aristocracy had declined in favor of a growing middle class with increasing discretionary wealth.

This gradual replacement of church, state or aristocratic patrons by middle class customers was associated with significant changes in the production of art. In earlier days the customary relationship between artists and patrons was direct: artists fulfilled orders of the patrons. The role of capital as nurse or governess of the arts under the traditional system is obvious: the patron - church, state or aristocrat - commissioned an artist to produce a painting, of which the choices of materials, scale of work, subject, and number of objects or figures to be depicted, etc., were affected by the patron's explicit wishes and/or budgetary considerations. As long as artists followed the dictates of patrons the risk factor was quite low. Written, legally enforceable, contracts facilitated such transactions, and guild regulations provided guidelines for the cost of artistic labor.

The new open market system first began to establish itself in Flanders, the Netherlands and Florence during the late Middle Ages.[1] As anonymous customers replaced the identifiable patron, artists lost the relatively secure position of executing commissioned works. Instead, artists had to produce on speculation for a largely unknown heterogeneous mass of people of different degrees of wealth, different tastes, types and levels of education, professions and social backgrounds. Consequently, artists had to consider aspects in the manufacture of their products which hitherto had been largely irrelevant: comparing the monetary and non-monetary benefits and costs of alternative actions within a market context. Thus, a mixture of producers' subjective perception of demand and objective signals from the demand side began to exert influence over the production of art. Art became a synthesis in this dialectic between producer and consumer modified by the available exchange technology, and the anonymous and expanding market stimulated process innovations and product differentiations.

In the past decades investigations of the effects of a prevailing exchange system on artistic production, marketing and consumption have become a focus for art historical study. Francis Haskell's seminal work, *Patrons and Painters, Art and Society in Baroque Italy*,[2] illuminated the period's patronage and its components and so set the framework for other similar investigations. Cynthia and Harrison White soon followed with their examination of the institutional changes in the nineteenth-century French arts environment. Since then other art historians, social historians, economists and sociologists have taken a more expanded approach by broadening the scope of their investigations to encompass economics and the institutionalized art market.[3] Such interdisciplinary research has shown that art history benefits from a methodology that crosses traditional academic boundaries and directs its investigations towards the various components which make up the framework of an art market.[4] We are advocating therefore an approach less constrained by disciplinary custom and one that presents the market, the place where the interests of producers, middlemen, and consumers meet, as a useful alternative starting point for art historical inquiry. The resulting new insight allows us to reconsider art objects in a new, expanded context. Within a narrower historical perspective, we also contribute to the discussion on art produced in Europe, specifically in Britain during the eighteenth and nineteenth centuries when this nation's art market developed from a proto-modern stage to full maturity. Furthermore, by employing quantifications and mathematical analyses, we expand the methodological discourse on art history.

The apotheosis of art that our western cultures constructed suggests that these culturally consecrated objects must be removed from vulgar considerations of mammon. One of the greatest attributes we assign to a cultural good is to describe it as 'priceless'. Yet many gallery aficionados can confirm that such 'priceless' works usually do have a price, albeit a high one. As the dealer, Lord

Duveen, replied when Paul Mellon complained about the sum asked for Thomas Lawrence's *Pinkie*: 'When you are paying high for the priceless, you are still getting it cheap'.[5] This apotheosis has been so persuasive that we instinctively react defensively against any attempts that might undermine this sacred status – scholarly examinations not excluded. Yet the models and analyses we employ and the explanations we propose do not intend to replace the validity, in methodological terms, of more traditional investigative approaches. However, there are instances where our interpretations challenge directly or by implications those offered by others scholars.

Our evidence shows that any understanding of the art produced within the market structure of a modern consumer society must take into account the myriad implications of artists acting as producers, dealers and critics as exchange agents and market makers, auctions as exchange platforms and buyers as consumers of luxury goods with a perceived asset quality.

The notion that an art product represents the result of interactions between art producer, middleman and art consumer does not suggest that some metaphysical Hegelian force drives this process. To the contrary, what fuel the innovations in the market are the creativity, ingenuity and sensitivity of artists to distinguish themselves; the actions of middlemen to compete effectively and the personal choices of consumers to express preferences with the act of consumption. Of course, numerous other cultural, political, or religious aspects also play formative roles but rarely to the exclusion of economic factors.

For economists, the term 'market' describes a framework within which owners of property rights make contact with one another for the purpose of transferring ownership, usually for money. It is not a monolithic, tangible structure but a mechanism composed of different parts all intended to facilitate this transfer of ownership of property rights. The successful establishment and subsequent growth of the art market, therefore, is associated with an internal evolution towards an increasingly complex structure the dynamic composition of which is the result of a constant interaction between supply and demand. Economists also consider markets to 'behave' in certain ways: they send signals to participants; they regulate prices; they are subject to structural changes; and they react towards other complementary or competing markets. Thus markets are not deterministic forces but rather a complex composite of human actions based on certain subjective decisions.

Before proceeding with an overview of the different chapters, some general comments are in order. The use of quantifications produces often very exact values that are computed on the basis of relationships between different sets of variables. In our case, this exactness should best be understood as a narrow range rather than a precise number. Working with records hand-written by different individuals over the course of two centuries is inherently difficult. Different spellings of the same name, idiosyncratic abbreviations, different ways of description, ink spots, tears, and faded writing are but some of the obstacles. While we made every effort to verify our data and analyses, some errors may have occurred. We are, however, confident that the findings and our conclusions are correct.

Our story spans 200 years during which a modern art market came into existence. Of course, this development is not confined to the precise dates stated in our title, but by 1900, the London art market had become fully international and the story of its genesis comes to an end. To exemplify this progress we selected those narratives from the available abundance that best illustrate and corroborate our various quantitative analyses. Quite possibly, other scholars of the period would have chosen differently. The wealth of evidence necessitated subjective choices. We have also included in our discussion many contributions of other writers to present a reasonably comprehensive account of the current state of scholarship relevant to our topic. Most likely, we have missed some. However, such omissions are not judgmental on our part. We hope that the website associated with this publication will become a useful platform for the exchange of information, further discovery and discussion for all those who wish to contribute to the knowledge of this period.

Overview of Text

Chapter one examines the changing arts environment in the Netherlands during the sixteenth-century to introduce the methodological concepts applied later to eighteenth- and nineteenth-century Britain. As a prelude, the discussion of the Netherlandish art market will show that the later developments in England were not unique to the country but were phenomena inherent to a transforming and expanding art market. Chief among these was the emergence of professional art dealers. Therefore, this section also introduces this exchange agent to illuminate the importance of middlemen and their impact on market growth, composition and product diversity.

Since the progress of the first modern art market in Holland was interrupted towards the end of the seventeenth century, we switch location and historical time to England at the beginning of the eighteenth century when London was on the verge of becoming a center of an international art market. Our discussion of this 'proto-modern' stage identifies and analyzes the relevant building blocks and traces the developments that result in the emergence of a modern art market as these separate entities come together in a cohesive framework. Similar to the Netherlands, this process was closely linked with middlemen's activities. Stated differently, we trace an ongoing trend of commodification. The term describes here the various adaptations of any product or entity of the production, distribution, exchange, and consumption phases that improve the exchange criteria, e.g., salability, of a thing or facilitate its exchange. We also found it useful to consider 'things' be they paintings, structural art market components, or aesthetic theories as having their own biography within a given cultural system. One of the aims of this study is to trace the changes within the biographies of the 'things' that make up the art market.

Chapters two, three and four focus on the changes of the British arts environment from the beginning of the eighteenth century, when there existed no picture galleries, no museums and no places where native artists could exhibit their work, to the 1770s when the country sported numerous independently organized artists' organizations, a royally sanctioned academy and public exhibition facilities visited by tens of thousands of art enthusiasts in which the star exhibitors were not foreigners but native born Englishmen. By then, the trade in contemporary pictures and prints had developed into an enormous commercial enterprise. Artists in general had become socially accepted within the circles of 'respectable' society and art criticism had entered its early stage. Chapter two discusses the transformations in aesthetic and economic theories and discourse towards accommodating an increasingly larger public. Chapter three examines the evolution of artists' social position from lowly 'mechanics' to their acceptance among polite society, the development of artists' organizations, art marketing and dealing. Chapter four introduces the newly emerged art writer/critic as an important ally in this economic emancipation. By aiding the consumption of cultural goods, these writers performed a function essential to the continuing expansion of an art market. Furthermore, the chapter also employs our extensive auction sales data to explore the changing character of art auctions in London from their beginnings as dealer-staged, unregulated sales events where *caveat emptor* ruled to their establishment as regulated public exchanges and market reference.

Chapter five discusses the first appearance of the contemporary art dealer in eighteenth-century Britain. The evolution of picture dealing from diverse proto-professional beginnings to international enterprises was based on a gradual recognition and alignment of shared economic interests between painters and professional middlemen. An important catalyst was the reproductive print. The vast print publishing enterprises of the last quarter of the eighteenth century gave middlemen and painters the first significant opportunity to explore the benefits and pitfalls of their nascent union. The chapter closes with a look at the effects of the Napoleonic Wars on this promising yet still fragile alliance. The event resulted in a temporary collapse of the British export trade for reproductive engravings and a shift of dealers' attention away from contemporary British paintings to more profitable arbitrage opportunities involving old masters. However, as the supply of such works dwindled and became corrupted with fakes, middlemen's interests focused again on native artists. In economic terms, this change marks the onset of the mid Victorian art boom.

Chapter six examines the changes in patronage as old and new wealth shifted from collecting Old Masters to buying works by living artists. This switch in consumption habits was associated with a noticeable increase in dealer activities. Therefore, we revisit the earlier theme of institutionalized art dealing and focus on the *modus operandi* of the now established Victorian picture dealer. A case study of two years of business activities of the prominent dealer Arthur Tooth provides unprecedented insight into the operations of a typical mid-Victorian art dealing enterprise. The data show that the institutionalized trade contributed to a far greater extent to the increase in stylistic variety and innovation that occurred during this period than conventional art history hitherto acknowledges.

Chapter seven focuses on mass-produced reproductive prints and professionally managed commercial art exhibitions, the two foremost methods by which dealers disseminated an unprecedented number of art products. We discuss specific publishing and exhibition ventures as examples of the scale and sophistication of these enterprises and revisit the increasingly important art writer whose role had expanded correspondingly to dealers' growing presence. The very exchange system of art defined the changing parameters of art writers' activities within the context of a common goal of increasing the consumption of art products.

Chapter eight investigates the meteoric rise of the London art auction firm of James Christie. The dwindling number of different art auction firms that were active in the market during the eighteenth century gradually resulted in a near monopoly of this one firm by the end of the Napoleonic war period. As the market turned away from old paintings, Christie's dominance enabled the firm to establish itself as the central exchange platform for contemporary paintings. To that end and in close cooperation with dealers, the auction firm facilitated certain market making and regulatory activities to check market volatility.

Chapter nine discusses the different effects of this dealer-centered market on paintings produced under such conditions. The changes that differentiate nineteenth-century British pictures from their eighteenth century predecessors can be explained, in addition to the traditional social causes, by the appropriation of the art market by institutionalized dealers for the purpose of selling art products to primarily middle class consumers for domestic use. The paintings we discuss can be viewed on the website described below.

The decline of the mid-Victorian art boom is the topic of chapter ten. The 'Golden Age' came to an end in Britain mainly due to the success of, and consequent economic dependency on, mass-marketed prints and the associated dealer-organized exhibitions. Confronted with the new medium of photography, rampant copyright violations and adverse changes in copyright laws as well as the availability of cheap substitutes, the expensive steel engraving could no longer compete. Further pressures on the existing market structure resulted from new aesthetic theories that arose partially as a consequence of the market's demand for innovation and undermined the worn product characteristics of Victorian painting. The Etching Revival movement is discussed as a paradigm of art producers proactively redesigning their products and successfully challenging prevailing aesthetics. We also examine in greater detail the history of the Grosvenor Gallery as a model for innovative competition in art marketing that is both symptom and agent of change. A similar role was played by dealers from the Continent who came to England hoping to profit in London's buoyant art market. Moreover, contemporary British painting was again threatened by a resurgence of interest in old master works which, by comparison to works by living artists, were undervalued.

Chapter eleven presents a summary and relates our findings to the present art market. The commoditization we traced throughout the preceding chapters continues to shape the arts environment. Aesthetic theories and their associated art products have multiplied paralleling the market's expansion; exhibitions have become enormous in scope; dealers have become even more crucial to the arts environment; critics further entrenched themselves; a near duopoly emerged in the international auction market; and numerous investment art funds, employing varying business models have become major players. Art market historians offer their services to art investors, and even academic art history, studio art and the international museum community have become an integral part of this multi-billion pound international market for cultural goods.

We hope to dispel the persistent prejudice that commoditization is inherently damaging to the aesthetic merit and quality of art products. Rather, we argue for a more balanced view that recognizes that artists, dealers and collectors come together voluntarily in a tripartite market for the purpose of exchanging property rights. Their respective decisions and actions to that purpose serve, one can assume, the facilitation of that exchange and are, for the most part, based on rational choices and, in turn, influence production, distribution, exchange, and consumption. The product of the various dialectics between these producers, middlemen, and consumers of art respectively can be good or bad by whatever subjective standards one wishes to apply. This is not to suggest that the art market as an exchange mechanism is 'perfect' and experiences none of the symptoms commonly associated with market failure. Such problems did transpire. During our period, 'bubbles' occurred and incidents of information asymmetry impeded transactions. Yet in such instances, market participants managed, for the most part, to turn potential failure into opportunities. Markets are, after all, in the words of the Austrian economist, Joseph Schumpeter a 'perpetual innovative whirl'.[6] The art market is no exception.

Description of database

Many of our conclusions are based on statistical and econometric analyses of a database composed of information largely compiled by Algernon Graves and George Redford, which lists 42,117 sales of paintings taking place in England from 17 March 1709 to 19 December 1913.[7] These data were verified and augmented by relevant information from catalogues in the London archives of Christie's.[8] Graves' *Auction Sales* has all auction transactions involving an artist whose work sold for £100 or more at some time during the time period covered. This is therefore not a complete account of all paintings sold during the entire period. We therefore constructed a separate database derived from Christie's auction catalogues that contain all pictures sale held at Christie's from 1840 to 1885, the time frame during which the mid-Victorian art boom occurred. Tests on both sets of data showed that Graves recorded approximately 10% of all paintings sold during this period with a bias towards the more valuable works.

Since the information provided by Graves is often incomplete for the period from 1709 to 1740 and a relatively small number of transactions are recorded post 1909, we truncated the data to sales from 1740 to 1909 for the various analyses. Table I.1 gives a summary statistics for this database. The total value of all sales was £11,380,004.

Table I.1: Overall Statistics for the Transactions.

	N	Mean	Median	Minimum	Maximum
Price (£)	34,797	327	158	0.4	24,250
Length (in.)	17,057	30	25	1	303
Width (in.)	17,058	29	25	1	374
Size (in.2)	17,055	1,115	650	1	54,540
Picture date	5,481	1841	1862	1463	1907

Graves' records are usually used for provenance research, as they describe under the alphabetically ordered artists' names the sales of their works. Each transaction lists the date of sale, the auction house conducting the sale, name of the seller, lot number, picture title, date, medium, size, buyer's name, and auction price. The resulting database contains paintings by 1,837 different artists; 3,890 different sellers; 3,551 different buyers; and 33,266 different paintings sold by 90 separate auction houses. Furthermore, there were 2,380 transactions involving 2,055 paintings that sold more than once during this period. Table I.2 gives a summary of the transactions by these categories. The significance of these results is discussed in later chapters of the book. One particular observation shows that the median price paid by dealers (£205) was higher than the amount paid by other buyers, except for institutions (£525). The higher price paid by institutions indicates the importance of the works purchased for major museums. The higher price paid by dealers over and above the prices paid by artists (£105), the middle class (£116), and the upper class (£151) indicates that dealers were not just using their superior knowledge to take advantage of sellers and other participants by purchasing bargains and paying less. Indeed, the data reveal that the dealer was a much more important participant in this market than just a bargain hunter.

Table I.2: Statistics by Category.

	Number of Transactions	Number with Price	Median Price (£)	Number with Size	Median Size (in.^{2})	Total Value (£)
Panel A: Types of Buyers						
Artist	47	47	105	6	759	9,701
Bought-in	2,182	2,150	149	288	1,033	602,980
Dealer	16,727	16,686	205	9,766	587	7,069,830
Institution	85	85	525	21	520	88,296
Middle class	19,732	15,039	116	6,775	696	3,346,864
Upper class	795	790	151	199	750	262,334
Panel B: Types of Sellers						
Artist	2,903	2,112	39	637	690	25,546
Dealer	1,478	1,311	142	611	1,008	341,866
Institution	176	71	147	28	399	14,132
Middle class	29,064	26,133	168	13,351	612	8,622,283
Upper class	5,947	5,170	168	2,428	736	2,156,177
Panel C: Gender Effects						
Artist, Female	350	301	210	178	645	147,980
Artist, Male	39,218	34,496	158	16,877	650	11,232,024
Buyer, Female	51	51	100	18	831	9,803
Buyer, Male	39,517	34,746	158	17,037	648	11,370,200
Seller, Female	1,746	1,653	137	655	612	528,059
Seller, Male	37,822	33,144	161	16,400	655	10,851,945
Panel D: Art Subjects						
Animal	2,290	2,124	158	1,023	713	635,131
Genre	8,065	7,275	179	3,638	546	2,395,497
History	1,547	1,326	152	550	1,008	414,657
Interior	356	311	158	157	374	102,611
Landscape	12,519	11,614	179	6,015	486	3,884,493
Marine	1,210	1,125	194	548	570	381,159
Mythology	1,470	1,024	142	423	1,160	339,545
Portrait	7,481	6,533	105	3,100	750	2,153,356
Religious	4,045	2,942	142	1,274	832	959,368
Still Life	576	523	158	327	252	114,188

Unlike Bredius' inventories or the analyses undertaken by John M. Montias or Alan Chong,[9] these records contain far more information than a simple listing of someone's possessions at a specific moment in time. Rather, the data show a work of art at the moment of change of ownership. Such information can reveals trends, fashions, consumption habits and their changes over time, as well as long-forgotten collectors, dealers' activities over time, statistics concerning values of art, changes in the definition of art as a consumer good and the consequences of these changes.

Our data also allow us to explore the effect of different characteristics of the artist or the painting to the price. Results of our regressions appear as Table I.3.[10]

Table I.3: Price Estimates for All Artists.

	OLS Estimate Total R-Square 0.1463		Garch Estimate Total R-Square 0.4347	
	Coefficient	t-statistic	Coefficient	t-statistic
Constant	(26.543)	(28.886)	(0.583)	(13.724)
Living (vs. Deceased)	(0.074)	(2.397)	(0.064)	(1.646)
Painting (vs. Drawing) *	0.817	23.507	0.642	13.859
Art Subjects vs. Genre				
Animal **	(0.272)	(5.728)	(0.208)	(4.113)
History **	(0.576)	(9.255)	(0.423)	(7.637)
Interior	0.053	0.480	(0.008)	(0.077)
Landscape	0.009	0.295	(0.020)	(0.676)
Marine **	(0.181)	(2.961)	(0.127)	(1.976)
Mythology **	(0.538)	(7.566)	(0.354)	(5.268)
Portrait **	(0.301)	(7.948)	(0.205)	(5.794)
Religious **	(0.479)	(10.194)	(0.409)	(9.119)
Still Life	0.151	1.939	0.034	0.369
Contemporary (vs. Old Master)	0.232	7.957	0.049	1.463
English (vs. Continental) **	(0.554)	(23.628)	(0.473)	(16.615)
Year	0.014	28.000		

* Significantly more than the alternative in both regressions

** Significantly less than the alternative in both regressions

The first sets of numbers are the ordinary least squares results (OLS). However, the final, year, variable is highly significant, indicating that prices were rising over this period. This general price rise makes interpreting other results problematic because other characteristics of paintings may have become more frequent over time and thus may appear to contribute to higher price when the real contributor is the general price increase.

Figure I.1 gives the smoothed average prices over time of four different types of artists, Old Master Continental, Old Master English, Contemporary Continental, and Contemporary English. The general trend upward is apparent.

The standard econometric correction to this autocorrelation problem is called Garch. Thus, the Garch regression coefficients and their t-statistics appear in the two columns to the right of the OLS estimates. These results allow us to draw the following conclusions:

1. Paintings sold for significantly more than drawings. This result is not surprising, but it must be included for the effect of paintings vs. drawings to be extracted and not interfere with the other conclusions.
2. Genre, Interior, Landscape, and Still Life paintings sold for prices that were not statistically significantly different. However, Animal, History, Marine, Mythological, Portraits, and Religious paintings all sold for statistically lower prices than Genre paintings.
3. Contemporary artists and Old Master artists sold at prices that were not statistically different from each other.
4. English artists sold for significantly less than did Continental artists.

Website

A Tulane University website, artmarket.tulane.edu, provides virtually all of the images referred to in this study. The website is an integral extension of the book because the text has no illustrations of paintings. Moreover, an additional wiki website hosts interactions with the outside world. Our database includes artists, dealers, auction houses, buyers, and sellers of whom often little is known. The wiki provides a medium for scholars, students, and general readers, to update information on these individuals and businesses with results of their own research, experience or family histories. The website of images and the MediaWiki with links to discussions are the electronic media linked to the publication of the book. Any feedback from users of these websites will be used to improve the sites. In progress is an interactive database of the art market transactions utilized in the research leading up to this book.

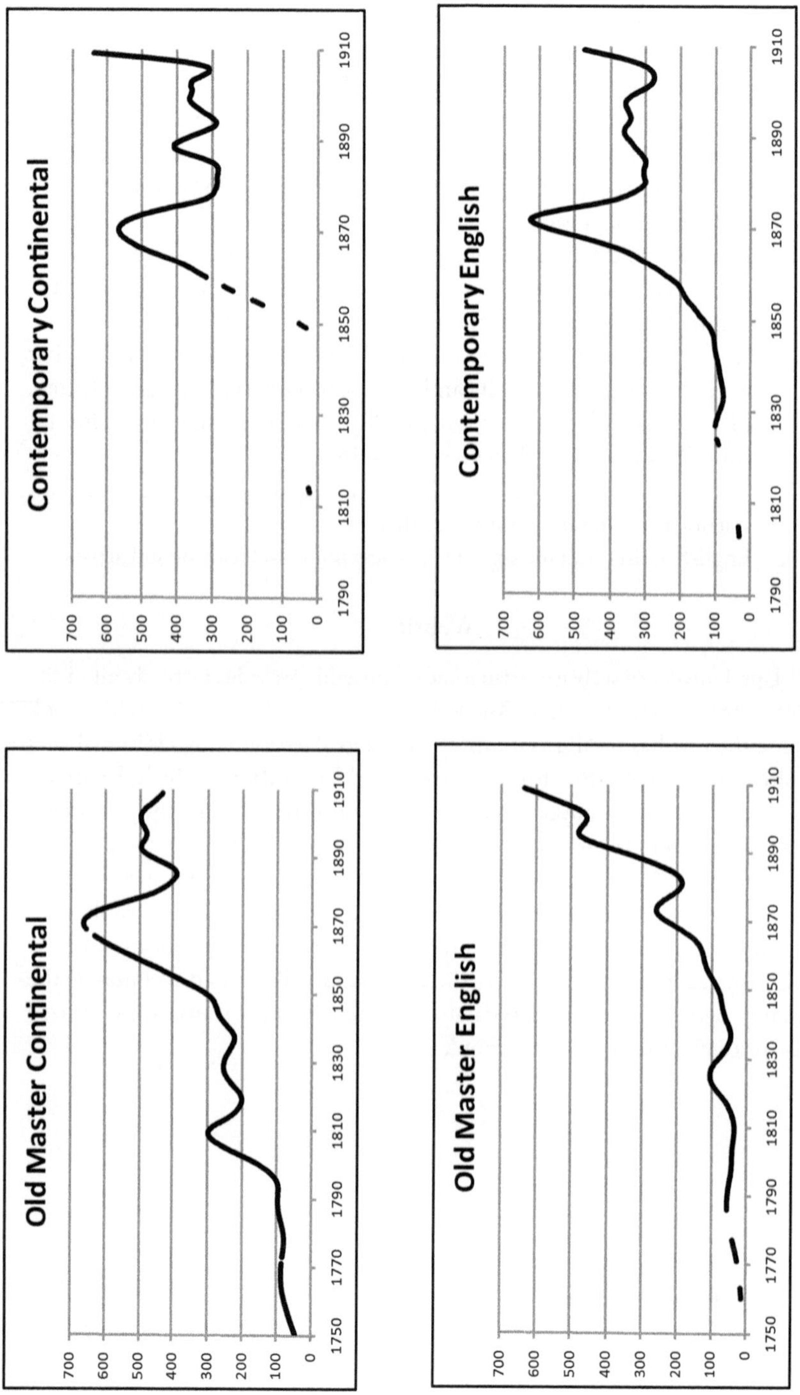

Figure I.1: Smoothed Average Prices in Pounds by Art Code.

1 THE EARLY STAGES: FROM THE NETHERLANDS TO GREAT BRITAIN

The Netherlands

An immediate consequence of the system of anonymous patronage in the Netherlands in the sixteenth century was a process innovation in marketing. Untying the production of art from marketing improved the effectiveness of exchange and, as a result, a modern art market came into existence. Separately, production and marketing became more efficient internally, in their interaction with each other and with other markets.

On the supply side, art producers adopted cost-reducing measures, such as switching from panel to canvas painting: canvas was cheaper, easier to prepare, lighter in weight, and less sensitive to climate changes.[1] Division of labour resulted in specialization in subjects, copying, formula painting and mechanical repetition of designs for workshop production.[2] Paintings, on average, decreased in size: smaller paintings were better suited for the urban residences of the new patrons, and sellers could display a larger number of selections, thereby increasing the opportunities for sales. Market considerations were also responsible for the outpouring of engravings, published in large editions and sold inexpensively to the general population. Specific stylistic changes, such as the adoption by certain artists of a more monochromatic execution and the popularity of landscapes or grisailles were further manifestations of producers' responses to changing market conditions.[3]

Process innovation in marketing led to the spread of art fairs, officially sanctioned art auctions, art lotteries and, ultimately, by the end of the fifteenth century, to the establishment of professionally operated art galleries.[4] The gradual institutionalization of specialized art merchants brought its own dynamics into the equation: the profit-motivated art dealer became the main vessel by which the market sent its signals to both the demand and supply sides.[5] However, by passing through middlemen, these signals were subject to modifications that reflected these dealers' economic considerations. Consequently, their interests affected both producers and consumers of art.

The extent of middlemen's influence over consumption habits and taste of art buyers on the one hand and the formal appearance of artists' products on the other is difficult to gauge. We will employ a model to help examine conceptually the question of middlemen's impact on the arts environment. The specific model we apply derives from an observation made by the anthropologist Igor Kopytoff that:

> the exchange function of every economy appears to have a built-in force that drives the exchange system toward the greatest degree of commoditization that the exchange technology permits ... In large scale and monetarized societies, the existence of a sophisticated exchange technology fully opens the economy to swamping by commoditization ... The internal logic of exchange itself pre-adapts all economies to seize upon the new opportunities.[6]

Apparently, markets evolve, due to internal dynamics, towards maximizing their function as exchange systems. These markets – or rather, the individuals who voluntarily engaged in exchange – seek out new opportunities, and also act and react in a manner that, in their subjective opinions, optimizes these conditions. As a result, commoditization occurs.[7]

Applied to the transformation of the arts environment in sixteenth-century Netherlands, Kopytoff's observation offers several explanations for those changes and identifies specific developments. The shift of patronage from the social elite to the middle classes resulted in new opportunities that the participants in the art economy seized. Consequently, the desire of these market players to promote exchange – that is, the 'internal logic of exchange' – drove the exchange system towards the greatest degree of commoditization permitted by the extant exchange technology and occasioned changes to improve it. The types of product innovation that aimed to improve production efficiencies were part of this trend. Similarly, the divisions of labour within the exchange system and the guilds' reaction to them also fall under the rubric of commoditization.[8] The emergence of intermediaries as exchange facilitators was, therefore, necessary for the expansion of the art market. The development into the specialized, professional art dealer was the next logical step.[9]

Professionalization came about gradually. Initially, a wide variety of individuals engaged in buying and selling of art works: painters themselves; frame-makers; second-hand dealers, often women called 'uijtdraegsters', operating at the lower-quality end of the market; inn and tavern keepers; and even some wine merchants.[10] During the first half of the seventeenth century as the art market experienced an expansion faster than the rest of the economy of the northern Netherlands, specialized dealers became more common.[11]

Generally, these dealers' function in this market was to bring about and improve the flow of art goods from producer to consumer, and the demand for their services was positively associated with the degree of artists' specialization and the variegation of consumer tastes. Self-interest tied their actions inextricably to improving the efficiency of the market and reducing market barriers. They challenged guild regulations pertaining to selling art or establishing art lotteries, began art auctions and, ultimately, set up fixed location retail art galleries.[12] The more effective dealers were, the more important they became as links between artists and collectors, thereby increasingly isolating producers from end consumers.

A by-product of this gradual loss of contact was a role change: art buyers ceased to be patrons of one or several artists and became instead customers of dealers. Correspondingly, dealers assumed the function of patrons and, consequently, became the hub of the market. As their influence grew and the dividends of wealth became increasingly centred in their hands, art followed their lead for wealth's 'rich rewards'. Dealers as personifications of the abstract exchange function were the very agents that drove the art market towards the greatest possible degree of commoditization within the available exchange technology. Therefore, middlemen's behaviour and general market efficiency influenced art production towards improving the products' marketability. Similarly, the dialectic between seller and buyer indicates that middlemen must have influenced the consumption habits and tastes of their customers.[13]

This economic approach offers an additional explanation for the transformation of the arts during this period. Many of the earlier mentioned formal and stylistic changes and variety in the appearance of pictures during this period are attributable, to varying extents, to market forces manifested by professional art dealers.

Inventory analyses show that the fortunes of living painters during Holland's Golden Age began a steady decline towards the end of the first half of the seventeenth century. Evidently, the developing art market was quite susceptible to changes in economic climate and, burdened by 'structural overproduction', failed.[14] The economic stagnation around mid-century, the catastrophic war with France that started in 1672, a tendency toward a more unequal income and wealth distribution and the growing trend of collectors to acquire paintings by old masters rather than contemporary works, all contributed to the market's contraction. Demand declined, as did the number of specialists. Once again, artists had to depend more on traditional patronage than the open market.[15]

Johann van Gool, writing 100 years later, claimed that this decline had intensified due to speculation and corrupt activities of dealers.[16] The application of a supply/demand model to this observation shows how speculative activities by dealers in contemporary art can lead to a downturn of the market. When contemporary paintings are perceived as investment goods, purchasers acquire art in anticipation of higher prices and for the purpose of selling it at some future date for a higher amount. If dealers speculate, their activities withhold from the market part of the regular supply of contemporary works. Therefore, *ceteris paribus,* prices increase until an equilibrium reflects this new supply and demand relationship. However, once this rise in prices satisfies the expectations of speculators, they put these previously withheld paintings back on the market. This sudden supply increase will affect a price decline even if demand stays constant. As prices decline, purchasers wait to buy in anticipation of future price decreases, thus adding pressure to an already downward moving market by reducing demand. Then investors may resort to panic selling further pushing prices down. As prices continue to decline, artists must reduce or even stop production. If paintings were strictly luxury goods, lower prices would eventually result in increased demand; however, if they are also treated as investment goods, disappointed investors may leave that market altogether. The above mentioned trend of collectors to acquire Old Master paintings over contemporary works indicates that part of this market's decline may well have been due to the actions of disappointed speculators.

Great Britain

By the eighteenth century, the Netherlands's economic fortune declined in favour of another nation whose growing prosperity initially rivalled that of the Dutch but soon overtook it. The centre of European economic activity had begun to shift across the Channel to England. By 1700, London, with a population exceeding 550,000 people, had become the largest and richest European city. The number of individuals there with sufficient wealth and leisure had expanded to a level where the satisfaction of their cultural aspirations became professionalized. As van Mander had opined, art soon followed this new wealth.[17]

Art patronage was no novelty in England. The Reformation had resulted in a redistribution of wealth, and many of the beneficiaries conspicuously displayed their fortunes by building grandiose houses with chambers and halls that needed decoration. During the seventeenth century, as the 'grand tour' was becoming fashionable, young upper-class Englishmen crossed the Channel, and their travels exposed them to the consumption habits of their Continental peers. True, John Evelyn's comment that it was an 'ordinary thing to find a common farmer lay out two-or-three thousand pounds in this commodity [paintings]'[18] may well be hyperbole. Nonetheless, the impact of the conspicuous display of wealth and artistic patronage found in seventeenth-century Europe on impressionable young men coming from an island with still lingering iconoclastic tendencies[19] and little native tradition of painting must have been extraordinary.[20] As the 'grand tour' became culturally institutionalized in England, some tangible evidence had to be shown as testimony for the journey's successful accomplishment. Already under Charles I (1625–49), it had become fashionable for the elite to own works of art and promote spending large sums of money on building one's collection.[21] This trend somewhat continued under Charles II (1660–85).[22] The passage of the Navigation Act in 1660[23] stimulated the British economy, and the building boom resulting from the devastating fire of London in 1666 helped divert new wealth into art.[24] Then, during the reign of William III and Mary II (1689–1702) enterprising Dutch picture dealers began bringing collections of paintings to England for sale at auction.[25] In the Treaty of Westminster in 1674, Britain finally had made peace with the Netherlands, and Dutch merchants took advantage of greatly relaxed enforcement of import rules concerning paintings to explore and expand this new market. By the 1680s these laws appear to have been entirely ignored, thus further reducing import trade barriers.[26] Moreover, William III's Dutch origin and the English/Dutch alliance against France from 1689–1712 must have yielded additional benefits to the trade between the two countries. Estimates suggest that somewhere between 300 to 500 paintings were imported annually from Europe into London during the last forty years of the century.[27] Contemporary sources confirm that dealers and owners of art on the Continent knew that the English were prepared to pay high prices; furthermore, their knowledge of art was thought to be generally less than their enthusiasm for collecting. Consequently, and not surprisingly, many of the imported canvases were of dubious authenticity. The unsavoury image created by such unscrupulous business practices was a frequent source of gossip on, and condemnation of, the art trade throughout the eighteenth and well into the nineteenth century with far reaching consequences.[28]

While imports thrived, the native arts in England were in an abysmal state at the dawning of the eighteenth century.[29] In his chapter on painters in the reign of King William, Walpole laments that 'This prince, like most of those in our annals, contributed nothing to the advancement of arts'. He describes the subsequent reign of Queen Anne (1702–14) as 'illustrated by heroes, poets, and authors [though it] was not equally fortunate in artists'.[30] Numerous reasons were given. John Pye, in his *Patronage of British Art*, published in 1845, cites a newspaper article reproduced in *Gentleman's Magazine* in 1737 in which the writer laments that Great Britain, unlike France, offered no annual prizes to her native artists.[31] Writing in 1753, Rouquet complains

> Wherever commerce flourishes, wealth is one of those things that are [*sic*] mostly considered; and as the arts are not the high road to wealth, consequently less value is set upon them. And here I may observe ... that the arts are not made an object of the public attention in England; for there is no foundation or institution in their favor ...[32]

This situation was exacerbated by the fact that Dutch artists had increasingly migrated to England since mid-century. Between the 1650s and 1700, approximately 116 painters from the Netherlands visited or emigrated to England. This flow increased after Charles II openly welcomed immigrants from Holland with his declaration of March 1672. Their production may have added between

118,000 to 237,000 most likely qualitatively superior works to the locally available stock.[33] The English market, centralized in London and less developed and regulated than those on the Continent, presented a 'rare instance of a perfect natural experiment without any inherited institutional structure in the form, for example, of guilds or other restrictions on sales'.[34] Better trained and more popular, these Continental artists worsened the already tenuous situation of native English painters. Pye mentions a letter published in the the *Adventurer* on 5 December 1752, in which an artist grumbled:

> I am, at present, but an humble journeyman sign-painter in Harp Alley; for, though the ambitions of my parents designed that I should emulate the immortal touches of a Raphael or a Titian, yet the want of taste among my countrymen, and their prejudice against every artist who is a native, have degraded me into the miserable necessity, as Shaftesbury says, 'of illustrating prodigies in fairs, and adorning heroic sign-posts'.[35]

Thus, foreign competition and imported old pictures, mainly cheap copies made in the art centres of the Continent specifically for the English market,[36] much impeded the development of local talent. Lack of support for, and even outright hostility towards, native artists by dealers further envenomed this situation.[37] Ironically, at the same time, collecting in general was growing in popularity and scope, and the period witnessed the emergence of a regular trade in works of art.[38] These buoyant conditions attracted local merchants and fostered, in the words of Pye, 'instead of artists, skillful dealers',[39] who put their marketing talents to work, organizing art auctions, lotteries and raffles.[40]

The English art market was, therefore, in a state of tension at the beginning of the eighteenth century. Wealth's 'rich rewards' were unequally distributed to the detriment of native English painters. Consequently, the economic history of art in England during the century exemplifies a process of native art producers competing for their share in an expanding market. For that purpose, painters had to find new opportunities without the supportive and flexible guild structure that existed in the Netherlands and in competition with an established trade in older pictures and cheap locally produced or imported copies.[41] During this period the nascent development of the infrastructure that makes up the framework of a modern art market occurred in Great Britain.

The Infrastructural Components

The relationships between the components that make up a market – production, distribution, exchange and consumption – are fluid. One of the built-in functions of the exchange system is to reduce barriers and ease tensions that might impede the flow of goods through the market or hinder the system's ongoing commoditization. The market, therefore, in an abstract sense and/or as personified by individuals acting as go-betweens, influences consumers as well as producers and simultaneously adjusts itself to improve its exchange capability within the specific economy it serves. This influence, as we mentioned in our earlier discussion of the Netherlandish market, goes beyond the manner in which art goods change hands, but also affects art theory, subject matter, techniques and styles.

The development of an exchange system is associated with the degree of progress of the available exchange technology applicable to a specific market. In London, the high density of consumption due to the city's size, wealth, and heterogeneity promoted among producers the development of new commercial techniques to capture the highly concentrated demand, stimulate it further and direct it into specific channels. This process 'marks the revolutionary stage in the development of a modern consumer society as we know it today'.[42] There is much debate about the phenomenon of the 'Birth of a Consumer Society'.[43] Did it happen? Why did it happen? How did it happen? Was it a revolution or an evolution? Those are but a few of the questions on which there is no consensus. Nevertheless, most social and economic historians of this period agree that significant changes in consumption were taking place. Innovative entrepreneurship, demographic changes, rising wages, expansion of the press, and a favourable intellectual environment are contributing factors.

The art market was ripe for commercial exploitation in Britain. In many respects, it was at a similar stage of development as the Netherlands' art market had been some 150 years or so earlier. Changes in demand were transforming the arts environment while painters and entrepreneurs sought novel ways to reach this new audience composed, as in the Netherlands, of an expanding and increasingly affluent middle class.

Associated with such middle-class growth was the country's urbanization. The urban environment was the seedbed for the large-scale development of professions, services and trades that customarily define this class. Towns are a prerequisite for tapping into the anonymous demand represented by this heterogeneously composed social group. England, from the eighteenth-century on, was one of the most urbanized nations in the world: by the end of the century, 31 per cent of the population resided in urban centres with a population of over 2,500. With their retail shops, newspapers, libraries and scientific societies, towns functioned as civilizing agents through which art and cultural goods could be disseminated to the public. Of particular impact was the phenomenal expansion of fixed-location retailing without which the distribution of cultural products would have been significantly impeded and the products less diversified. Specialized commercial art galleries did not yet exist in provincial England, but the 'urban Renaissance' consisted, in part, of countless private and public building projects, the decoration of which must have benefited native art production.[44]

Expanding markets for consumer goods are generally associated with an expansion of the printed media and its use as direct and indirect advertising. Like the Netherlands, England enjoyed a relatively high literacy rate. Exact numbers are difficult to ascertain. The customary test – the ability to sign one's name – by itself, is not an accurate indicator of literacy. Nevertheless, marriage certificates show that the eighteenth century witnessed in Britain a significant increase in literacy among the urban population, while the rural sector seems to have regressed.[45]

More telling than such statistics is the unprecedented growth in book and newspaper/magazine publishing. Advertisements for books were the largest single group among contemporary newspaper ads, a category that itself experienced tremendous growth.[46] For most of the century, printing and publishing of books occurred under the same roof. Therefore, the increase in numbers of provincial and London printers is a useful indicator of the expansion of the publishing industry. In 1724, there existed seventy-five printers in London and twenty-eight in the provinces; by mid-century, their numbers had swelled to an impressive 128 and 120 respectively.[47]

The story of the newspaper publishing industry was similar. At the beginning of the century there was not a single newspaper while at the end 244 different provincial newspapers were published, containing domestic and foreign news, essays on manners, fashionable conduct, instructions for connoisseurship, poems, serial books, etc. The largest amount of space was occupied by its main revenue source, advertisements placed by London merchants. This not only confirms the rising importance of the provincial markets but also a growing demand for consumer and luxury goods.[48] The London daily press, similar in content, boasted by mid-century weekly sales of around 100,000 issues; each issue of magazines like the *Spectator* may have passed through as many as twenty hands.[49] Also, an increasing number of magazines was available, featuring exclusively such topics as conditions of life, curiosities, essays about manners, social morality, connoisseurship, improvement, etc., rather than politics or religion. The appeal of the most successful daily, the *Spectator*, is usually credited to its special style of literature involving talking to the public – essentially the middle class – about itself.[50] The press, thus, greatly contributed to the advancement of an appreciation for the arts in the fertile field of middle-class cultural aspirations. Regular reviews of art exhibitions were uncommon in the early decades as such events were rare. However, mixed in with articles on opera, theatre, literature, or polite conduct, readers of the *Spectator* could find the occasional essay promoting the enjoyment of paintings, the announcement of an art auction, or the visit to a private picture gallery.[51] Moreover, booksellers and publishers not only employed artists directly but, as a trade group, they were chiefly responsible for the initial mass dissemination of reproductive prints without which the mid-Victorian art boom would not have occurred.

The increase in numbers of literary products favoured primarily authors. Writers, like painters, at the beginning of the century, depended on aristocratic subsidy. A growing middle class – fundamentally the market for writers' products – provided authors, like painters, with the opportunity to abandon traditional patronage and compete in an open market. Over the course of the century, painters adopted some of the methods of the publishing industry, such as distribution and sales by subscription, to reach the same audience. Writers succeeded earlier and partially paved the way for painters: the structural similarities of both industries underscore the close connection between these two cultural products. The offer by the publishing house of Murray in 1813 to Byron of 1,000 guineas for the copyrights of 'The Giaour' and 'Bride of Abydos', and the £3,000 Longman paid in 1814 to Thomas Moore for the rights to a poem, anticipated the huge fees paid to mid-Victorian painters for the publishing rights of some of their paintings.[52] Similarly, the eighteenth-century magazine *Review*, which was entirely devoted to literature and science,[53] was a forerunner of the Victorian *Art Journal* or the *Athenaeum*, the specialized art magazines whose contribution to the mid-Victorian art boom was crucial.

Unlike most products of the publishing industry, however, art is classified as a luxury good. Consumption requires that the purchasers possess some surplus capital beyond the basic needs of food, clothing and shelter. On that higher level, the perception of an inherent asset value may place the consumption of certain types of art in the category of autonomous spending, that is, spending unaffected by the size of income, but by other things, such as optimism about the future.[54] Whatever the case may be, the development of a country's art market from infancy to maturity requires optimally a steady expansion of the general economy. Over most of the eighteenth and nineteenth centuries, Britain fulfilled this condition as its economy, throughout the period, enjoyed extraordinary wealth and growth.

At the start of the eighteenth century, England was already a rich country by the standards of the time. Although the population was still predominantly rural, the substantial urbanization, led by the growth of London with its 11 per cent share of the population,[55] fueled further industrial and commercial activity. While the majority of the population was still poor, the economy produced considerable surplus above basic subsistence needs, with much of that surplus benefiting those in the top 10 per cent or so of the income distribution.[56] Included in this 10 per cent were large sections of the urban professional and merchant population. Within these 200 years also falls the Industrial Revolution, usually placed between 1760 and 1840, when the country began to experience the fundamental redeployment of resources away from agriculture.[57] Even before this, the economy had already steadily expanded at an accelerating rate. Moreover, the percentage of the total population of the occupational groups usually associated with the middle classes grew from 38 per cent to nearly 50 per cent, while their share of the overall income distribution increased from 50 to 60 per cent throughout the eighteenth century, and real income rose steadily until the onset of the Edwardian period.[58]

The growth of Britain's economy was also associated with another revolution, a financial one that preceded the industrial one and without which the latter may not have happened. It began when William III ascended the throne in 1689 and brought with him his Dutch financial advisors. These gentlemen, spearheaded by Bishop Gilbert Burnet of Salisbury, introduced the sophisticated financial tools of the Netherlands, which had been fundamental to that country's economic growth, particularly to the spread of retail trade and commercial fairs.[59] These innovations found fertile ground. For some time, England, like the Netherlands, had been among the beneficiaries of a series of forced relocations of the international mercantile elite due mainly to religious reasons and wars. Now settled in England, these merchants had connections in place and trading habits established that would reap immediate benefits from certain financial innovations.[60] Chiefly among those were negotiable foreign and local bills of exchange; transferable shares in corporations that were traded in a reliable secondary market; and governmental issued perpetual annuities free of default risk. Consequently, between 1688 and 1695 eighty-six new joint-stock companies were formed and the combined worth of all English joint-stock companies increased fivefold in the subsequent twenty-two years.[61] Therefore, from the formation of the Bank of England in 1694, to the spread of provincial banking starting in the 1770s, to the legal regulation of the Bank of England notes in 1844, the development of the financial environment was an engine of growth not just for the economy at large, but also for the arts. Trading in paintings on a large scale requires a monetized society with sufficient resources of regulated currency to transfer property rights of expensive moveable goods. Particularly the early import-driven art market of London must have benefited from a reliable system of international bills of exchange. Similarly, local sales of art likely benefited from local bills of exchange that were superior to the old-fashioned bill obligatory. Furthermore, for the market in inexpensive reproductions to reach mid-nineteenth century levels, monetization had to have trickled down even to the lower rungs of the social ladder. By then, a well-established network of intermediaries provided access to the nation's financial markets and their products.[62]

England was also unique in that throughout the entire period under examination the island enjoyed relative internal peace. Incidents of social unrest occurred, but the riots surrounding the Wilkes affair in 1763 and 1769, the Gordon Riots of 1780, the Luddite activity in 1811 to 1817, or the Chartist reform movement of 1838 to 1840 did not disrupt the social and economic fabric of England as the French Revolutionary and Napoleonic Wars (1792–1815) or the near European-wide revolutions of 1848 did the Continent. Neither was Britain victim to the destructive effects of war on its native soil. English troops were certainly involved in widespread and long-term military campaigns, but they all occurred in someone else's yard. While a supply/demand model suggests that the destruction of art due to war or Iconoclasm sends signals for replacement to the market, the overall ill effects on structural resources disrupt, at least temporarily, the efficiency of the market. The English art market was able to reach maturity by mid-nineteenth century, without having suffered any setbacks caused by the ruination of its infrastructure.

The effects of an unimpeded development of the nation's economy and its unparalleled wealth were among the chief reasons behind the fact that England was a center of the international art market throughout the entire two hundred years under examination.

Furthermore, in the case of Britain, the composition of the art market is quantifiable. England was a trading nation, the workshop for the world and a nation of shopkeepers. Keeping records, be they of inventories or transactions, is a characteristic of economies that rely heavily on domestic and international trade. For this study, we are indebted to the records preserved by George Redford, Algernon Graves, the art dealing firms of Agnew and Arthur Tooth as well as the superbly maintained archive of Christie's and its staff. Their painstaking record keeping work significantly facilitates any investigation of the English art market.

Towards the Public

> The English Painters have one obstacle to surmount, which equally retards the progress of their abilities, and of their fortune. They have a set of men to contend with, whose profession is to sell pictures; and as it would be impossible for this sort of people to trade with the pictures of living artists, and especially of their own country, they take it into their heads to decry them, and to amuse those whom they have access to, with the absurd notion, that a picture becomes more valuable in proportion to its antiquity.
>
> M. Rouquet, *The Present State of the Arts in England* (1755)

Despite a favorable infrastructure, for most of the first half of the eighteenth century, the prospects of an aspiring native English painter for a financially rewarding and intellectually stimulating career in his own country were discouraging. There was no lack of interest in the arts in general among the social and moneyed elite; however, the English art market had not evolved to a level at which it would offer institutionalized avenues for native art producers to offer their products to anonymous consumers. The often-voiced complaints about the harmful effects of imported old original pictures or cheap copies, the unfair competition by better-trained foreign artists and the overall non-supportive attitude of collectors towards English painters were evident market barriers. Yet the root of the problem lies elsewhere.

During this period, the absence of physical facilities and consumption habits that could help painters present their works for viewing and sale directly to the general public left artists with only two options. They could attract, by whatever means, potential clients to their studios or sell works through the agency of dealers. While the former was certainly practiced, the alternative, the employment of middlemen, was, as Rouquet's above comment indicates, far from being successfully implemented.

Why did dealers, whose very presence was a consequence of an expanding market, stay away from dealing in works of contemporary English painters? After all, one of the chief function of dealers, the very one that stimulates market growth, was seizing new opportunities. Assuming that these dealers made rational business decisions suggests that dealing in products of native English painters may not yet have presented commercial prospects worth pursuing.

Included among any businessperson's decisions is the realization of profit. Rouquet's statement attests to the reality that dealing in contemporary native paintings simply made no business sense, that is, it had no profit potential, and was thus not only 'impossible' but, in fact, threatened the already extant trade in paintings. The matter-of-factness of Rouquet's observation given without any qualifying remarks suggests that the reasons for this were, at least to him and, by inference, to his readers, self-evident. Rouquet implies with the term 'impossible' that the prevailing conditions in the market for contemporary English paintings were such that art dealers could not pursue a profitably trade in such works. One must bear in mind that Rouquet wrote at a time when the traditional system of patronage, that of personal contact between artist and patron, was still firmly in place. Moreover, since portrait painting was the main source of income for native artists,[63] physical proximity was essential. Such propinquity of producer and consumer eliminated the need for intermediaries. For that reason it was 'impossible for this sort of people to trade with pictures of living artists, and especially of their own country ...' Viewed in this light, the disparaging of contemporary English painters' works was but a form of protectionism practiced by middlemen in defense of their lucrative business in cheap local copies and imported old master paintings of widely varying quality and attribution. Dealers 'decried' contemporary native works because they perceived contemporary British painting as a serious threat to their established financial interests.

One of our main themes is how contemporary British painters reacted to the favorable circumstances associated with the general increase in demand caused by middle class growth in both affluence and numbers. Their story throughout the eighteenth century and beyond is one of native producers of art searching for, and ultimately establishing, the necessary means with which to exploit new opportunities presented by an expansion of patronage and the associated general transformation of the arts environment. The establishment of the Royal Academy (RA) in 1768 marks the successful conclusion of a process innovation by which artists as producers physically and institutionally separated the marketing of their products from their studios while still maintaining control over it.

Market expansion also presented new opportunities to dealers: the division among artists of work place from show place brought with it the potential for a considerably larger and more heterogeneous audience that was also increasingly growing accustomed to viewing and buying paintings outside of painters' studios and without direct contact with the artists. As this new consumer habit became more ingrained and the physical separation of production from marketing locale became more established, opportunities for middlemen as exchange agents grew and their economic significance expanded. In fact, the contribution of dealers to market growth in contemporary painting was crucial. Our analyses of auction transactions show that the mid-nineteenth century's explosive growth of the market for contemporary paintings in Britain was directly associated with dealers' activities.

Selling paintings by public auction also became common practice in England during this period. After its introduction in the 1680s, auction sales of paintings boomed. In the absence of regular public exhibitions of art, museums, and commercial galleries, attending auctions as spectators or bidders was among the few opportunities open to the public to view paintings. Moreover, the establishment of this system of selling art was also an essential feature of the infrastructure of a modern art market. Similar to the way a stock exchange functions for securities, art auctions enhanced the liquidity of their goods by presenting to both buyers and sellers an independent alternative by which to exchange property rights. Furthermore, the growth in the number of auction houses, the number of sales, and their monetary value was yet another consequence of, and stimulus for, an expanding market. The introduction of auctions to the exchange system for art represented a structural process innovation and a further specialization within the market.

The eighteenth century was also witness to an unprecedented growth in production and dissemination of reproductive prints. Without them, the extraordinarily high prices paid for certain contemporary paintings during the mid-Victorian art boom would not have been economically justifiable. Unlike original paintings, for which a marketing system was still under construction, an existing network of booksellers from which the specialized print seller gradually branched off as the market expanded, facilitated a widespread distribution of prints early on.

During the second quarter of the eighteenth century, the initial domination of foreign-produced plates yielded to domestic production giving increasing importance to prints as a source of revenue for artists, engravers, and print sellers. Prints also aided not only the development of native talent but, additionally, of a mass market for artists' products. The relationship between original design and the mass-produced derivative print began to exert a formative influence on the image to accommodate an increasingly larger and more heterogeneous mass audience.

The recognition of positive financial effects of mass-produced derivatives on a market for luxury goods echoed in eighteenth-century discourse on art. The exclusive and elitist nature of Shaftesburian civic humanism gradually gave way to views on art that permitted greater diversity of subject matter and audience composition. As the new audience for painting grew, the exploitation of its potential as buyers of art needed a theoretical frame within which this possibility could develop and find moral justification. This process of democratization of art consumption was part of a larger disquisition concerning general economics and related questions of social policy. At the onset of the century, the discussion was primarily concerned with the manners and morality of a paternalistic aristocratic elite. Soon, however, the language modified to accommodate commerce within the context of civic virtues and the definition of establishment broadened to embrace social status and values of middle-class citizens. By mid-century, when political economy emerged as an important discipline of social thought, the moral overtone dwindled. An individual's economic activities replaced as measures of worth notions of status and hierarchy as the natural basis of social existence, and the formation of society was discussed in terms of its dependence on the operations of the market. Like the discourse on art, economic debate followed a path towards addressing an increasingly larger audience whose contribution, existing or potential, to the general economy and to the economy of art gave it a steadily expanding significance. In this market of ideas, Kopytoff's observation on the exchange purpose of economies applies as well. In this case, this function gradually reduced and ultimately omitted moral language from the content of theoretical discourses on art and economy and thus eliminated certain exclusionary barriers to the extent where one's economic activity alone, rather than civic virtues, remained the only qualifying aspect.

Before venturing into a more detailed examination of the individual topics outlined above, a brief review of some of the literature on the arts environment of eighteenth-century Britain will help place this discussion within the context of the existing discourse. Besides the primary and secondary sources cited throughout the text, there are several works that serve as critical counterpoints to our own approach. Lawrence Lipking's *The Ordering of the Arts in Eighteenth-Century England* interprets the body of eighteenth-century writing on art and aesthetics as an effort to establish through theory some sense of order in the fields of painting, music, and poetry.[64] These discourses, Lipking explains, can be viewed under a model that associates changes in theory with changes in audience composition as they relate to the expanding middle class. The relationship between audience, artists and theoretical discourse pushed the latter towards theories that could address simultaneously the new and expanding middle class audience as well as offer philosophical justification and guidance for painters to explore different pictorial imageries to similar ends.

This relationship of theory, practical application and audience is the focus of John Barrell's *The Political Theory of Painting from Reynolds to Hazlitt.*[65] The author proposes that the theory of painting advanced by the individuals discussed in his book – Sir Joshua Reynolds, William Blake, James Barry and Henry Fuseli – was a political theory that shared many of the terms, arguments and concerns of contemporary writers on politics and economics. He points out that the attempt to promote a public mode of painting with an inherent and explicit political function was ultimately unsuccessful. Consequently, painting came to be seen as an art that offered only private pleasures to a private audience. Similar to Lipking, Barrell describes a commoditization occurring in the field of theoretical discourse on painting. Since these theories connect to the production and consumption of a commodity, they are part of a market's framework and respond to the same built-in force that drives an exchange system towards whatever commoditization the extant exchange technology permits.

David Solkin expands Barrell's discussion by taking a more holistic approach in his *Painting for Money*. He concludes that market forces were indeed the agents responsible for the change in the traditional subject matter of historical paintings. Solkin points to a trend in British painting towards pictorial modes with the broadest possible attraction to the new middle-class audience. However, his use of the terms 'market', 'market forces', and 'commerce' suggests that he sees them, in this context, as synonymous with the term 'middle class'. While, indeed, the new end consumers were largely middle class, they represented only one aspect of the multi-faceted framework economists define as 'market'. The phrase 'market forces' is even more complex, as it describes a market's internal dynamics. Thus, discussing commissioned works, such as portraiture and certain conversation pieces, together with paintings done on speculation and those for public exhibition neglects the differences between these categories. A commissioned portrait represents more the explicit wishes of the end consumer, while at the other extreme, a work intended for an anonymous market, can give insight into the producer's subjective assessment of demand. Similarly, paintings designed for mass reproduction can aim to appeal, as the example of Hogarth shows, to an audience beyond the groups usually associated with middle class patronage. None of the above comments invalidates Solkin's conclusions. Quite to the contrary, they endorse his general argument for an art created for, and shaped by, market forces. However, further distinctions should be considered to explain the changes in pictorial imagery occurring at the time.

To an extent, Iain Pears takes up this task in his *The Discovery of Painting*. Pears argues that English interest in painting derived from a process of cultural unification of the upper ranks of society. He proposes that discussions on the topic encouraged the aristocracy and the middling ranks to identify a set of common interests and attitudes. This consensus, he contends, was the main motivation that complemented and assured a steady expansion of the art market. He dismisses explanations that ascribe the growth of interest in the arts to an evolution of a sophisticated market. Nevertheless, Pears devotes considerable space to a discussion of dealers and auctions, two of the components that, together with others, spearheaded the art market's evolution. Unquestionably, the cultural unification the author deems as ultimately responsible for the growing interest in paintings was an important ingredient. However, viewing it as a monolithic magnet capable of exerting enough force initially to bring about this interest and then maintain a momentum sufficiently powerful to fuel the market's expansion implies that intellectual interest in paintings and their consumption are either one and the same or that the latter is an inevitable consequence of the former. Interest alone does not have to engender consumption. Obviously, the latter is the *sine qua non* of market expansion. The question to ask, therefore, is by what or whose agency was intellectual interest turned into consumption? Since consumption generally involves the exchange of property rights and thus falls within the function of the market, we must investigate that market to understand the changes in the arts environment in the commercial society of Georgian England.

One of the common denominators of the above discussions is the central role these authors assign to contemporary theoretical discourse on art. Literature on the arts experienced an unprecedented expansion during this period, one that was paralleled in the book industry in general. The appearance of theories by which to measure the merits of individual paintings is in itself an indicator of an expanding art market: theories offer a differentiation beyond the standards of manual execution. The dialectic between theory and practice posits a mutually formative influence. If theories address a commodity such as paintings, the theories should exhibit similar commoditization as the paintings. This very process can be traced in eighteenth-century theoretical writings on art as well as in the discourse on luxury and consumption.

2 THE COMMODITIZATION OF THEORIES OF ART

The London publication in 1638 of Franciscus Junius the Younger's (1591–1677) *De Pictura Veterum* as *The Painting of the Ancients*[1] brought the study of art in Britain into the domain of humanistic scholarship. The writer was an exceptionally erudite man; an intimate of Rubens, van Dyck and Inigo Jones; and also the librarian and curator for the great collector, Thomas Howard, second Earl of Arundel. His book was part treatise, part history and part oration presenting quotation after quotation, ultimately moving into philosophical discussion. The author argued that painting must be acknowledged as a liberal art, that it comes from the mind not the hands and eyes. Earlier, similar attempts by such individuals as Richard Haydocke or Lomazzo and Nicholas Hilliard, *c.* 1598 and 1600 respectively, to advance the social position of art had been largely unsuccessful. However, Franciscus's suggestion that knowledge of painting was a prerequisite for a gentlemanly education found a receptive audience among empiricist philosophers and others concerned with similar issues. Yet Franciscus's tome had several shortcomings. For one, it dealt with paintings no one could see, a concern raised by Rubens in a letter to the author in 1637.[2] Furthermore, the writer's advocation of gentlemanly learning was difficult to turn into practice. Anecdotes concerning Zeuxis or other ancient painters offered few practical tools for honing one's connoisseurship. Moreover, other than portraits and the occasional import from the Continent, there were few paintings available for erudite discourse. Thus, Franciscus's account of the paintings of the ancients existed in a kind of vacuum and was ill-equipped to stimulate discussion on theoretical principles of painting.

This impracticality of *The Painting of the Ancients* was rectified by one of the celebrated literary figures of the Restoration, John Dryden (1631–1700). Urged by several 'Gentlemen Virtuosoes and Painter', including the successful portrait painter Godfrey Kneller (1631–1700), the poet translated in 1694 the posthumously published 1668 Latin version of Charles Alphonse Du Fresnoy (1611–68) *De arte graphica* as *Art of Painting*.[3] Du Fresnoy's attempt to provide a set of rules based on contemporary experience and applicable to the process of making and comprehending works of art was well suited as a guide for artists and art lovers to evaluate paintings. Roger de Piles, the author's friend and editor, declared in the preface to the first edition that 'you will find it capable of giving the most nice and delicate sort of knowledge, not only to the lovers, but even to the Professors of that Art'. For painters he had the encouraging words that from now on they 'may work with pleasure; because they may be in some manner certain that their Productions are good'.[4] The book's appeal was considerable.[5] Later editions dropped the dogmatic tone of the original Latin verses in favour of an English text. By the 1780s, the publication had evolved to accommodate an audience that was not only numerically larger but also more sophisticated and accustomed to viewing paintings, and the 'Muse of Fresnoy' was outfitted with a 'modern vest'.[6] Thus, over the course of a century, the evolution of this one book echoed the development of the market that it served.

The same phenomenon can also be observed in the development of aesthetic discourse.[7] Most of the eighteenth and early nineteenth-century writers contributing to the debate were preoccupied with criteria of taste and aesthetics to develop different contexts in which to position art in a modern commercial society. At the onset of the century, the discussion occurred within the discourse of civic humanism. Articulated most clearly by the Earl of Shaftesbury, civic humanism considered the arts as a republic structured similarly to a political republic: the highest purpose which painting should seek was the promotion of public virtues. Consequently, history painting ranked highest, since it was best equipped to address rhetorically an exclusively qualified audience of free male citizen members to advocate private acts of public virtue. The Earl considered history paintings as conduct books for the ruling elite of property owners, well suited for the education of their young.[8] The contradictions inherent in an approach which barred, by definition, a numerically and economically increasingly significant segment of Britain's commercial society from participating in the consumption of art, facilitated, if not forced, a modification of the restrictive character of the Earl's aesthetic philosophy to the changing reality of England's social and economic conditions. Furthermore, Shaftesbury's theory, as it addressed the social position of painters as producers of art, also ran counter to artists' efforts to promote their activity as one that was rooted in intellectual contemplation not just manual labour. As long as painters were mere illustrators of sophisticated ideas conceived by their learned social superiors, advancement for them beyond the lowly, socially restrictive rank of 'mechanics' would be severely circumscribed.

One of the first attempts to modify Shaftesbury's version of civic humanism was launched in 1715 by the portraitist Jonathan Richardson (1664–1745) whom Walpole describes as being 'undoubtedly one of the best English painters of a head that had appeared in this country'.[9] The artist may have been motivated partly by a desire to defend his own lucrative activity as a portrait painter when he embarked his theoretical apologia of portraiture. Since this genre occupied an even lower rank than landscape painting in the Shaftesburian hierarchy,[10] Richardson proposed an expansion of the narrow social role civic humanism assigned to painting. Rather elegantly, Richardson applied Shaftesbury's demand for a didactic function of painting to portraiture by arguing that an artist wanting to depict commendable virtues could do so by painting 'a brave man, and one honestly and wisely pursuing his own interest in conjunction with that of his country'.[11]

There were two dimensions to Richardson's position. On one level, it suggested that it was permissible for a gentleman to pursue other non-leisurely activities as long as they were in accord with the welfare of the nation. On another level, and as a consequence of the first, Richardson's reasoning proposed that painting these worthy men's portraits was an activity that, although private and outside the field of leisure, promoted the virtues personified by these sitters. These portraits therefore agreed with civic humanism's lofty purpose for painting to advocate private acts of public virtue. Richardson attempted not only an extension of the definition of 'gentlemen' to include those engaged in commercial pursuits, but also an inclusion of himself, as a painter, among their ranks. He took his argument further by assuring collectors that their purchases were demonstrations of patriotism, since the pictures they bought would help with the 'reformation of our manners' and the money spent 'may turn to better account' than almost any other form of investment.[12] Patriotism and social prestige coupled with profit potential optimally suited middle-class consumers in the mercantile class society of eighteenth-century Britain.

By extending the definition of 'gentlemen' and including painters among their ranks, as well as providing social and economic justification for the consumption of paintings, Richardson offered a theoretical foundation for 'polite' members of the commercial middle class to consume art while simultaneously elevating the social status of the artist. His writing also represents a first attempt by a painter to provide a middle-class alternative to aristocratic civic humanism by proposing that social or public virtues could be exercised by a wider class of men than the more exclusive theory permitted.

Yet civic humanism's insistence on a moral dimension for art may not have suited those consumers who neither needed nor wanted such virtuous and lofty, yet restrictive, conditions attached to the enjoyment of their wealth.[13] What was needed was a justification of consumption that operated outside the stringent moral requirements attached to civic humanism.

Among the first and most radical to respond to this call was Bernard Mandeville (1670–1733) in his *Fable of the Bees*.[14] His controversial work was an explicit attack on Shaftesbury's assumption that the operation of society can be represented in moral terms. Mandeville attempted to demonstrate that it was not individuals' moral virtues but their vices, particularly consumption, that sustain a civilized society. He also argued that there existed no moral sanction for the hierarchic order of society advocated by the Earl. Mandeville, instead, viewed the social hierarchy as delineated by wealth, motivated and maintained by self-interested vices of fallen men, and one in which none of the social classes could claim any natural or moral predisposition to rule. The only division in society was, according to Mandeville, between consumer and producer. Consequently, economic relations in the market determined social relations. While in the discourse of humanism, luxury was considered to be the prime source of corruption for both state and individual,[15] for Mandeville 'luxury' was merely a category of consumer goods and, as such, it was included in the vernacular of economic analysis and has remained in use ever since. Moreover, Mandeville, originally from the Netherlands, evidently considered a descriptive [in the Dutch mode] rather than dogmatic art better suited to the character of a modern, commercial world.

The author relates his attack on Shaftesburian dogma in an amusing fictitious account of six dialogues in which two men and one woman debate the role and merit of pictures. In a lively discussion, the two men pontificate on the Earl's doctrine while the woman, seemingly ignorant of classical learning, presents Mandeville's view. In the end the Shaftesburian camp wins. However, this is achieved only by condescendingly dismissing the woman rather than responding to her argument: 'These things may seem strange to you, Madam, but they are of immense use to the Publick'.[16]

Several aspects become apparent from this dramatization of a juxtaposition of conflicting theories: the high-minded ideas of Shaftesbury cannot be maintained in the face of reason; and their seemingly altruistic motives are in reality – as the final patronizing gesture towards the woman demonstrates – poorly disguised weapons of aristocratic oppression. By implication, Shaftesburian history painting is rejected on the same grounds. The dialogue also reveals the shortcomings of Italian art, as representative of the theories of civic humanism, versus the merits of the more truthful and personal Dutch paintings. Furthermore, since female attendance at art auctions, one of the few venues for ladies of quality to view art, was not uncommon, the woman's role may have been created specifically to appeal to a nascent female audience.

While Britain's art market was still in a proto-modern phase, civic humanism represented in economic terms a barrier to unimpeded exchange of goods between the majority of art producers and potential consumers. Two entities opposed civic humanism's exclusivity. On one side was the burgeoning number of property-owning businessmen whose vital economic function in Britain's commercial society challenged any restrictions to social, political and economic participation until they, as a class, achieved full recognition with the passage of the first Reform Act in 1832. On the other side was the opposition from painters on economic grounds. A classification as products of 'mechanics' or manual labourers associated the prices of artists' works exclusively with production costs, while an acceptance of their works as carefully contemplated intellectual accomplishments would, besides enhancing painters' social standing, also add a less tangible element than labour and materials to the value of their paintings. The price of the product of genius is more ambiguous than compensation based on input of hours and raw materials. As Raymond Williams pointed out, it is no coincidence that the meaning of the term 'genius' changed from 'characteristic disposition' to 'exalted special ability' precisely at the time when painters were becoming small businessmen.[17] In purely economic terms, defining paintings as manually executed *intellectual* [authors' emphasis] commodities constitutes a form of product differentiation that facilitates the application of other systems of valuation to these products. Within the context of supply and demand, one of the prerequisites for the record prices achieved by many paintings in the first decade of the twenty-first century is the acceptance of a system of valuation that is independent of, and disregards, considerations of input costs.

Mandeville's focus on consumption of luxury, his division of society into consumers and producers and his insistence on economic relations as the determinants of social relations anticipated the emergence, in the 1740s, of Economics as a new scientific discipline of social thought. Economics removed, as to some extent Mandeville had tried to do, the moral framework altogether from the definition of luxury. However, rather than defining the motivation for the consumption of such goods as self-interested 'vices' of consumers, economics viewed these 'vices' as natural human propensities that are best expressed in the market to the benefit of all. The traditional concerns of civic humanism were thus modified and eventually replaced by analyses of the workings of a free market economy and its function in society. David Hume, for instance, wrote in 1742 that if the labour released due to agricultural improvements 'apply themselves to the finer arts, which are commonly denominated to the arts of luxury, they add to the happiness of the state'. However, he still distinguished between 'vicious' luxuries, with no benefit to society and 'innocent' luxuries, such as the arts, which are advantageous to the public. Traces of humanism were also still apparent, albeit with a different emphasis, in Josiah Tucker's introduction to *The Elements of Commerce and Theory of Taxes* (1755). Here the 'natural Disposition of Mankind to Commerce' has become a firmly established fact; so has the notion of 'rational choice' – Tucker used the term 'Self-Love' – as 'the great Mover in human Nature.' The paternalistic role given to the aristocratic elite by traditional humanistic theory is not abandoned but re-assigned to a 'legislature', and the discussion revolved around the means by which this body can direct this natural 'disposition'.[18] A similar position was also advocated by James Steuart. In his volume II of *Principles of Political Oeconomy* he stated that 'the principle of self-interest will serve as a general key to this inquiry; and it may, in one sense, be considered as the ruling principle of my subject ...' Yet he is quick to disclaim that this self-interest can be applied to the conduct of a statesman. 'Self-interest, when considered with regard to [statesmen] is public spirit; and it can only be called self-interest, when it is applied to those who are to be governed by it'.[19]

By the 1770s, civic humanism had all but disappeared from the language of political economy. In his famous statement Adam Smith posited that 'this division of labour, from which so many advantages are derived, is not originally the effect of any human wisdom, which foresees and intends that general opulence to which it gives occasions', but instead is the necessary result of 'the propensity to truck, barter, and exchange one thing for another'.[20] In this passage, human wisdom, whether manifested through aristocratic or other stewardship, receives no credit for the benefits of an expanding economy. To the contrary, the advantages are the consequences of a 'propensity' rooted in the expression of self-interest.[21]

The development of eighteenth-century political economy was an essential contribution to the changes in the eighteenth- and nineteenth-century art world. Political economy, like aesthetic theory, adapted to the needs of a modern commercial society. The exclusivity of moral underpinnings and its associated preoccupation with stewardship were gradually abandoned in favour of an inclusiveness based on scientific explanations of the workings of the economy and their effects on the composition of society. The discourse did not address specifically the production and consumption of art, yet its evolution, nonetheless, mirrored in many aspects the developments within the theoretical debates on art. It also reflected the general movement of eighteenth-century British society, particularly its middle class, towards greater participation in social, cultural and political spheres. Furthermore, a philosophy advocating a social hierarchy rooted in economic relations offered to painters a more suitable avenue for advancement than civic humanism's restrictive concepts. This is not to suggest that painters *en masse* flocked to read Adam Smith; however, the commoditization of political economy was a necessary contribution to the ongoing transformation of the arts environment. It empowered painters, free from the dictates of traditional patronage, to assume a position as equal and independent members among the ranks of other producers of goods. The desires of individual patrons were exchanged for an exposure to the vagaries of the market.

Eighteenth-century economic debate addressed painters only as far as their role as producers of luxury commodities was concerned. It said little about their products. Art-theoretical discourse, Richardson notwithstanding, was in the 1740s still largely rooted in civic humanism. Within this camp, however, subtle but significant modifications occurred which obfuscated the delineation between public and private virtues. These changes indicated that the moral prerequisites for the appreciation of paintings were not an aristocratic elite's exclusive property but could be obtained by a wider class of people. In the mind of the philosopher and teacher George Turnbull (1709/10–83), for example, paintings depicting private virtues were acceptable because they had the capability to engender similar positive feelings potentially in all of us. Turnbull provided the theoretical foundation that allowed for the introduction of contemporary themes into history painting so that it could appeal to a larger audience. He proposed a further divergence from Shaftesburian aesthetic theory by advocating descriptive details in paintings. This would move the image away from the representation of ideal nature and allow the 'Subject and Scene [to] be easily distinguished by those who are well versed in History'.[22] Relating this statement to Mandeville makes the radicalism of Turnbull's suggestion apparent: the seemingly incompatible antagonism between theories of idealization and description that is at the heart of Mandeville's fable is successfully reconciled.[23]

Turnbull's view was not isolated. Already in 1710, opinions advocating a more expanded definition of history painting could be found. Richard Steele, for example, argued that history painting should 'not for the future have so romantick a turn, but allude to incidents which come within the fortunes of the ordinary race of men'. In Steele's opinion, history painting should replace its mythological subjects with what he considered to be meaningful ones – 'the characters of real life, and the persons of men and women whose actions have rendered them laudable or infamous'.[24]

Among artists, Hogarth in particular was influenced by such views.[25] Moreover, the influx from the Continent of early Rococo paintings, which had begun to appear on the London market shortly after Watteau's death in 1721,[26] may have contributed to 'the gradual emergence of an imagery which spoke in increasingly positive terms of a life of material opulence ...'[27] Hogarth was the artist who succeeded in finding a mode of representing conspicuous consumption of luxuries as a contribution to the public good. His conversation pieces from the early 1730s blended the native tradition, largely based on Netherlandish models, with the popular Watteauesque manner imported from France.[28] His depictions were no longer of the aristocratic elite, but of the affluent members of the commercial class surrounded by accoutrements of their wealth. Hogarth's painting of the Wollaston Family (http://artmarket.tulane.edu/page67.html), for example, shows an obviously affluent group involved in social intercourse in a luxurious interior setting. Another group portrait, commissioned by the great aristocratic collector, Sir Andrew Fountaine (http://artmarket.tulane.edu/page68.html), avoids any reference to Shaftesburian stewardship but depicts the main character involved in what could be a commercial transaction, albeit of a cultural nature. These new, 'commercial humanist' type of pictures proved immensely successful for the artist.[29] He had indeed found a way to expand his clientele that was philosophically justifiable to his audience as well as himself. As a result of a complex relationship between, and within, audience composition, aesthetic theory, moral philosophy and painters' social position, a new, contemporary pictorial mode had emerged. As representations of a blend of two interests these images are not just visual reconciliations of many of the larger social and philosophical issues described here, but are also examples of artistic products created in an art market during its proto-modern phase. Within a few short years, Hogarth would herald the arrival of the new art market of the commercial age with the publication of prints after his 'modern moral' paintings and the inherent dependence of such ventures on 'the public at large'.[30]

Yet, in spite of their modernity, Hogarth's conversation pieces and his modern morals subjects were still tied to the civic humanist theory of painting. Both genres still conveyed a moral message. The former addressed refinement and consumption; the latter, as the name implies, judged various aspects of social behaviour. Before paintings could be classified as commodities produced for an anonymous market consisting of consumers whose only common denominator was that they belonged to a 'republic of means' rather than one of taste and virtue, the medium had to shed its didactical requirement. Paintings could still convey moral lessons; however, this aspect was not an essential prerequisite, only one among many qualities a painting might possess. Thus, theories of art began to move away from the traditional interdependence of republic of taste and political republic to more general considerations of aesthetics.

This development is reflected in Hogarth's theoretical work, *The Analysis of Beauty written with a view of fixing the fluctuating principles of Taste* (1753). In Rouquet's words, 'this work was written to prove that there is a line whose bending may be determined, and that the existence of this line constitutes the beauty and gracefulness of an object ...'[31] Having arrived at a suitable pictorial mode and a successful business model, the entrepreneurial Hogarth could now expand into pure aesthetics. The inclusion of such sophisticated aspects of connoisseurship as the curvature of a line in works generally considered to be 'comedies with a pencil'[32] broadened the potential level of appeal of, and appreciation for, his paintings. The prints of his modern morals paintings spoke with wit and satire to the common folk, while the artist's quest for beauty could transcend such vulgar notions of amusement and address the refined minds of the cognoscenti.

With Joshua Reynolds (1723–92), the founding president of the Royal Academy, the shift towards pure aesthetics and intellectual connoisseurship over didactical qualities became institutionalized. In one (wordy) sentence of his *Discourse IX*, delivered at the opening of The Royal Academy, on 16 October 1780, the artist states:

> The art which we profess has beauty for its object; this it is our business to discover and to express; but the beauty of which we are in quest is general and intellectual; it is an idea that subsists only in the mind; the sight never beheld it, nor has the hand expressed it: it is an idea residing in the breast of the artist, which he is always labouring to impart, and which he dies without imparting; but which he is yet so far able to communicate, as to raise thoughts and extend views of the spectator; and which, by a succession of art, may be so far diffused, that its effects may extend themselves imperceptibly into publick benefits, and be among the means of bestowing on whole nations refinements of taste: which if it does not lead directly to purity of manners, obviates at least their greatest deprivation, by disentangling the mind from appetite, and conducting the thoughts through successive stages of excellence, till that contemplation of universal rectitude and harmony which began by Taste, may, as it is exalted and refined, conclude in Virtue.[33]

In this impressive pronouncement, Sir Joshua expressed a complex composite of ideas. The object of his art was a non-specific intellectual beauty which, despite the shortcomings of the artist to express it, could be perceived by the audience and, under the right circumstances, result in public benefit. There is a romantic tone to this statement; the mysterious, abstract nature of this beauty, intangible, hidden, never beheld or expressed; the artist's struggle to depict it and the ultimate futility of the effort; the imperceptible, yet powerful, manner in which the contemplation of this beauty, of this 'universal rectitude and harmony', can transform and improve whole nations. Furthermore, Reynolds advocates painters as men of ideas, revealing his debt to earlier humanist theorists such as Junius, Du Fresnoy, and Richardson, and the emphasis on the selfless, life consuming exertion of artists to express these noble ideas underscores his romantic leanings. The structured, exclusive approach of Shaftesbury has all but disappeared to make room for a platform which assigns to painters a social rank equal to that of other professional men of ideas. There also occurred a shift of emphasis from the artist to the audience, as it is now the responsibility of the spectator to realize the benefits, social and otherwise, of the art professed by Sir Joshua. Paintings no longer required audience validation but could stand independently as intellectual products of professional men. The paintings no longer needed to instruct but only to display the world as an instructive metaphor that might be perceived by enlightened men.[34] Reynolds's canon eliminated the last vestiges of a restrictive definition for art: all it required now was beauty of an indeterminate kind that resided 'in the breast of the artist'. Thus, the make-up of artistic products was entirely left up to artists, and all those whose thoughts and views could be elevated and broadened were qualified consumers. Reynolds's subtlety democratized and potentially enlarged the consumer base for a product that he promoted as a manifestation of refinement and taste, that is, the utility of art consumption was image cultivation.

This switch of responsibility also laid the foundation for the cultural institutionalization of art criticism. As the appreciation and consumption of paintings broadened its demographic base, the expanded audience required guidance along the yet unfamiliar paths of connoisseurship. Reynolds's philosophy favoured an analytical approach to art writing and connoisseurship that was based on a breakdown of stylistic and compositional sources and fit comfortably within British Empiricist tradition.

Reynolds's modifications of the rhetorical aesthetic of civic humanism reduced the restrictions imposed on consumers and producers of art by the traditional discourse. At the same time, however, he dictated a new hierarchy of genres, ranging from history painting at the top down to landscape and still-life at the bottom.[35] Such rankings of products have economic implications: prejudice creates barriers that limit opportunities for some producers of art while giving advantages to others. Consequently, the next phase in the commoditization of aesthetic theory should be one that opens the playing field equally to all producers of art, subject only to the forces of the market.

This step was taken by William Hazlitt (1778–1830) at the beginning of the next century. In his essay 'On the Imitation of Nature', (25 December 1814) he objected to Reynolds's hierachy and argued for its breakup. Hazlitt thought that painters were best served by focusing on subjects of interest to them and in the depiction of which they excelled, rather than chasing some elusive concept of beauty.[36] In his *Criticism on Art and Sketches of the Picture Galleries of England*, he argued that the great masters of the past had relied 'not on the creation of a fantastic, abstract excellence, existing nowhere but in their own mind, but in their selecting and embodying someone view of nature, and which their particular genius led them to study and imitate with success'.[37] Great art, according to Hazlitt, was, as John Barrell states, 'a transaction between nature and individual genius, and a private transaction'.[38] We can also recognize in Hazlitt the fundamentals of a form of art criticism still in use today, that is, an open competition between equally ranked producers of artistic products expressing their personal interpretations in a manner best suited to their individual talents. Hazlitt describes this individual talent or genius as the ability to produce not a 'balance' of 'good qualities' but one chosen thing very well that is accomplished by a 'division of labour, an almost exclusive attention to some one object, which is necessary in Art, as in all the works of man'.[39] Such language must have sounded quite familiar to an audience of middle-class merchants and manufacturers whose accomplishments were based, to varying degrees, on the application of economic principles and the belief that focus and hard work were the keys to success. The unattainable genius of Michelangelo or Leonardo was replaced by Adam Smith and the Protestant work ethic.

Hazlitt's pronouncement had significant implications for the audience. In the absence of empirically derived or otherwise applicable criteria of judgment, it was now up to the consumer to discern the degree of success to which each painter realized her or his chosen interpretation of the external world. Thus, by mid-nineteenth century a private dialogue between individual artists and individual members of the audience had replaced the confining function assigned to both by civic humanism.

This commoditization of theory, which increasingly moved the arts away from the control of a social elite towards a free market environment, engendered voices of concern. Hazlitt himself was troubled by the fact that now the 'great vulgar and the small', the 'pretenders of taste', composed the 'herd of spectators' at the RA exhibitions. Lacking 'natural taste' for paintings, their judgment did not recognize true artistic merit and factitiously created 'candidates for fame' whose success was based on the production of 'popular effect by the cheapest and most obvious means, at the expense of everything else'.[40] Earlier, concern was also expressed by Henry Fuseli (1742–1825). His criticism of contemporary portrait painting which, in a society in which 'liberty and commerce have more levelled the ranks ... and more equally diffused opulence, ... can personify nothing but [the sitter's] opulence or his pretence' and [in which a portrait] is reduced to mere 'furniture' conveys his misgivings regarding an art for private consumption. In fact, as Fuseli's discussion on the causes of the flourishing of the arts in ancient Greece reveals, the privatization of modern society was, in his mind, the chief reason for the decline of the art of painting. He certainly acknowledged the positive effects on production and sales of paintings of a society with 'more equally diffused opulence', but at the same time he warned that 'luxury in times of taste keeps up execution in proportion as it saps the dignity and moral principle of the Art; gold is the motive of its exertions, and nothing that ennobles man was ever produced by gold'.[41] Fuseli's contemporary, William Blake (1857–27), although involved as a small entrepreneur in direct sales of his own hand-decorated prints, cautioned against a private art in a commercial nation, blaming the profit-driven activities of 'ignorant picture dealers' for bringing 'all the Rubbish of the Continent' and 'sell[ing] these Smears and Daubs at an immense price'.[42] Blake's pronouncement also testified to the separation of and antagonistic relationship between the market for contemporary art and the market for imported Old Masters. Perhaps most succinctly, this apprehension about private art for private consumption was expressed by the critic John Williams, better known as Anthony Pasquin (1761–1818) in his *Memoirs* (1769):

> The mightiest evil to be regretted is, that the vulgar, who have no knowledge of propriety, should, from their numbers, their riches, and consequently their power, have the national patronage within their dominion; and yet these bipedal reptiles must be uniformly soothed and solicited, under such forcible designations as THE PUBLIC.[43]

In the conclusion of his *The Political Theory of Painting from Reynolds to Hazlitt*, John Barrell states that

> the increasing concern with genius as what marks the difference between one painter and another, and with art offering private satisfaction to private men – these phenomena, I believe, are best attended to and best understood in terms of the history of the survival, the adaptation, and the final abandonment of the civic humanist discourse.[44]

However, if we substitute civic humanism as the central reference point with Kopytoff's earlier described commoditization model, a different conclusion suggests itself. At issue was not a dialectic surrounding the theories of Shaftesbury. Instead, we witness an interactive multilateral dynamic the momentum of which facilitated the transformations of theory, producer, product and consumer to adapt to the conditions of a developing art market and embrace its inherent opportunities. Therefore, in order to illuminate the manner in which these changes in the theoretical superstructure modified the wider arts economy of this period, the discussion will now turn to market's respective players.

3 THE PAINTER AS *HOMO ECONOMICUS*

To what extent economic considerations were at the root of change in aesthetic theory is impossible to say. In any case, assuming a direct cause-and-effect relationship between these two entities would be an oversimplification of the issue. The transformation within the theoretical discourse on art possessed its own internal dynamic; furthermore, other, external influences contributing to this evolution originated from such diverse areas as political economy, political and moral philosophy, as well as demographic and social changes. Economic concerns of painters seeking to remove restrictive barriers to an unimpeded exchange of art products between producers and consumers were only one of the agents of this change.

Nonetheless, the ambition of native British painters to seize the opportunities offered by an expanding consumer base is central to the structural and institutional developments of the British arts environment. It is to these efforts that such producer-controlled marketing entities as artists' clubs, private academies, independent exhibition facilities, and copyright protection are indebted.

Contemporary and/or near contemporary writings on the eighteenth-century British art scene share the observation that the dealer-controlled trade in old imported pictures and cheap copies or potboilers – made locally or abroad – thrived throughout most of the period, while the market for original works by native contemporary painters was rather poor. Rouquet blamed the English attitude in general and criticized that they 'amuse themselves pretty much with the arts, without paying any great regard to the artist'. But he also levelled accusations at dealers:

> Behold, say they [dealers], speaking of a modern picture, it still shines with that ignoble freshness which we perceive in nature; time is far from having covered it with its learned smoke, with that sacred mist which some day or other must conceal it from the vulgar eyes, when none but the initiated shall perceive the mysterious beauties of its venerable antiquity. Such are the blemishes with which those insolent brokers charge modern pictures, and with such discourse they exclude from the cabinets of the curious, the performances of living painters, who are never employed but with repugnance, and when it cannot be avoided.[1]

Walpole similarly decried in his essay on Hogarth the 'ignorant virtuosi of the age' and voiced his 'indignation at the impudent tricks of picture-dealers', whom he saw continually recommending and vending 'vile copies to bubble collectors'.[2] The term 'bubble collectors' most likely derived from the scandal-ridden collapse, in 1720, of the South Sea Company which had lured gullible investors into acquiring its over-promoted shares. Walpole may have described a type of collector susceptible to dealers' promises of unrealistic, highly speculative profits from an investment in paintings. However, the actual occurrence of a bubble in the old master market around that time is difficult to verify due to the paucity of data.

James Barry also joined the chorus of condemnation of dealers arguing that the increased demand for art tended to multiply the importation of foreign pictures and as a result

> artful men [dealers] have not failed to avail themselves of this passion for ancient art, as it afforded a fine coverlet for imposition, for vending, in the name of those great masters, the old copies, imitations, and studies, of all the obscure artists that have been working in Italy, Flanders, and other places for two hundred years past ... so that this ill fated country of ours is to be crammed with nothing but rubbish from abroad.[3]

John Okley, a correspondent of the *St James Chronicle*, saw middlemen of any type as the chief culprits and in an article published in April 1761 summed up the dilemma:

> It is a known melancholy Truth that the Tribe of Auctioneers, Connoisseurs, Picture Brokers, Dealers, Menders, Cleaners, &c. &c. for their Divisions and Subdivisions are endless, have all my Time engrossed and monopolized the *Trade* of Pictures, and by their Authority, Interest, and Artifices with the Great, have made it a matter of ridicule to purchase any modern Production, or encourage an English Artist.[4]

These statements all attest to the existence of two apparently mutually exclusive art markets in a state of hostile competition. One consisted of a flourishing trade in imported old paintings of varying degrees of quality and similar locally painted merchandize under the control of middlemen; the other, opposing one, was a depressed market in original works by native living painters.

Two circumstances retarded the progress towards reconciliation and ultimate alliance between these seemingly opposed interests. On one side, native English artists like Hogarth and Blake focused their endeavours on establishing channels through which to sell their works directly to the end consumer. This strategy not only eliminated the need for middlemen, but it was perceived to endanger dealers' financial interest by tapping into the same market. This alleged threat also implied that the demand for paintings was thought to be relatively inelastic. While all the relevant data show an increase in overall art consumption, the contemporary perception was less certain. For one, the distinction between

Old Master collectors and collectors of contemporary works which, as buying patterns at auction show, was well established by the middle of the nineteenth century, had not yet occurred. Artists and dealers sold to the same clientele and, judging from the commentaries, the competition was ugly. In contradistinction, Table 3.1 shows the later purchasing patterns.

Table 3.1: Buying Patterns from 1840–1910.

	Number	Percentage
Only Continental	675	23.74%
Mixed	686	24.13%
Only English	1,476	51.92%
Only Contemporary	1,146	40.31%
Mixed	677	23.81%
Only Old Master	1,014	35.67%

Moreover, artists were opposed by picture dealers who focused their resources on those opportunities that had the actual or perceived potential for the highest financial return. Ultimately, the resolution of this conflict would require a third art product beyond old paintings and contemporary works: the reproductive print after contemporary paintings. From the merger between the established print/book selling trade and the dealer in old paintings, the modern dealer in contemporary works was born. This process, however, was slow and circuitous. Indeed, one of the defining characteristics of the eighteenth-century English art environment was an opposition between dealers and native artists.

Therefore, we discuss the two topics – contemporary paintings and Old Master paintings – separately. An economic connection between these two related luxury goods existed, of course; but opportunity in one camp retarded or even reversed progress in the other and hinged around the focus of middlemen's attention. As long as dealers had a steady supply of old imports from the Continent augmented by 'vile copies' produced by local artists 'employed but with repugnance', there was no reason to do business with contemporary native painters unless it 'cannot be avoided'.[5]

Under certain conditions, however, specifically when the market for old imports is tainted with a suspected supply of bad-quality goods, this competitive relationship can stimulate growth in the contemporary painting market. The frequently mentioned flood of 'rubbish from abroad' at some point actually fuelled demand for contemporary production.[6] For example, associated with the dwindling supply during the eighteenth century of continental old pictures of good quality was an improvement of the economic conditions of living artists in England. Then, after a century of systematic searching of the Continent for saleable old paintings by dealers of mixed competence and integrity, the upheavals surrounding the French Revolution and the Napoleonic Wars brought fresh works of good quality and provenance on the market. Consequently, middlemen concentrated on this new opportunity to the detriment of living native artists. It was not until this new supply was depleted, before dealers finally redirected their focus on the market in contemporary paintings. This switch and the corresponding reallocation of middlemen's resources ultimately led to the 'Golden Age'.[7] That shift, however, did not happen until the second quarter of the nineteenth century when it fundamentally changed the financial condition of contemporary painters and the arts environment in general.

It is doubtful that even the most optimistic art observers could have anticipated the Victorian 'Golden Age of Living Painters' in 1714, when Walpole, at the ascension of George I, commented that Britain had 'now arrived at the period in which the arts were sunk to the lowest ebb'. Only Sir Godfrey Kneller seemed to have risen above the undistinguished circle of mediocrity – although, Walpole mentioned, this noted portraitist was 'prostituting' his name by 'suffering the most wretched daubings of hired substitutes to pass for his works'. Consequently, 'where he offered one picture to fame, he sacrificed twenty to lucre'.[8] Kneller's specialty – portraits – was the one branch of painting in which a painter could hope to earn a reasonably reliable living.[9] However, artists often had to engage in other, related activities to complement their earnings.

One of these income-supplementing options was sign painting. Pye describes a market in Harp Alley specifically for the sale of shop signs which could be seen all over London. According to Pye, sign painting 'appears to have been the greatest resource of the British painter for employment'.[10] Others worked as coach painters and designers of banknotes, theatre tickets and funerary monuments. Many of these painters also provided cheap run-of-the-mill pictures to auctioneers and dealers.[11] Some, as the picture merchant William Buchanan noted, even doubled as dealers, since 'the lucrative speculation in older pictures was probably more profitable [for painters] than selling their own works'.[12] The first recorded native English dealer in paintings, Thomas Manby, was a landscape painter who had worked in Italy where he assembled a collection of paintings and subsequently sold them in London.[13] Arthur Pond, as well, besides being a successful painter and picture restorer, operated as a dealer and respected consultant to collectors with, evidently, significant influence over the buying habits of his clientele.[14] Others doubled as shipping agents, restorers, book illustrators, copyists or assistants to other artists.[15]

Painters' need to subsidize their activities or engage in purely decorative work confirms the underdeveloped state of the British art market for contemporary native painting. Walpole occasionally refers to specialties of certain painters, but these individuals were mainly foreigners who had immigrated to England in search of opportunity.[16] Native artists who were able to specialize in specific genres were few. The marine painters Peter Monamy (1689–1749) and Samuel Scott (1703–72), the horse painters James Seymour (1702–52) and John Wootton (1686–1765), or the fowl and game painter Charles Collins (d. 1744), were the exception rather than the rule.[17]

Unfortunately, such 'mechanical' work as sign painting or theatre ticket design ran counter to precisely those efforts which aimed to elevate the activity of painting from one belonging to the manual trades to one ranking among the liberal professions. Executing decorative designs by hand for others allowed little room for the intellectual prerequisites of a liberal profession. Moreover, the dependency on employment to earn a livelihood compounded the prejudices concerning the 'servile' nature of a painter's activity. It follows that a change in social status was linked to changes in painters' economic conditions. Consequently, native British artists, recognizing this interdependency, focused their efforts on two strategies: organizing and marketing.

From Coffee Shops to a Royal Academy

George Vertue (1684–1756) reports that during the seventeenth century attempts had already been made to establish art academies along Continental lines. One was called 'Museum Minerva', founded around 1636; another was at the house of the diplomat, art advisor and miniaturist, Sir Balthazar Gerbier (1592–1663), and it appears that John Evelyn had entertained plans for an artists' organization.

Also, there was a 'Society of St. Luke', mentioned by Whitley, which apparently owed its existence to Van Dyck's habit of inviting artists and connoisseurs to his house at regular intervals. These customary meetings ceased with Van Dyck's death in 1641 but were revived later by Sir Peter Lely (1618–80). However, this Club disintegrated in the 1730s, apparently because most of its members joined a rival group that gathered at Slaughter's coffee house, conveniently located right in the middle of London's artists' colony, on St Martin's Lane.

In 1704, Vertue was a member of an academy that congregated at the 'Rose and Crown'. These early organizations were largely social clubs. Meetings at trendy coffee houses and pubs must have been more of the convivial and lively sort often associated with artists' drinking establishments rather than offering much opportunity for the systematic study of painting.[18]

On St Luke's Day, 18 October 1711, a small group of artists announced the founding of the first academy with the specific purview of systematizing the study of painting and offering its curriculum to professional artists and interested amateurs. This organization differed from the older groups: its didactic and professional purpose was made apparent by offering the use of live models. If this was limited to male models is uncertain: Hogarth's remark stressing the availability of female models at another school, one founded by John Vanderbank (1694–1739) around 1720, may have been intended to distinguish the latter from the former. In any case, classes and meetings were held in a large room on Great Queen Street, near the residence of Kneller, who had been unanimously elected governor. The new academy had initially eighty-six members and twelve directors among who were Jonathan Richardson (1665–1745) and James Thornhill (1675–1734).[19] Voting members included such well-known artists as Vertue, Closterman (1660–1713), Vanderbank, and the sporting painters, John Wotton and Peter Tillemans (1684–1734).[20] An annual membership fee of one guinea was charged which in combination with the organization's mission of teaching helped to elevate the status of painting as an occupational pursuit. The fee also differentiated painting from related activities surrounding the production of other luxury goods. The academy clearly was not a school for young, aspiring painters: any hint of a similarity to a trade apprenticeship was conspicuously avoided. Most of the subsequently described groups, including the Royal Academy, can be traced to this artists' organization.

Around 1713, Thornhill proposed to secure royal or governmental backing for the group. English painters were aware of the support extended by the French state to its native artists, and some wanted to explore similar arrangements.[21] However, Kneller was strongly opposed. Therefore, the young organization divided, and Kneller resigned as governor in 1715. It is unclear why the matter of official support became a divisive issue for this group. Perhaps Kneller was already on his way to become the official court portraitist to the newly imported king and did not care to have official royal patronage of a chartered group interfere with his privileged post. His often-described mercenary character would certainly be consistent with such motives.

In any case, Thornhill was subsequently elected to the vacant position but was deposed in 1720 by Vanderbank. The ex-governor then attempted to set up a competing academy in Covent Garden. This venture, however, proved unsuccessful and soon had to close. Vanderbank, meanwhile, as governor of the original group, vacated the old premises and moved to St Martin's Lane. Many of the noted artists of this period, such as Hogarth, Louis Laguerre (1663–1721) and George Knapton (1698–1778), were among the members of the St Martin's Lane Academy, as it was often called. The membership fee had gone up to two guineas for the season lasting from October to spring.

The school flourished until 1724, when it was discovered that its treasurer had embezzled funds and the academy had to shut down. Thornhill attempted to set up another school along similar lines in his private residence as soon as Vanderbank's St Martin's Lane Academy closed. However, even though membership was free, the enterprise met with little success and before long closed.[22]

The failures of these early academies, however, were only temporary. Shortly after Thornhill's death in 1734, his son-in-law Hogarth formed an academy in Peter Court on St Martin's Lane. Since the demise of the old facility in St Martin's Lane, Old Slaughter's coffee house had become 'the Tip Topp Clubb of all, for men … in Arts & Gentlemen lovers of Art'. Hogarth had apparently recognized a need to consolidate these individuals in a more professional setting. It has been suggested that Hogarth was also motivated by his conviction that the future of English painters did not lie with the aristocracy but should be sought among the middle classes. The establishment of this group was an important milestone in a series of events that turned Hogarth and many of his fellow artists towards this new source of patronage.[23]

Hogarth's group formed the nucleus of the later 'Society of Artists' from which a splinter group provided many of the founding members of the Royal Academy. The royal institution was, therefore, the direct descendent of the St Martin's Lane Academy. A familiar theme was voiced among this new group. Pye reports that members complained about the 'degradation of their own state of vassalage' blaming the 'influence of dealers in ancient works'. Since thus far these painters had been unable to 'emancipate themselves from this thraldom of the picture-dealer or to elevate themselves above the practice of decorating coaches and painting signs' such concerns were the main topic of conversation at their meetings.[24] Clearly, economic considerations were involved in the formation of this group.

Similar concerns also played a role in subsequent efforts at forming academies. For example, the 1755 publication *The Plan of an Academy for the Better Cultivation, Improvement and Encouragement of Painting, Sculpture, Architecture and the Arts of Design in General*, laments the 'prodigious sums England has laid out at foreign markets for paintings'.[25]

In general, the idea of setting up art schools of varying types was catching on. From 1735 to 1754, the noted collector and physician to the King, Dr. Richard Mead (1673–1754), opened an academy in his house to give art students the opportunity to copy works in his private collection. Moreover, he allowed access to professional copyists, some of whom were in the employ of the dealer/painter Arthur Pond. Also in 1735, George Michael Moser, a Swiss enameller and draughtsman conducted a small drawing school in Salisbury Court. In 1738 the group expanded and moved to new facilities in St Martin's Lane and then merged with Hogarth's St Martin's Lane Academy in the early forties. In 1749 John Gwynn (1713–86) published a pamphlet that criticized the deplorable condition of native artists and the poor regard among the English for their own art. He urged that the founding of an academy was the best way to remedy this situation. Contemporaneously, Vertue explored similar notions. Even some members of the aristocracy wanted to play a part in this melee, and in 1758, the

Duke of Richmond made a philanthropic attempt to establish an academy by opening up his extensive private collection to art students.[26]

Art academies were also established in other urban centres around the island. In Edinburgh, an 'Academy of St. Luke' was formed in 1729. In 1734/35, the painter Richard Cooper (1705–64) organized a Winter Academy there. In Glasgow, in the 1750s the Foulis Academy was set up. Liverpool witnessed the formation of an academy in 1769. Then in 1786 an academy of painting in Oxford was proposed. There was even an attempt to set up a rival English Academy at Rome that was advertised in the *Daily Advertiser*, 8 June 1752.

Most of these early academies were patterned after the French model: artists copied old masters and executed figure studies from plaster casts of mostly Roman copies of Greek statues. Use of live models was rare, and women were not admitted. The Italian version, the artisanal workshop, seems to have been avoided, although it was certainly pursued on an individual level. Kneller, for instance, managed his atelier on the same 'principles as the fabricating of carpets at Kidderminster', implementing such manufacturing practices as specialization and division of labour.[27]

Several aspects of these attempts to set up professional art schools warrant further comments. Charging a fee for membership in a non-regulatory body emphasized these organizations' distinction from trade guilds, such as the then nearly extinct Painter-Stainer Company,[28] which had performed a regulatory function for most aspects of the business of painting from apprenticeship to production to sale. However, as artistic painting adopted more intellectual overtones, criteria of artisanal workmanship became less suitable. If painters were to achieve a classification as independent professional men, they had to discard any remnants that reminded of 'mechanical' trades.

The theoretical discourse was still concerned with the hierarchical ranking of genres at the same time when painters, such as John Wooten and Peter Tilleman who, as equestrian specialists should have occupied a rather lowly rank, were among the voting members of Kneller's original academy. Clearly, this (theoretical) hierarchy was not uniformly accepted among all painters. Furthermore, the academy membership indicates the recognition among artists that a division within their ranks based on specialization was counter-productive to their professional ambitions. The 'democratic' character of membership requirements already anticipated later moderations of theory. Sooner or later, theoretical discourse had to recognize that specialists in 'lower' genres were successfully operating in the changing patronal environment. Thus, rather than becoming inapplicable, theory had to adapt. In this instance, it appears that the market place was among the agents of this transformation.

Besides providing places for practice and organizational structures to advocate a changing occupational image, these facilities also served as a form of protectionism for native producers of art against the perceived threats to their material conditions by dealers in old pictures. The St Martin's Lane group, for example, was quite outspoken in blaming the 'degradation of their own state of vassalage' to the 'influence of dealers in ancient works'.[29] Barriers were such that advancement, both economic and social, was thought possible only through organized effort. Operating a studio on the principles of manufacture and trade – as Kneller did – while simultaneously promoting the aura of an enlightened liberal profession as a group, appears to have been reconcilable.

This protectionism suggests yet another dimension. The economist G. Akerloff argued in a seminal paper on the effects of information asymmetry that the alleged existence of 'lemons' may be detrimental to the market for used cars.[30] The suspected presence of 'lemons' will keep potential sellers of good quality used cars away from the secondary market as they recognize that sales at full value cannot be accomplished. This causes a decline in the average quality and, therefore also price. Since supply and quality are a function of price, both will be subject to further reductions. Apprehensive consumers' absence from the market further compounds the downward direction and may potentially result in a market collapse. Akerloff proposed that sellers could counter this trend by offering some type of quality guarantees.

We readily acknowledge that it is a far leap indeed from used cars to old paintings and, to some, possibly an inopportune analogy. Yet under the familiar scenario of a perceived presence in the market of old paintings of bad quality and questionable authorship – the frequent comments to that effect suffice to attest to the existence of this suspicion – several similar consequences are likely to occur. Owners of old works of good quality, unable to realize full value, become disinclined to sell; average quality of old paintings on the market declines; demand and prices fall; consumer confidence drops and wary buyers stay away causing further downward movement of prices. However, the market for paintings offers to risk averse, pent-up demand the option of shifting to close substitutes, that is, contemporary works. On the supply side, certain dealers will leave the unprofitable market of low quality old pictures and seek opportunity elsewhere, possibly in the contemporary painting market. Or, going back to Akerloff, they may attempt to regain consumer confidence by offering certain specific quality guarantees as our later discussion on the development of the auction business will show. Similarly, contemporary painters may also resort to offering quality assurances for their products, namely in the form of establishing organizations in which membership is restricted and based on some internally agreed-upon standards of product quality.

In this light, Reynolds' *Discourses* take on the character of product-specific quality guarantees offered by one particular organization, the Royal Academy. Due to its stature, the organization was even in the position to proclaim and enforce them as uniform standards. It could be argued further that the empirical nature and general tone of several of the publications on aesthetic theories discussed earlier make these writings into useful consumer guide books for purchasing paintings. Under this model it becomes apparent that both the proliferation of artists' organizations and the changing nature of aesthetic writing were building blocks of the economic structure of the art market in addition to being social phenomena.

This numerical growth of artists' groups attests to an expansion of the market for contemporary paintings. Under such conditions of increasing competition, the product differentiation model also applies to rivalling artists' organizations. To compete effectively, each cohesive group must proclaim some unique aspect that sets it apart from others in the eyes of consumers. Doubtless, the greatest and most exclusive distinction for an artists' organization in England was the receipt of a royal charter. Several efforts were made towards that goal, starting with Thornhill's divisive attempt in 1713. But it was not until 1768 before the grand prize of official recognition as The Royal Academy was finally won. The significance of this organization to the history of the British contemporary art market deserves a more detailed account of its genesis.

Early in 1755, the organization in Peter Court, St Martin's Lane, which had been started by Hogarth around 1734, opened negotiations with the 'Society of Dilettanti' and submitted a pamphlet titled *The Plan of an Academy for the Better Cultivation, Improvement and encouragement of Painting, Sculpture, Architecture, and the Arts of Design in General,* authored by Reynolds, Jean-Francois Roubiliac (1685–1759), William Hoare (1707–92) and other leading painters of the period.[31] The organization had already considered an earlier proposal submitted by Robert Dingley in 1748. However, this scheme, which called for yearly exhibitions of pictures, statues, models and architectural designs, did not come to fruition due to the society's insistence to maintain control over the proposed academy. Nonetheless, it led with the participation of a number of artists from St Martin's Lane to the founding of the 'Society of Artists'.[32] Since the dictatorial attitude of the 'Society of Dilettanti' did not change towards the new proposal offered by the St Martin's Lane group, negotiations broke off.

Around this time, Hogarth became a member of the 'Society for the Encouragement of Arts, Manufactures and Commerce' (or 'Society of Arts'), founded in 1754 by, among others, William Shipley (1715–1803), a drawing master from Northampton. This organization, however, according to an advertisement in the *Gentleman's Magazine,*[33] was intent not on instructing young people to become artists but to train them in the industrial arts.[34] Therefore, the efforts to establish an academy with the help of Shipley's group also proved to be fruitless.[35] Nonetheless, the connection with his 'Society of Arts' turned out to be beneficial for those St Martin's Lane artists who, together with others had formed the earlier mentioned 'Society of Artists'. In 1759, the latter group rented rooms from the 'Society of Arts' to stage a first exhibition, scheduled for the next year. The event was successful and occasioned the 'Society of Artists' to ask for permission to use the same facilities again for the next exhibition scheduled for 1761. The new request contained a proposal to charge one shilling admission; however, this was rejected by the 'Society of Arts'. Moreover, Shipley's group now also demanded vetting privileges. The members of the 'Society of Artists' considered these issues significant enough to sever their connection with the other organization.

Then, Reynolds, together with the architect James Paine (1717–89), found an alternative showroom in Spring Gardens that belonged to the auctioneer Christopher Cock. Cock's dealings with contemporary British painters went as far back as the early 1740s when pictures by John Wotton and Peter Monamy made their first appearance at his sales.[36] This represents one of the earliest records of auctioneers' involvement with works by well-known contemporary painters. The commercial union between living artists and auctioneers, not always a happy one, was to develop later into a crucial building block of the mid-Victorian contemporary art market boom. For now, however, the group simply used the facility for exhibitions until, encouraged by the granting of a royal charter by George III in January 1765, it purchased a house in Pall Mall with the intention of opening an art school. Because of disagreements over appointments to various positions within the new school of the now renamed 'Incorporated Society of Artists of Great Britain', several artists led by Reynolds decided to branch off. Finally, at the end of 1768, Reynolds and his followers emerged as victors and were awarded the much-coveted prize: George III's recognition of the group as his official 'Royal Academy'. Most of the leading artists were understandably drawn to this royally sanctioned new organization. The 'Incorporated Society' was unable to compete and discontinued functioning by 1791.[37]

Within a few years, The Royal Academy became one of the most dominant forces in the British arts environment and a defining component of the British art market. Emerging as the pre-eminent show place for contemporary paintings, the Academy challenged subsequent generations of painters to recognize its supreme authority. Due to its very function in the exchange mechanism for art, it became one of the agents of the future of British painting.

Associated with the formation of the RA and the other organizations were various and varying attempts to market paintings, independent of middlemen, to the new middle-class patrons. One avenue by which artists and potential patrons were brought together was through such clubs as the 'Rose and Crown',[38] the 'Kit Kat', [39]or the 'Beefsteak'.[40] In the absence of an established independent exchange mechanism, these clubs provided a transitional structure for producers and consumers to transact business. Despite each organization's specific character, there was also much they had in common. Generally, their membership was composed of a heterogeneous mix of writers, publishers, artists and patrons who often shared a leaning towards oppositional politics. Some, like the group that met at Slaughter's Coffee House, even championed certain styles of art.[41]

An equally important role in selling artists' products directly to end consumers was played by the expanding print media. Through advertisements placed in newspapers and periodicals, painters invited the public to their ateliers. At first, there appears to have been some reluctance among artists to utilize direct media advertising. Perhaps there was concern that conventional advertisements would align them in the public's eye with the lesser trades of bookselling, print selling, and auctioneering. Therefore, they often disguised their notices as news items for the column on recent events in the capital.[42] This bias against the media, however, was soon overcome. The ever business-ingenious Hogarth, for instance, continuously used newspapers to advertise his new publications or studio sales to circumvent dealers.[43] His choice of subjects betrays an entrepreneurial awareness of two of the governing principles of modern retailing: innovation and product differentiation. Since his small conversation pieces earned him insufficient income to feed his family, he decided to try a 'more model mode, *viz.*, painting and engraving modern moral subjects, a field not broken up in any country or any age'[44]

Besides the press and social gathering places, painters used still other methods to attract clientele. There was always the traditional word of mouth. But offering drawing and painting lessons to affluent members of the middle class as well as displaying engravings after portraits with booksellers and in luxury shops also became part of a painter's marketing kit.[45]

No one specific course was readily available for artists in their search for economic prosperity. The old system of direct patronage still existed, yet it offered fewer promising opportunities. Painters were prepared to try anything that had a reasonable promise of success. Many of these endeavours, such as offering lessons or exhibiting works in non-gallery settings, are still practised today and typify artists who lack professional representation in the market. These activities are not only descriptive of a contemporary art market at an infant stage but, on an individual level, of the state of a given contemporary painter's career under a mature market environment.

Although marketing methods had become more refined, the need for direct contact between producer and consumer to transact business severely circumscribed commercial growth. At such moments of tension, the dynamics of the exchange system challenge participants to seek out alternative opportunities that usually engender further commoditization. It is a testimony to the importance of middlemen that the next crucial step was accomplished through their agency.

The socio-economic advancement of painters as artisanal shopkeepers – for that is what they were as long as production and sale occurred under the same roof – was constrained. There was little distinction, in that respect, between a silversmith or furniture maker and a painter. What was called for was a redefinition, in economic terms, of paintings in the eyes of consumers, that is a change in their commodity character. Since pictures as tangible goods consisted of certain, fairly narrowly defined, input of materials and labour, the change had to take place in the intangible realm, the 'aura'.[46] As long as contact between product and consumer occurred within an existing, familiar context, such transformation was difficult to achieve. Therefore, a new, contextually different, environment for the display of paintings for public consumption had to be found.

Publicity and Status: the first Exhibitions

In the first third of the eighteenth century, options for viewing paintings, aside from painters' studios, were limited to auctions, although works by better-known living British artists rarely made it to the block. The one exception seems to have been Don Saltero's coffeehouse, where as early as 1708 art and all sorts of curiosities for public viewing could be found. Unfortunately, it is not known if these works were for sale or to attract customers to the establishment or if any of these works were by contemporary British artists.[47]

The opportunity for change came in 1732, when the entrepreneur Jonathan Tyers reopened Spring Gardens at Vauxhall after leasing them from the proprietor, Elizabeth Masters, in 1728. The Gardens had first become famous under Charles II for their lovely walks. Now, the developer added elegant supper boxes decorated 'with interesting paintings by Francis Hayman (1708–76) and William Hogarth'.[48] Along the paths, lit by over 1000 lights, the landscaping boasted artificial ruins and arches, statues, even a waterfall, all creating an ambience intended to heighten the enjoyment of paying visitors on their casual stroll to the music room, the Chinese pavilions, or the Gothic orchestra. The opening ceremony on 7 June 1732, a lavish *ridotto al fresco*, was a great promotional success and helped establish the Gardens as the fashionable resort of the day. Even the Prince of Wales attended the event and remained a loyal patron until his death in 1751.

A contemporary ballad describes the popular appeal of Vauxhall:

Now the summer months come round
Fun and pleasure will abound,
High and low and great and small,
Run in droves to view Vauxhall.
See the motley crew advance,
Led by Folly in a dance,
English, Irish, Spanish, Gaul
Drive like mad to dear Vauxhall.
Each profession, ev'ry trade
Here enjoy refreshing shade,

Empty is the cobbler's stall
He's gone with tinker to Vauxhall,
Here they drink, and here they cram
Chicken, pasty, beef and ham,
Women squeak and men drunk fall.
Sweet enjoyment of Vauxhall.[49]

Evidently, the Gardens attracted not just the respectable set, but folks from all walks of life, including squeaking women and intoxicated men.

Regardless of the immediate success of his enterprise, Tyers continued refurbishing, and on 7 June 1736 the newly decorated facilities made another debut. *Scots Magazine* reported in 1739 that at least fifty large paintings were on view at various locations throughout the Garden. Among scenes of playing children and rustic amusements, there were four Shakespearean subjects; four contemporary history themes by Francis Hayman; Hogarth's *Henry VIII and Anne Boleyn*; four canvases depicting contemporary naval engagements by the sea picture specialist, Peter Monamy; and twelve scenes from Richardson's popular novel, *Pamela,* by Joseph Highmore (1692–1780).

The various paintings displayed at Vauxhall were chosen by the respective artists to suit the Garden's heterogeneous mixture of patrons.[50] According to the Shaftesburian hierarchy, these paintings were distinctly non-elitist. Ranging from depictions of frolicking peasants to children's games *a la* Dutch 'drolleries' to openly erotic scenes, the pictures were a far cry from the display of heroic acts of virtue demanded by the Earl.

The consumer orientation of these pictures is also evident within a chronological context. The earlier canvases decorating the supper boxes were backdrops, secondary to the other diversions of food, drink, music, or people-watching. Hayman's later Shakespearian subjects of around 1745 were displayed more conspicuously. Elaborately framed and installed in their own classical pavilion, their prominence unencumbered by any other furnishings, the paintings were the primary attractions. Visitors had to walk up from the Gardens over several sets of stairs to view the canvases. The works' literary/historical content not only ranked them substantially higher in the hierarchy of subjects, but the general enthusiasm for theatre must have occasioned patrons to take the extra time to inspect a painter's treatment of these familiar themes. Although not yet self-sufficient since their exchange function was still tied to another product – Tyers' Gardens – the paintings at Vauxhall took a first significant step towards becoming autonomous cultural commodities.

Unfortunately, we cannot establish if the participating artists were the first to become aware of the opportunity and then approached the developer, or if Tyers had taken the initiative. Pleasure gardens were beginning to be recognized as rather profitable enterprises, and Spring Gardens had to differentiate itself from its competition. Therefore, the idea of displaying contemporary paintings may have been the developer's. Alternatively, Hogarth's entrepreneurial character and business strategy suggests that he might have been the first among the artists to meet Tyers and, recognizing the potential of the Gardens for exhibiting contemporary art, propose the scheme.[51] In any event, Hogarth was granted perpetual free entrance to the gardens, perhaps in appreciation for having come up with the concept.[52]

The gardens' popularity was enormous. A guidebook was published, and the benefits to artists' careers of having works on exhibit there were well recognized. Walpole even went so far as to credit the display at Vauxhall of Roubiliac's sculpture of Handel with having 'fixed Roubiliac's fame'.[53] Private commercial initiative and entrepreneurship, not public funds, had successfully transformed Vauxhall into England's first public picture gallery on a grand scale.

David Solkin describes the Gardens as a model for

> an economics of art production responsive to the character of the modern public sphere – an economics predicated first and foremost on the need to satisfy the interests of an exceedingly large audience, many of whose members had little understanding of or sympathy for the finer points of connoisseurship.[54]

In short, Vauxhall was a model of process innovation in art marketing and as such offers a further example of commoditization of the arts environment. The Gardens also represent a product innovation in the newly emerging leisure market. Not only did Tyers succeed in building a profitable enterprise, but he did so by creating an exemplary Romantic environment, an escape removed from the realities of the everyday world – in fact, a theme park. Of particular importance to our story is that the display of paintings at Vauxhall was the result of the agency of a middleman. Through Tyers' efforts, the presentation of contemporary pictures was, for the first time, separated from artists' studios and, untarnished by any direct association with trade or craft, brought into an environment accessible to all. Moreover, these works were shown in a new exotic context that facilitated their aura's transformation. Their commodity character had been successfully changed. Vauxhall achieved the presentation of paintings as part of a new, enticingly different experience, as a form of novel and fashionable entertainment enjoyable for royalty and commoners alike. Spring Gardens introduced the activity of viewing pictures as an innovative product to be used in a new, potentially highly profitable and expanding enterprise – the commercial exploitation of leisure. Without this exchange qualification, paintings would have generated interest at best only on a personal level. To attract attention beyond that degree among members of the business community, these artistic products had to offer some type of economic incentive.

Clearly, Vauxhall was not organized specifically as an exhibition facility for paintings. Pictures were just one among many other attractions. Nonetheless,

Tyers had created with Vauxhall a prototype for the increasingly popular commercial exhibitions of paintings which developed in Britain subsequent to the opening of the Gardens. Emphases would shift according to the aims of each undertaking, but the principle – the recognition of the economic potential of art exhibitions as commercial leisure products for consumers of all classes – was, and still is, always present.

The favourable audience response to the Vauxhall project must have encouraged participating painters to explore other novel avenues to show their works. It was Hogarth who recognized the many potential benefits of conspicuous involvement of artists in philanthropic activities. If one were to seek a personification of the artist as *homo economicus*, the entrepreneurial pioneer Hogarth was without peer in the environment of eighteenth-century Britain. His time witnessed the first great period of philanthropic activity in England, with its most notable achievements being the charity schools and hospitals. Hogarth appears to have been connected in some way with almost all the great philanthropic and humanitarian projects of his time – from the Parliamentary Committee on Prison Reform to the Foundling Hospital, from St Bartholomew's Hospital to the London and the Bethlehem.

As with many philanthropists of the time, Hogarth's humanitarian motives were usually supported by an awareness of how circumstances could benefit his own purposes – aesthetic as well as commercial. Within five years after his appointment to the board of governors of the newly established Foundling Hospital in 1739, Hogarth and other painters associated with his St Martin's Lane Academy donated several of their works to decorate the public rooms of the hospital.[55] Prominent inscriptions identified the paintings – suitable depictions of biblical acts of charity – as donations by the respective artists. This emphasis of the gift character of the pictures proclaimed not only the hospital governors' prudent fiscal management, but also the philanthropic character of the artists. Their charitable acts also took them into excellent company: the hospital was financed by public subscription with contributions from a mixture of titled and middle-class sources. Even George II was among the donors.[56] The altruistic artists must have thought that those affluent enough to donate money may have some left for buying paintings. Then there was the lagniappe of affording 'the public an opportunity of judging whether the English are such indifferent artists, as foreigners, and even the English themselves pretend'.[57]

By 1746, around twenty artists had donated their works and were formally appointed governors. It was decided to host an annual banquet on November 5 to discuss the donation of further works. One can think of this event as the forerunner of the yearly ceremonial dinner of the Royal Academy still held today.[58]

The Foundling Hospital project went one important step beyond Vauxhall. By associating with trendy philanthropists and advertising their own benevolence to the public, the artists involved achieved their first significant progress towards respectability as a community. Like Vauxhall, this undertaking was also immensely successful, and a visit to the hospital 'became the most fashionable morning lounge of the reign of George II'.[59] Therefore, what Tyer as a professional middleman had done for the popular appeal of paintings, the painters themselves achieved through the Foundling for the long sought-after elevation of painters' social status. From these combined platforms the commercial exploitation of exhibitions of contemporary art could be launched.

Courting the Public: the First Commercial Group Exhibitions

Over a decade passed before the lessons of Vauxhall and the Foundling came to fruition. Whitley quotes:

> Foundling Hospital, Nov. 5, 1759. At a meeting of the Artists, resolved: That a general meeting of all Artists in the several branches of Painting, Sculpture, Architecture, Engraving, Chasing, Seal-Cutting, and medalling, be held at Turk's Head Tavern, in Gerrard Street, Soho, on Monday the 12th inst., at Six in the evening to consider a proposal for the honour and advancement of the Arts, and that it be advertised in the Public and Daily Advertiser. John Wilkes, President. Fra. Milner Newton, Secretary.[60]

The outcome of this fateful meeting at Turk's Head Tavern, presided over by John Wilkes, the later notorious adversary of George II and editor of the *North Briton*, marks the beginning of the British phenomenon of self-financing, public showings of art, organized by independent bodies of artists. According to a contemporary author, the accessibility of the donated works at the Foundling had 'made those artists more generally known than others; and this circumstance it was, that first suggested an exhibition; which was no sooner proposed than approved'.[61]

Consequently, in December 1759, Francis Hayman, helped by his friend, Samuel Johnson and in his capacity as chairman of the Turk's Head Tavern group – later to become known as the 'Society of Artists' – wrote a letter to the president of the 'Society for the Encouragement of the Arts, Manufacture and Commerce'. Better known as the 'Society of Arts', the organization, as mentioned earlier, had been founded by William Shipley in 1754 with the help of several wealthy art lovers to offer monetary rewards for winning entries in competitions for different areas, including drawing.[62] Hayman asked for permission to use the organization's recently acquired room in the Strand in which prizewinners' efforts were usually exhibited. Regular commercial galleries had not yet come into existence, and the young organization had no premises of its own. The Turk's Head group wanted the space to 'raise a sum for the purposes of charity, by the annual exhibition of their works ...'[63]

Some issues between the two organizations over the precise means by which to 'raise a sum' had to be resolved first. Finally, in April 1760, five months after the meeting at the tavern, the first commercial exhibition of contemporary paintings in England opened its doors to the public. It boasted an impressive 130 works by 69 artists. Most of the leading London papers took note of the event, without, however, specifically mentioning the 'Society of Artists'. The press was mainly concerned with the awards presented annually by the 'Society for the Encouragement of the Arts, Manufacture and Commerce' to certain artists, and a debate ensued on the choice of recipients and their works.[64] Apparently, the newly formed 'Society of Artists' had not yet succeeded in carving out its own distinct identity. Nonetheless, the enterprise, judging from the sale of 6,582 catalogues – the ultimately chosen method to generate revenue – during the two weeks of the exhibition, was successful. Daily demand for catalogues grew steadily as news of this exciting novel event spread. The curiosity surrounding this 'experimental exhibition was so intense, that the room was continually crowded to inconvenience'.[65] Gross receipts amounted to £164 11sh.; after deducting expenses of £58 12sh 6p, a net profit remained for the stated 'purpose of charity' consisting of the establishment of a pension plan for needy artists. While the art for charity concept of the Foundling project had provided the model for the exhibit, its philanthropic spirit did not prevail. Contrary to the resolution of the earlier general meeting and the letter to Shipley, the committee in charge resolved that the monies should benefit the advancement of their academy.

The excitement and thrill this event must have caused among the thousands of visitors unfamiliar with anything of this sort is difficult to appreciate today. Aside from its popularity, among the most important consequences of this project was the recognition among painters that they were producers of a commodity that could generate its own financial returns. Reflecting on this fact, Pye wrote in 1845, '... the effect of the exhibition soon diverted the attention of the artists to more important matters, by opening to them a source of new prospects and new hopes, arising out of the possession of a revenue of their own, – the first qualification of Englishmen for unquestioned respectability'.[66] The close association Pye describes of relative financial and economic independence with the much-coveted notion of respectability underscores the commercial character of the British arts environment of this and subsequent periods. As long as affluence remained a measure of respectability, painters would orient their products towards that end. The successful marriage of picture merchants and painters that resulted in the mid-Victorian contemporary art boom was so effective because it united producers and middlemen of compatible minds and goals. The key to its success was its consumer orientation. It is no surprise that from this point on annual shows of contemporary art became a common feature in London.

One year later, dissension over money issues caused a split in the ranks of the 'Society of Artists', ironically partly due to the tremendous success of the first venture. Evidently, the rooms were 'crowded and incommoded by the intrusion of great numbers whose stations and educations made them no proper judges of statuary or painting and who were made idle and tumultuous by the opportunity of a show' and consequently '[g]reat inconvenience [had] resulted from inferior people crowding the exhibition room last year'.[67] To keep such individuals out, the 'Society of Artists' demanded that this time no one would be admitted without first paying for the one-shilling catalogue. This was not acceptable to the 'Society of Arts' as the host organization, insisting that the exhibition should be free. There may also have been additional misgivings among the members of the 'Society of Artists' about the fact that not they, but the already well-established host organization and its awards had received the lion's share of publicity. No agreement could be reached and the majority of the 'Society of Artists' decided to look for space elsewhere, finally relocating to Christopher Cock's auction rooms at Spring Gardens. The others remained with Shipley to exhibit at the previous year's location. Consequently, in the spring of 1761, London had two annual exhibitions of contemporary works.

On 17 April 1761, a front page announcement in the *Public Advertiser* informed the public of a change of location of an upcoming exhibition to Spring Gardens. No official name was used; instead, the notice was signed by F. M. Newton, secretary of the 'Committee chosen by the body of artists who exhibited last year'. Ten days later, on 27 April, the office of the 'Society for the Encouragement of the Arts, etc.' advertised on page three of the *Public Advertiser* the commencement of ticket sales for its annual exhibition. Finally, on 2 May, the rival Turk's Head artists' organization countered by publicly shedding its anonymity and informing the readers of *The St James Chronicle* that 'The Society of Artists of Great Britain give notice of the opening of their exhibition on Saturday, 9 May'. The identical announcement appeared in the *Public Advertiser* on 6 May[68] and subsequent publicity was excellent. Both the *St James Chronicle* of 7 May as well as the *The Public Ledger* of 11 May featured a complete catalogue of the exhibited works that listed artists alphabetically and provided a brief description of the numerically ordered works.[69] On 9 May, the *St James Chronicle* printed an excerpt of the pamphlet 'A Call to the Connoisseur' which discussed, in a down-to-earth manner, the content of the show. Three days later, the *London Chronicle* followed up with a lengthy discourse on aesthetic theory, dwelling on such hot topics as 'imitation of nature'.[70] Moreover, not just the events themselves made news but, as a letter to the *St James Chronicle* on 2 June indicated, so did the rivalry between the two artists' organizations.[71] Rarely a day passed during the length of these two competing exhibitions without some art-related article appearing in one or more of London's leading papers or periodicals. While the previous year's event appeared to have attracted little media attention, the second occasion suffered no such neglect. Reading through the almost continuous coverage creates the impression of rather adroit use of the press by both artists' organization. The *St*

James Chronicle, in particular, was a cooperative partner for promoting painters' interests. Beyond the earlier-mentioned publication of theoretical discussions on aesthetics, there were also several letters to the paper signed by a Mr. Oakley that were outright promotions of artist-organized sales. The first, published on 23 April, derided dealers and auctioneers and praised the new union among artists. The letter was reprinted in the same paper on 2 May and again on 5 May. The second letter to the *St James Chronicle*, published 14 May, promoted the exhibition at Spring Gardens. Then on 28 May, a lengthy commentary on Mr. Oakley's writings could be found in the same publication. A few days before, on 23 May, the paper had featured a letter discussing Hogarth in which the writer stated that he had paid twelve or fourteen shillings for this artist's prints 'and would not take 50 for them'. This kind of barely concealed puffing suggests that perhaps Hogarth himself had been the author. Another paper, the *London Evening Post* of 27 May, published a review of the Spring Garden show written in the form of a letter by a young officer to his father. The emphasis on the author's military rank and the identity of the addressee underscored the respectability of the exhibition. On the same page the reader was treated also to a poem 'occasioned by seeing a picture of Mr. Hogarth at the Exhibition...' Such respectable rapture made excellent publicity. As did charity: reminiscent of the Foundling project, an announcement of a donation by the Society for the Encouragement of the Arts to Middlesex Hospital, the British Lying-in-Hospital, to the Asylum, and also to different needy artists appeared in the *General Evening Post* on June 4, near the closing of the exhibitions.[72]

In less than a quarter of a century, the arts milieu in England had profoundly changed. Vauxhall had established paintings as popular public attractions; the Foundling enhanced the social status of artists, and, finally, the first commercial exhibitions demonstrated the economic potential of this combination. Pye writes,

> In this way British artists, – after having vainly endeavoured to acquire countenance and protection of the crown, and of the wealthy and powerful, – by reposing on the million, as Hogarth had done twenty-five years before, made their first advance in such a manner, both morally and conventionally, as to extend a beneficial influence to every artist who contributed to this exhibition, without inflicting upon him the inconvenience of pecuniary favours or obligation.[73]

The precise commercial results of these early, artist-organized, exhibitions are difficult to gauge. The sources mention nothing about paintings being offered for sale. It appears that revenues came only from the sale of catalogues that also doubled as admission tickets. One can only speculate if and how any sales of paintings might have occurred at such occasions. Conceivably, artists may have hoped to attract buyers through the catalogues. Perhaps listing prices or attaching them to exhibited works was thought to lend too commercial of a character to these events which could be damaging to painters' recently gained improvement in social status. Direct sales during, or in conjunction with, these exhibitions may have been attempted, but evidently without much success. In one instance, in 1762, concurrently with the closing of that year's exhibition an auction was conducted which obligated the show coordinators to subsidize reserve prices set by a committee if a work should sell for less. Apparently the loss to the organizers was substantial and the enterprise was not repeated.[74]

The history of such artist-organized events shows that these undertakings were, in fact, better suited for promotion and advertising than for effective marketing of contemporary paintings. At fault was not the exhibition concept, but the absence of professional middlemen as stake-holding organizers and managers. The presence of promoters does not guarantee success; however, their activities, financial risks and rewards are, by definition, tied to the commercial results of an event as a whole rather than to any one participating individual or product. Therefore middlemen would have focused primarily on those aspects they judged to have the greatest potential of yielding commercial success: sales.

'One Man' Shows

Certain foreign painters, more independent and entrepreneurial than their group-affiliated native-born colleagues, began organizing their own exhibitions. Canaletto (1698–1768), for instance, had come to England for the specific purpose of circumventing his dealer, Joseph Smith, an Englishman residing in Venice, who had sold the painter's works to English collectors for huge profits. Bringing one's own works directly to an established market and publicizing their availability for sale was the simplest way to avoid middlemen. Canaletto did so by advertising showings of individual paintings in 1749 and 1751. To protect their own market in cheap copies of the artist's paintings and drive him away from England, the London picture trade responded by spreading rumours that Canaletto was actually an impostor.[75]

Another painter, the Swiss John Stephen Liotard (1702–89) also offered a collection of his work through the media during his first stay in England in 1754. Later, in 1773, the artist, who enjoyed the distinction of wearing oriental robes, assumed a dealer's role for a publicly advertised and rather successful auction of a mixed collection of his own works augmented by numerous Dutch and Italian Old Master paintings.[76]

Neither business method was new to England. British artists had been trying similar means to attract business. The difference in Canaletto's case was that his actions openly threatened the interest of the very dealers who had already developed a market for his work in Britain. The artist's motive for leaving England was ostensibly his inability to paint Italian scenes from memory.[77] Yet he may also have realized the benefits of returning to Italy to paint, while leaving the selling of his paintings to middlemen. Liotard simply capitalized on the popularity of Old Masters and employed them as well as a conventional selling method to market his own work. Considering that prices ranged from thirty-one guineas to 200 guineas, the scheme appears to have worked. Nonetheless, 15/16 April 1774, one year later, the painter turned to the auctioneer James Christie to dispose of a number of his own works together with some of the Old Masters that had remained unsold during his earlier private auction.[78] The artist's reasons for this action are unknown. In view of his forthcoming departure from England, he may have decided that it was inconvenient to deal personally with the organizational aspects of an auction and, therefore, chose a specialist to do the job.

Hogarth, 'after projecting schemes to promote his business in some extraordinary manner', had less success with direct marketing. The auction sale organized by the artist of his six-picture series *Marriage a la Mode* in 1751 attracted but a single offer.[79] In this instance, his business savvy abandoned him. Auction sales of paintings by native living artists were still uncustomary. The attempt to sell in such a novel fashion works which openly satirized certain habits of fashionable society – the very demographic group that made up this project's potential consumer base – was, as a marketing strategy, doomed.

In such varied ways, English painters and some of their foreign colleagues dealt with the challenges of their new role as independent producers devising ways to market their products. All these methods exist to this day; however, they inevitably gave room to more efficient ways, better suited to an expanding art market.

A New Variable: The Royal Academy

The most serious challenge to these early, artists-organized, independent group exhibitions and sales venues resulted from the founding of the Royal Academy. Starting with its first annual show on 26 April 1769, the royally sanctioned institution quickly became the most coveted space for painters to show their works. With the establishment of this official body, the struggle of native British painters for social emancipation and relative control of their economic fate was brought to a successful conclusion. Artistic and economic concerns changed focus as painters' financial success became a factor in their ability to compete against each other both inside and outside the Royal Academy.

From the start in 1769 a clear distinction existed between exhibitors at the Academy and those who showed their works elsewhere. That year, a *Diana Disarming Cupid,* a *Death of Adonis,* or a *Hector and Andromache* as well as other, similar depictions of classical themes could be admired at the RA, while far less lofty images of a *Horse and Mare*, a *Girl by Candlelight* or a *Ship on Fire* were displayed at the Society of Artists exhibition at Spring Gardens.[80]

The original reason, as earlier noted, for the existence of two competing artists' organizations was a disagreement, back in 1761, over admission costs. The faction from which ultimately the RA developed, had insisted on being more exclusive by levying a fee, while the other group had been adamant about free entry. Implicit in these opposing positions is a statement about target audience. The pictures hung at the RA, for the viewing of which one had to pay, reflected, to a degree, Shaftesburian concepts, while the contributors to the Spring Garden exhibition rejected elitism on the basis of money or theme.

These refinements in exhibition concepts, the growth in variety of subjects and styles, the changes in picture sizes, the founding of new artists' societies and the emergence of specialized dealers were all manifestations of economic competition in an expanding market. The presence of the Royal Academy simply added one more, albeit very significant, variable to the scenario.

Artists as businessmen acted and reacted in diverse and creative ways in this new economic environment. The relatively unknown Nathaniel Hone (1718–84), for example, gave birth to the 'sensation picture' concept that was to develop into one of the most successful art business models of this and subsequent centuries. In 1775, rumours spread that his work, *The Conjuror* (http://artmarket.tulane.edu/page69.html), had been rejected by the selection committee of the RA because it included a depiction of the highly respectable painter, Angelica Kauffmann (1741–1807), dancing naked holding a smoking torch. Apparently unperturbed, the savvy Irish painter capitalized on the publicity caused by this rejection. In direct competition with the Academy he organized a private showing of this canvas with about sixty of his other works, charging one shilling to see the scandalous canvas.[81] There were only three other exhibitions in London at that time, and Hone's show was welcome material for the press. The front page of *The Morning Chronicle* of 19 May 1775 even featured a discussion on whether or not Hone's canvas was actually a barely concealed plagiarism charge levied against Sir Joshua. Attendance must have benefited from such news coverage.

Pictorial sensations as a marketing device, although not always including depictions of naked celebrities, became a corner stone of Victorian picture dealing and effected a redefinition of the commodity character of an entire type of painting. The entrepreneurial Hone applied the lessons of Vauxhall with an understanding of public relations to create a new success formula. Henceforth, artists as well as dealers sought to imitate the key ingredients of Hone's project, namely the commercial opportunities inherent in publicity and broad-based public appeal.

Among the most successful of these early artist/entrepreneurs was the American John Singleton Copley (1738–1815). In a stroke of business genius, the painter decided against displaying his already well-known *Death of Chatham* (http://artmarket.tulane.edu/page70.html) in the RA. Instead, he organized in 1781 the first one-picture show, a private exhibition of this work in Spring Gardens. The event was extensively advertised and covered editorially in the press.[82] Over 20,000 visitors paid to see the gigantic pictorial sensation, earning Copley some £5,000 – or around £530,000 in 2010 value[83] – in admissions alone. In the cash-poor economy of eighteenth-century England, this sum was truly extraordinary. Additional revenue was generated through the sale by subscription of low cost engravings after the original work. Prudently, the artist entered into an arrangement with the print dealer, entrepreneur and alderman, John Boydell, to handle the daily business aspects of selling the print. Copley kept the original painting until its sale to Alexander Davidson in 1806 for 2,000 guineas – less than half of the amount realized by entrance fees. Ticket revenues had exceeded by far even the most extravagant amount any artist could have hoped to earn from a simple sale of an original work. The celebrated Sir Joshua could command only around one tenth of Copley's total box office take. According to an article on page 2 of the *Public Advertiser* of 2 June 1781, Copley's enterprise was considered the prototype and reference point for single picture exhibitions: 'The immense and continued success of Copley's Picture shows what very affluent gains would result from an exhibition in London ... of any other individual picture of great decided fame'. The success and scope of this enterprise as well as the limited size of the art audience can best be appreciated by the fact that the private showing of this canvas was responsible for a drop of one third of the attendance revenues of the contemporaneous exhibition at the RA.

In 1791, with even greater financial success, Copley launched a similar event with another huge canvas, *Floating Batteries at Gibraltar* (http://artmarket.tulane.edu/page71.html). Although he had worked on this picture for six years, there was less financial risk involved than in the first project since this painting had been commissioned for 1,200 guineas by the Corporation of London, of which John Boydell, the print dealer, was also a member. Boydell also paid Copley's expenses of £200 to travel to Germany to paint the portraits of the Hanoverian officers who had helped the English during battle. Finally, by 1795, the gigantic picture was ready. However, due to its enormous size, 18 by 25 feet, the artist had to use a tent to exhibit it. Twice he was forced to change location due to neighbours' complaints about noisy crowds but, finally, upon invitation by the king, Copley was able to stage the event at a site near Buckingham House. Over 60,000 visitors paid to see the exhibition. Beyond such immediate rewards, the artist's association with the dealer Boydell that had resulted from the success of these two paintings, set an important precedent and led to other joint business ventures.[84]

Exhibiting original works to sell engravings by subscription was certainly not Copley's invention. Hogarth, for instance, had tried this marketing device when he invited the public to see his *Sigismunda* (http://artmarket.tulane.

edu/page72.html) at Langford's auction house from 16–18 February 1761 for that very purpose.[85] However, *Sigismunda* did not qualify as a sensations picture and, consequently, no admission to the exhibition was charged. Copley's business model fundamentally revolutionized the arts environment: as a joint venture between an artist and an experienced dealer it brilliantly combined a sensational event to which attendance required the payment of an admission fee with aggressive marketing of a low-cost, derivative product.

The recognition of, as Pye wrote, 'the possession of a revenue of their own', independent of host organizations tempted other artists to explore this new scheme. Contemporaneous with Copley's first project, the London *Daily Courant* of 4 May 1781 mentioned on page two an exhibition of works by P. J. von Loutherbourg (1740–1812). Some years later, in 1784, Thomas Gainsborough (1727–88) withdrew all eighteen of his pictures from that year's Royal Academy exhibition and discontinued showing there after the hanging committee refused his demands for a special installation of his portrait of the three eldest royal princesses. Instead, he began to hold frequent private exhibitions, thereby avoiding both Academy politics and competition by proximity.[86] James Barry (1741–1806) staged two exhibitions in 1783 and 1784, and Benjamin West (1738–1820) also organized a private showing of his oversized canvases, *The Death of Nelson* (http://artmarket.tulane.edu/page73.html) and *Christ before Caiaphas* around the same time.[87]

News of this novel money-making concept also reached the Continent. In his foreword to a similarly organized private exhibition of his canvas *The Sabines* (1799) (http://artmarket.tulane.edu/page75.html), the French painter, Jacques-Louis David (1748–1825) mentioned West's projects and lauded this type of public exhibition. 'Is this not an idea as just as it is wise, which brings to art the means of existing for itself ... thus to enjoy the noble independence suited to genius ...? ... [C]ould there be a more dignified and honourable means of gaining a share of the fruit of his labours than for an artist to submit his work to the judgment of the public ...'[88]

Copley's enterprise set the business model upon which key financial projections of art production and contemporary art dealing relied in England for the next century. The redefinition of the commodity character of a single work of art into three separate independently marketable products tripled the earning capabilities of paintings for producers and middlemen alike. Painters henceforth sold not only original works, but also the derivative properties of exhibition rights and copyrights separately and to different buyers.

One of the consequences of the abandonment of traditional patronage in favour of appealing to the public through open exhibitions was the competition for the attention of potential buyers. Therefore, art production henceforth occurred within the context of painters searching for various means by which to distinguish their individual products to attract the attention of anonymous consumers. Product differentiation was most noticeable within the highly competitive arena of the Royal Academy, where an artist had to 'keep his name before the world'.[89] In the preface to *Art on the Line: The Royal Academy Exhibitions at Sumerset House 1780–1836*, David Solkin writes that 'the RA supplied its audience with highly individualistic demonstrations of theatricality and novelty, fundamentally in tune with the intensely competitive spirit of contemporary entrepreneurial capitalism'.[90] Solkin's statement articulates in more modern terms the concerns of contemporary observers of the art scene. Farington, for instance, recorded in his diary a conversation with the painters R. Smirke (1752–1845) and T. Lawrence (1769–1830) during which he opined that the 'pure style accompanied by great simplicity is not now attempted: but bravura in execution, and contrivance for extraordinary and affected effects are now the prevailing considerations'. Farington's friend, Sir George Beaumont, thought 'the practice of many artists [had] become very meritricious [*sic*]'.[91] This was not just an observation limited to cognoscenti but also extended to the broader public. In July 1832, an essay in *Fraser's Magazine*, for example, proclaimed that unless 'it is very conspicuous, from its size or situation, in order to obtain notice in the exhibition room, a picture must have something that will catch the eye at once ...'[92] To achieve this all important eye-catching ingredient, painters resorted to ingenious methods of pictorial product differentiation. This artistic agency in the face of economic competition is behind much of the explosion of styles and rich diversity of subjects that characterized the art production of this and subsequent periods.

In the case of Benjamin West, the immense size and haunting theatricality of his *Death on a Pale Horse* (http://artmarket.tulane.edu/page76.html), exhibited in the Great Room in 1796, assured the artist of a prominent placement on the wall. This visual spectacle also guaranteed him success in the competition for catching the visitors' eyes. Similarly, the painter James Northcote (1746–1831) intentionally set out to create a 'large composition which should demand the attention of the publick at the Exhibition of the Royal Academy' and, most likely, also the print trade's notice. His 8 x 12 feet spectacle, *Portraits Painted from Life, Representing Capt. Englefield with Eleven of his Crew Saving Themselves in the Pinnacle from the Wreck of the Centaur, of 74 guns, lost Sept. 1782* (http://artmarket.tulane.edu/page77.html), was exhibited at the RA in 1784.[93] Fuseli was so successful in carving out a distinction for his products that he achieved a kind of 'fusilesque' brand recognition that enabled him to compete, as he did with his *Death of Dido* (RA. 1781), with the likes of Joshua Reynolds, merely by exhibiting at the RA his own highly idiosyncratic treatment of the very subject chosen by his competitor.[94]

Even landscape painting was affected by this need to employ attention-grabbing pictorial devices. As Ann Bermingham points out, landscape painters were 'forced to inflate the size of their works and to heighten their visual impact by dramatic manipulations of perspective, colouring and subject matter', and thus 'abandoned the style that had previously been the hallmark of the English school'.[95]

The exaggerated colouring, composition and subject of Francis Danby's (1793–1861) 1828 RA exhibition piece, *An Attempt to Illustrate the Opening of the Sixth Seal* (http://artmarket.tulane.edu/page79.html), is but one such case in point. Constable put up 'six-footer' exhibition pieces, and John 'Mad' Martin (1789–1854), as well, responded similarly to the competition. The difference between his first RA exhibition piece in 1811, plainly titled, *Landscape Composition*, and his *Joshua Commanding the Sun to Stand Still* (http://artmarket.tulane.edu/page113.html) shown there five years later reveals this painter's awareness of artistic devices aimed to enhance his product's visibility. J. W. M. Turner (1775–1851) first showed his attentiveness to market competition with his utterly atypical 1807 exhibition picture, *Blacksmith Shop*, an obvious response to the previous year's highly successful picture *Blind Fiddler* by David Wilkie (1785–1841). Later, Turner took the rivalry even one step further by applying his remarkable talent and speed to finish his sometimes almost unrecognizable compositions on site after the entire exhibition had been installed and his competition had revealed itself.[96] Benjamin West actually thought that Turner had become 'intoxicated and produced extravagancies'.[97]

It was, therefore, not only the 'sensation picture', ranging from the scandalous type of Nathaniel Hone to the heroic versions of Copley, West, or Northcote, that was a consequence of the demands placed upon painters by the new market environment. Economic conditions also affected landscape painting in important ways. Commoditization, however, did not stop there but would show its formative effect on the visual image in some way or another, subtle or obvious, in the majority of works of art created with the specific intent to sell them to an anonymous consumer group.

The production of many of these 'eye-catching' pictorial sensations had specific inherent problems. These canvases, while they indeed garnered public notice or even notoriety were extremely costly to produce and difficult to sell. A twenty or even twelve-foot wide picture could not as readily find a suitable private home in which to hang as a three-foot wide one. Hogarth was aware of this problem and was convinced that there would never be a market for these opuses since 'our apartments are too small to contain them'.[98] Therefore, means had to be found by which these expensive, yet career-necessary, products could recapture their high input costs. Exhibiting them in an artist-organized group exhibition, such as the RA, was, financially speaking, a less than optimal solution for a producer with an already established reputation. The RA distributed revenues earned through entrance fees without giving special consideration to the financial contribution generated by specific works. Therefore, staging independent showings was, as Copley's example shows, a rational choice by painters towards maximizing the return on their labour. So was the employment of professional middlemen to turn such events into sales venues for inexpensive reproductions to exhibition visitors.

In short, market conditions demanded that artists produce attention-getting pictures with mass-appeal as well as function as exhibition planners, public relations and publicity agents, print publishers and even print sellers. The artists were therefore investors in as well as project organizers and promoters of sophisticated business enterprises. The transformation of history painting that occurred during this period was, therefore, market-driven, as the economics behind the development, production and marketing of these consciously differentiated, attention-grabbing pictorial sensations demonstrate. Similar notions of product differentiation also offer plausible explanations for the increasing individualization of styles and subjects typical of nineteenth-century painting. Furthermore, the natural next economic step when faced with the expanded range of activities in which painters began to engage was a division of labour. Thus, the appearance of specialized dealers in contemporary art was similarly a consequence of the evolving art market.

Some Conclusions

We would like to present some results of the analyses of our data of auction transactions on which various notions proposed in this chapter are based. An examination of prices of paintings in relation to size revealed that there existed a decreasing return to scale: each additional input of artistic labour produced a marginally decreasing return. Sorting by price and subject showed that history paintings, the leaders of the traditional Shaftesburian hierarchy of genres, not only produced the lowest price/size yield but were also infrequently bought at auction by dealers. Only 3.47 per cent of dealers' purchases belonged to that category.

Several observations can be offered. Our analysis supports the above theoretical model concerning the need for subsidiary income properties of history paintings. A direct exchange did not reward, in monetary terms, the required investment in labour. *Ceteris paribus,* the production of such pictures should have ceased unless these paintings underwent a transformation that could generate for their producers revenue in addition to a straight sale. The resulting production and marketing of subsidiary products necessitated an expanded range of activities that, as mentioned above, led to the employment of middlemen. This entry of new players into the market introduced its own set of dynamics to the production and exchange mechanism. These dealers, for example, stayed away from investing in history paintings on the *secondary* market precisely because the works' subsidiary income-earning properties of copy-rights and exhibition rights had already been exploited. Moreover, the paintings' usually large size made them not only difficult to resell, but they also occupied expensive commercial gallery wall space which could be put to more profitable use by displaying a wider choice of smaller pictures.

We also observed that the most popular sizes overall were 20 x 30 to 24 x 36 inches, the still classic 'sofa size' (Table I.1). We further noticed that Dutch seventeenth-century paintings were smaller, regardless of subject, than those produced in other countries contemporaneously. Moreover, English eighteenth-century paintings were considerably larger than those painted by British artists in the next century.

From these facts we concluded that again the market affected this particular aspect of the physical make-up of pictures. The Netherlands's urban consumer of paintings lived in a more confined space and, thus, smaller works were more suitable. However, the expected buyer for contemporary British paintings of the eighteenth century was, most likely, still thought by artists to be found among the gentry who possessed more spacious country homes, while the target consumers in the nineteenth century were members of the urban middle class.

As manufacturers of cultural commodities, painters oriented their products towards the consumer. Furthermore, their path towards professional emancipation and unimpeded participation in the market displayed sound recognition of the principles of competition in an expanding market.

4 CRITICS AND AUCTIONS

The Economics of Art Criticism

By the time painters approached the public sphere at mid-century, cultural criticism was well established in Britain. The growth of England's book industry in the seventeenth century had offered new opportunities to authors, but also to a new subgroup of writers, the literary critic. Confronted with an expanding audience, these writers recognized that their essays had to be directed towards an increasing and demographically more diverse audience. Indeed, literary criticism experienced, albeit earlier than painting, its own similar commoditization to adapt to the progressively broadening and more heterogeneous consumer base for literary works.[1] The growing popularity of art auctions and the advent of public exhibitions of works by contemporary painters provided writers with new topics, and a new literary genre was born: popular art criticism as it is still practised today.

The first public showing of paintings in April 1760 generated little response. However, soon thereafter, journalists recognized the opportunities to write about art for a still developing audience.[2] Initially these contributions, often solicited from the public by newspapers or periodicals, simply advertised an event together with rudimentary instructions in viewing paintings to an audience not yet conversant in matters of art. In one of the few surviving reviews of the 1760 exhibition, published in the *Imperial Magazine*, the author was clearly more concerned with promoting the show. But at the same time he offered basic if rather vague observations useful to a less informed audience not just for viewing but also for polite conversation about pictures. 'In these pieces', he wrote about four works by Reynolds, 'you see a copious and easy invention, the most graceful attitudes, great truth, sweetness, and harmony of colouring; a light bold, mellow and happy pencil ... one living proof that genius is of all ages and countries and that Englishmen need not travel abroad to see fine things'.[3]

As audiences became more accustomed to viewing art, writing about it also changed. Finer points of connoisseurship, such as more obscure iconographic aspects and historical accuracy of the depiction of certain classical themes, entered the discussion. Gavin Hamilton's (1723–98) *Achilles Lamenting the*

Death of Patroclus was scathed by an anonymous reviewer in *The Gazetteer and New Daily Advertiser* in 1765, questioning rhetorically the right of a painter, 'when he vies in the scene which he undertakes with a poet, to depart from the description of the latter'. One of the objectionable aspects of the picture was Hamilton's placement of Patroclus 'upon armour, as if it was just taken off his body; but that was left in the field: neither could Achilles be said to have his own in his tent, as it was his he had lent to Patroclus'.[4]

The above described development in literary genre was characterized by its consumer orientation. Unlike Reynolds's ruminations on esoteric aspects of beauty, these writings were intended for popular consumption and designed for precisely that market. A more discriminating, intellectual approach would have impeded an exchange mechanism that aimed to facilitate the consumption of artists' products by a growing, intellectually non-elitist, audience.

Painters soon recognized the crucial influence these new writers could have on their careers. Publishers as well noticed the positive effects critical essays on art had on the sales of their magazines, and art criticism assumed a pivotal role in the English arts scene.[5] Unlike on the Continent, particularly in France, where art criticism was often an arena for political debate, British art writers assumed an essential function in an art *business* environment. The art critic John Wolcott's arrangement with the painter John Opie (1761–1807) which called for the writer to receive a percentage of the artist's earnings in exchange for puffing him in the press may have not been so unusual.[6] Writers actively advanced schools, individual artists, or particular dealers. They were also involved in commercial exhibitions and the publication, promotion and sale of reproductive engravings. As agents of communication, instruction and criticism their impact on the arts was as subtle as it was inevitable. Henceforth artists and dealers had to reckon with this additional player.

These art critics were agents of culture who, by educating the consumer in matters of art appreciation, created order, promoted the consumption of cultural goods and thus positively influenced the commodity character of paintings. At the same time, they also enlarged the market for their own products.

On another level, however, critics also retarded commoditization. Within the cultural system of order, paintings occupy a specific place defined by their shared biographical characteristics. Unless the art market has a built-in mechanism that prevents excessive commoditization, paintings could give up their distinctiveness within their own order but also in relation to other cultural goods. Among the consequences would be the loss of the function of art writers. Therefore, it was and still is in the self-interest of critics to stop excessive commoditization of paintings by promoting individuality and uniqueness, two of the salient prerequisites of not just modern art but also of successful retailing in a competitive market. In this task, art writers were in alliance with painters.

The assertion of painters' personality and genius, which accompanied their evolution into independent small entrepreneurs, was also part of the same check mechanism. Kopytoff describes the counter-forces to the exchange function's push towards maximum commoditization in more general terms as 'culture and the individual with their drive to discriminate, classify, compare, and sacralise'. This means a two-front battle for culture as for the individual, one against commoditization as a homogenizer of exchange values and the other against 'the utter singularization of things as they are in nature'.[7]

Art writers' function was two-fold. Culture creates order within the apparent disorder of its environment by establishing well-defined areas of homogeneity through classification and discrimination. If this process of homogenizing goes too far, groups of cultural commodities can lose their distinctiveness, and culture's function of cognitive classification is weakened.

The relationship between artist, art writer, dealer and audience would become a crucial factor in the arts environment. The preponderance of narrative and literary subjects in post-mid-eighteenth century and, even more so, in Victorian art is to some extent attributable to art writing and its indebtedness to literary criticism. Purely aesthetic themes, such as Whistler's nocturnal subjects, were more difficult to write about and less entertaining to a mass audience largely uninitiated in cutting edge aesthetic debate. Yet choices made by art writers necessarily involve different considerations than those of artists and/or dealers. Therefore, the impact of art criticism on the commoditization of the arts environment of this period was not always as clear cut as it was, for instance, in the case of dealers.

Towards a Trading Platform: the Development of Art Auctions

The benefits of art writing on the art market extended also to the increasingly popular art auctions. While English painters explored various means through which they could realize the potential economic benefits associated with changing market conditions, art auctions had already become a customary method for dealers and private collectors to trade in old paintings and newer copies of varying quality and price. This system of selling art was among the Dutch imports of the latter half of the seventeenth century and was used as a mechanism for selling luxury goods of highly personal utility such as imported paintings in an as yet underdeveloped English art market. Buyers were not subject to perfect price discrimination; instead, rather than having to offer the highest price they could pay, they only had to bid one increment above the sum of the underbidder. In turn, competitive bidding assured the seller that in each case the maximum price was paid under the specific auction's condition. Moreover, auctions helped to establish a value for a commodity for which a market price had not been fixed or was difficult to establish.[8]

Although auctions had been used since the early years of the seventeenth century to dispose of a variety of different goods, the first record of art works sold that way dates to 1674.[9] During the 1680s, as it became the established method for art dealers to offer their goods and services, it experienced a boom, with over 300 advertised sales occurring between 1688 and 1694.[10] Estimates based on extant auction catalogues suggest that as many as 35,000 paintings may have been offered on the block between August 1689 and March 1692 alone.[11] This translates into a 12 month average of over 13,000 pictures or approximately 300 lots distributed over 43 auctions each year. The relatively low number of recorded imports during this general period - averaging fewer than 500 per annum[12] - indicates that the majority of these auctions consisted of consignments of old and new locally produced pictures and existing older stock of European origin rather than recent imports.[13] Some of these early auctioneers may have also offered their services directly to local artists.[14] As auctions entrenched themselves they provided for the top end of the market a physical space and social context for intellectual connoisseurship, erudite writing about art and discriminating consumption of it. For the lower end these sales offered an exchange platform for a commodity that was only gradually distinguishing itself from common household goods.[15]

After a period of uneven growth following the boom years, auctions by the 1730s had become the main channel through which paintings changed hands in London.[16] The high frequency of sales likely nurtured a perception that these art works were easily traded and therefore possessed a certain asset value. Auctioneers aggressively solicited consignments with the promise of 'ready money' to 'any persons [that] have any pictures to sell'.[17] Moreover, segmentation by quality/price, sales location and audience – itself indicative of an expanding market - must have occasioned some speculative consumption among more knowledgeable buyers hoping to arbitrage.[18] The rather indiscriminatingly assigned attributions of many of these paintings to well-known artists suggest that a possibility of 'discovery' was certainly implied. Such generic descriptions as 'seapiece' or 'little fruit piece' do not discount the perception that bargains may hide among the offerings. Since these early catalogues do not list prices, it is impossible to determine the quality range and if and to what extent such scenarios occurred. Even in today's far more informed market, dealers and private collectors still attend sales of lower quality goods and/or in secondary locations to similar ends.

Already early in its genesis, in 1689, the industry began to refine its business methods. Policies and regulations were imposed to improve the conduct and speed of sales, to protect the auctioneer from frivolous or fraudulent bidders and to assure timely payment of purchased goods. Apparently it was through the initiative of Edward Millington, the best known among these early auctioneers, in conjunction with a sale in 1689 in Tunbridge Wells that these rules were first published.[19] For the most part they have stayed in effect until the present day. Some auctioneers, including Millington, also commissioned pamphlets on the appreciation of art in order to educate potential customers.[20] Rouquet specifically commented on the efficiency and consumer orientation of these sales.[21]

By the early 1720s, London papers advertised almost weekly auctions of paintings by Titian, Carracci, Cortona, Bassano, Claude, Poussin, van Dyck, Rubens, etc.[22] Judging from the prices fetched, the majority of these paintings were either older or recent copies. These early events were initially staged by dealers at coffee houses and taverns such as the Barbadoes Coffeehouse, Batson's Coffeehouse and Tom's Coffeehouse, all located in Cornhill, or Will's Coffeehouse in Westminster.[23] By mid-century, however, fixed location sales conducted by professional auctioneers had become the norm.[24] Among the earliest pioneers of the profession was the above mentioned Edward Millington who already in 1692 was conducting regular sales at his location, 'The Vendu'; by 1694, so was Cock and Edward Davis by 1697.[25]

Art auctions were well attended by the social elite as well as the middling ranks as both buyers and spectators.[26] This 'bourgeoisification'[27] did not go unnoticed: 'Nothing can be more entertaining', wrote Rouquet, 'than this sort of auctions; the number of persons present, the different passions which they cannot help by shewing on these occasions, the pictures, the auctioneer himself and his rostrum, all contribute to the entertainments'.[28] A poem on the subject published anonymously in *The Man of Taste Occasioned by an Epistle of Mr. Pope on that Subject* in 1733 offers a glimpse from a participant's side.

> In curious paintings I'm exceeding nice
> And know their several beauties by their price.
> Auctions and Sales I constantly attend,
> But chose my pictures by a skilful friend.
> Originals and copies much the same,
> The picture's value is the painter's name.
> My taste in sculpture from my choice is seen,
> I buy no statues that are not obscene.[29]

Consumer enthusiasm was evidently little dampened by the fact that sales were riddled with fakes. Rouquet describes these auctions as 'a kind of gaming, where the knowing ones employ all the wiles and artifices imaginable to make dupes of the unwary; and too often they succeed'.[30]

While art auctions were centred in London, auctioneers also promoted their business in provincial locations. Millington, as already noted, took his business to the fashionable resort of Tunbridge Wells 'for the diversion and entertainment of the gentlemen and ladies'.[31]

If there were any commercial galleries in the early decades of the eighteenth century, they disappeared without a trace. The only exception was the establishment of the dealer James Graham around 1715 about which little is known.[32] Consequently, art auctions were the only environment in which the English public could get initial exposure to paintings. Rouquet even likened Londoners' attendance of pre-sale viewings to Parisians' visits to the annual exhibition of the members of the French Academy.

Auctions of paintings, however, were not just exchange platforms but also engines of consumption. 'This sort of sales', Rouquet observed, 'have spread a pretty general taste for pictures in London; a taste which they not only excite but form; there you learn to know the different schools and different masters'.[33] Not just gentlemen, but ladies were also targeted consumers. Millington specifically catered to women in his sales by advertising in the *London Gazette* the 'convenience of galleries' reserved for 'ladies and gentlewomen'.[34]

Occasionally, spectacular prices were achieved, with apparently little positive consequence on the wellbeing of living painters.[35] Evidently, more affluent buyers focused on one expensive picture - a 'centrepiece' - and then bought inexpensive pictures or copies to fill up their walls. This practice depressed the prices living painters could charge for copies or their own original compositions.[36] Nevertheless, from time to time, native artists used the auction system, albeit with mixed results, by either staging their own sales or exhibiting their works in existing auction facilities. Paintings by native and/or contemporary British painters also showed up on the block as part of private collections offered for sale. Cock's auction of a collection belonging to the Earl of Oxford on 7–11 March 1741, for example, included a number of portraits by Kneller, Lely, Richardson and Riley; five marine scenes by Peter Monamy and three paintings by John Wootton. Evidently, there were exceptions to the often lamented reluctance of the English social elite to patronize living native painters.[37] Among the buyers were Lord Holderness, the Duke of Bedford and Sir Burrell. Even the much maligned trade was present at the sale: Vandergucht bought Kneller's portrait of Dryden.

The remaining half of the century witnessed an increase in the number of works at auction by such artists. The general economic and social advancement of painters and increasing difficulties for importing paintings due to the outbreak of war with Spain in 1739 and France in 1744 must have augmented this trend. Consequently, the London art market relied more on recycling local stock. The impact of the reduction in imports on the amount and variety of lots available at auctions was mitigated by several excellent and large collections that came on the market during that decade. Imports from Holland picked up again at the end of the decade, and the 1750s also saw the dispersal of the collections of

John de Pesters and Thomas Hart at Prestage's. The same house also sold the Earl of Waldegrave's pictures in 1763. In general prices fluctuated; buy-ins occurred and dealers occasionally supported their own pictures at sales.[38]

Around the 1770s, London auction houses became the primary exchange platform for many of the great collections from the Continent whose owners sought to remove their treasures from an increasingly politically unstable environment and threat of revolution and war.[39] This flood of pictures not only contained the seeds of England's National Gallery but contributed – more circuitously but no less effectively - to the growth of the market for contemporary English paintings during the next century. At the same time, the auction rooms also profited from sales of numerous private local estates that included a broad mixture of Continental and English works.[40]

During this last quarter of the century, besides older English works such as Dobson, Lely, and Kneller, contemporary paintings by Gainsborough, Reynolds, Kauffmann, Copley, George Stubbs (1724–1806), and Dominic Serres (1719–93) began to appear regularly on the block.[41] The consignors of such works were mainly members of the professions or professional dealers.[42] By this time, London auction houses were firmly established as the largest clearing houses for art, and better-known contemporary painters' works began to be traded more commonly.[43] This trend increased, and by the next century the use of auctions to trade in the works of living artists became a nexus of the mid-Victorian contemporary art market.

Auction economics explains the relatively late appearance of contemporary paintings - other than cheap copies or run-of-the-mill potboilers - on the auction market. They also clarify why this method is not well-suited as a primary sales venue for living artists' works. The unpredictability and therefore relative inelasticity of supply that favours auction sales is jeopardized when living artists use them to reach their primary market. The artist can increase production in response to high demand with the possible eventual consequence of driving prices down. Consequently, contemporary English pictures in the eighteenth century were usually sold at auction in a secondary market scenario.[44] Yet even such transactions harboured risks. Although original art works by definition have no direct substitutes, there exists in theory a price ceiling determined by the cost of a copy by the same painter. None of the transactions recorded in our data shows a consignor identical to the painter whose work is auctioned off. In cases where the date of the work is given, it is always substantially earlier than the sale date. Artists as sellers of their own works are only listed in cases of estate sales. Occasionally, dealers' names are listed as sellers of contemporary works; however, the data do not allow us to make definitive conclusions about such sales. Without a well-ingrained custom of artists selling to dealers to sell to private consumers who then use auctions as liquidity needs arise to sell back to the trade, auctions are a suboptimal exchange option for contemporary painting. Dealers, however, during most of the eighteenth century, still used auctions predominantly to sell their inventory to the primary market, a tendency that would decline in the nineteenth century for reasons we will address later.

Throughout the eighteenth century, the changing character of art auctions reflected an expanding market. They started out as events to sell to the public collections accumulated abroad by foreign dealers for that specific purpose.[45] This business model caught on and attracted local entrepreneurs who, as the market expanded, began to augment imported works with older local stock and recently produced pictures.[46] Further market growth led to specialized auctioneers with fixed locations while the conventional dealer developed towards the direction of a fixed location retail gallery operator. In many ways, the auctioneer had less risk. Goods were sold on consignment and the auction house earned a commission of usually around ten percent of the hammer price.[47] When works were bought-in, the auctioneer still received compensation, sometimes amounting to the same amount as if the lots had sold.[48]

Among professional auctioneers, further specialization occurred and in time the specialist art auctioneer emerged.

During the first half of the eighteenth century, the auction business developed along two separate paths. One was taken by such firms as Langford, Cock, Prestage, and later, Christie's, whose owners catered to the upper echelons of society in terms of both wealth and status. The other path was taken by a less distinguished type of auctioneers whose origin was in the Upholders' Company, the liveried company of upholsterers which had been granted the right to sell second-hand household goods in the sixteenth century. Until the eighteenth century, this group had conducted fixed price sales, but it increasingly began to use auctions as this venue became established. The upholders also collaborated with the tightly regulated appraisers' trade, while the other auctioneers provided this service in-house through non-binding pre-sale estimates. By the end of the century, however, this guild, like those of the Painter-Stainers or Barber-Surgeons, had all but disappeared.[49]

The eighteenth century also witnessed the first legal regulations of the auction business beyond the conditions of sale first published in Millington's catalogues in the previous century.[50] These laws dealt with licensing and the mechanics of conducting business such as bidding up of pictures by an accomplice rather than the frequently mentioned problem of attribution. The most important case in this context was Jenwardine vs. Slade in 1796: two pictures sold as originals had subsequently been declared copies. The judge, Lord Kenyon, argued that since in many cases it was impossible to trace the authorship of a painting and since the works had been sold with an attribution based on the *opinion* of the seller, no fraud was committed.[51] *Caveat emptor* still prevailed, a fact that must have retarded overall market growth. However, this inefficiency of the auction market must have stimulated business for professional dealers.

Economic theory suggests that to increase volume the art auction business would require at some point the implementation of consumer protection policies and/or the sale of art goods with reduced authenticity risks. The mid-Victorian contemporary art boom occurred partly for precisely those reasons.

Before the demographics of auction buyers changed from being mainly dealers to mostly private consumers, few warranties were offered by leading auction houses. It was assumed that purchasers were aware of risks and made their decisions on the basis of their personal knowledge and connoisseurship. When auction houses began to target private and thus less experienced buyers, certain consumer protection devices were established. Similarly, the lucrative business in certificates of authenticity, first practised by Arthur Pond, is another example of commoditization since such documents enhance the saleability of the art works in question. Of course, this practice also negatively affects individual consumers' connoisseurship since reliance, for better or worse, is deferred to another authority.

Associated with the above-described development of the auction business towards enhancing its consumer appeal and improving the exchange of goods was a gradual establishment of the auction market as the point of reference for the art market in general. In theory, auctions are an impartial mechanism for parties to transfer property rights. Auctions began to perform a somewhat similar role for paintings as the stock exchange performs for certain financial products. By mid-nineteenth century, auction prices had become the price indexes of the picture market, and reports on sales took on the character of financial reports, a trend that has continued and grown in importance to this day.

This value and trend setting aspect of auctions developed further in the twenty-first century. Appraisals of paintings for income or estate tax purposes must include comparable examples sold at auction. Thus, donations to qualified institutions favour those art works the comparables of which have performed favourably on the auction block. There is also a close and multi-lateral relationship between public institutions, auction prices, and private collecting/donating. A record price at auction for a specific work may result in an increase of donations of comparable works to museums as private owners recognize the tax advantages. In turn, museum exhibitions stimulate commercial activity and thus affect market/auction prices. Moreover, works already in public hands have an effect on the value of comparable works in private possession, etc. We have to recognize, therefore, the influence of financial considerations on the placement of works of art in the public domain which are often precisely the works of art available to us for study.

5 THE EVOLUTION OF PICTURE-DEALING

Pears estimates that up to 40 per cent of recorded picture sales between 1711 and 1760 were organized by dealers to sell inventory.[1] Their impact on the art economy is further corroborated by the earlier described frequently critical, if not outright hostile, comments made by native painters about the picture trade.[2] Research into dealers' role in the growth of the arts environment during the eighteenth century is still in its infancy and may well remain fragmentary due to the paucity of data. Nonetheless, the available information on dealer-organized sales suggests that these events may have affected noticeable fluctuations in the art market in general. The decrease in sales during the 1720s and 1730s, for example, coincided with a relatively low level of dealer activity, while the import boom in paintings of the early 1740s occurred amidst an increase in trade presence.[3] Furthermore, inventory analyses show that the majority of dealers' business consisted of sales of inexpensive original pictures or copies made by native artists of original works.[4] Auctions data show that the average price of paintings sold during the first half of the eighteenth-century was around £15 with a median of £7.3. Pears determined that out of approximately 25,000 recorded transactions, only 545 fetched above £40.[5] While most of the cheaper works often had impressive sounding attributions, their low prices indicate that most of them were copies or of uncertain authorship. This suggests that the most reliable source of revenue for dealers came from supplying relatively inexpensive works to a fairly modest, in terms of wealth, yet numerically large, customer base. The employment of contemporary painters – English or Continental – as copyists attests to the fact that there existed a limited and unreliable supply of good original works. To procure these good original works, dealers had to risk substantial capital, travel extensively for extended periods of time on the Continent, and buy collections that then still needed to be packed and shipped perilously to London at great expense before they could be offered for sale at dealers' private homes or auctions. The successful conduct of such enterprises was, particularly in the eighteenth century, a complex logistical project fraught with physical and economic dangers. Arrangements with international merchant banking houses, like Fagniani in Rome, had to exist to facilitate payments for purchases, shipping and insurance. Experienced packers were needed to prepare the paintings for transport by land and sea. Safety of the cargo during adverse weather conditions, times of war, civil unrest or banditry was a constant concern. Finally, to re-coup the significant investment, the art still had to be sold for a substantial mark-up.[6]

One of the successful early entrepreneurs of the first half of the century was the Scotsman, Andrew Hay. Hay focused primarily on France and Italy as his main sources of supply and, apparently with his own capital, bought extensively during numerous trips and then sold these goods at his own auctions back in England. Between 1725 and his retirement in 1745, Hay travelled to Italy six times, twice on foot, and fourteen times to France.

Another dealer who operated similarly but rather less successfully was Samuel Paris. Evidently, a somewhat adventurous business style coupled with questionable fiscal responsibility forced him to stay away from England for nearly fifteen years. Nonetheless, Paris managed to avoid serious legal consequences and after his return to the island organized at least seven auctions between 1738 and 1742.[7]

From the early 1740s to the late 1750s, the dealing scene was dominated by the colourful presence of Robert Bragge. Attaching the title of 'Doctor' to his name, the dealer promoted himself as a gentleman-connoisseur rather than as a mere merchant. In fact, his sales catalogues displayed a noticeably greater attention to descriptive details and provenance than those of his immediate predecessors in the trade.

Concurrently operating was Arthur Pond. Although he dealt on a somewhat smaller scale than Bragge, Pond offered his customers a guarantee of authenticity in the form of the word 'true' and his signature written on the back of thusly authenticated works to reinforce their confidence in a market riddled with fakes.[8]

In the spring of 1770, the dealer Goodall offered a group of over one thousand imported old paintings. An extensive collection of old masters assembled by the dealer Gerard Vandergucht appeared at Christie's on 6–8 March 1777. The same gentleman sold another similar collection, again through Christie's, on 14 and 15 March 1788, and the prominent dealer Benjamin Vandergucht's inventory went on the block at the same auction house on 11 March 1796. Noel Desanfans was another noted dealer of this period, and around the same time the dealer and later dictionary author Michael Bryan made his first appearance on the international art dealing scene.[9]

Many of those who made their living by trading in art works had, like the landscape painter-turned-dealer, Thomas Manby, started out as artists or professional antiquaries before venturing into the business. The dealer Buchanan mentioned in this context such individuals as James Irving, James Campbell, George A. Wallis and Jacob More.[10] The dealer and later auctioneer, John Greenwood, had similarly started out as an engraver and painter.[11] Even successful portraitists like Hudson or Closterman dealt in art.[12]

There also existed certain gentlemen 'virtuosi' and 'connoisseurs' who supplemented their personal collecting through dealing.[13] Identification of these individuals is difficult. They may have sold works by consigning them to auctions organized by more established dealers. Graves *Auction Sales* for this period lists numerous sellers of whose identity nothing else is known; many of these sellers could have operated in such a manner. Alternatively, they may have profited from purchasing paintings for other private collectors on a commission basis or by adding a surcharge for their services, as, for example, John Talman had done with Lord Somers in the acquisition of the collection of Padre Resta.[14] Working as a runner for professional dealers was another option. Diplomats, bankers, and political exiles added further to this colourful mix, such as Dr. Hickman, the associate of the Duke of Kingston in Paris and the Parisian banker Mr. Selwin.[15] Even secret agents, like the notorious Jon Macky, occasionally dealt in art as a cover for their clandestine work.[16]

This heterogeneous fringe of the art trade is indicative of a proto stage of a market's genesis. At the same time, it characterizes an unregulated business without standardized professional pre-requisites. Such low barriers were among the engines of growth in a business environment that, in many ways, still wrestled with its medieval past.

Even in present day art dealing, this fringe performs a vital function. The business is still unregulated and without uniform standards. Despite the well-intentioned efforts of various trade associations, this is unlikely to change. In economic terms, the function of these groups is mainly one of enhancing consumer confidence, rather than of enforcing professional standards internally. Thus they are simply marks of commoditization. In today's mature art market, there still exists below the level of professional dealers a great number of semi-professionals quite similar to, and equally as colourful as, the 'proto-professionals' of the eighteenth century. Most established professional galleries and private dealers still rely to varying degrees on loose networks made up of individuals outside the conventional structures of the art business to facilitate buying and selling. While the expansion of the market called for the firm entrenchment of the professional picture dealer, it did not do away with the 'proto-professional' roles from which this occupation evolved.

Unlike today, however, in the eighteenth century those dealers whose identities are known to us rarely appeared as buyers of paintings at auction. Instead, they used auctions mainly to sell their own inventories. This characteristic of the auction market was to change dramatically during the next century: the large majority of auction purchases would be made by dealers while, conversely, dealers as sellers at auction were relatively infrequent. Among the most noteworthy discoveries of our analyses was this central role played by dealers (Table I.2).

Figure 5.1 shows the decreasing presence of dealers as sellers and the increasing presence of dealers as buyers.

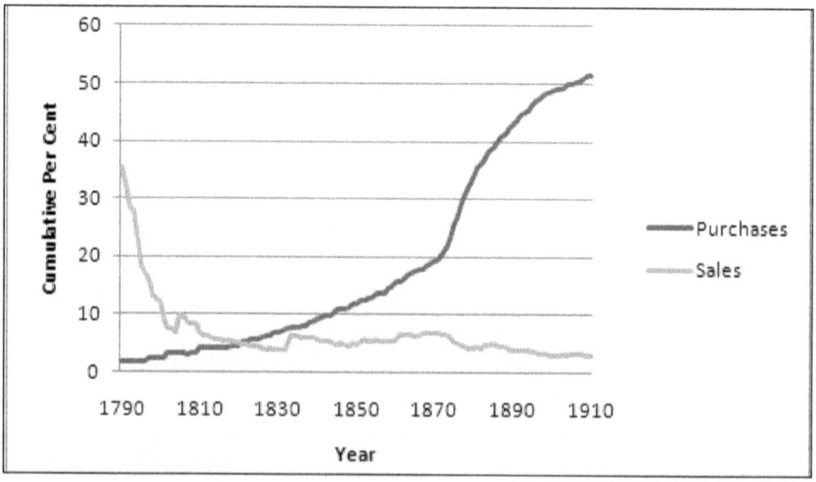

Figure 5.1: Cumulative Per Cent Represented by Dealers.

Auctions were to remain the province of middlemen and their main source of inventory well into the last quarter of the twentieth century, when the 'retailization', or to be more precise, the 're-retailization', of the auction market occurred. The 'proto-professional' character of art dealing was a consequence of an insufficiently developed market, particularly in terms of reliable supply, which did not permit the establishment of dealers with fixed locations on a pervasive scale.

Some manifestations of market maturation, such as Desenfans's or Bryan's private treaty sales and Arthur Pond's guarantees of authenticity, were already evident during the eighteenth century. The period also witnessed the emergence of the profession of picture dealing and its evolution into large-scale entrepreneurship. This development can be traced from the nameless 'picture jobbers' of the late seventeenth and early eighteenth centuries via painter/dealers like Pond of the middle decades to the huge enterprises of mega-dealers like Desenfans and Bryan at the end of the period.

During the next decade or so, the search for new opportunities and the need for a steady supply of reliable goods drove other dealers away from old paintings towards a crucial economic alliance with contemporary painters. Dealers' relationship with the auction industry changed correspondingly.[17] It no longer served as the primary venue through which to sell inventory, but was used by dealers to send signals to the market. The prerequisite was an expansion of the market for contemporary paintings to the point when a clear separation between production and marketing provided these now seasoned middlemen with the chance to apply their marketing skills. Vauxhall, the Foundling Hospital, artist-organized group exhibitions, private treaty sales and single 'sensation picture' shows were but milestones on this path to a convergence of interests.

The Eighteenth-Century Print

The main catalyst in this transformation of the contemporary painting business and the genesis of the dealer in modern art was the reproductive print. The eighteenth-century was Britain's great age of printmaking. Reproductive prints during this period may have outnumbered original works at least fifty to one.[18] Images produced at low costs and in large numbers provided artists and print sellers with the ideal mass market product. In Hogarth's words, 'this I found was most likely to answer my purpose, provided I could strike the passions, and by small sums from many, by the sale of prints which I would engrave from my own pictures, thus secure my property to myself'. Walpole commented that 'they are become [sic] almost the favourite objects of collectors, and in some degree deserve that favour, and are certainly paid for as if they did'. This popularity was, in the opinion of another contemporary insider of the art scene, William Graves, because prints 'cost much less than Paintings' and that 'Knowledge of them is more easily attained, and as they comprehend all sorts of Subjects, they are equally as useful and entertaining'.[19]

Engraving appeared in England around 1490. Before Hollar's arrival in 1638, the medium was largely confined to portraits or used to get commissions for original works.[20] However, during the early decades of the eighteenth century, themes became more varied to include both classical scenes composed by the great masters of the Continent as well as contemporary English subjects, initially by foreign artists and later by native painters. The main catalyst for this change was Queen Anne's employment in 1711 of the French engraver Nicholas Dorigny (1652–1746) to engrave Raphael cartoons for her at the huge cost of £5,000. For unknown reasons, the Queen abandoned the project. So Dorigny offered the prints by subscription and advertised them at the price of 4 guineas a set in the *Daily Courant* on 18 February 1713/14 to be viewed and sold at Garraway's Coffee House. '[F]rom his [Dorigny] arrival to England' Vertue wrote, 'I may justly date the rise of the reputation of sculpture graving ...'[21]

The first major publication of a contemporary British theme, Dubosc's engraving of Louis Laguerre's (1606–1656) paintings of Malborough's battles, commissioned by a group of print sellers at £80 per plate, occurred also during this decade. Dubosc then followed this project with another series of engravings after Thornhill's paintings in St Paul's cupola.[22]

Other foreign engravers, particularly from France, were drawn to England during this period to reproduce many of the great paintings in English collections. Accordingly, the engraving market changed from a previous almost total reliance for supply on imports to a predominantly London-based home industry.[23] Engravers' dependence on publishers/print sellers and painters of the original work had a frequently-commented-on financially depressing effect on this trade. Vertue thought that as long as '[the engraver] is the labourer for other men's vending or profit he must be content with low prices and small rewards'.[24] The enterprising Hogarth successfully challenged this situation by performing all steps of production and marketing himself. In the publication of *A Harlot's Progress* in 1731, Hogarth eliminated the need for a publisher/seller by assuming the role personally. The set was offered by subscription, attracted over 1,200 subscribers and firmly establishing the artist's reputation. Since he often engraved personally, Hogarth also controlled the production process.[25] A revealing comment by the artist in his *Autobiographical Notes* exposes the influence of economics not just on production and marketing but also on formal appearance. He explains that ' ... neither great correctness of drawing or fine Engraving were at all necessary but on the contrary would set the price of them out of the reach of those for whome [*sic*] they were chiefly intended'.[26]

While Hogarth succeeded in his first publishing venture, the industry in general developed towards increased specialization. Prior to 1733, there were only two specialized shops selling prints in London, while by the end of the century, print shops existed in every major town.[27] For this growth to occur, the engraving trade commoditized production, marketing and subject chosen. By the next century this industry would reach hitherto unknown levels of sophistication, yield unparalleled monetary rewards for painters and dealers, and leave its defining mark on Britain's culture.

Without specialized print shops, publishers initially relied for their distribution – the key to the success of selling mass products – and their marketing methods on an existing network of booksellers.[28] Since authors and booksellers/publishers often employed engravers as illustrators, readers were already familiar with prints. This traditional connection also gave print publishers some familiarity with the book publishing trade's well-established production, financing and marketing methods.[29]

The relationship between the book selling industry and the spread of contemporary art through reproductive engravings went beyond marketing and distribution. Most of the major publishing ventures of the last decades of the eighteenth century involved themes from the established English literary tradition familiar to many of those who patronized bookstores. Consequently, the first popular introduction of contemporary English paintings via reproductive engravings had a distinctly literary and narrative character.[30] Moreover, the huge export market to the Continent facilitated the spread of English literary themes and narrative subjects in general. Therefore, the economic origins of contemporary art marketing, that is, its ties to the book industry, are among the reasons for the typical narrative quality of much of Victorian English and nineteenth-century European painting in general.

Beyond familiar literary themes, the engraving industry also adopted the book trade's dominant marketing technique: selling by subscription. Relatively low risk, profit potential and the availability of established retail outlets lowered entry barriers and made this form of publishing ideally suited for the budding print industry.

Pye offers some financial accounts of specific publications. For instance, J. O. Robinson and Mr. Hurst – who had purchased in 1819 the stock of the late great print publisher Boydell – paid Thomas Lawrence (1769–1830) £3,000 annually for the exclusive right to publish engravings after his work. William Woollett's (1735–85) engraving after West's *The Death of General Wolfe* (http://artmarket.tulane.edu/page80.html) alone earned the engraver over £6,000.[31] Pye also cites a speech delivered by the Earl of Suffolk in the House of Lords in 1804 in which the latter states that at one time the annual revenue from the export of engravings had exceeded £200,000.[32]

Invitations to subscribe were usually published in the media or mailed directly to prospective clients. Recognizing the benefits of product differentiation, artists and publishers began to distinguish original prints from reproductive prints, as well as proofs before letters, proofs with letters, and the limited edition thereof.[33] Sometimes a speculative potential was suggested to consumers by advertising that prices would be raised after a subscription list was filled. Abraham Rainbach commented in his 1843 memoirs that these schemes were meant as 'inducements to connoisseurs and lovers of rarity, to form collections of choice exemplars'.[34]

One serious encumbrance to unimpeded growth, however, resulted from the market's own expansion. Before mid-century, print collecting had reached such popularity that piracy became a viable threat. Again it was Hogarth who addressed this problem. His efforts resulted in the passage of the Copyright Act of 1735. This 'Hogarth Act' was based on the literary Copyright Act of 1709 and protected artists' and publishers' ownership of their products for fourteen years from the time of publication.[35] The protection offered by this law must have been partially behind the continuing expansion of the print market, both in size and profitability. In addition, when Parliament imposed an import duty on foreign made 'worked copper' in 1738, local production increased further.[36]

By the last quarter of the eighteenth century, the print trade had developed from a small cottage industry into a huge enterprise. Whitley mentions that by 1787 the print market in Britain had changed from being dominated by imports to such an extent that now English engravings were among the leading exports.[37] 'By this art alone it may be said the British school is known and admired in every country of Europe and America'.[38]

These ventures had become the most profitable segment of all art-related commerce. Due to the affordability and variety of themes, prints dispersed artists' products to a much larger segment of the population than could be reached with original works. Moreover, the revenue potential of mass-produced derivatives gave contemporary painters the possibility to produce the 'sensation' pictures needed to establish and maintain their reputation in a highly competitive public arena.

The recognition of mass appeal as a crucial determinant of painters' careers began to have a formative impact on their works. Many of the paintings produced in England during this period can be better understood by considering their function in a mass market for derivative products. Waterhouse, for instance, contends that Copley painted *Watson and the Shark* (http://artmarket.tulane.edu/page81.html) with the specific expectation that its engravings would be bought by the emerging mass audience for art.[39] West, the other successful American artist/entrepreneur, also was aware that history paintings could only compete in the new market if their high production expenses could be offset by earnings from their reproductive engravings and exhibition rights.[40] In the commercial environment of the eighteenth century, these painters had to consider in addition to audience demographics also different aspects of production, distribution and sale of their products. Subject, composition and formal execution all affected the commercial success potential of any given painting.

The size of this mass market in the eighteenth century is difficult to establish. Inventories list 'pictures' in many provincial households, but often the low values placed on them suggest that they were prints rather than original paintings. Towards the end of the century, the size of the publishing enterprises of, for example, Boydell, indicates that he anticipated sales in the hundreds of thousands of copies. He depended heavily on exports, making this number inconclusive with respect to the English market alone.

Despite this considerable growth of the print industry and its importance to the contemporary painting market, the occupational status of engravers was judged by contemporaries as being merely an essential manual component in the distribution of art goods. A remark published in the *Spectator* stated that 'an engraver is to the painter what a printer is to the author'.[41] William Blake (1757–1827), hardly one to favour convention or the artistic establishment, rebelled against the inferior status of engravers by publishing his own designs in addition to prints he executed after other artists' works. This bias was also responsible for engravers' exclusion from membership in the Royal Academy. Great effort and polemic was expended to keep them from gaining acceptance into the royal body.[42] In economic terms, this exclusion of engravers from membership in the newly founded institution was an act of protectionism by painters to guard their only recently attained social, professional, and thus economic status. Engravings were fast becoming the financial engine of the expanding art economy. As J. Landseer testified before the Select Committee of the House of Commons on the Arts, 'by the graver's art, it has been as truly as elegantly said, "copper has been turned into gold," for it is a vein of wealth both to the artist and to the state'.[43] Admitting engravers as peers to the exclusive club of the Academy would have amounted to yielding control of the top rung of the economic ladder. It was therefore in the self-interest of the Royal Academicians to erect barriers to prevent an usurpation of their hegemonic position, one that could result, so economic reasoning suggests, in a role reversal. Rather than leading the production chain, painters might have been forced into the auxiliary role of design makers in the employ of engravers.

Before this could occur, however, the print industry transformed. One of the by-products of this change was the decline in the production of the kind of painting that depended for its success on the sale of reproductive engravings. Consequentially, the importance of the engraving profession diminished. But until the last quarter of the nineteenth century, the significance of the print industry within the contemporary painting market was in visual and economic terms defining.

The Effects of the Napoleonic Wars on the British Art Market

The buoyancy of the contemporary arts environment of the last quarter of the eighteenth century must have given dealers and native painters much cause for optimism. A brief survey of the London *Times* of this period shows the vitality of this market segment. Between the beginning of July and the first week of August 1799 alone, advertisements announced the exhibition of parts of the famous Orleans collection in the gallery of the dealer Bryan, Fuseli's exhibition of his Milton Series in the Royal Academy,[44] William Elmer's show of Sportsman's Pictures, and the publication by subscription of views of London by Noah Black.

Besides these private undertakings, there existed now also a newly established Royal Academy that offered a steadily increasing number of painters a prestigious showcase for their works. The number of works exhibited at the RA had increased from 136 in 1769 to 1,100 by the turn of the century. This growth was largely due to the increase of non-members in the annual exhibitions. In 1769 only seventeen such artists contributed works compared to thirty-three members. By 1784 the number of the former had swelled to 229 while the latter had declined to twenty-three. This numerical imbalance between member versus non-member exhibitors created an economic tension with far-reaching consequences, since the vast majority of art works was produced by non-members. Even discounting for the value of exhibiting in the prestigious company of Royal Academicians, the revenues generated by entrance fees were mainly associated with the labour of non-members. Unfortunately, their status barred them from voting on fiscal or other matters concerning the operations of the Academy, such as the ever-important decisions of the hanging committee.[45] This unequal distribution of contributions and benefits led in the next century to the establishment of rival exhibition organizations like the Old Watercolour Society or the British Institution founded, respectively, in 1804 and 1805. These competing organizations were symptoms as well as engines of further market expansion by facilitating the market participation of a steadily increasing number of artists. As we discuss later, associated with this process was also a growing diversification among painters' products in the form of increasing specialization, stylistic distinction and heterogeneity of subjects.

Exhibiting at the Academy was indeed considered essential to keeping ones 'name before the world';[46] yet the institution was not ideal for promoting sales. S. C. Hall, the founder of the influential *Art Journal*, commented that as late as the early 1840s, often not a single work sold during the private viewing of the annual exhibition of contemporary art at the RA.[47] This was not a matter of etiquette. The purpose of the event was to provide an exclusive opportunity for the social elite to view and purchase what was considered that year's best production by England's most esteemed painters. Artists turned elsewhere for better commercial outlets. 'One man' and 'sensation picture' exhibitions had already been introduced, and since the business model was successful, it continued.

Numerous artists also participated in print publishing enterprises. The huge undertakings of the leading art dealing/publishing entrepreneurs of the period, Boydell or Macklin, offered contemporary English painters an attractive income possibility and set the stage for other enterprising middlemen to try similar, smaller ventures. Boydell's 'Shakespeare Gallery', Macklin's 'Poet's Gallery', Bowyer's exhibition in conjunction with his publication of Hume's illustrated 'English History' and Fuseli's 'Milton Gallery' were responsible for introducing an unprecedented type of art exhibition – the theme show. These and similar ventures provided an ideal training ground for enterprising individuals interested in exploring new commercial opportunities in the art market.

Despite such innovative entrepreneurship and general buoyancy of the market, it still took nearly half a century before a significant general improvement in the economic conditions of living painters occurred. The reason for this is again the behaviour of dealers. Just at the time when the contemporary art market had evolved to a point that offered opportunities for merging the interests of producers and dealers, competition from old master paintings impeded the full fruition and exploitation of this merger. Consequently, the growth of the market in contemporary paintings slowed. The Victorian writer Wilkie Collins commented on this rivalry in his *A Rogue's Life* during an account of the novel's hero's visit to the premises of a dubious old master dealer.[48] The promising prospects of a union between painters and dealers were frustrated during the last quarter of the eighteenth century by the vast quantity of paintings that appeared on the market due to the political upheavals on the Continent. The union was delayed until well past the commencement of Queen Victoria's reign. The effect of these events on the British art market in general and contemporary painting in Britain particularly is one of the most persuasive examples of the influence of economics, specifically middlemen's resource allocations, on the arts environment.

Writing in 1824, the Old Master dealer, William Buchanan, remarked that 'the last thirty years have produced events in the history of Europe which ... forced from their ancient sanctuaries those treasures of Science and of Art, that had long been the pride and glory of the states to which they belonged'.[49] He was referring, of course, to the French Revolution and the Napoleonic War era. England, although involved militarily, benefited economically from the disruption this conflict caused to its competitors while leaving the island's own infrastructure intact. The dealer Thomas Winstanley noted in the late 1820s, that

> the immense fortunes which have been made by individuals during the late war – the abundance of wealth accumulated by those who have been successful in money transactions of late years, and various other sources of riches from which Great Britain has drawn both collectively and individually the power of possessing whatever is precious – is another cause of the great prices now to be obtained for articles of high taste and virtu ... Paintings are universally acknowledged to be objects worthy of possession ...[50]

The combination of these two factors, the increased supply Buchanan mentioned and the corresponding growth of demand described by Winstanley, substantially enlarged the market for old paintings and created new opportunities for middlemen. Again Winstanley:

> ... agents are employed not only in this country but in every part of Europe, to purchase, at almost unlimited prices, Pictures of the highest class. Large prices have been paid by ... Dealers ... it is not uncommon to find that they are outbid at public sales abroad, and meet with formidable rivals at home in the agents of Foreign Amateurs and Dealers, who every season visit London for the purpose of purchasing as well as of selling.

He adds, '[i]t is well known that since the termination of the late continental war, every corner of Europe has been searched – and, as it were, hunted for Pictures, both by the Collector and Dealer ... Eminent dealers have sought for Paintings in every city, town, and almost every village in Holland, Flanders, and Germany, to satisfy the cravings of their English customers'.[51] Pye corroborates Winstanley:

> Scarcely was a country overrun by the French, when Englishmen, skilled in the arts, were at hand with their guineas ... [i]n proportion as the number of capital pictures which gradually came to England increased, the more did a taste for them spread, so

> that demand becoming greater, the prices continued to rise. The natural consequence was, that whoever in Europe wished to sell pictures of great value sought to dispose them in England. [Even Lucien Bonaparte, Napoleon's brother, went to Christie's in 1815 to sell his collection.] Accordingly, the number of pictures consigned to England became astonishingly great … when the storm of the French Revolution burst over the different countries of Europe …[52]

Already during the decade of the 1760s, the annual average number of imported pictures into London had doubled to 880.[53] Moreover, our analyses of auctions during this general period confirm the accuracy of Pye's observation. Coxe, Clayton, Langford, Squibb, Walsh and the newcomer, James Christie, began to attract a growing number of foreign sellers as early as the mid 1770s.[54] Dealers like Vandergucht, Desanfans, Greenwood or Bryan were responsible for some of the biggest sales. Other consignors during the 1770s included the Count of Schulenburg, Baron Jan Got de Grote, Signor Biondi and numerous individuals described in the catalogues as 'from abroad' or 'French Nobleman'. For the next forty years or so, in the wake of the great wave of change that swept over the Continent, an unprecedented number of the prized pictorial treasures of Europe were dispersed through London sales rooms to new owners in England. The provenances of many of the greatest paintings in England are sufficient documentation that these political upheavals in Europe and the business opportunities that arose from them were, to a large extent, the seedbed for the magnificent private collections that ultimately formed the core of the National Gallery in London (founded 1824).[55] Capital seeks opportunities for maximizing returns and middlemen focused on the obviously profitable importation and sale of Old Masters. Again Winstanley:

> … many Pictures, purchased even at the best sales of the most valuable Collections have been resold at a very large advance … It is then only natural that all those engaged in the traffic of Pictures, commonly called Picture Dealers, will uphold the value of the works of the old Masters in which they have probably embarked their fortunes, and to obtain the possession of which they have exerted all their skills, industry, and enterprise.[56]

This support of the prices for old Masters works was occasionally coupled with virulent attacks on the market for contemporary paintings. Farington recorded a remark by his friend, the architect W. Porden, that dealers in old pictures 'have at present prejudiced Lord Grosvenor's mind so far against the merit of modern art as to interrupt his design of making a Collection of modern pictures …' Even owners of works by such celebrated artists as Sir Reynolds expressed concerns about liquidity and prices.[57]

The detrimental effect on living painters of this allocation of dealers' resources to the market for old paintings was compounded by the high prices many contemporary artists asked for their works. According to Winstanley, such demands 'preclude[d] them from becoming anything like an article of commerce'.[58] Farington deemed some of the prices so 'extravagant even to be ridiculous. Douglas for *The Riposo* 3 figures 300 guineas. Mulready, for a Carpenter's Shop 300 guineas'. Compared to the £30 both George Romney (1734–1802) and William Beechey (1753–1839) charged for a three-quarter portrait, or the £70 annual salary paid to the housekeeper of the RA,[59] the sums mentioned by Farington corroborate Winstanley's assessment of out-of-market pricing.

Taste and collecting habits among British art consumers, therefore, cannot be held solely responsible for the relatively underdeveloped state of the contemporary painting market. Economics suggests an additional explanation: dealers recognized that each additional unit of investment, be that in time, capital or both, in dealing in old pictures produced greater financial returns than an equal investment in the alternative business of contemporary paintings. Therefore, as businessmen, they chose to allocate their resources to the more profitable activity. As soon as the marginal returns changed, however, another shift occurred, this time towards contemporary works.

An example of the significance of middlemen to individual artists' careers, the art market in general, and the understanding of cultural cross-currents was the introduction of Constable's works by the dealers John Arrowsmith and Claude Schroth to French audiences during the 'British' Salons of 1824.[60] Of particular interest is not the consequence of dealer support on Constable, the individual, but its historical impact, for which credit must be assigned to the agency of these two dealers. It is impossible to determine if the artist's paintings would have found their way to the 1824 Salon without dealers' enterprise; economic reasoning, however, suggests that the likelihood would have been slim. The presence of Constable's paintings in Paris was a direct consequence of trade initiative. By the summer of 1826, when Constable received Schroth's notification of the latter's decision to discontinue their commercial relationship, more than twenty of his pictures had found their way to France. Therefore, the significance of his works on the subsequent development of French painting must be credited, in no small part, to these two dealers. Clearly, the English painter's technique and vision of nature earned him such high accolade among French artists. But without Schroth's and Arrowsmith's initiatives, the extensive exposure of Constable's paintings to this group may not have happened. In his foreword to the exhibition, *Crossing the Channel*, Patrick Noon wrote: 'Audiences today generally associate the great strides towards modernism with later French movements, such as Impressionism, yet it is manifest that those movements found their source in the intellectual tumult and shared purpose of the 1820s'.[61] Constable's artistic persona was an inseparable part of this capricious environment. However, the two dealers as engines of this far-reaching cultural exchange were an integral element of this 'tumult'.

The allocation of middlemen's resources had become a major factor in cultural economics. However, economic theory models human actions and one should not expect an inevitable change in a painter's career as a result of dealer patronage, as was the case with Constable. Neither should one look for a monolithic switch from one type of dealing to another at a specific point in time. Nonetheless, auction sales records show a statistically significant increase among dealers' purchases of contemporary works starting as early as the 1830s.

It would also be incorrect to assume that all contemporary painters fared badly during the Napoleonic War years. Certain artists did rather well. John Hoppner (1758–1810), for example had a record year in 1802, when he earned £3,000. William Daniell (1769–1837) mentioned in 1808 that he had never earned less than £1,200 a year. John Opie (1761–1807), on the other hand, could only manage to get 20 guineas for a three quarter portrait, while Constable charged three guineas for a portrait with hands and two guineas for one without.[62] The latter two cases are a more accurate reflection of the general economic climate of the contemporary painting market.

The detrimental effects of this general redirection of middlemen's resources during this period were compounded by the loss of the Continental market for the English engraving industry. Pye, himself an engraver, commented, ' – whilst it incidentally afforded the opportunity of enriching [Britain] with immense treasures in works of art – [the Napoleonic Wars] suspended altogether that commerce by which British artists had been mainly enabled to live'.[63] The resulting failure of Boydell's and Bowyer's publishing businesses was yet another blow to the financial fortunes of many of England's contemporary painters.[64] Elaborating on his aforementioned observation, Pye described how in 1804 Boydell disposed of his entire stock by lottery. The publisher's bankruptcy not only eliminated his support of certain living artists but it also placed an unprecedented number of their works on the market. One year later, Bowyer followed suit. The appraisals assigned to Boydell's stock had to be approved by both houses of Parliament, and the assessed amounts disclose the values of the copyright versus the paintings after which engravings were fashioned. The plates from which the prints were pulled were priced upwards of £300,000, while the original pictures were appraised at a mere £46,266.[65]

The substantial difference between these two valuations implies that the mass-produced engraving was functioning on some level as a subsidy for the cost of artistic labour. The original painting, while necessary, was a far less valuable entity than its associated copyright. Economics suggests that under such conditions, the make-up of the original work on which the reproduction is based will reflect the producer's perception of its market function. As we discuss in a later chapter, the very appearance of a great many of the pictures produced during this period demonstrates the validity of this theoretical model. Moreover, the number of works that evidence these attributes is large enough to consider this phenomenon an important characteristic trend among nineteenth century English painting and essential to the understanding of Victorian art.

Further financial demands, in addition to the decline of the engraving industry and the appearance on the English market of vast numbers of old paintings from the Continent, were placed on dealers by other collections whose owners simply wanted to capitalize on the general buoyancy of the Old Master market. Among the better-known examples are the Trumbull collection sold by Christie's over several days in February 1797; the pictures owned by Baron Fagel, the Dutch Secretary of State, sold at Coxe on 23 and 24 May 1801; or the superb collection of Dutch paintings owned by the Countess of Holderness on the block at Christie's on 6 March 1802. Names of other, less noted collectors can be found in the auction catalogues of this period kept in the archives of Christie's, London.

Analyses of auction sales confirm this statistically significant growth in incidents of sale. They reveal also an increase in average price of Old Masters paintings beginning around 1800 (Figure I.1). Both trends peaked between 1810 and 1815 and then slowly dropped. This higher average price level was less a consequence of demand outpacing supply, but largely due to an increase in average quality. This can be documented by computing average price without the contents of such famous sales as the Calonne sale at Skinner in March 1795, the already mentioned Trumbull sale at Christie's in February 1797, the dealer Bryan's sale at Coxe in May 1798, and the associated Orleans sale at Coxe in February 1800. These collections had come on the English market as a direct or indirect result of the French Revolution and were noted for their high quality. Without them, the increase in average price of old master paintings was less significant, a fact that suggests that the bulk of old paintings on the English market were, qualitatively, at best average.

Such sales and other dealer-organized exhibitions began to receive a great deal of press attention. The showing of the legendary Orleans collection managed by the dealer Bryan, which opened on 26 December, 1798, received almost continuous coverage during the six months it remained on view.[66] As usual, the public was invited for a one shilling entrance fee. The dealer Buchanan offers in his memoirs some insight into the business model of this event. Evidently, Bryan, in order to procure this prized collection, had taken on the Duke of Bridgwater, Lord Carlisle, and Lord Gower as investors in a joint venture. Their agreement entitled them to select a number of paintings for their own use with the remainder to be sold at a specifically organized exhibition. This type of venue, sale by private contract, had been tried earlier in 1786 by Noel Desenfans as an alternative to auction sales. Prior to that, the dealer had apparently suffered a loss when he engaged

Christie to dispose of a collection of pictures and was obliged to pay commissions on bought-in lots.[67] The new method caught on and was successfully adopted by the trade to market works by living painters during the Victorian period. Bryan's Orleans project turned out to be quite profitable and ranks among the watershed art market events of the period. Buchanan reported that the sale of the pictures passed up by the investors realized around 41,000 guineas and more than paid for those paintings, valued at 31,000 guineas, they kept for themselves.[68] Even the framing costs could be paid out of the exhibition proceeds.[69]

This upswing in the Old Masters market, however, was only temporary and merely delayed the progress of the economic conditions of the contemporary arts environment. In many ways the boom bred its own demise. Corroborating the earlier observation concerning the generally mediocre quality of the majority of old paintings imported from the Continent, Winstanley lamented around 1828 that with the many truly great pictures which came to England over the preceding thirty years, there was a vastly greater number of inferior paintings whose only recommendation was that they 'came from the Continent'. These were 'thrown unreservedly into the public market in this country' by dealers of 'less eminence ... who have no other feeling for the Works of Art but as they produce profit'.[70] The customs files from 1833 to 1838 alone show that the total number of old paintings imported from the Continent amounted to a staggering 45,642 pieces. The duty charged on these pictures, which had been reduced in 1826 to the rate of five shillings for each painting plus an additional one shilling per square foot, earned the crown a respectable £11,870.[71] This tariff policy, however, had some evidently unforeseen, consequences. 'In reducing the duties from almost an exorbitant to a nominal charge', so a July 1839 editorial in the *Art Union* proclaimed, 'Government could not have contemplated the mischief that resulted from the change – an influx of worthless and injurious copies ...'[72] The English market was virtually flooded with 'canvases that had never been seen by the artists to whom they were attributed'.[73] The essay's author, S. C. Hall, founder of the *Art Journal*, maintained that out of approximately 81,000 pictures imported into England, only about 200 were, in fact, painted by the artists to whom they were attributed.[74] Even though Hall's agenda might have tempted him to hyperbolize, the old painting market in England was doubtlessly inundated with questionable imported goods. Confidence in this market further eroded due to a large-scale home production of forgeries. There were entire 'manufactories' where recently painted 'Old Masters' were carefully aged and then sold by the score to the unsuspecting public. One such establishment in Richmond was even known as the 'Canaletti Manufactory'. Another one, run by a Mr. Zachary, was located on the Adelphi Terrace. There, freshly done pictures were treated with heat and smoke. Such 'baking' would transform a newly painted work into an old master: the heat created cracquelure, while the smoke would leave the desired darkened appearance of the canvas. Varnish would be applied subsequently to prevent detection through smell and/or rubbing off of the soot.[75]

The existence of large numbers of imitations in a market where genuineness is the main determinant of value is indicative of an imbalance of supply and demand in favour of the latter. As the artist Richard points out to the protagonist in Collins's *A Rogue's Life*, '[e]nlightened collectors of old pictures pour into the market by fifties, while genuine specimens of ... any Old Master you like to mention, only dribble in by ones and twos'.[76] The demand for old paintings was stronger than the available supply of legitimate works could satisfy. Consequently, copies and outright forgeries were added. Mixed with an already prevailing information asymmetry in the field of old master in general, this 'lemon problem' greatly increased the risks consumers faced. At the same time, modern English and Continental paintings still sold poorly. The dealer Hobday's exhibition of contemporary French pictures which opened in a prime location at Pall Mall in the former premises of the auctioneer Porter on 2 June 1828 was such a commercial failure that it drove the organizer into bankruptcy.[77]

In view of these various developments, a market model can be constructed for the period starting around 1780 to the end of the 1830s. The above described promising changes in the contemporary painting market were challenged by a rapidly increasing flow of higher quality old paintings imported from the Continent. The profit potential of this improved old master market attracted middlemen and their resources and pulled them away from contemporary paintings to the detriment of living painters whose economic fate then received another blow, the collapse of the export-based engravings industry. The combined resources of the exchange mechanism of the market – dealers and auctioneers – then focused almost exclusively on the old painting market. By exploring new business models, professional dealers aggressively expanded the consumer base for old pictures sometimes to the point of attempting to prejudice the public against contemporary works. At the same time, the London audience became increasingly accustomed to attending commercial exhibitions and acquiring paintings outside the more traditional and familiar auction room setting. Auction firms competed equally forcefully, refining their own industry and facilitating the geographical relocation of a quantity of cultural treasures unequalled since antiquity. The consequences of this enormous transfer of art reach to the present day and are only beginning to be better appreciated.[78] These auction houses, however, occasionally also sold contemporary works, usually as a result of liquidity sales of artists' estates but also as part of other private collections. Therefore, the market for such works, although overshadowed by old paintings, remained active. Over time, dealers appeared increasingly among the identifiable buyers.[79]

Due to the gradual depletion of supply on the Continent of good quality old paintings and the still growing demand at home, the market became corrupted with copies and forgeries. Consumer confidence waned and a substitution effect occurred among both consumers and dealers. At the same time, a growing, talented and vibrant community of contemporary painters, competing for their share of this expanding art economy, was refining both their products as well as their marketing tools. Overall, it was a situation pregnant with change.

6 THE VICTORIAN ERA

The expansion of the market in contemporary and Old Master paintings that occurred in Britain during the latter half of the eighteenth century took place within a context of unprecedented economic growth, a virtual population explosion, demographic change towards greater urbanization and a general redistribution of income. These trends continued, save the occasional fluctuation, until the beginning of the 1870s. One of the pre-requisites of a boom in consumption of luxury articles is surplus consumer capital. The income-shift away from wages towards rents and profits favoured the already more affluent members of society, the middle and upper middle classes. Furthermore, Britain's industrialization had a head start and thus yielded financial benefits to England's population before other nations industrialized. 'Art follow[ed] wealth for its rich rewards' and, indeed, after the recovery from the 1836 to 1842 depression, London established itself as the centre of an international art market in general as well as the premier international market for contemporary art. Auction records from this period show the first significant influx of paintings by still living artists from the Continent. These records also indicate that many of the artists, whose names later became synonymous with the Victorian period, were bought as early as the 1830s by both middleclass and aristocratic buyers, suggesting that collecting habits were not predominantly defined by class. Middle-class collecting not only preceded the Victorian era but, as auctions during the immediate post-Napoleonic Wars period show, it was not distinct from the collecting habits of the aristocracy, but, in fact, emulative.[1] Dealers also began to market foreign works through their galleries providing further opportunities for English audiences to see and acquire such works.

A major change in patronage had occurred. W. Collins commented that in the early 1850s,

> traders and makers of all kinds of commodities have effected a revolution in the picture world ... [They] started with the new notion of buying a picture which they themselves could admire and appreciate, and for the genuineness of which the artist was still living to vouch ... These rough and ready customers ... turned their backs valiantly on the Old Masters, and marched off in a body to the living men. From that time good modern

> pictures have risen in the scale. Even as articles of commerce and safe investment for money, they have now (as some disinterested collectors who dine at certain annual dinners I know of, can testify) distanced the old pictures in the race.[2]

The painter C. R. Leslie made a similar observation in a letter to his daughter in 1851: 'The increase in private patronage of Art in this country is surprising. Almost every day I hear of some man of fortune, whose name is unknown to me, who is forming a collection of the works of living painters'.[3]

Several factors contributed to this transformation. For one, unethical business practices on a widespread level, such as dealing in fakes, are inherently temporary. In England their spread was checked by a self-appointed watch dog of the art trade and champion of contemporary British painting, Samuel Carter Hall, who founded in 1839 the highly influential *Art Journal*.[4] Trained for the bar, Hall claimed two mandates for his publication: to induce people to patronize British art and to 'destroy by conclusive evidence and continual exposure, the extensive and nefarious trade in "old masters"'.[5] It appears that he succeeded on both counts. In his *Memoirs*, Hall proclaimed that the decline in the Old Master market and the 'commencement of the career of prosperity' of British artists was, in fact, attributable to his very activities. The specific event he held responsible for this change was a lawsuit filed against him in March 1855 for slander by the dealer Hart whose forthcoming sale of Old Masters Hall had proclaimed a fraud. Although the jury pronounced in favour of the plaintiff, for Hall there was not 'the slightest doubt that to the case Hart *vs*. Hall may be traced a commencement of the career of prosperity that has since awaited the productions of British artists'.[6] This mono-causal proclamation may be hyperbolic, but change was underway and unquestionably, the *Art Journal's* campaign played a significant role.[7] But a more influential agent of this systemic transformation was the wholesale entry of dealers into the contemporary art market and it is to them this discussion now turns.

The Victorian Picture Dealer

> He has taken the place of the patron, and to him has been owing, to a great extent, the immense increase in the price of modern pictures.
>
> Samuel Carter Hall, Art Journal, December 1871

The richness of our data for the Victorian era helped us to discover previously unknown, important facts concerning the activities of dealers. Certainly, Hall's comment is corroborated by our quantitative analyses.

Figure 6.1 gives the cumulative percentage of purchases by type of buyer, namely dealers, middle class and upper class. Beginning around 1840, dealers became the major buyers in the auction market for paintings, and by 1900 the dealers dominated the auction market. During these sixty years, only around 190 different dealers – less than 7 per cent of the total number of buyers – bought

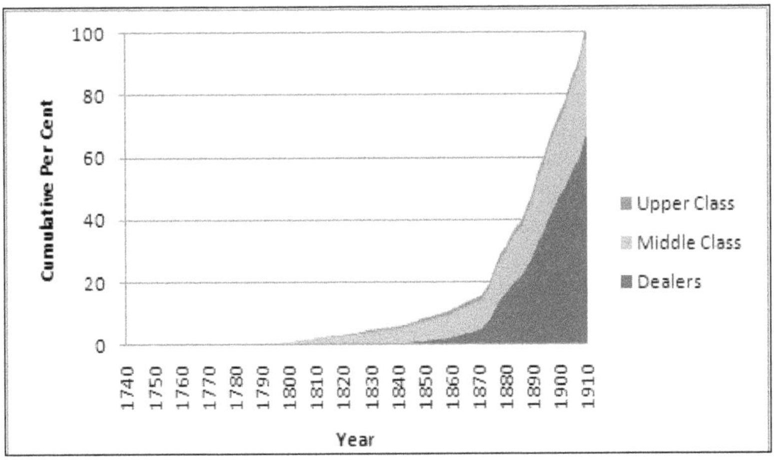

Figure 6.1: Cumulative Per Cent of Purchases by Type of Buyer

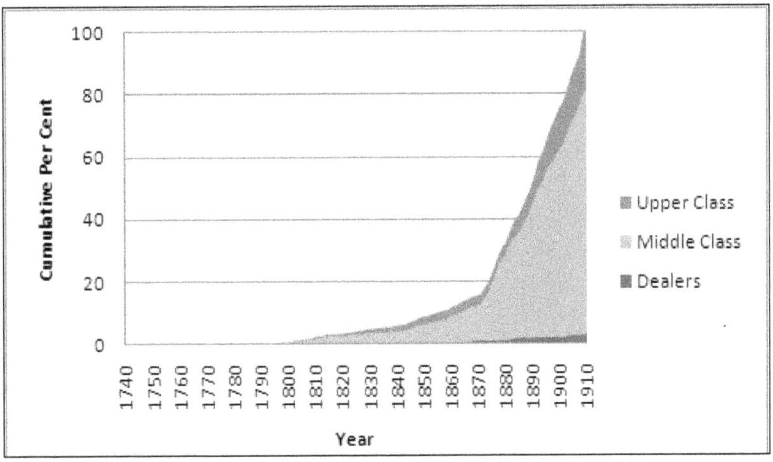

Figure 6.2: Cumulative Per Cent of Sales by Type of Seller.

over 66 per cent of all paintings recorded in our data, while the remaining 34 per cent of purchases were distributed over 2,665 different private consumers.

Figure 2 then gives the cumulative percentage of sales from the same types of sellers. The figures clearly show the dominance of dealers as buyers after 1850 and the infrequence of dealers as sellers throughout the entire period. Figure 2 also identifies the upper class as net sellers in the latter part of the time period.

This expansion of professional middlemen's activity coincided with significant increases in prices, in incidents of sales of paintings by contemporary English painters and, marginally even more so, in sales of works by living painters from the Continent (Figure I.1). This increasing interest in contemporary painting is corroborated by the subscription lists of the Art Union of London. From its foundation in 1837 to 1844, the number of subscribers grew from a few hundred to fourteen thousand. By the end of the decade, the concept had been copied in Manchester, Liverpool, Birmingham, Norwich, Plymouth, York, Dublin, Belfast, Edinburgh and Glasgow.[8] Auction data, moreover, show a strong correlation between the number of different buyers and the number of dealers buying in the market. The number of individual buyers recorded in Graves nearly tripled from around 300 in the 1840s to over 850 by1900. The number of different dealers was around forty-four at the beginning of the period and rose to over 120 by the turn of the century. As a percentage of the total number of separate buyers, the trade, as a group, averaged 12.6 per cent for the period, with a peak of 16 per cent in the decade of the 1860s and a low of 10 per cent in the 1890s.[9]

Further analyses of the relationship between the trade and the contemporary painting market show that between 1840 and 1900 dealers purchased an overall average of nearly 48 per cent of all works by living British artists and over 44 per cent of all contemporary Continental paintings, or a total of 46 per cent of all contemporary works recorded by Graves. By comparison, dealers during this period were buyers in 40 per cent of all transactions involving Continental Old Masters and in 40 per cent of all sales of English Old Masters. Viewed over time, in the first category, the market experienced a substantial drop in trade support until the end of the 1860s, when it began to rise again from 11 per cent to nearly 63 per cent by the end of the century. In the second category, dealer buying stayed fairly flat, around 15 per cent, but then also rose, beginning in the seventies, to nearly 62 per cent.

Examined by decade, the significance of dealers in this expanding auction market becomes even more evident.[10] During the 1840s dealers only bought 7 per cent of contemporary works by artists from the Continent with the remainder going to middle class purchasers. However, this figure more than quadrupled in the 1850s to 33 per cent. During the 1860s, dealer purchases of contemporary Continental paintings grew to over 37 per cent of the total. The number increased to above 63 per cent during the next decade and then dropped to 55 per cent in the 1880s followed by a peak to nearly 70 per cent in the nineties. From then on, dealer purchases of contemporary paintings from the Continent levelled off at just above 66 per cent.

Contemporary English paintings enjoyed greater dealer support earlier. In the 1840s, over 30 per cent were purchased by the trade, and this figure rose, although not as dramatically as the aforementioned category, to 63 per cent in the 1870s then dropped to 55 per cent in the next decade and rose again in the 1890s to 66 per cent and levelled off.

Old masters still remained a significant part of the auction market throughout the period. Relating old masters to the contemporary art market identifies specific consumption trends. In the 1840s, for instance, the old master market was four times the size of the contemporary paintings market. Within one decade, however, the latter market had surged ahead and grown to 1.5 times the size of its rival. It grew to double the size of the old master market during the 1860s, to 2.5 times in the 1870s and three times the size in the 1880s. During the 1890s the contemporary painting market shrunk to 1.5 times of a now expanding old master market. By the turn of the century both markets had reached parity.

These observations invite some comments on the question of whether this increase in dealers' activities was a reaction to changing consumer habits or whether dealers themselves provided the initial impetus. The low incidence of dealers buying contemporary Continental paintings at auction during the 1840s and the fact that the majority of such works – 93 per cent – were purchased by private consumers show that trade interest in that market was, at least to begin with, minimal. Contemporary English paintings attracted greater trade interest, yet the total volume of dealer purchases of both contemporary painting categories was still only at 18.5 per cent. However, by the 1850s, the percentage of trade purchases of works by living artists from the Continent had quadrupled while trade acquisitions of works by living English painters had increased to 33 per cent. Thus, dealer participation in the contemporary painting auction market had increased by well over 400 per cent during a time when the relationship of size of the combined markets of contemporary English and Continental paintings to the old master market had changed by 500 per cent in favour of contemporary paintings. Therefore, dealers were not only responsible for purchasing more than four times the percentage of such paintings but did so in a substantially larger market. This suggests that originally the trade reacted to changes in the market rather than initiated them. However, the increase in dealer activity during the subsequent decades together with the continuous growth of the contemporary painting market in relation to old masters, established the middleman as the agency responsible for sustaining the growth momentum.

Graves's data also identify a recession in the British art market in the late seventies and early eighties, consistent with narrative accounts and coinciding with the contemporaneous general contraction of economic growth (Figure I.1).[11] Furthermore, the records also demonstrate the general expansion of the market in old paintings – both Continental and English – that took place during the last two decades of the nineteenth century. Moreover, the data place the peak of the 'Golden Age for Living Painters' in the mid-1870s. This shift in these two markets was associated with the change of focus of dealers' activities. For a number of reasons that will be addressed below, the contemporary market in England was in decline. At the same time, increasing buoyancy in the Old Master market offered greater opportunity for profit and dealers shifted or increased the level of their activities appropriately.

A profound structural change had occurred in the art market. As mentioned already, throughout the eighteenth, and for the first decades of the nineteenth century, middlemen rarely bought inventory at auctions. Rather, they used them mainly to sell old works while, overall, their business in paintings by living artists was negligible. From the 1840s on, however, dealers largely ceased to be auction sellers but, instead, became the dominant buyer group at these sales (Above, Figure 6.1 and 6.2). Data show that Agnew, for example, participated as buyer in 748 different auction events, the dealer Colnaghi in 404, Vokins in 369, Tooth in 364, McLean in 350 and Wallis in 303. However, in only 25 different auction events did any of them, specifically Wallis, participate as sellers during the period of 1840 to 1880. Furthermore, while not abandoning Old Masters, dealers shifted focus towards living artists. Consequently the auction market for contemporary paintings soon came virtually under their control. Records show that some of the leading dealers, Colnaghi, Graves, Rought and Farrer, for example, bought such works at auction already in the late 1830s. Wilkie, David Roberts, Bonington, Stanfield and the French marine painter Isabey were among these early purchases.

Contemporary observers were aware of this change. Modern pictures, W. Collins observed, had become 'articles of commerce',[12] and, as the dealer T. Rought wrote in 1850 to the collector Gillott, 'all the old dealers [were] in spite of themselves now going into the Modern ...'[13]

In many ways, painters had paved the way. Artists-organized exhibitions and organizations like the British Institution through which artists could sell directly to the public challenged the hegemony and legitimizing clout of the RA and helped accustom consumers to new ways of viewing and purchasing art. Entrepreneurs from varying backgrounds saw opportunity and simply appropriated and refined these marketing methods.[14] It must have been during these early days that these individuals began to develop the *modus operandi* that we discuss below. Even Hall conceded that the campaign he had planned for his publication was aided by 'some of the picture-dealers in the manufacturing districts, who created a desire ... in prosperous Manchester and its rich locality'.[15] Yet as late as 1848 he still urged his readers to ''void ... the Dealers' and, instead, buy at artist-organized exhibitions.[16] This pronouncement, however, had little effect on middlemen's encroachment on the contemporary art market. Artists and dealers even collaborated to sell through venues that were ostensibly the exclusive domain of painters.[17] Artists were aware of this increasing influence of middlemen. Reflecting on the years 1850/51, Holman Hunt observed that 'affluent connoisseurs, whatever their independent instincts might be, did not in modern England decide upon art by their own judgment, but were guided by the voice of the majority and of dealers'.[18]

The rise of middlemen's market participation was similarly noted by the press. The *Illustrated London News* commented in 1862 that 'surely these are the golden days for the picture dealers and publishers'.[19] Then, in 1864 it was finally acknowledged that 'it is now in the rooms of the most eminent picture dealers that we must look for those productions of our painters ...'[20]

Contemporary art writing also acknowledged artists' preference to conduct business with dealers rather than private collectors. P. G. Hamerton, for instance, noted in his *Etchers and Etching* that artists and dealers 'understand each other and waste little time ... The dealer is wider and more catholic in his judgment than the amateur; he does not buy to suit the taste of one person, but to suit all tastes, and a picture which might not gratify him as a private purchaser is satisfactory to him as a merchant, if only he knows that it will not remain long on his hands'.[21]

Similar preference prevailed among the collecting public. Hamerton wrote in 1868 that 'so long as buyers would rather give five hundred pounds to a dealer for a picture than three hundred for the same picture to the artist, the dealer was necessary to the artist himself'.[22]

Finally, in December 1871, Hall articulated for the first time one of the central tenets of the age: 'The influence of the dealer is one of the chief characteristics of modern art'.[23]

The business in contemporary paintings continued evolving towards maximizing its commercial potential. The earlier undertakings of Macklin, Boydell or Bullock were but prototypes, smaller and less complex, of the enterprises of mid-Victorian art dealing. Revenues generated by the sale of reproductive prints and entrance fees to dealer-organized exhibitions created an unprecedented buoyancy and middlemen manipulated and controlled this market to their best advantage, a fact that did not go unrecognized.[24]

Thus, the model of a contemporary painting market emerges defined by middlemen trading in cultural luxury goods that, in each dealer's subjective opinion, fulfilled the inherent requirements of business-based considerations. Mass-appeal, 'sensation' potential and product differentiation were fundamental aspects in this process – precisely the qualities characteristic of nineteenth-century English painting. The multiplication of styles, the literary, narrative, or homely appearance of pictures, the explosion of landscape painting and the revival and perpetuation of baroque-like visual epics were all manifestations of a highly competitive arts environment hinging on the activities of dealers. A complex dialectic of supply and demand was reconciled through their agency and delineated by considerations defined by the economics of fixed-location retailing of luxury goods.

Our analyses shows that in apparent contradiction to the rules of arbitrage the average amount dealers spent on paintings at auction was substantially higher than that spent by any other category of buyers, save institutions like the National Gallery or other museums (Table I.2). Data show that institutions favoured exceptionally important works. Furthermore, institutions are publicly funded and thus under different budgetary considerations than dealers or private consumers. Moreover, there are non-monetary benefits, such as national prestige and enrichment of a nation's cultural inventory, associated with costly acquisitions.

For dealers, however, such a stratagem appears to violate conventional economic reasoning. Middlemen, as arbitrageurs, should purchase as cheaply and sell as expensively as market conditions permit. One explanation for this tendency among the trade to bid high could be that dealers, since they effectively dominated the market as buyers, had to compete among themselves for the best works. However, data show that mid-Victorian dealers pursued, generally speaking, non-competitive buying strategies, in that each of the major trade buyers bought in his clearly defined 'stable' and rarely transgressed into someone else's territory. Analyses of purchasing practices of sixty-five dealers during the period show that, with the exception of Agnew, Colnaghi, Gooden, Vokins and Wallis, none bought in all of the four categories of Continental Old Masters, English Old Masters, contemporary Continental, and contemporary English paintings. Even in these four cases bias is evident.[25] The rest of the dealers concentrated on either one or two categories combining either English and Continental Old Masters or contemporary English works and paintings by English Old Masters. Certainly many of the dealers bought works by the same artist, but individual sales catalogues show that they rarely bought works by the same painters at the same auction.

Specialization went even further. The trade not only paid more, but also showed preference for certain types or subjects. The overall favourite was landscapes: dealers bought over 50 per cent of all landscapes sold at auction between 1840 and 1900. Animal and figurative or genre paintings followed: over 47 per cent and 45 per cent respectively went to the trade. Mythological and history paintings were least in demand.

The trade also had a penchant for marines and animal subjects by contemporary Continental painters. At the same time, dealers avoided these artists' portrait subjects. Living British painters also found greatest interest among the trade for their marines, landscapes and animal and genre subjects, while their interiors were least favoured.

Among Continental old masters, still lives were most sought after by the trade while mythologies, history paintings and religious subjects found little support. As to works by native old masters, dealers bought landscapes and portraits while leaving histories, mythologies, and religious subjects for others to buy.

Associating the top thirty-five dealers with different subject categories further substantiates their specialization. Only Agnew bought paintings of all ten types. The majority of the other dealers limited themselves to much fewer categories. Five dealers, Cox, Gooden, Permain, Polak, and Sampson bought genre, landscapes and portraits. McLean and Wallis occasionally acquired animal paintings in addition to the aforementioned, while Tooth might add a rare marine to this selection. Only Colnaghi and Lesser, mainly old master dealers, bought also religious subjects and Vokins included also a few histories and still lives.

There were, of course, exceptions to these observations but they reflect the typical behaviour of the English art dealing trade during this period. We will discuss at a later point some of the implications of these practices, particularly their effects on the production of contemporary paintings.

Meanwhile, concerning the notion of competition between dealers as an explanation for their unorthodox bidding strategies, the data do not provide a satisfactory explanation. To that end, several other factors should be considered. Approximately the same number of different buyers and sellers were active in the market overall – our data lists 3,551 and 3,890 respectively – yet dealers, though numerically small as a category, bought at over seven hundred separate auction events while not a single seller sold at more than twenty-five different sales dates. This identifies the majority of sellers as liquidity traders, rather than speculators believing that public competition for the paintings offered at auction would yield the best results. To test this assumption, we identified paintings that sold at auction multiple times throughout the period. Among the over 3,500 different such sales, not a single individual used the auction system more than once to buy and sell the same painting. This absence of auction speculators alone is sufficient proof that this method was not profitable. Further analyses of these multiple transactions confirm that Victorian art investors attempting to earn money from art speculation by using auctions to buy and sell their art portfolio would have been better off with conventional and safer 3 per cent government consoles rather than with the average annual return of around 2 per cent offered by the art auction market.

Art speculators, of course, existed. But the way to profit was to sell paintings through auction that were purchased earlier directly from the respective artists. Hall gives a partial original cost and return accounting of the collection of the ship owner, Elhanan Bicknell, that sold at Christie's in April 1863.[26] On the twenty-six oils and nine watercolours listed, Bicknell had spent £6,810 and his heirs received £39,015). Hall does not mention these works' acquisition dates making a computation of an annualized return impossible. Nonetheless, the gross figure represents a 572 per cent return on Bicknell's initial investment. Shortly after the sale, Hall provided a detailed account of the financial history of Bicknell's collection in the *Art Journal* of June 1863.[27] The publication of such staggering returns from an investment in contemporary British paintings must have contributed to the perception of profitability of art market speculation. However, Bicknell had almost exclusively bought directly from artists. His rare auction purchases realized an annual average return of 10.5 per cent. Yet, while the majority of works he had acquired this way made positive returns, not all did so.[28]

Perpetuating an aura of profitability of private investments in contemporary paintings was clearly in the interest of artists, middlemen and consumers with a stake in the market. A conversation described by W. P. Frith between the contemporary painting collector, Jacob Bell, and his father during which he accused his son of wasting his money on art confirms this contention. After being told that these paintings could be sold for twice their original cost the father replied that he sees 'no sin in thy buying more'. Frith commented that 'investment, a love of display, and a spirit of speculation ... are the guiding-star of many of the picture buyers of the present day'.[29] Again, money followed art for its just rewards, and the allure of profit was a powerful incentive for consumption.

However, what sellers may have perceived as a competitive market was actually a system of informal collusion and networking among dealers. Such practices were not unknown to art world insiders. Hall, indeed, wrote an entire article in the August 1852 issue of the *Art Journal* on specific aspects of this trade collaboration.[30]

Dealers often worked with each other in such enterprises as print publication or large exhibition ventures and, as dealers' stock books show, in other ways as well. Moreover, the London dealer scene was quite small, and major dealers knew each other personally as well as each others' respective businesses. It would not require any clandestine formal agreement to engage in tacit cooperation. In fact, this practice can still be observed today. We should add, however, that *de facto* rings did exist and, most likely, far more frequently than the number of documented cases indicates.[31]

A market controlled to such extents by middlemen, invites speculation on how it may have been manipulated to maximize its usefulness. In a business in which middlemen customarily purchased goods for inventory directly from producers, buying on the secondary market with its associated additional transaction costs must have fulfilled some other, additional function.

Perhaps an answer can be found in the public nature of auctions. Sales were discussed not just by the art press, but also by daily newspapers such as the *Times*. The results of auctions, therefore, were powerful signals to consumers on the present state of the market. Consequently, dealers paying, as a group, on average substantially more for paintings at these public events was an effective way to advertise a healthy state of the market.

For example, in a letter of 27 June 1862, barely four months after the Plint estate sale had unexpectedly put over three hundred, mostly Pre-Raphaelite, works onto the block, J. E. Millais made the telling remark that 'nearly all the picture sales we have seen in the papers have been false'.[32] The corresponding catalogues of the spring 1862 season at Christie's list, as usual, almost exclusively dealers' names as buyers. However, hidden from public view, the catalogues also record the first failures of works by such celebrated artists as Landseer, Frith, Ansdell and Bonheur to reach their reserve prices. In the same letter Millais lamented the saturation of the market with contemporary paintings. 'There is evidently a smash in the picture trade ... there are so many works by Phillip, Frith, Ansdell and the lot in the hands of [the dealer] Gambart, that if they fail they must be sold anyhow'.

The context of Millais's remarks suggests that dealers performed regulatory action to defuse a potentially volatile situation by providing liquidity for the products in which they traded. This practice was not limited just to dealers. Artists, as well, monitored and protected the value of their work. Turner, for example, habitually and openly bid on his paintings and occasionally bought them back and was praised by the press for doing so.[33]

Art works offered at auction are usually protected by confidential reserve prices. Sellers generally desire the highest possible reserves while auctioneers and buyers are more interested in lower amounts. Numerous conditions, including the general state of the market, the relative significance of the lot and personal aspects of the seller determine the ultimate reserve price, and bidding customarily starts at slightly below this figure. An auction can thus reflect a particular bidder's competition with the seller as represented by the reserve rather than an actual competition between rivalling potential buyers. Unfortunately, neither our data nor the sales catalogues indicate whether there were under-bidders or merely reserves responsible for final hammer prices. Furthermore, while Christie's day books corresponding to the sales catalogues list the reserve prices to enable the auctioneer to design the selling strategy for each lot, they do not show if competitive bidding had taken place at levels below the reserve.

For these reasons dealers' responses to reserve prices are complex. Occasional buy-ins, i.e. the failure of specific lots to meet their reserve prices, were tolerable and, under certain conditions, quite useful, but pervasive failures could trigger panic reactions among consumers.

One of the more disastrous auctions of contemporary British and Continental works occurred in April 1883 with the sale of the collection of the Catalan Banker Jose Murietta. Despite the usual line-up of dealers, the buy-in rate was exceptionally high. The application of a price projection model on the buy-ins to test if they had performed 'correctly', or above or below market expectation showed that the amounts for which they were bought-in were substantially higher than the market should have been prepared to pay for the paintings in question. It appears therefore that the increase in buy-ins of contemporary works in the 1870s and 1880s was less a function of changes in taste but more the consequence of inflated price expectation by sellers.

In addition to promoting market stability, the trade may have paid high prices to support or even advance the values of paintings by artists already in their inventory. Economic research has documented that bidding is more aggressive when bidders have a previously established financial interest, or 'toehold', in the entity for which they bid.[34] Awareness of such economic principles is apparent in Rossetti's correspondence. The dealer Gambart had complained to the artist that Rossetti's indiscreet disclosure of the price of 200 guineas paid by the dealer for a painting which the latter then sold for 1,600 guineas would 'bring an end to the possibility of doing business'. Rossetti responded that the best way to prevent 'any injury to you for the future through reports of low prices received by me for my pictures will be to ask higher ones'. The painter was well aware of the profitable consequences of Gambart's sale to his own present and future production. Just a month earlier he had written to his uncle that 'it is, of course, my interest to help him [Gambart] getting the highest price he can for my works, and not express the least discontent at his being the first to profit to such an extent by the market he creates for them. I will take care that my turn comes too'.[35]

Further, albeit circumstantial, support for the argument that the British art trade may have used the public nature of auctions to regulate the market for contemporary paintings is offered by the occurrence of dealer to dealer sales via auction. As already mentioned, one of the systemic differences between the art markets of the eighteenth and the nineteenth centuries was the relationship of dealers to auctions. During the earlier period, the trade used auctions, often organized by individual dealers, to disperse goods while they rarely appeared as buyers. The reverse was true for the Victorian period. Familiar names, such as Flatou, Gambart or Wallis, appear occasionally as consignors, but this occurred mainly due to financial difficulties or retirement. Moreover, dealer sales through auction are associated in our data with a substantially above average buy-in rate: approximately seventy-five different dealers appeared as sellers, selling a total of 930 paintings out of which over 180 (19 per cent) were bought-in as compared to over thirty thousand remaining sellers who are associated with around two thousand (6 per cent) failures to sell. This is entirely rational market behaviour, since dealers attempting to sell inventory at auction which they were unable to sell through their galleries would encounter few, if any, bids from fellow trade members or the general sale attending public.

Successful dealer-to-dealer sales through auction, however, happened frequently enough to suggest that they were not coincidental. Graves's data identify at least four hundred and twenty such instances, that is, over one-third of all trade consignments to auction were purchased by other dealers.

In an environment in which major dealers knew each other and often worked together, it seems to make little economic sense to incur the transaction costs of an auction sale unless the marginal increase in benefits of such action was larger than its cost. Adding to the perplexity is the aforementioned fact that, in general, members of the trade avoided buying pictures that may have been unsuccessfully offered by other dealers. In some cases, perfectly orthodox explanations for dealer – auction – dealer transactions may have existed. For instance, paintings acquired from private sources and kept away from public view, could reasonably be disposed of through auction; also 'experimental' works without established price records can be tested at auction. Beyond this, there can be numerous personal reasons impossible to reconstruct. Other instances, however, resist conventional rationalization.

One particular transaction that led us to explore this issue involves the 1848 painting *Coming of Age in the Olden Times* (http://artmarket.tulane.edu/page81.html) by W. P. Frith.(1819–1909). On 1 June 1864 the work was auctioned off at Christie's to the dealer Flatou for the strong price of £1,207. The painting had a somewhat tainted commercial history since it had failed to make its reserve in 1860 when W. Turquand had consigned it to the same house. It must have been sold privately in the interim since the consignor in the sale to Flatou was John McArthur. Then on 24 March 1865, the canvas re-appeared at Christie's, consigned by Flatou and knocked down to Agnew for £1,464. Both amounts were auction record prices for Frith, over 300 per cent above his average price level and unsurpassed for the next nine years. Taking transaction costs into account, Flatou must have barely broken even. This Frith was Flatou's only recorded sale at auction this year, so financial need was, most likely, not the reason for selling. Agnew evidently managed to get rid of the work, and it made its last auction appearance during the Victorian Age in February 1900 when it fetched a mere £367. Equally curious is another transaction we found which lists Agnew as both seller and buyer of the same lot, a view of Newark Abbey by Turner, at a Christie's auction on 22 May 1869.

Such incidents may well have been intended to influence the public's perception of the state of the market for specific artists' works. In the absence of documentary proof, however, our proposal remains circumstantial. Millais's remark and Hall's report in the *Art Journal* reflect only their own opinion and while we believe their assessments to be correct and price manipulation to have existed, it does not address the specific scenario of dealer – auction – dealer transactions. Hard proof for our proposed notion may simply not exist. Yet the model fits the circumstances and offers a plausible explanation. Moreover, this method of price manipulation of contemporary art is still much in practice today and still as difficult to prove.[36]

The above discussion does not intend to create an image of London picture dealers as unprincipled and deceitful. Certainly, as Hall points out, there were individuals who 'trade in the most unscrupulous ways' questionable even under the most liberal criteria of business ethics.[37] In general, however, one notices refreshingly high standards in their commercial activities.[38] The painter F. Shields even described his dealer J. Rowbotham as 'a man of sterling worth and simplicity of character, an upright Christian ...'[39]

In today's art market, regulatory activities are largely performed by the two leading auction houses, Sotheby's and Christie's in collaboration with the trade. One example is their management of the re-appearance on the market of the overpriced, often mediocre, works acquired by Japanese collectors in the early 1980s. Another example is the handling of art sales during the financial crisis of 2008 – 2010. Both houses established specific methods to exercise some control over the flow of such goods on to the auction market. In a related context one might recall the detrimental effects of programme trading during the 1987 stock market crash in the United States. Since then systems have been installed to suspend trading and allow the market to cool off. In the absence of such sophisticated technology, Victorian art dealers may have availed themselves of simpler means of intervention but to similar ends.

Intervention was necessary particularly when large collections of contemporary paintings unexpectedly went on the block and challenged existing demand. In a market in which stability was very much a factor of the public's *perception* of value, appearance was all important, rather than something akin to current price/earnings ratios. Prices of contemporary art exist, under the best of circumstances, in a 'bubble' environment. Its primary market is created by dealers, and it is essential that their financial support of artists' works extends to the secondary market in order to maintain liquidity and stable or even increasing values that were and still are expected by the collecting public. The undertakings of Victorian picture dealers, huge in terms of general scope and financial commitments, warranted such market practices. The economic fate of countless individuals, from artists, printers, engravers, and large and small retailers to various types of collectors, some of whom had invested extraordinary amounts in contemporary paintings, depended on the perceived state of a multifaceted market that was well integrated in the economic mainstream. The size of England's contemporary painting market of this period was impressive. Wood's dictionary lists over 11,000 different artists active during the Victorian period.[40] The author suggested to us that at least half of those were full-time professional artists.

Erratic fluctuations of prices of publicly traded works would have undermined the public's confidence and led to panic selling with the possible result of a market crash. Middlemen could intervene when necessary and developed certain strategies to create a relatively stable market environment for contemporary paintings and facilitate further growth.

Market fluctuations, of course, did exist in the nineteenth century. Data identify a particularly noticeable decade-long downward trend of average prices during the early 1870s (Figure I.1). In part, this may have been due to the retirement of the dealers Gambart and Wallis in 1871 which removed two major buyers from the market.[41] Another troubled period was during the years 1858/9 when numerous dealers, among them R. Colls, J. Gilbert, W. Wethered and H.

Wallis were facing financial difficulties.[42] Our data also show that Wallis, from February 1858 to February 1861 used auctions to sell a sizable amount of his inventory. In 1861 Gambart and Flatou were also large volume sellers at auction. In these instances average auction prices showed no downward inclination between 1858 and 1861; apparent is only a very slight marginal decline in the upward slope of the average price curve for Contemporary English painters in the first half of the 1860s which afterwards resumes its previous angle of ascent. It appears that the hard times experienced by some members of the trade did not affect auction prices this time. The reason for this may lie in the fact that the majority of buyers at the above mentioned sales were other dealers who bought in order to keep prices from collapsing.

Such measures enabled capital to continue to be 'nurse and governess of art'. The regulatory actions performed by dealers were an essential ingredient in paving the road towards the unprecedented explosion of artistic and patronal activity in Victorian Britain. Middlemen's support of the arts, while lining their pockets, was a major contribution to the growth of production and consumption and thus facilitated the existence of more art in Britain.

Laissez-faire still ruled, and private enterprise, in the form of dealers, assumed the role of commercial patron. However, once dealers' business focus moved away from contemporary native works towards the end of the nineteenth century, the market for Victorian paintings collapsed, and it would take nearly seventy years before a recovery occurred. Besides changes of consumer taste, shifts of perceived profit opportunities for middlemen again provided the forward momentum and thus also lay at the heart of this decline and fall – and subsequent recovery.

Arthur Tooth & Sons, 1870/71: A Case Study.

To examine a Victorian art business in the context of the above observations we analyzed the purchases and sales for the years 1870/71 recorded in the stock books of one of the dealers listed in our records, Arthur Tooth & Sons.[43] The firm was smaller than Agnew or Gambart and ranked in size among the second tier with such dealers as Colnaghi, Permain, Vokins or McLean. During this period, the gallery focused mainly on contemporary works by British painters and became a major presence on the auction market from 1870 onward.[44]

In terms of numbers of pieces Tooth's business consisted mainly of transactions to the trade of works by a small group of artists for whom he may have acted as some type of agent.[45] Yet his main revenue was generated by a handful of lucrative sales of expensive works by several of the period's established names to other dealers and private collectors. However, rather than relying only on a few steady sellers and the occasional 'big hit', the dealer continuously refreshed his inventory with less costly works by a wide array of different artists most likely to test their market appeal. These purchases alone pumped an impressive total of £10,510 into the production side of the market and no less than 12 different painters received in the excess of £300 during this period from this one gallery alone.[46] In these endeavours, Tooth operated within a network of dealers that bought around 75 per cent of these pictures, presumably to try selling them to the public. Tooth's ledger, therefore, not only confirms Hall's allegations that 'the horde of dealers ... are enabled to profit ... by conspiring and acting together' but it also reveals particular details of this alliance.[47] If any of these new artists sold well, then Tooth continued buying their pictures; however, three-fourths of the time the dealer only bought one or two works. They moved slowly, tied up his capital and incurred unnecessary opportunity cost. Since they were mainly sold to the trade, the lack of demand indicated that dealers had difficulties placing them with collectors. He also frequently acquired inventory from dealers and auctions, often more expensive paintings. These he sold either to the public or, again, to the trade. Apparently, in his business with other dealers he took on specific works from their stock that he thought he could sell to the private market, and if unsuccessful, he would recycle them to give others a turn. Of the 861 pictures he purchased during this period, Tooth recycled around 330 pictures. Sometimes, such transactions incurred little if any net profit, occasionally even a loss.

As part of this informal dealer network, Tooth facilitated in just two years the entry of an impressively large number of new works into the market: 403 came directly from the artists who produced them. Not only was such a practice quite profitable, but the business of retailing in luxury goods demanded the continuous refreshment of a well diversified inventory. The fact that nearly 90 per cent of all the British painters traded amongst this group had previously shown their work at one or several of the officially sanctioned exhibition venues indicates that in addition to the Royal Academy these institutions were integral platforms for artists' exposure to dealers. The network also appears to have cooperated on sales of well-known names, usually in higher price ranges, to private collectors. To accomplish both, they bought from, sold to, and, presumably, consigned to, each other to share the cost and risk of trading in established works and continuously introducing new products. In the physical space of the gallery, the juxtaposition of untried and established art in close proximity had a positive effect on the commodity character of new products. The 'aura' of the established art rubs off on and validates the new products. It also delineates their range of differentiation. The retail trade's need for product and price diversity, frequently changing inventories, as well as the ongoing establishment of contemporary paintings as speculative goods drove the forward momentum. Together these factors stimulated innovation in subject, medium, and style.

Trade collaboration thus optimized the influx of new producers and new products into the market as well as maximized the opportunities for sales of works by new and better-known painters to the public. In this manner, Tooth and other similarly operating dealers collectively helped to finance the market entry of a great number of Victorian painters and established themselves as the hub of the contemporary art market.

Moreover, Tooth's ledger reflects a bullish, low entry-barrier market. The cost of maintaining such low barriers for untested inventory was partially subsidized by a small number of high-value transactions involving established artists whose works were sold directly to end consumers. The risk associated with testing these new products was spread across the network through the purchases of these paintings from Tooth by other members of the group and vice-versa in a collective attempt to find end-buyers.[48] The resulting systemic low barriers encouraged production, and the associated market expansion stimulated increasing product diversity. Thus, Tooth's operation offers an explanation on a micro-economic level for the link between growth in middlemen activity and general market expansion: the virtual explosion in the number of professional artists during the latter half of the nineteenth century was directly associated with the business model of professional middlemen operating in tandem. Furthermore, the escalating appearance of different styles that epitomizes late nineteenth and early twentieth century European painting is, in no small measure, similarly attributable to the trade practices. As Robert Jansen pointed out, even the various Secession movements of this period frequently hinged around specific dealers and depended on them for commercial success. While these groups often came into existence initially in direct opposition of what was seen by them as a controlling influence of the trade and/or the academy/salon system, their eventual establishment and recognition was usually linked to professional dealers who recognized the commercial potential of conspicuously differentiated new art products.[49] Although our observations predate these Secessions, Tooth's operation provides a glimpse of how the associated necessary, and likely unprecedented, market expansion was managed.

Consequently, contemporary British artists created works that were clearly distinguishable as their own, even to the point of quasi trade mark. Nicknames like James 'Waterfall' Smith or 'Birds Nest' Hunt are but reflections of successfully distinguished products initiated by this dealer-driven market growth. The painter Charles Ricketts (1866–1931) described these products as those of an age of 'competitive painting, i.e. competition to secure attention against other artists, other aims and other schools'.[50]

Economics suggest that at some point this ongoing need for differentiation develops products and product identities the merits of which are no longer measured by traditional means, such as, for example, quantifiable input of labour or degrees of technical skill. In Britain, for paintings and similar visual products this process began in the nineteenth century with the Etching Revival and the Aesthetic Movement and led to the contemporary art of the 21st century, where concept/idea outweighs, if not altogether supplants, the older, labour-based, approach to the extent that physical involvement of an artist in the execution of a work is today no longer necessary.[51]

Beyond the stimulating effects on stylistic diversity and innovation, dealers collectively also exerted a positive impact on market stability which, in turn, led to further expansion. Tooth's business records together with Graves's data reinforce the notion that the trade performed the role of market maker similar to certain present-day stock market specialists: de facto guaranteeing a market for the goods in which they traded.[52] Dealers availed themselves of methods that ranged from the above described pooling of resources, risk sharing, and cooperative trading to using art auctions in what appears to be efforts to influence the public's perception of the state of the market in general as well as price levels of specific artists' works. The already mentioned article in the *Art Journal* attests to the existence of such practices.[53] While such methods can be illegal or unethical, the general practice of dealers supporting the works of artists in which they trade is commonly expected and, optimally, serves to buttress the market against overreactions.

The expanding role of middlemen was not only responsible for market growth and stylistic diversity. Similar observations can be made about the dimensions of paintings in response to the changing market character. Since the 18th century, when English artists began to explore new ways to bring their works before the public, the issue of size had become more complex. What had previously been largely a response to specific patrons' wishes became intertwined with considerations of production and marketing. Since paintings were the only means by which painters could compete for the attention of the exhibition-attending public, producing works with eye-catching dimensions was one way to achieve that. So was, of course, subject matter and execution.[54] However, as we already pointed out, while these canvases indeed caught the public's eye, they were, due to their production cost and size, difficult to sell to an audience that was increasingly composed of an urban middle class living in houses and earning incomes that could not readily accommodate paintings of such dimensions or price. The issue became more intricate when professional middlemen with fixed retail locations started taking an interest in contemporary paintings. Their demand for a diversified, changing, and sizeable inventory, as well as their consumer orientation sent signals to the artists.[55] Consequently, paintings became, on average, smaller than they had been during the preceding century.[56] In fact, an analysis of size in relation to price shows that artistic labour had a decreasing return to scale: the smaller the painting the greater the income yield of each unit of size. This was not limited to artistic labour, but also extended to profit: each additional unit of size produced a marginally smaller profit.[57] The domination of 'sofa-size' and smaller pictures in Tooth's inventory reflects this dealer's rational behaviour and explains, in economic terms, the general trend toward smaller, market-orientated sizes. Moreover, scale has a subtle and difficult-to-measure, yet wide-reaching effect on artists' choice of subject, composition, manner, and style of execution.

To summarize, Arthur Tooth's records describe a business model that is consistent with the prudent operation of a fixed-location retail business in a buoyant market of luxury goods with added speculative commodity character. The dealer continuously refreshed his inventory; maintained a high turn-over rate; mixed new and established works; he may have availed himself of the auction market to protect his economic interest and provide liquidity; and he operated as part of a group of approximately thirty dealers apparently organized in a loose network that extended beyond London and functioned in the market as both arbitrageurs as well as market makers.[58] Without this latter function, that is, the assurance of liquidity for the products traded, the modern art market, as it functions today, could not have established itself or flourished. Under this business model, painters were challenged to compete for their individual share of an ever increasing market in which institutionalized middlemen were the engines of growth. Artists contributed works that were not just more suitable in size but also increasingly more distinct from competitors' works and more diverse. Dealers invested their expertise in promotion and marketing, their access to clients, their exposure to risk and their share of capital. Joined together by common interest, artists and dealers occasioned the hitherto unprecedented expansion of art production and consumption that lies at the root of the extraordinary visual and underlying intellectual diversity that we witness today. The germination of this seed can be observed in the pages of Arthur Tooth's old business ledger.

7 'WORKING THE ORACLE': THE TOOLS OF THE TRADE

The Mass-Produced Print

> Art should not be content to minister to the tastes of the few alone, to whom the possession of its best labour is a luxury; but its healthy influence should be felt among the millions.
>
> *Art Union*, July 1847, p. 261.

Typical Victorian picture dealers like Agnew, Gambart, Wallis or Tooth differed in many respects from most of their predecessors. Rather than just buying and selling individual works to private collectors, they also engaged in the publication and sale of reproductive prints. Although earlier publishers like Boydell, Macklin or Bowyer had pioneered this type of business activity, Victorian dealers took it to new heights. Their operations evolved from retailing artistic luxury articles to include publishing and selling derivative mass products nationally and internationally. The press celebrated these firms as missionaries of culture that brought the benefits of art to the underprivileged.[1] Like Hogarth a century earlier, these entrepreneurs applied one of the central tenets of modern capitalism: greater profits can be derived from the sale of many goods cheaply to a mass market than by selling luxury goods to the elite. The earning potential of these mass-market goods boosted the high prices of the original works from which they derived and increased the general cost of artistic labour.

This business model allowed dealers to tap into a substantially larger customer base, 'a still more numerous body of the community not possessing the means to purchase the original works of our painters, but who are able to acquire and do acquire, the next best substitute – engravings, and imitation drawings or chromolithographs'.[2] The expanded consumer base also offered dealers considerably higher and steadier cash flow expectations and reduced risk.

The role of the print industry in the transformation of art dealers from small merchants to large-scale entrepreneurs with substantial capital and revenue requirements had profound consequences. In Boydell's time, the financial success of a publication was restricted by certain inherent technical limitations. Then, engravings were customarily done in copper plates and generally restricted to smaller and simpler images. Copper's softness, while making the actual engraving process easier, limited the plate's longevity and the quality of each impression visibly deteriorated after a certain number of executions. Usage for publication beyond this point required further work by the engraver to restore the line quality. In 1845, however, the invention of electrotyping applicable to steel plates revolutionized the engravings industry and made it possible to publish steel engravings in editions numbering tens of thousands of impressions with hardly any loss of detail.

The use of steel plates for engravings dates back to the 1822, when the technique was introduced by Thomas Lupton at a meeting of the Society of Arts. However, the trade first responded slowly, most likely due to related cost factors, until the engraving industry adopted this new cost-effective technology. A boost to the business was provided by the elimination of the English duty on glass, essential for framing a fine engraving, even though the cost of home-produced glass remained rather high.[3] These two developments – electrotyping and the end of the duty on glass – gave birth to the immensely popular and distinctly English art product: the two guinea proof in a five shilling frame. Its influence on taste, its impact on the lives of artists and dealers, and its effects on the development of pictorial imagery and the art market in general are without peer. F. G. Stephens, art critic and Pre-Raphaelite supporter, wrote in a pamphlet published in 1859 in conjunction with Hunt's exhibition of his *The Finding of the Saviour in the Temple* (http://artmarket.tulane.edu/page98.html) at Gambart's gallery that 'indeed, a national service is rendered by the publication of really noble transcripts from noble pictures ... Where pictures cannot go, the engravings penetrate'.[4]

The publication and sale of a steel engraving required substantial capital. Gambart, for example, paid Holman Hunt 5,500 guineas for his *The Finding of the Saviour in the Temple* (http://artmarket.tulane.edu/page98.html), the pictures' copyright and exhibition rights, the highest amount yet paid for a work by a living British artist. In a memorandum to the print dealer George Pennell of November 1860, Gambart outlines additional costs of 3,000 guineas for printing and a gross earnings' projection of 88,000 guineas for the entire edition.[5]

Such high entry costs necessitated that images for publication be chosen on the basis of their earning potential. The *Art Journal's* description, in 1850, of print publishers as men of 'taste and judgment, as well as capitalists' who 'select such works as are adapted for engraving ... and afford [them] a return for the large sums invested ...' plainly couples the selection process with commercial appeal. The same article also portrayed these businessmen as 'a class ... to whom both artists and public are largely indebted, and who may be regarded as the medium of communication between the two'.[6] Mass-appeal was the key to success, a fact that had not escaped those involved in the business. According to Agnew, Victorian painters owed their fame and fortune – as did their dealers – to the popularity and circulation of engravings.[7] Moreover, as 'medium of communication', publishers could channel, interpret and direct signals from the supply and demand side of the market for maximum benefit to their enterprises. Henry Graves, for instance, told the House of Commons in 1845 that the success of the industry was based on 'giving them subjects which are suited to their tastes ... you may do fine things, and they will not buy them ...'[8] Indeed, P.G. Hamerton, in the late 1860s criticized the entire English school for their endeavour to please an uneducated public and, for that purpose, aiming at making their work 'pretty and popular rather than great'.[9]

Recognizing the benefit of this mass market on the copyright value of original works, painters negotiated their prices accordingly. Holman Hunt, for example, considered the potential earnings of the publisher/dealer from the sale of subscriptions to the engraving of his *Finding of the Saviour in the Temple* (1854–1860, http://artmarket.tulane.edu/page98.html) when he sought advice on the pricing of this work.[10] Edwin Landseer was paid between April 1836 and March 1841 by the print-selling firm Hodgson and Graves alone the sum of 1,300 guineas for various copyrights: 100 guineas each for *The Abercorn Children* (http://artmarket.tulane.edu/page83.html) and *The Highland Whisky Still* (http://artmarket.tulane.edu/page84.html); 200 guineas for *The Highland Grovers*; 300 guineas for *The Sutherland Children* (http://artmarket.tulane.edu/page86.html); 600 guineas for *Horses Drinking* (http://artmarket.tulane.edu/page87.html) and *The Duke of Beauford's Dog*.[11] Even more impressive were the £1,200 Elizabeth Thompson received in 1874 for the copyrights of her *Roll Call* (http://artmarket.tulane.edu/page89.html).[12] The Fine Art Society was charged £300 by Edward Poynter for the rights to publish his *Atalanta's Race*.[13] One of the period's most successful painters, W. P. Frith, was commissioned by Jacob Bell to paint *Derby Day* (http://artmarket.tulane.edu/page11.html) for £1,500 and then sold the copyrights to Gambart for the same amount before the painting was even begun. In another instance, the dealer Lloyd sold Frith's *Life at the Seaside* (http://artmarket.tulane.edu/page91.html) to the Royal Family for the same price he had purchased it from the artist. Lloyd could afford such patriotic largesse since his profits came from an arrangement with the Queen that allowed him to have the original painting engraved. Frith reported that the Art Union of London subsequently paid £3,000 for the plate alone.[14]

Not surprisingly, under these new economics, many British artists and those Continental painters whose success was linked to the British market, such as Tissot (1836–1902) or Legros (1837–1911), considered mass appeal and the associated copyright value in the choice of subject and execution of their works. The target consumers were, as Thomas Lawrie, Agnew's agent in Glasgow wrote in 1871 in a letter to the firm's London branch, 'fond of pictures that tells [*sic*] them something'.[15]

This preference for narrative content was, as mentioned before, partly a consequence of the print industry's earlier indebtedness to the book trade. As recently as 1800, booksellers had been the main patrons of engravings.[16] Later, periodicals like the *Penny Magazine* or the *London Journal* spread the appreciation of graphic products to an ever wider audience.[17]

By mid-nineteenth century the expanded consumer base for prints had increased the price of copyrights and thus the earning potential of artistic labour. Economics suggest that under such circumstances the revenue-generating entity dictates the design of the product: the print influenced the painting rather than the reverse. Hunt even went so far as stating that 'if copyright in works of art were not legally safeguarded, invention, which costs most time, would be discontinued by the painter, and he would consider only the meaningless surface of a canvas'.[18]

The prices of these all-important copyrights were determined by supply and demand. Demand, however, included each individual dealer/publisher's subjective assessment of each image's mass-appeal. Thus, a successful choice extended beyond simply the subject depicted in the print and other, subtler criteria had to be taken into account. The resulting pictures reflected, to varying degrees, the formative influences of such economics on product design.

Even original etchings were affected by it. The members of The Etching Club, founded in London in 1838, were of the opinion that etchings should be priced in accordance with the amount of manual labour associated with the products' design and execution.[19] This type of commoditization ran counter to the old mission of aesthetic philosophy to disassociate manual labour from the value of artistic products. However, such pricing was suitable for the sale of cultural products among a population more familiar with Protestant work ethics than the notion of creative spontaneity. The ubiquity of highly finished, detailed prints characteristic of the period shows the pervasiveness of this labour-based concept of value.

Potential mass reproduction of the original design and availability of copyrights were thus crucial ingredients of product price. Redford recorded an incident relating to the value added to a painting by its copyright. During an auction at Christie's on 17 May 1879, bidding for Landseer's *Twa Dogs* (http://artmarket.tulane.edu/page92.html) had stopped at 850 guineas; then, after the auctioneer announced that this image had not yet been engraved and, therefore, the copyrights were included with the picture, bidding resumed and the lot sold for over twice that amount – £1,753.[20]

Since painters, like other producers, also aim to maximize the returns from their labour, their products is, intentionally or unintentionally, shaped by economic aspects. However, in this growing mass-market for inexpensive derivates such considerations were associated with signals from middlemen. For these reasons salient features of much of Victorian and European nineteenth-century painting were a consequence of the growing significance of the institutionalized dealer's *modus operandi* as the economic hub of the arts environment, its source of money and patronage.

Within a decade after the duty on glass was abolished in 1845 the number of print publishers/dealers in London doubled to eighty-five and it continued to grow thereafter, although at a slower rate.[21] John Burnett wrote in 1850 that not only this increasing number of publishers 'but above all the prodigious increase of the retail trade, require so large a variety of prints, that an engraving becomes out of fashion in a few weeks ...'[22] The dealer/publisher Ernest Gambart recalled that

> the whole exports [*sic*] of English engravings at the time [1843] did not amount to more than five thousand pounds per annum ... The imports of engravings from the Continent might have amounted to about ten thousand pounds per annum ... the importation of French prints in 1845 by my house alone amounted to more than twenty thousand pounds and our exports of English engravings to about a quarter of that sum.[23]

In just two years, the England's print market had grown at such a rate that one firm alone could now afford to import double the nation's previous total. A caption in the *Art Union* in 1845 described a parallel development in the export trade of English prints: '... a desire to possess our print is, indeed, so rapidly gaining ground abroad, that Messrs. Gambart expect very shortly to export more than they import'.[24] Agnew's business ledger also reflects this tendency. In 1847 the firm made its first substantial investment in its print publishing division; by 1861 the still family-owned business had published and marketed editions of over one thousand different prints.[25] In such a rapidly expanding market, painters had to compete with each other by increasing product differentiation.

The ability to print much larger editions further improved the economics of reproduction and reduced the risks of publishing prints after the most important, most elaborately executed paintings. Consequently, an increasingly larger section of the population had the opportunity to own a product of artistic 'genius' at an affordable price. Agnew even published Hunt's *Shadow of Death* (http://artmarket.tulane.edu/page93.html) by selling engravings on an instalment plan through workingmen's organizations across England.[26]

Nothing suggests that engravings were considered to be anything less aesthetic or less original than the paintings after which they were fashioned. Not only were engravings held in the highest esteem, but the 'aura' of the original work was actually improved by the publication of prints. As Jacquelynn Bass pointed out, 'modern techniques of reproducing works of art confer a mystical aura upon the "original" that is quantifiably verified in the marketplace'.[27] The 'aura' of prints was further enhanced by the press which treated announcements or advertisements by print dealers of publications of engravings as major news events.[28] Reviews themselves commoditized as the character of reproductive prints evolved from being simple reproductions to independent works of art.

Initially, discussions in the press focused on the reproduced original work. The *Art Union* of October 1845, for example, described an engraving after Raphael as 'one of the most remarkable productions of the great master; it is painted in his second manner – that which has contributed so much to his glory ...'[29] Nothing was mentioned about the print. Later, when original and reproductive print had become two separate commodities, critics reviewing exhibitions in the *Times*, *Art Journal* or *Athenaeum* devoted particular attention to finer points of connoisseurship and were not shy about employing outright hyperbole.[30] Furthermore, such books as T.H. Fielding's 1844 publication of *The Art of Engraving with the various modes of operation*, must have positively affected the appreciation for prints. The character of fine engravings as luxury articles was further augmented by the location of their retail outlets in London's West End, an area of the city renowned for its luxurious shops. Henry Graves and Co. was located at 6 Pall Mall; P.D. Colnaghi's gallery at 14 Pall Mall; Ackermann's at 191 Regent Street; McLean's at 26 Haymarket.

Associated with this rapidly expanding market was also an improving technical sophistication to increase the high degree of finish and detail of prints in order to embrace and emphasize the labour-based norm by which Victorian paintings were judged. Since elaborate detail and high degree of finish represented easily comprehensible, tangible, yardsticks for quality and value of paintings, the same standards applied to reproductive prints. Therefore, not only were painters motivated to create products which fulfilled these criteria, but engravers also had sound economic reasons to incorporate readily apparent, labour-intensive aspects in their products.

By the late 1840s, the expansion of the print publishing industry occasioned several print dealers to explore the idea of forming a trade organization and adopt certain measures considered essential to the continuing growth of the industry. Thus, on 9 January 1847, *The Athenaeum*, reported to its readers that on 17 December 1846 a letter signed by ten leading print dealers was circulated announcing the intention of forming an association with the main purpose of preventing an openly declared number of proofs to be exceeded.[31] The proposal was widely supported since dealers recognized the advantages of regulatory devices to forestall misrepresentation and fraud regarding the rarity of prints.[32] Regular meetings of the Print Sellers' Association began on 5 February 1847, and it was agreed that future prints had to be declared on publication, the number of proofs before letters and lettered proofs clearly stated, and each print stamped by the Association.

It is partly to this organization that one can trace the origin of limited edition prints to which the financial fates of many of the artists of the twentieth and twenty-first centuries are tied. The statutes of the organization, similar to general product warranties, assured consumers that the purchased article was correctly represented, genuine and endorsed by the Association.

Prints were customarily published in several states. Each state, although in quality of image almost identical to the others, was priced differently: the most expensive edition, the artist's proofs, had the fewest number of prints and, hence the name, was usually reserved for the artist as part payment for the copyright; the second most costly state, the proof before letters, contained a larger number of sheets; then, slightly cheaper and, again, in increased edition size, followed the lettered proofs; at the bottom of the hierarchy came the print, sold for the lowest price and in unlimited numbers. Landseer's (1802–73) image, *Monarch of the Glen* (http://artmarket.tulane.edu/page94.html), for example, was priced as follows: Artist's Proof: ten guineas; Proof Before Letters: eight guineas; Lettered Proofs: five guineas, Prints: three guineas.

Before the nineteenth century, a proof-print was understood to be an impression pulled while the engraving was in process to allow the artist and/or engraver to examine the product and consider the next steps. In a Proof Before Letters, the publication line does not appear in the margin above the print but is printed in the centre below the image. The publication line includes the name and address of the publisher, place of publication, any copyright details, the artist's name on the left and the engraver's name on the right. Usually Proofs Before Letters were printed on India paper and bore the Printsellers' Association stamp in the lower right corner, if the publication was endorsed by this organization. The Proofs After Letters, or Lettered Proofs, featured the title on the lower margin and, again, carried the Association's stamp if appropriate. The cheapest version, the Print, was published without any numerical restrictions, other than those technically imposed, and produced when the plate had begun to lose its sharpness. Occasionally, an edition included a small number of complimentary Presentation Proofs, usually around twenty-five, for distribution to special clients and friends.[33]

A similar system with minor modification is still used today in the multi-billion dollar market of contemporary limited-editions. Besides the obvious benefits of product differentiation for an essentially identical product line, the creation of limited editions also allows publishers, artists, and investors to calculate a considerably more detailed revenue prospectus for each publication. Moreover, since price is a consequence of supply and demand, the creation of a limited supply, that is, scarcity, of a product results in higher per unit prices without increasing input costs. Such economics were not lost on Britain's artists. A notice published in *The Illustrated London News* on 27 October 1855 informed readers that the friends of the painter Thomas Shotter Boys had been

> invited on Wednesday last to that gentleman's premises, 467 Oxford Street, to witness the breaking up of twelve of his most celebrated plates. A voluntary destruction of property to such an amount is almost unprecedented; But Mr. Boys wisely deter-

> mined the step in order to enhance the value of their prints to previous purchasers and to ensure a readier sale of the last lot of impressions to the trade and public.[34]

Furthermore, price hierarchies appeal to social hierarchies, and the production of subtly differentiated products that were differently priced in indirect proportion to their available numbers, mirrored the English social structure and must have appealed to the deeply ingrained English class consciousness.

The success of the reproductive print coupled with the size of the market stimulated the introduction of other, rivalling, forms of reproduction methods such as chromolithography, mezzotint and photogravure. However, competition was not limited to the use of different reproduction technologies. O*riginal* prints were also able to establish themselves as distinct graphic products and compete effectively. By using many of the well-tested marketing methods of reproductive graphics, these products challenged the hegemony of the reproductive print ultimately contributing to this industry's demise.

The Function of Exhibitions

Eighteenth-century exhibitions in the form of artists-organized public showings of their works pale by comparison to such enterprises after professional middlemen appropriated the general concept and turned it into a viable business model to suit their needs. The precedents set by Hone, West, and Copley of publicly exhibiting works of art for an admission fee had caught on and evolved to become the singularly most effective marketing tool for paintings and their by-product, the print, during the Victorian art boom.

Professional merchant/promoters also paved the way for certain Continental painters to organize commercial exhibitions of their works in England. It was these kinds of entrepreneurial economics and drive that facilitated the introduction of new ideas to both the English artists' community and lay audiences.

Guillaume Léthiere (1760–1832), for example, exhibited in 1816 his *Brutus Condemning his Sons* (http://artmarket.tulane.edu/page95.html) in London. The project, arranged by an enterprising British showman named William Bullock, was apparently lucrative and occasioned Theodore Géricault (1791–1824), after hearing about it from Léthiere's son, to try, in 1820, a similar undertaking with his own recently completed, controversial *Raft of Medusa* (http://artmarket.tulane.edu/page96.html). Géricault hired the same promoter, and the gigantic canvas was shown with great success and press coverage in London at the Egyptian Hall and, after six months, shipped to Dublin for exhibition. Adhering to the well-tested business model, the promoter also offered lithographs after the original picture during both events.[35]

Publicity was a crucial ingredient for success and from the mid-1840s on, nearly every week the London *Times* featured on its front page announcements of some type of commercial exhibit of paintings. The notices usually included invitations to subscribe to soon-to-be-published prints or solicitations to purchase sheets from existing editions. Indeed, a type of 'exhibition mania' had begun to develop. In one instance in June 1860, the dealer Gambart alone had four exhibitions running concurrently.[36] Since organizers could operate under much higher revenue projections, these undertakings reached an unprecedented scope.

Gallery shows typically featured works of one painter or a small group with some unifying theme. Under ideal circumstances, one painting, often specifically created for the event, served as the main attraction – the visual sensation – to distinguish the particular exhibition and lend it the aura of 'must see'. Press contacts provided the necessary hyperbole to make this commercial enterprise into a major news event. After paying the customary cover charge of one shilling that often included a catalogue visitors could choose from the more expensive original works offered for sale and were solicited by the sales staff to purchase or subscribe to whatever prints were offered.

A crucial factor was the visual focal point, the 'sensation' picture. Its importance to the success of gallery exhibitions or nationwide and even international tours can be appreciated best when taking into account that the rights to exhibit a painting did not automatically accompany physical ownership of the original work but had to be purchased separately. The same was the case with copyrights. These two derivates had the potential for yielding far greater returns for middlemen than a one-time sale of an original work. In a case involving Hunt's *The Light of the World* (1853, http://artmarket.tulane.edu/page97.html), Gambart had failed to acquire the original canvas but managed to purchase, for £200, the still available copyright. He then entered into a publishing partnership with the collector, Joseph Gillott, and the venture grossed in the first year at least £10,000, far exceeding any amount the dealer could have realized from the sale of the original.[37] Gillott, as a collector, had little interest in the Pre-Raphaelites; his arrangement with the dealer was strictly commercial and stands as an example of art as an investment in the strictest sense.

Artists and dealers were aware of the earning potential of an effectively performing 'sensation picture'. Prices for the individually saleable derivative properties of a painting were independently determined by dealers' perception of a particular work's qualities to perform a specific economic function. Presumably, artists considered audience appeal in the design and execution of those works that were intended to fulfil this role not only as they perceived it but also as interpreted by middlemen.

Painters responded to these market conditions with similar business savvy as their eighteenth-century predecessors. Hunt, for example, himself the son of a businessman, offered an informative account of his negotiations concerning the sale of his *The Finding of the Saviour in the Temple* (http://artmarket.

tulane.edu/page98.html).[38] Already in 1853, during his dealings with Gambart concerning the painting *Light of the World* (1853, http://artmarket.tulane.edu/page97.html), the artist showed his understanding of the relationship between mass-appeal and the price of the work's copyrights.[39] This time the painter felt compelled to ask his friend, the writer Wilkie Collins, for business advice emphasizing that there were 'many reasons to think that the public will be really interested in it ... I am told it will make an attractive and remunerative exhibition, and this will persuade some publisher to buy the copyright'. Collins suggested that Hunt approach Charles Dickens who had the reputation of being rather clever in commercial matters. The ensuing conversation testifies to this painter's understanding of the economics of the Victorian art market, particularly concerning an artwork's different income properties. When Dickens queried the artist on the various sources of revenue the painting might generate, the painter included in his reply a calculation of potential exhibition revenues based on a daily average of between 400 and 600 visitors paying each one shilling to see the painting. Hunt pointed out that 'painting subject pictures is an expensive profession', which can only be pursued if the huge investment of money, time, and labour in the production of such paintings yields appropriate financial returns.[40] The artist also contemplated undertaking the entire publication/exhibition enterprise himself but conceded that a dealer is really much better suited for the task.

Economics were also at issue during a conversation between Hunt and Eastlake, the president of the RA, when the latter tried to induce the artist to lend this canvas to the annual exhibition at the Academy. The painter declined since he was not interested in giving up the potential earnings of the picture's exhibition rights by loaning it to the institution. The fact that in less than six months the entrance fees alone to the exhibition, which opened at Gambart's German Gallery in April 1860,[41] had nearly recouped the dealer's total investment of £5,500 provides a measure of the value of this derivative product. Visitors numbered often a 1,000 a day, and the first year's door receipts were estimated by William Rossetti to amount to over £9,000.[42]

The economic relationship of original work to its derivatives was also in Hunt's mind when he toyed with the novel idea of donating to the nation the original painting *The Shadow of Death* (1870–3, http://artmarket.tulane.edu/page93.html) and selling only the exhibition and copyrights.[43] He must have been aware that removing one of the painting's commercial properties would, according to the rules of supply and demand, increase the value of the two remaining ones. Furthermore, giving it to his country and thus removing the painting from the market, in a certain sense de-commoditized the original work and further enhanced the value of the two remaining purchasable properties.

Standard business deliberations, such as input costs, capital needs and earnings projections, as well as the more sophisticated economics of elasticity relationships of supply, demand and price had become closely associated with a painting's production. Not surprisingly, certain artists, Hunt just being one example, began to relate to their work precisely in terms of an industrial venture.[44]

Potential profits from successfully staged exhibitions of these 'sensation pictures' were huge. Like their late eighteenth-century brethrens, Victorian artists had to compete for public attention between themselves. But unlike their predecessors, they faced an environment controlled by professional middlemen. The visual sensations they had to produce to catch and remain in the lime-light had to satisfy businessmen experienced in the art of promotion and aware of the factors that entered into commercial ventures involving works of art. Only ten years had passed between the purchase, by the dealer Farrer, of Millais's *Christ in the House of His Parents* (1850, http://artmarket.tulane.edu/page99.html) from the walls of the RA for £150[45] and the sale of Hunt's *The Finding of the Saviour in the Temple* (1854–60, http://artmarket.tulane.edu/page98.html) to Gambart for £5,750. This increase within a decade in the price of artistic labour is persuasive evidence for the successful establishment of a business model under which painters, middlemen and press cooperated to maximize the financial rewards of the first systematic approach to mass marketing of artistic products.

These enterprises involving 'sensation pictures' are more reminiscent of Hollywood-type launches of 'block buster' movies than some of today's highly promoted art exhibits. Not only is one subjected to a seemingly endless stream of advance publicity to attract the highest possible consumer response in the shortest amount of time, but shortly after a film's appearance in the theatres, the availability of the movie's main derivative product, the DVD, is equally aggressively marketed. Movie production companies at first attempted to outlaw video cassette players but now base their earnings projections to a greater proportion on the profits from DVD sales than ticket sales.[46] Evidently Victorian art dealers had a better understanding of the profitability of derivative products since there is no evidence that the trade ever felt that a reproductive print stood in any competition with the original painting.

The analogy with today's motion picture industry also extends to the area of general marketing. Using familiar hyperbole, the promotional efforts associated with these nineteenth-century visual entertainment events to create anxious anticipation among the public began already in the earliest stages of production. Press contacts cultivated by artists and dealers performed their required function in this promotional machinery with impressive results.[47]

An impressive example of advance publicity occurred in the case of W. P. Frith's *Life at the Railroad Station* (1862, http://artmarket.tulane.edu/page100.html). On 8 December, 1860, the *Illustrated London News* reported that the artist had received a commission for the staggering sum of £10,000. To add suspense, the paper kept the identity of the patron secret until 22 December, when it revealed that the canvas had been ordered by the dealer/publisher, Flatou, in a clever manoeuvre to outdo his competition in pictorial sensationalism. Two years passed before the painting was finished, but the artist managed to extract only an additional £750 for the work's exhibition rights. In this negotiation Frith was not as shrewd of a negotiator as Hunt, since *Life at the Railroad Station* went on to gross for the dealer in the excess of £4,000 in entrance fees alone. According to the *Illustrated London News* of 20 September 1862, some 83,000 visitors had paid to see this now famous picture and 'the subscription list for the engraving is also very large. Mr. Flatou runs little risk, therefore, of being ultimately a loser by this venture'.[48]

A further illustration of successful advance publicity involved Frith's *Derby Day* (1858, http://artmarket.tulane.edu/page101.html). Prior to its exhibition at the RA in May 1858, publicity articles appeared in the *Athenaeum*, on 13 February, and 13 March, as well as in the *Art Journal* on April 1. When the painting was installed, it had gained such popularity that a rail had to be put in to protect it from the enthusiastic crowd.[49] Another instance involved Hunt's good friend, F. G. Stephens, a journalistic champion of the Pre-Raphaelite Brotherhood. On 25 February, 1860, some three months before the public exhibition of the *Temple* picture, the writer informed his readers in the *Athenaeum*, that the artist's 'long expected work ... is on the very eve of completion, and will be placed before the public in April next ... The splendour and solidity of the mere workmanship are rare amongst us, – its dramatic power, second to none ...'[50] This article appeared prior to the commencement of the negotiations that ultimately resulted in the sale of this canvas to Gambart. Such publicity certainly strengthened Hunt's position since it enhanced the earning potential of the derivative properties of the painting. However, Stephens's promotional support extended also to the dealer. In conjunction with the opening of the exhibition of this painting at the German Gallery, the writer in a lengthy article again in the *Athenaeum*, called the painting 'almost unequalled in our time ...'[51] Undoubtedly, such puff translated into hard cash for the gallery's proprietor.

The earning potential of these dealer-organized exhibitions was augmented by taking many of these shows on nationwide and even worldwide tours. Gambart, for instance, toured Hunt's *Temple* picture (http://artmarket.tulane.edu/page98.html) throughout England for nine years until 1869 and even considered sending it to America. Unfortunately, he could not find a partner to share the financial risk.[52] Hunt also contracted with Agnew to produce a copy of his *Shadow of Death* (http://artmarket.tulane.edu/page93.html) for the specific purpose of sending it on tour.[53] Rosa Bonheur's *Horsefair* (1853–5, http://artmarket.tulane.edu/page102.html) went on a six year-long world-wide tour starting in 1856 and, as a result, was dubbed 'circumnavigator'. The huge canvas went to Australia and also the US where it subsequently ended up after its final exhibition at Colnaghi's in London in May 1862, when Gambart sold it to the New York collector, William P. Wright.[54] The world tour of this painting caused some consternation about how many versions or copies really existed. The controversy came out into the open in a letter published in the *Times* on 26 April 1865. Gambart's response published the following day explained that there were three versions, the original work, an engraver's copy and one 'reworked original', all necessary components to this vast enterprise.

How these international business ventures influenced artistic production in the countries to which such exhibitions were sent remains conjecture. At the very least, as the earlier discussion surrounding Constable, Arrowsmith and the 'British Salon' of 1824 shows, it can be argued that without the entrepreneurship of this new class of professional art dealers, international cultural exchange would have occurred differently and at a slower pace.

The London artist community was quite aware of the impact this professionally run marketing of art products could have on painters' careers. The painter William Bell Scott (1811–90) described it as 'working the oracle'.[55] Even non-resident painters tried to participate in the financial rewards by orienting their works towards attracting the interest of English dealers. Artists like Alma-Tadema (1836–1912), Tissot or Legros were highly successful in this. Degas, however, was not, and his failure is instructive on a subtler level. The artist, somewhat familiar with the English market through favourable accounts provided by his friend Tissot, had painted his *A Cotton Office in New Orleans* (http://artmarket.tulane.edu/page103.html) with the intention of selling it through Agnew's to a Manchester cotton magnate, Mr. Cottrill. It is unclear whether this art dealer ever saw the picture; even if he had, he would have rejected it. For one, although the canvas depicted numerous figures, it lacked any easily communicable narrative to convey to a potential buyer and engage a viewer's eye. One should only recall the earlier mentioned letter by T. Lawrie, that his customers were 'fond of pictures that tells [*sic*] them something'.[56] Moreover, the scene was too real to suit the Ruskinian demand for a censored representation of nature. The artist had not confined himself to depicting accurately only those aspects that would fulfil the didactic, aesthetic, religious and patriotic requirements of a painting with commercial potential. Furthermore, the physiognomy of the figures ran contrary to the prevailing English preference for caricature-like facial characteristics. Hogarth's style was still greatly admired, and the Victorian public in general was quite interested in the subject of caricatures. Every issue of the *Art Journal* for 1863, for example, contained illustrated feature articles on this subject. Finally, as a candidate for engraving, Degas's work had no chance. Thematically it lacked mass-appeal and the unorthodox, non-Albertian perspective would have been ridiculed by Victorian art writers.[57] Clearly, in order to be successful, the product required certain criteria which Degas's work did not fulfil.

The significance of a smooth cooperation between essential components of a commercially successful exhibition becomes even more evident in case studies where one of these factors is missing. In one instance in 1865, Ford Maddox Brown (1821–93) failed to interest Gambart in staging a major one-man show with the painter's *Work* (1852–65, http://artmarket.tulane.edu/page112a.html) as the centrepiece. The artist, therefore, organized the entire event on his own, failing miserably in the process. Inexperienced in these matters, he had neglected to offer subscriptions for engravings. After the exhibition, the painting was unsuccessfully offered at Christie's. Initially, the canvas with copy and exhibition rights had been sold by the artist around 1861 to Thomas Plint for £1,320. After the ill-fated exhibition, which severely curbed the picture's 'sensational' qualities and thus its earning potential, the market decided that it was worth even less than its reserve of £550.[58]

Another example that went wrong was an unprecedented enterprise undertaken in 1857 which brought over 350 modern English paintings for a three-city commercial exhibition tour to the United States. This was the first organized attempt to introduce contemporary English painting to American consumers and the endeavour exemplifies a prototype for exhibition enterprises *per se*. Such large ventures were usually organized by committees whose members were picked for their ability to contribute to the project. In this case, the group consisted of a characteristic mixture of moneyed aristocracy, influential members of the press, art dealers and celebrity artists, all of whom were asked to solicit additional artists to consign works to the planned exhibition. Several months before its first opening in New York in October 1857 and throughout its entire duration, the show was promoted in the American art press. To create the aura of official sanction, the promoters had selected appropriate locations in the participating cities: the National Academy of Design in New York, the Pennsylvania Academy in Philadelphia and the Athenaeum in Boston. Despite the sale of over 40 per cent of oils and almost 50 per cent of all watercolours during the course of the tour, plans for future events were cancelled. The painters whose works sold during the tour must have been pleased, but the organizers who only received a commission evidently could not financially justify repeats. The committee had failed to include a suitable work by a 'celebrity' artist for the specific purpose of performing the role of 'sensation picture', and offer engraving of this painting as well as a selection after others. Properly promoted, this picture could have been elevated to the status of 'must see'. This would have not only increased earnings from gate fees, but high volume sales of engravings would have significantly added to the overall revenues of the project. Perhaps the uncertainty of exploring a new market resulted in an overly cautious approach, and the investment required for the production of a 'sensation picture' with engravings was deemed too risky. The omission of such well-tested essentials may well have been due to the fact that the experienced dealer Gambart after an initial involvement in the project bowed out.[59] How a wider, more frequent exposure of the American public to contemporary British art would have affected the subsequent development of American paintings can only be hypothesized.

The organization of art exhibitions was, for better or worse, not exclusively the domain of professional dealers. There was, of course, the all-powerful RA that, in spite of frequent criticism, stood at the centre of the British art world. However, rival organizations had sprung up almost as soon as the Academy was founded. There was, for instance, the considerably less prestigious British Institution, founded in 1805. In addition to its annual exhibition of Old Masters, the Institution became a useful way to market better-than-average potboilers that would not have passed the scrutiny of the Royal Academy's acceptance committee. Visitors paid the usual shilling admittance, and a five percent commission was charged by the organization on the sale of pictures.[60] Another organization was the Society of British Artists, founded in 1823 and particularly popular with landscape painters. Others included The Old and New Watercolour Societies, established in 1804 and 1832 respectively, the Free Exhibition, the Cosmorama and the National Institution, begun in 1847 at the Egyptian Hall. The same facility also housed the Dudley Gallery, which later moved to Regent Street, changed its name to the Portland Gallery, and closed in 1861.

By mid-century, many of these institutions had become stale and too encumbered by vested interests to satisfy the demands of an expanding, heterogeneous artists' community. Consequently, painters again sought alternative venues to show and sell their work. Similar to other venture capitalists – for this is what these artists had become – they promoted the formation of independent bodies that set up their own committees to organize commercial art exhibitions outside established venues. The considerable expenditures of such ventures demanded fiscal prudence and sound business judgment in the planning and execution of these exhibition enterprises. Accordingly, organized cultural activities in England were strongly shaped by their economic feasibility. Indeed, this close connection of money and muse was, at the time, a uniquely British phenomenon. As a result, exhibitions of contemporary art – organized outside of conventional forms of patronage, yet dependent on financial success – had to operate under new sets of rules.

This development of artist-controlled exhibitions coincided with certain events. The first founding of rival organizations to the Academy around the turn of the century occurred during the depressed state of the contemporary painting market during the Napoleonic War period while the first Free Exhibition in 1848 witnessed the wholesale entry of middlemen into this market. Most likely, economics were partly responsible for this trend to organize. First, painters consolidated in a shrinking market and sought ways to bypass the formidable entry barrier put up by the Academy and its selection committee; then, as consumption habits shifted in favour of living artists and demand for their work grew, these organizations expanded from necessary support and subsidy structures to potentially profitable business ventures. Their internal make-up, however, was not designed to perform all the tasks demanded by commercial enterprises. Since economic expansion is associated with specialization, the remarkable growth in exhibition activity during the latter half of the 1840s must have attracted outside specialists to perform necessary organizational and business tasks. This increase in artist-controlled exhibitions also attracted competition from professional merchant/promoters who, recognizing opportunity, began staging their own contemporary art exhibitions.

The growing dealer participation in this expanding market is confirmed by auction data as well as by the contemporary press. Increasingly, announcements and/or reviews of art exhibitions in the *Times*, the *Art Union/Art Journal*, or the *Athenaeum* began to appear. The media initially even took sides in the competition between dealers and independent exhibitions. The March 1848 issue of the *Art Union*, for example, advocated visiting artists-organized exhibitions and avoiding auction rooms and dealers.[61] This hostile attitude would soon change, however, as the trade and press recognized their interdependency and cemented their relationship.

The general rivalry between artist-organized and dealer-organized events added further momentum and fed the already mentioned 'exhibition mania'. Within the four years that separated the opening of 'The First Exhibition of the Free Exhibition' in the summer 1848 and the closing of the 'Great Exhibition' in the fall of 1851, London witnessed, for example, such important events as the first commercial introduction of works by Barbizon School painters organized by John Arrowsmith in 1848.[62] This exhibit completed a cultural exchange that Arrowsmith had helped initiate twenty four years earlier when he made it possible for French landscape painters to examine Constable's work first hand in his gallery and the Paris Salon. Also, in 1849, at the Free Exhibition held at the Hyde Park Gallery, the first painting by one of the members of the recently founded Pre-Raphaelite Brotherhood, Rossetti's *The Girlhood of Virgin Mary* (http://artmarket.tulane.edu/page104.html), was first seen by the public.[63] In the same year, London dealers introduced the annual 'Winter exhibitions', effectively making the art season an all-year affair; and by 1850, the city was literally swamped with different art shows, organized either by artists' committees or by dealers.[64] In June of the following year, the exhibition of pictures by contemporary Continental artists held at Litchfield House, despite preliminary organizational problems and tepid press support, initiated in England the beginning of widespread trade and private patronage of Continental painters. Correspondingly, the incidents of auction sales of contemporary Continental paintings, their average prices, as well as the associated trade buying activity all markedly increased in the decade subsequent to this event.

However, the most monumental undertaking of this sort occurred a few years later in Manchester: the Arts Treasures Exhibition of 1857, which, so contemporary comments suggested, was 'destined to change ultimately the face of things'.[65]

The buoyant conditions resulting from the combination of dealer-managed shows, gallery sales, publications of prints and independently organized exhibitions expanded considerably the opportunities for women aspiring to become painters. The number of women who took advantage of these favourable economic circumstances during this period was astonishingly high. Out of the over 11,000 painters listed in Wood's dictionary more than 3,200 – nearly 30 per cent – were female. This level of participation of women as producers in the art market appears to be entirely without precedent in the history of western art.

Unfortunately, the data provide little concrete information on female artists in the market place: neither auction catalogues nor Tooth's inventory list women painters in any significant numbers. However, their absence from these conventional exchange platforms may well reveal a key factor behind the founding, in 1857, of the Society of Female Artists by the British feminist Harriet Grote. Economics suggest that the establishment of an exhibition venue exclusively serving female artists must have been at least partly a response to certain well-entrenched barriers erected by the male-dominated art establishment to keep women from unencumbered participation in the period's booming art market. In addition, the Society responded to the demand for increasing differentiation in an expanding market for exhibition venues. A niche existed for offering inexpensive art produced by women for women, and the enterprise was well received by precisely the audience it targeted.[66] Furthermore, within a larger historical context, the Society of Female Artists was also one of the building blocks of increasing female economic empowerment in Victorian England. The new economics of the contemporary art market, radically different from the patronage structure that preceded it, facilitated women's entry into the economic mainstream. While the majority of these female painters gained neither great fame nor fortune by their work, their presence in the market in such large numbers is testimony to their tenacity to search out and compete for economic opportunity in an environment utterly controlled by men.[67]

For the remaining years of the century and beyond, commercial, privately or trade-organized art exhibitions were the main tool to market contemporary art on an increasing scale. The participation in what started out as purely commercial undertakings has become today a measure of an artist's career. As testimony to the commoditization of the arts environment, the once derided picture merchants of the nineteenth century have now attained such status and power that the bestowing of their patronage is a determinant of a painter's commercial and critical success. Even tenure and promotion of studio artists in academia are very much influenced by their commercial gallery exhibitions history, and commercial exhibitions also factor into the make-up of textbooks on contemporary art.

Art Writers as Agent of Commerce

> We are overwhelmed with a tribe of critics who are fully imbued with every kind of knowledge which is useful to the picture-dealer, but with none that is important to the artist.
>
> John Ruskin, Arrows of the Chace

The success of commercial art exhibitions depended, to varying extents, on art writers and critics. The market for their products had rapidly grown in the wake of the increasing number of exhibitions following the establishment of the annual showings of contemporary art at the RA.[68] The earliest reviews could be found in general periodicals and newspapers until 1785, when Charles Taylor started the first publication, the *Artist's Repository,* dedicated to featuring general topics of art and, specifically, to reviewing contemporary art showings. From then on, discussing art and art exhibitions became an important part of many of the period's periodicals' regular content. Indeed, by 1848, as many as 20 different art writers could be counted among the attendees of the opening of the annual RA exhibition.[69]

Like painters, these journalists competed to find their audience and their niche; yet there appears to have been a consensus on the corrupt practices of the RA. A comment in *Arnold's Magazine* in June 1834 encapsulates these sentiments: 'Of all our public institutions, however tainted with the prevailing vice of favouritism and intrigue, we know of no one more openly, and, as it appears to us, more justly accused of it than this'.[70]

Such condemnation must have endeared these writers to many of the artists who felt wronged by the pervasive nepotism of the RA's Selection and Hanging Committees. These attacks must have also delighted the growing number of dealers whose galleries and exhibitions provided artists with new commercial outlets and also offered additional material about which art journalists could write.

The benefit to the art trade of art journalism was well understood by both painters and dealers. In fact, the proposal, in 1838, which led to the establishment of the leading nineteenth-century art journal, the *Art Union/Journal,* was initially made to the magazine's founder, S. C. Hall, by the painter Charles Landseer, and financing was offered by Mr. Hodgson, one of the partners in the print publishing firm of Hodgson and Graves.[71] Artist and print publisher knew that the promotion of general interest in the arts, a prerequisite for patronage, would be positively affected by the publication of a magazine exclusively devoted to the visual arts. Furthermore, even though most of the earlier publications, such as the *Repository of Art*, the *Annals of the Fine Arts*, the *Somerset House Gazette* or the *Library for the Fine Arts*, had not survived,[72] the market for literary products dealing with the arts had now expanded sufficiently to warrant the publication of a new specialized periodical.

Art appreciation, particularly of contemporary painting, was still at a nascent stage in the 1840s. Appropriately, the new publication promoted the general consumption of art among its readers rather than engaging in sophisticated, critical rhetoric on the formal merits, or absence thereof, of the art reviewed. Hall also differentiated his new publication from the earlier periodicals by staunchly defending the RA as an institution: 'To prejudice and injure the Royal Academy is to prejudice and injure the Fine Arts of Great Britain'.[73] In Hall's words, his magazine 'was to be a just representative of the interests of artists and art'. To meet this lofty goal, the publisher went as far as promoting the investment potential of works by living artists and even publishing what can be best described as financial analyses of the contemporary painting market.[74]

The general tone of Hall's publication as well as many of the later periodicals[75] was didactic and frequently descriptive of the minutest details of a given painting. The literary background of many of the writers lent itself to re-telling painted stories, and narrative subjects were clearly favoured – a fact not lost on artists.[76] Indeed, there was concern that artists were induced by critics to paint works that lent themselves to the literary approach of their writing and were easy sellers for dealers.[77] The abundance and success of narrative paintings, so characteristic of the period, attests to the accuracy of this observation. Towards the end of the period, as the mid-century consensus on aesthetics was challenged by a flood of stylistic innovations, Elizabeth Pennell, the wife of the artist Joseph Pennell, lamented that to catch a critic's attention, artists must create 'novelty at all costs'.[78] Writers also were often criticized for the abundant use of terminologies borrowed from the world of aristocratic connoisseurship the meanings of which were as vague then as they are today.[79]

Victorian art writing was by no means uniformly positive as far as specific works were concerned. Reviews could be quite scathing, yet they still maintained a popular, didactic tone and promoted viewing. Dickens, for example, went all out in his condemnation of Millais's, *Christ in the House of his Parents* (http://artmarket.tulane.edu/page99.html), writing, 'In the foreground of that carpenter's shop is a hideous, wry-necked, blubbering, red-haired boy'. Even more cutting was his description of Mary as a woman 'so horrible in her ugliness that she would stand out ... as a monster in the vilest cabaret in France, or the lowest gin shop in England'.[80] Such words could hardly have pleased the artist. Nonetheless, the hyperbolic, even subtly blasphemous, description of young Jesus and the unabashed, seedy-sexual reference to the Virgin's appearance must have enhanced the work's popularity among spectators.

The increasing number of independent, privately organized exhibition venues and the countless commercial shows organized by dealers challenging the once all powerful RA also contributed positively to the growing demand for art writers' products. The effectiveness of these sales venues and, consequently, their continuation, was affected by press coverage. This tri-lateral interdependency between artists, middlemen, and art writers, particularly its effect on artistic production, was a consciously recognized and accepted dimension of the Victorian arts environment.[81]

Art writers then as now were biased and readily embraced specific causes. To the earlier mentioned example of Stephens's journalistic support of Hunt one can add the running commentary by the same writer in the *Athenaeum* throughout 1871 and early 1872 promoting Millais's *Christ in the Carpenter Shop* (http://artmarket.tulane.edu/page99.html). Stephens's championing of Pre-Raphaelitism even went as far as giving Rossetti veto power over anything the critic wrote on the painter in the *Athenaeum* from 1871 on. The writer also actively endorsed the merits of inexpensive prints.[82] P. G. Hamerton devoted much of his writing for *The Portfolio* to the promotion of etchings; William Morris advocated his own version of Socialism in *The Commonweal*, and David C. Thomson supported the Barbizon painters while he was a sub-editor for the *Art Journal* in the 1880s.[83]

At times critics' involvement went to the point of personal engagement in selling particular artists' works. Hall, the undying campaigner for contemporary British painters, not only claimed for himself a large part of the credit for their success, but actually performed the role of salesman for the painter Linnell.[84] Markus Huish, the editor of the *Arts Journal* from 1881 to1892 also served as the director of the Fine Arts Society from 1879 to 1911. His successor, Thomson, was the manager for the London branch of the French publisher Goupil Maison followed by a stint in the same capacity at Agnew while he was the magazine's subeditor between 1881 and 1888.[85]

Such close cooperation between critics, dealers, and artists was not an exclusively English phenomenon. A Continental example of this dealer/critic relationship that developed during the nineteenth century is the writer and art critic Alfred Sensier's promotion of Courbet, Rousseau, Millet, Michel, Diaz and others of the Barbizon School.[86]

As mentioned earlier, dealers also cultivated their contacts in the press, often through placing advertisements. Harry Quilter once complained that dealers and publishers expected favourable treatment in exchange for placing advertisements. Comyns Carr even quit Hall's employ when the editor suggested a more flattering tone for reviews of specific exhibitions which organizers were frequent advertisers.[87]

On a social level as well, dealers like Gambart or Agnew built mutually advantageous relationships with leading art journalists like Hall, Taylor of *The Times*, or Stephens of the *Athenaeum*.[88] At times even attractive business opportunities were made available to these writers. Gambart, for instance, promoted and managed a lecture tour for Ruskin in 1858 during which the writer presented talks on 'Unity of Art' in Manchester and on 'Modern Manufacture and Design' in Bradford.[89] These provincial urban centres were art markets with promising growth potential, and Ruskin, the acknowledged man of taste, had the kind of reputation and skills to foster such development. The esteemed critic was also persuaded by the same dealer to include reviews of the French exhibitions in his *Academy Notes* from 1857 to 1859.[90] A similar example is Tom Taylor's involvement in the earlier-described exhibition tour of modern British paintings in America in 1857–8.

Aware of the interdependency of the market's major components, painters also catered, deferred and paid homage to critics. '[T]he man who paints for popularity cannot afford indifference to press notices upon which it is fed', opined Elizabeth Pennell.[91] Hunt certainly was quite sensitive to the benefits to the Pre-Raphaelite cause of Taylor's appointment,[92] while a near apotheosis of Ruskin is apparent in a comment by Burne-Jones after having received a reply to a letter he had written to the great critic: 'I'm not Ted any longer, I'm not E.C.B. Jones now – I've dropped my personality – I'm correspondent with RUSKIN [Burne-Jones's emphasis], and my future title is "the man who wrote to Ruskin and got an answer by return"'.[93]

Writers in turn courted certain artists. Ruskin's early success, for example, was very much associated with his outspoken and often hyperbolic praise of England's greatest living painter, J. M. W. Turner who, at the pinnacle of his success, certainly did not depend on the critical support of a then rather unknown writer.[94]

Ruskin was not only Britain's supreme judge of taste but also the classic example of a critic and art writer in the arts environment of the period. Arguably, no writer on art had greater influence.[95] The identification as the champion of Turner must have enhanced the critic's commercial value and factored into Gambart's decision to engage Ruskin's help in marketing the second publication of Turner's *Harbours of England* series in 1856. Despite the buoyancy of the market, the critic's contribution to the success of this enterprise was deemed crucial by the dealer, as the first issue of this series had commercially failed in 1826.[96]

The writer's most widely recognized promotional cause was his early and lasting support of the initially much derided Pre-Raphaelite Brotherhood.[97] Yet not all members of the group always took the great arbiter's comments seriously. Rossetti, for instance, wrote to his friend, the sculptor Thomas Woolner (1825–92) on 16 April 1853, that

> Ruskin goes into raptures about the colour and grouping [of a work by Rossetti] which, he says, are superior to anything in modern art – which I believe is almost as absurd as certain absurd objections he makes to them. However, as he is only half informed about art, anything he says in favour of one's work is, of course, sure to prove invaluable in a professional way, and I hope, for the sale of my rubbish, that he may have the honesty to say publicly in his new book what he has said privately.[98]

The painter professed little respect for Ruskin's formal knowledge of art but welcomed the positive influence of the critic's ignorance on the market for his work. Rossetti's reference to his work as 'rubbish' and the causal connection he made between Ruskin's lack of knowledge of art and the beneficial effect this had on a painter's career is difficult to reconcile with the public image of elevated sincerity of the Brotherhood in general and the hyper-sensitive, romantic image of the painter/poet Rossetti. A few years later, on 23 May, 1856, Rossetti commented in a letter to Maddox Brown: 'Millais had written to me that Gambart wants me to paint something, so I imagine Ruskin is beginning to bear fruit – that is, after his kind'.[99] Rossetti connects critic and dealer in a manner which suggests a manipulative cultivation of Ruskin on the artist's part to attain commercial rewards; at the same time the 'fruit' of this cultivation extends to nothing more than commerce.

Ruskin also successfully expanded his critical writings into the area of political economy, thereby adding a certain social missionary and reform dimension to his identity.[100] As a romantic socialist, the critic had clear ideas concerning the economics of art in society. In lecture II of the Political Economy of Art, presented in Manchester in 1857, he argued that the government should collect and display the works of dead masters in public galleries and also encourage private patronage of living artists. However, applying a somewhat unorthodox interpretation of the rules of supply and demand, Ruskin suggested that 'the first and best way in which to encourage such private possession is, of course, to keep down the price of them as far as you can', because it 'will make painters produce more pictures'. Such intervention in the market, in the critic's mind, will 'increase a thousand-fold the demand for the commodity, and therefore its wholesome and natural production'.[101] Yet, keeping prices of a commodity artificially low will ultimately result in reduced numbers of producers as they switch to more profitable activities, unless the intervention is in the form of subsidy. The 'thousand-fold increase in demand' will stimulate an increase in supply to equilibrium level determined by the extent of the subsidy to producers. In the absence of a subsidy, however, a reduced number of producers will produce the increased quantity demanded by cutting production costs in the form of labour and/or material. In the case of painters, the most easily changeable variable is time, and the result of Ruskin's proposal would have been the proliferation of cheaply, that is, quickly, produced paintings. Ruskin's above reference to paintings as a 'commodity' is quite apropos: he argues in favour of a radical commoditization through government intervention. He seems to have been unaware that this specific aspect of his political economy of art opposed his labour-based measure of quality of art.[102] Furthermore, how painters could, or why they would want to, fulfil Ruskin's demands of 'not merely to delight [the viewer's] senses, not merely to amuse his fancy, not merely to beguile him into emotion, not merely to lead him into thought, but to do *all* [Ruskin's emphasis] this', on a reduced compensation per unit of labour is difficult to rationalize.[103]

Ruskin's advocacy of government intervention in the contemporary art market entails a noteworthy implication for the later and more famous Whistler versus Ruskin trial of November 1878. The critic's proposal to lower artificially the prices of contemporary paintings to occasion artists to produce more pictures would result in the production of more paintings in less time. Or differently stated, less labour would be evident in each painting. This was exactly the aspect which Ruskin later attacked in Whistler's *Nocturne in Black and Blue: The Falling Rocket* (*c.* 1874, http://artmarket.tulane.edu/page105.html). The defendant Ruskin and his witnesses, the painters Burne-Jones and Frith, considered Whistler's painting, which had taken the artist only two days to produce, unfinished and, therefore, the price of 200 guineas inappropriate. Nothing suggests that the critic and occasional political economist was aware that one of the consequences of his proposed market intervention would have been a flood of pictures precisely like the one that had so offended him.

There is another economic dimension to Ruskinian aesthetics. The restrictive measures for determining the merits of paintings advocated by Ruskin presented, in economic terms, obstructions to producers wishing to enter a potentially lucrative market. Whistler's challenge of Ruskinian aesthetics, therefore, can also be described as an action by an art producer to realize his opportunities in this market by attempting to break down these market barriers. For artists to compete effectively under the above-described changing conditions and expanding market, product differentiation was essential. 'Novelty at all costs', as Elizabeth Pennell had astutely observed. Since paintings' commodity character includes also an aesthetic dimension, a differentiation on the latter grounds was a logical and readily available option. It provided art writers with new topics and causes with which they could set themselves apart; it provided art dealers with an expanding variety of aesthetic goods from which to chose; and it freed penned up artistic creativity and production. This perhaps most far-reaching redefinition of the product character of paintings was spearheaded by producers.

Such challenges to the prevailing commodity character of paintings were also manifestations of another change. The multi-dimensional confluence of interests of artists, dealers and critics, and the resulting marketing collaboration that characterized the Victorian art boom was at its peak a virtually unstoppable tide engulfing with remarkable efficiency an ever-growing number of consumers to whom conspicuous consumption of appropriately designated cultural products was promoted as a patriotic, moral, and financial good. However, its own force brought about its break-up. The modern art market finally expanded beyond its last limitations and its 200 year genesis was coming to an end. Henceforth, it would be defined by open competition among producers, professional marketers and art writers for an ever increasing number of consumers of art.

8 THE FORMATION OF A NEXUS: A STORY OF CHRISTIE'S

In a rough analogy of the art market to the stock market painters are firms which produce products (here paintings rather than stocks or bonds), dealers are specialists and brokers, critics are analysts and the auction house is the stock exchange. Throughout most of the eighteenth century, the auction industry was characterized by the presence of numerous auctioneers disbursing collections generally assembled by middlemen to sell to the public. Liquidity sales appear to have been less frequent. The nineteenth-century scene, to the contrary, can be told as the story of one auction house – Christie's – primarily involved in the disposition of private estates to the trade.

This auction house alone conducted 92 per cent of all sales between 1840 and 1900 recorded by Graves: 90 per cent of all transactions involving Continental Old Masters; 92 per cent of sales of English Old Masters; 95 per cent of Contemporary Continental works and 93 per cent of Contemporary English paintings passed through Christie's. The remaining 8 per cent were spread across approximately thirty other firms. Since Graves recorded the top end of the market and only about 10 per cent of the estimated total volume of auction sales, we checked Graves's records against our records of the dealers Tooth and Agnew. Both data sets show that, indeed, Christie's was the overwhelmingly favoured auction house for these two dealers. In the years 1870 and 1871, the 150 paintings Tooth bought at auction all came from Christie's, while Agnew made over 90 per cent of its auction purchases between 1870 and 1880 at the same house. Comparing Graves's data from 1840–1900 to that from 1790–1840 shows that earlier on a much larger market share was taken up by Christie's competition. Only 62 per cent of all transactions involved the firm: 57 per cent of Continental Old Masters, 71 per cent of English Old Masters, 21 per cent of Contemporary Continental and 78 per cent of Contemporary English paintings with most of the overall growth occurring in the decades of the 1820s and 30s. The market had changed from one made up of many different 'exchanges' to one in which one exchange unmistakably dominated and became the nexus of the market. Sometime between 1840 and 1860, Christie's left its competition markedly behind.[1]

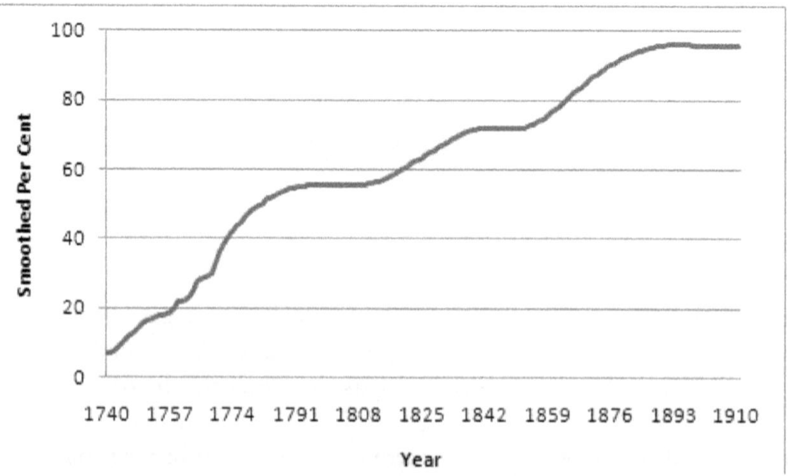

The rise to virtual supremacy over a nation's fine art auction industry by one firm and the maintenance of this position for well over sixty years and possibly beyond is remarkable and likely unprecedented. This near monopoly was among the favourable conditions behind the buoyancy and expansion of the art market, particularly, of the market for contemporary paintings.

In a market model, the auction house provides liquidity, a prerequisite for the expansion of proprietary transactions involving commodities of a highly individual utility and/or speculative character. Consumers of art works knew that their collections were assets that could be turned into cash through auctioneers' agency. They were also aware that these art works appreciated in value. Both factors, as mentioned earlier, must have contributed to some degree to the initial growth of art auctions in the eighteenth century. The financial regulations following the South Sea financial disaster of 1720 and the subsequent structuring of the national debt offered to the often cash-poor English upper class attractively secure investment opportunities. One could raise the money necessary to participate in such schemes by the sale of paintings through auction. Similar financial considerations may have motivated middle-class auction bidders and sellers. Non-financial reasons – emulative behaviour, for example – also could have been contributing factors. Whatever rationales occasioned the industry's growth, the earlier mentioned amount of imported works listed in customs records, together with the estimated number of paintings sold at auctions during the last decade of the seventeenth century indicate the existence of a large locally owned stock from which by the 1720s London auction houses could draw consignments. Since most of these pictures were inexpensive 'run of the mill' works well within the reach of the middle classes, their participation in the art market must have been encouraged by this liquidity availability.[2]

For most of the eighteenth century, auction transactions were mainly limited to the Old Masters market, although occasionally the estates of recently deceased painters were also sold. Widespread trading in contemporary paintings did not occur until the second quarter of the nineteenth century and, increasingly, dealers were among the buyers at these auctions. To what extent occasional earlier sales of paintings by artists from the English School were associated with this trend remains conjecture. Our data list around thirty artist studio sales between 1770 and 1839 of which nearly two-thirds were conducted by Christie's. All were well attended by dealers.[3] There must have been many more of these disbursements of painters' estates with the result of distributing progressively more works by artists of the modern English School among the trade and the public in general.[4] The favourable publicity surrounding the 7 July, 1827 sale of the collection of contemporary English paintings formerly owned by Lord de Tabley certainly emphasized the profitability of buying modern pictures and may have helped to create the later pervasive aura of speculative potential in the market for modern paintings.[5] Interestingly, J. W. M. Turner was present at this sale, most likely, as was his habit, to protect the value of his paintings. Of the six canvases by his hand he bought two, paying in one instance a record price of 515 guineas.[6] Other buyers included members of the aristocracy, the gentry as well as several dealers. It appears that the later much more noticeable shift in trade and general consumer preference away from old paintings from the Continent towards works by still living artists may well have had its roots earlier than the date of Hall's well publicized campaign against fraudulent old masters indicates.

In any event, the much touted speculative aspect of contemporary paintings promoted the use of auctions as the exchange platform where profits could be realized. If the earlier description of auctions as useful tools for market manipulation is correct as our discovery of at least one hundred sales at which consignor and buyer were identical suggests, then the absence of competition between different auction providers made such use of auctions simpler and more efficient. Competition would have benefited mostly the consignors in the form of lower commission rates. However, the presence of a large number of rivalling auction facilities would have made it more difficult for middlemen to oversee the market, undertake regulatory measures and gain the cooperation of auctioneers. Again, the analogy with the stock market is useful. A small number of high volume exchanges can be monitored and managed by specialists more effectively than numerous small ones. The increasing electronic inter-connectedness of different stock markets internationally reflects this fact.[7]

A possibly even greater contribution to the decline in competing auction facilities was their change in function within the framework of the art market. As long as public sales remained the principal means by which middlemen sold property, established auctioneers were motivated to compete for consignments by, for instance, reducing transaction costs.

Our data do not tell us the precise means by which different auctioneers competed for sellers, but they do show the existence of competition. During the late 1760s and throughout the decades of the 1770s and 80s, for example, when Christie first offered paintings, specific sellers clearly used several different auction facilities in London. John Ansell, the framer, dealer and short-term partner of James Christie, for instance, used Christie in 1771 but then turned to Walsh in 1775 and Squibb in 1781. Conversely, John Bertel first employed Walsh in 1775 but then switched to Christie's to sell his huge collection in 1783.[8] However, once auctions transformed to becoming one of the primary sources of supply for dealers, and auctioneers had to rely for their goods on the inherent unpredictability of liquidity transactions, competition for consignments was less significant.

Our data show that the majority of paintings offered at auctions during the Victorian period originated from estates of recently deceased individuals or, in some instances, business failures, personal debts and/or bankruptcies. Consignments in the form of liquidity trades, such as estate liquidations, are by nature less suitable to competition as the likelihood of potential heirs or executors shopping for the best transaction costs is slim. The low number of individual repeat sellers also suggests, as we point out earlier, that the Victorian auction market was not an environment suitable for speculators – contrary to the pervasive aura. Indeed, buying and selling paintings through auction resulted during this period in an opportunity loss. Of course, on the positive side, this fact underscores the efficiency of this market. It should be noted that press reports, like Hall's financial accounting of the Bicknell sale, usually juxtaposed the amounts paid directly to artists or dealers with hammer prices.[9] This stratagem promoted, although erroneously, contemporary painting as a good investment in general, and the use of artists and dealers as sources of supply, as well as the auction house as the exchange where profits can be realized.

While the above contention offers an explanation for the association between market growth and a prevailing near-monopoly condition, it gives no insight into the methods by which this market dominance was achieved. The classic publications on Christie's by Whitley, Marillier and Roberts discuss the firm's genesis and major sales in addition to offering entertaining anecdotal accounts.[10] However, scholarly research into the early business history of Christie's is still in its infancy.[11] It may reveal certain business strategies employed by James Christie and his successors that facilitated the firm's impressive achievement. Some observations, however, can be made already.

No doubt, Mr. Christie was in the right place at the right time. But that place was already occupied by well-established competitors. Major consignments from both Continental and English sources were sold in the 1770s by such houses as Cock & Langford, Squibb, Walsh and Peter Coxe.[12] Langford handled, among others, the huge estate of the Duke of Argyle in the spring of 1771, that of the painter Jonathan Richardson in 1772 as well as the sale of the collection of the collector James West in 1773. Walsh landed the Bertel consignment in 1775 in addition to several large collections from the Continent. Nonetheless, the recently arrived James Christie attracted a number of important accounts in the 1770s that sold at his newly established firm.[13] Considering that his first picture sale did not take place until March 1766, this was a particularly impressive accomplishment. Among these consignors was the dealer Greenwood; Samuel Dickinson; M. Liotard, a relative of the painter J. S. Liotard and the banker Sir G. Colebrook who chaired the board of directors of the East India Company.[14]

Beyond his ability to secure important consignments, James Christie also understood the importance of the media to the growth of his business. He became part owner of two London daily newspapers, the Whiggish *Morning Chronicle* in 1769 and its rival, the pro-Tory *Morning Post* in 1772.[15] A prudent businessman, he covered both sides of the political spectrum and also reduced the firms' costs of frequent advertising.

Moreover, by whatever means, most likely through the employment of agents, Christie secured a number of the consignments that came on the market during the period leading up to the French Revolution. Christie's auction catalogues from this time list numerous Continental consignors such as the Biondi collection sale on 21 February 1777, or one described as 'property from abroad' on 16 April of the same year. Other notable foreign consignments came from the French (?) Count Schulenburg, the Hanoverian Count J. Got de Grote, the city of Rome, the Parma collection as well as property from the Calonna Palace. Christie also worked closely with the dealers Noel Desenfans, Gerard and Benjamin Vandergucht and Walsh Porter.

Besides collaborating with specific dealers, Christie may have also tried to promote his business by performing, in certain instances, private banking services. Farington recorded in his diary that the picture dealer Simpson told him that Christie, around 1799, had lent Chace Price the impressive sum of £14,000, evidently to cover some irregularities involving government funds.[16] What motivated the auctioneer is not known. Price was a young man about town, and Christie may have thought him to be of some use in securing consignments. More telling, however, is the fact that he had such a large sum at his disposal.[17] An auction business usually keeps only a small percentage of revenues. However, to boost his income Christie may have taken equity positions in some of the consignments brought to him by the dealers with whom he worked on a regular basis. The dealer Bryan's joint venture involving the Orleans collection is not likely to be unique.

It may have also been at that time that James Christie began to provide advances on consignments to entice cash-strapped sellers from the Continent or the British Isles to favour his firm over rivalling companies.[18] The practice of offering advances or loans, customarily around 50 percent of the pre-sale estimate and secured by the physical possession of the object(s) in question, is still used today to secure important consignments. However, such arrangements change the relationship of the auctioneer to the goods offered. The auction house is no longer merely an agent but instead becomes a stake-holder. Recent legislation requires that such financial interest be disclosed. There is also the inherent risk for auction firms that they might become owners of such properties if they fail to sell and consignors are unable to repay the loan. For James Christie, this practice would have required the availability of substantial capital in a notoriously cash-poor environment. Even though in the late 1790s, according to Farington, Christie already took in commissions of between £10,000 and £16,000 annually,[19] it would be no surprise if James Christie were to have had relationships with merchant banking houses and/or private venture capitalists. Moreover, Christie was occasionally frowned upon for not paying consignors on time.[20] This fact invites speculation that he may have used consignors' funds to pay advances. The firm's bank records are still kept by Coutts Bank in London and it might be possible to answer some of these issues by examining Christie's account activities in association with auction sales. A single large withdrawal from the proceeds of an auction composed of many different consignors could well have served the purpose of securing, via advance payments on goods, a profitable-looking consignment for a future sale.

Christie also conducted the first major auction of modern paintings when Boydell's bankruptcy released an unprecedented number of such works on the market in May 1805. Among the different aristocratic and middle-class buyers were also several dealers such as Bryan, Sequier, John Green and Gooden and most likely others whose identities as dealers we did not recognize. In the context of a developing secondary market in contemporary paintings, the Boydell sale and the later auction of the collection of Lord de Tabley were thus significant milestones. These sales together with studio sales may have given Christie a competitive advantage by establishing the firm as the best place to buy and sell modern works. While the firm after mid-century outperformed its competitors in all four painting categories, contemporary English and Continental paintings showed the steepest ascent. In sales of Continental Old Masters, Christie's moved slightly in front of its competition in the first decade of the century but did not surge ahead until around 1880; similarly, in the category of English Old Masters, the marginal lead advances noticeably in the 1870s.

From the 1840s onward, the earlier described patterns of the auction market became the norm and prevailed for the rest of the period: Christie's had become the nexus, dominating overwhelmingly the auction market for contemporary works and only slightly less so the market for older paintings; dealers were by far the largest group of buyers.

To what extent James Christie's business acumen was responsible for the demise of many of his competitors is impossible to say. Nonetheless, many of the larger auction firms discontinued their operations in the decades following the founding of Christie's. Our data show that Cock and Langford stopped in 1776; Walsh in 1777; Greenwood in 1794; Skinner's activity markedly declined after 1800. Coxe, one of the main competitors, ceased to do business in 1817, two years after Squibb had closed its doors. Competition, of course, still existed but experienced a steady decline throughout the entire Victorian period.

By the middle of the nineteenth century, the auction house was firmly entrenched as the leading art auctioneer in Europe and it maintained this position in part by closely cooperating with the retail trade. There are numerous examples of the use of auction catalogues to advertise and promote events staged by dealers. For example, the catalogue for the 23 March 1861 sale of paintings owned by the dealer Flatou prominently announced that he was intending to focus all of his attention on the publication of an important work which was especially being painted for him by an artist whose identity was not yet revealed. One year later, in the sale catalogue of 29 March 1862, the exhibition of this picture, the *Railroad Station* by W. P. Frith was conspicuously advertised. Other instances are Christie's pre-sale view for the 3 May 1879 auction of modern paintings owned by Jonathan Nield of Dunster House, Rochdale at the Manchester gallery of Agnew; the same occurred in conjunction with the 5 May 1879 sale of the collection of William Fenton of Dutton Manor, Ribchester.[21]

Besides collaborating with the trade, the company's management during this period showed also an understanding of the economics of auctions by providing longer, more factual and less hyperbolic descriptions of lots for sale. According to auction theory, presenting more information on these items yields financial benefits to the seller.[22]

Image management of Christie's as a business and target marketing of the goods it sold may have been behind an arrangement under which several pre-sale views were held at the offices of the prestigious accounting firm of Price Waterhouse.[23] Individuals who employed chartered accountants were, in terms of income, potential art buyers. Moreover, the implied endorsement of contemporary paintings by financial specialists must have enhanced the works' perception as investments or, at the very least, as non-frivolous expenditures.

The general commoditization of the arts environment during the modern period transformed art auctions from sales venues for retailers to becoming the central nexus in the exchange mechanism for art. Internal process innovations and refinements paved the path towards maximizing this function. In addition to enhancing the liquidity of fine art and offering a convenient source of supply to the trade, the auction industry developed a crucial role as a regulatory tool of the art market in general. Auctions also became the pulse with which to gauge the market's economic state. The industry reached its maturity during the Victorian era and remained essentially unchanged until the last three decades of the twentieth century.

Since then, the same process of commoditization that had shaped the system's structural character in the nineteenth century, has affected a transfer of functions between its two main participants. Increasingly, dealers are becoming significant sources for consignments, and the majority of buyers are private individuals. This development is by no means uniformly welcomed by the trade. In fact, the charges of price fixing and anti-trust laws violations levied against Christie's and Sotheby's in New York, which came to a head at the beginning of the year 2000, were but the latest manifestations of the efforts of the trade to wage battle against the ongoing encroachment of the auction houses on what, for nearly two hundred years, was considered the domain of middlemen.

The auction industry has pursued, since approximately the early to mid 1970s, a strategy of 'retailization', that is, re-designing the conduct as well as the related tool of its business towards better meeting the needs of the end consumer of art. This process included, among others, the change in appearance and presentation of the content of auction catalogues, the establishment of 'special clients' services and the increasing involvement in private treaty sales. This presents a tangible threat to the function, and thus the economic position, of the traditional middleman. Furthermore, the art market as a whole is continuing to become more efficient in its information distribution. The resulting decline in arbitrage opportunities negatively impacts dealers. The resistance to these developments of certain members of the trade may well be a futile struggle against the inevitable tide of historical change. As the past has shown, energies should be devoted to re-defining the role of the middleman, to embracing the new conditions as well as the opportunities inherent in a rapidly expanding market environment. To compete effectively dealers can form again cooperative trade associations and promote them as viable liquidity options to private collectors. The spring 2000 announcement of CINOA (the Confederation Internationale des Negociants en Oeuvres d'Art), the Zurich-based umbrella organization which includes thirty trade associations from twenty-one countries, the formation of CINOA.com, a fixed-price Web site to sell fine and decorative arts consigned by the organization's 5,000 member dealers, or the Dallas, Texas based ArtBanc are examples of such alternative trading platforms.

In the old master market the traditional manner of dealing in works of dead artists, whereby large gross profits were generated due to inefficiencies in the market resulting from asymmetric information distribution will continue to transform under the growing and easy availability of price information to private buyers and sellers. The industry will change as transaction revenues decline to levels that no longer permit the investment of large capital in inventory and the maintenance of expensive retail locations. However, in theory, declining per-transaction profits could be offset by a higher velocity of goods, that is, the frequency with which specific art works change ownership. Middle and upper middle-class consumers in Europe or the US change house ownership more frequently than ownership of paintings. If, for instance, art buyers' behaviour was to change and they treated paintings as part of a periodically changing interior decor, the velocity of pictures would increase substantially. Such a trend would also affect further commoditization of contemporary paintings to suit that purpose, impact consumers' choices of works by deceased painters and undermine the notion of long-term investment in a given work of art.

Concerning the consumption-inducing investment aspect of art, the market's ongoing commoditization has led already to the employment of financial instruments and analytical methods adopted from the securities' world and modified for application to the art environment. In this development, the auction industry, too, performs a vital function.

9 COMMODITIZATION AND THE ARTIST AS PRODUCER: PRODUCT DIFFERENTIATION AND THE DOMESTICATION OF PICTURES

Writing towards the end of the 1850s, Tom Taylor, the art critic for the *Times*, commented in the foreword to the *Autobiographical Recollections by the late Charles Robert Leslie*, that the new market environment carries the risk 'that it will multiply the manufacture and increase the homeliness of pictures, to say nothing of less direct and obvious consequences'.[1] His remark both quantified and qualified the effects of the changing art market. The observation that the expanding consumer base for artists' products attracted new producers is easily documented. The population of painters residing in London, between 1840 and 1845 alone, saw an average annual increase of 70 per cent.[2] The earlier described growth in exhibition societies in London and the provinces further evidences the entry of new producers into the market. Our auction sale records also confirm this increase. Furthermore, a simple numerical comparison of artists listed in Waterhouse's standard encyclopaedic work on British eighteenth-century painters with those in Wood's dictionary shows that over five times as many artists worked and exhibited in Britain during the Victorian era than during the entire preceding century.[3]

The second part of Taylor's statement presents a more challenging argument. 'Homeliness' has a prejudicial connotation today that may not have existed at the time of Taylor's writing. Considering the context in which the term was used, we interpret it as describing without implied bias objects that were produced for private domestic use. The painter, W. P. Frith, for example, praised the 'delightful treatment of homely' subjects of the prominent watercolourist, Helen Allingham. Homeliness' in art had also received official parliamentary sanction in 1845, because 'the more homely scenes of common life ... are oftentimes the only intelligible mode in which Art can speak to a large portion of the community'.[4]

Taylor's remarks have also economic implications. The increase in 'manufacture' of pictures happened in two ways: entry of new artists into the market, and an increase of output among existing producers. The most extreme form of this increase in output, reproductive engravings, has already been discussed. A further consequence was the wholesale production of 'potboilers' frequently mentioned by artists. So called because 'they keep the kitchen range alight',[5] these were usually small pictures with simple compositions in oil or watercolour or replicas of major works generally produced for the trade for quick sales.[6] Demand for such easily marketable products sometimes even had a retarding effect on innovation. Millais's son, for instance, records that dealers' requests for copies of his father's paintings *The Black Brunswicker* (http://artmarket.tulane.edu/page94a.html) and *The Huguenot* (http://artmarket.tulane.edu/page95a.html) 'worried him into painting no less than seven or eight watercolour replicas ...'[7] Artists also occasionally returned to the traditional and well-tested income source of portrait painting.[8]

Since an expanding producer base is associated with increased competition it also stimulates product differentiation. A manifestation of this, and also one of the most noticeable features of Victorian paintings, is the easy identification of artists with their work. Painters, in general, behaved no differently than other producers and were aware that financial success required sound business thinking. Hunt, in fact, mentioned that the only painters he knew who achieved work of note were those who showed the disciplined behaviour of businessmen.[9] Accordingly, to establish themselves and their product's identity in the market, painters commonly stayed with a specific type of painting, once its marketability was established, until a decline in sales would signal that a change was necessary. Market-savvy artists might introduce experimental test products during prosperous times in order to gauge market response to a new product variety. Typically, however, they stayed with a proven success formula.

Frith, for example, comments throughout his writings that his modern life subjects' initial success was the incentive for him to continue painting such themes, despite the fact that he found contemporary dress unappealing. Of particular interest is the artist's remark that 'unless a subject of tremendous human interest could be found – such an interest as should make the *spectator* (our italics) forget the dresses in it – [painting] modern life [subjects] was impossible ...'[10] Foremost in his mind for choosing a subject for painting was the reaction of the audience. Once Frith had established his pictorial mode, he even canvassed the public's taste when the increasing pressure to come up with new modern themes led him to advertise a reward in the newspaper to anyone with a useable suggestion. '... [g]et newer subjects – all depends on subjects', he noted in his diary.[11]

The painter had started his career painting English literary themes or historical subjects. His first painting exhibited at the RA in 1840 was a scene from *Twelfth Night, Malvolio before the Countess Olivia*; in 1842 he exhibited a depiction from *The Vicar of Wakefield* (http://artmarket.tulane.edu/page15.html), a topic to which he would repeatedly return; the next year's contribution was another Shakespearean subject, this time from *The Merry Wives of Windsor* followed, in 1844, by a depiction of John Knox and Mary Queen of Scots together with a further scene from *The Vicar of Wakefield*.

Frith claimed that his aversion to modern dress was overcome only after he encountered the writings of Charles Dickens while searching for fresh storybook subjects during the early 1840s.[12] Yet the above mix of literary and historical themes made up the artist's selection for the RA until the beginning of the 1850s. The earliest known attempt at a modern topic was a small study dating from 1851 that became known as *Sherry Sir* (http://artmarket.tulane.edu/page18.html), after it was engraved by Frank Holl. The somewhat salacious title given by the publisher without the painter's consent greatly displeased Frith. But when he tried to have the title changed, he learned that the print had only started to sell after it had this been thus 'christened'.[13] Firth's first serious attempt at a modern life subject came in 1853, with *The Sleepy Model* (RA 1853, http://artmarket.tulane.edu/page19.html), the picture he presented to the Diploma Gallery on his election to the RA in the same year.[14] The selection of a modern subject for such an important occasion may have been due to the fact that Frith, since the summer of 1851, had been working on his first monumental trademark picture, *Life at the Seaside* (1854, Buckingham Palace, http://artmarket.tulane.edu/page12.html), and was anxious to test his peers' reaction to his change from literary to modern topics. The importance of this decision is revealed by his diary entry of 30 September 1851: 'Began idly to make a sketch from Ramsgate Sands, which, if successful, will considerably alter my practice'. It was successful and, indeed, altered his practice. Still, one year later Frith was still uncertain about the picture's success potential, despite assurances from a friend, the artist John Leech, that the painting would be 'a great hit'. Frith's reply was: 'Who can tell?'[15]

His doubts were entirely unfounded. The exhibition at the RA in 1854 of this painter's first modern life subject, *Life at the Seaside*, was a stunning success, both critically and monetarily. Frith henceforth stayed with this formula for his major works. His diary for 28 April 1854, the private viewing day at the Royal Academy, records: 'Eastlake presented me to the Queen. She was delighted with *Seaside*. Wanted to buy it – found she couldn't, and gave me a commission for a similar subject. Everybody likes it. I find myself and Maclise the guns this year'. The canvas had already been bought by the dealer Lloyd for 1,000 guineas, 'who', so Frith told President Eastlake, 'for a profit would sell it to her Majesty or anyone else'. However, a few days later, the dealer, after learning of the Queen's interest, sold her the painting at cost but retained the lucrative exhibition and engraving copyrights, which were subsequently bought by the Art Union of London for £3,000.[16]

Frith's first major modern life theme generated a 300 per cent return for the dealer's initial investment, attesting to the successful coupling in the arts of popular and financial success. Henceforth, the painter's main income would result from sales of exhibition and engraving copyrights of similar canvases like *Derby Day* (1858, Tate Gallery, London, http://artmarket.tulane.edu/page11.html), *The Railway Station* (1862, Royal Holloway College, Egham, http://artmarket.tulane.edu/page13.html), *The Salon d'Or, Homburg* (1871, Rhode Island School of Design, http://artmarket.tulane.edu/page20.html), and *Private View Day at the Royal Academy* (1883, Christopher Pope, Esq., http://artmarket.tulane.edu/page21.html) – every one of them 'sensation pictures' *par excellence* that reflected the steadfast employment of his pictorial strategy. Frith wrote 'the great success that had attended my modern-life subjects encouraged me to further effort in the same direction, and I forthwith arranged compositions for three pictures of London street scenes ... for which I was to receive the incredible sum of ten thousand pounds from Mr. Gambart ... ',[17] the same amount that the dealer Flatou would pay him for just one painting, *The Railroad Station* (http://artmarket.tulane.edu/page13.html), just eight years later. Within the span of less than a decade Frith's modern life subjects had become a veritable gold mine for the artist: from £1,000 for his *Seaside* (http://artmarket.tulane.edu/page12.html) in 1854 to ten times that amount for his *Railroad Station* eight years later. By adhering to this proven formula for financial success and allocating resources where they generated the greatest yield, Frith demonstrated rational business thinking. In one instance, however, Frith returned to a purely historical subject for a major canvas intended for public exhibition, when the dealer Gambart commissioned him to paint *The Last Sunday of Charles II* (RA 1867, http://artmarket.tulane.edu/page21.html). Frith must have been elated that this picture too had to be protected by a rail from overly enthusiastic viewers.[18]

Besides their imposing size – a prerequisite for 'sensations pictures' – these works had in common the depiction of a large number of people involved in one central theme and painted with careful attention to individualized physiognomy. This main crowd was subdivided into numerous small groups which anecdotally cohered and filled these pictures with a complicated web of narrative incidents that could be viewed as whole compositions as well as vignette by vignette. Similar to popular panoramas and dioramas, for which viewing the public was already accustomed to paying admission, great attention was also paid to topographical and architectural authenticity. Occasionally the artist would include recognizable individuals. In his *Railway Station,* the famous detectives Haydon and Brett can be seen arresting a criminal, and the dealer Flatou, who commissioned the canvas, is shown talking to the engine driver. Oscar Wilde was included as one of dominant figures in *A Private View at the Royal Academy in 1881,* while Frith placed his wife and himself in the centre of *The Salon d'Or,*

Homburg, appropriately away from the gambling table looking with suitable disapproval at the slightly disreputable, yet highly intriguing, goings-on.

In the choice of his subjects, the artist proved repeatedly that his brush was firmly on the pulse of popular taste. His first 'sensation picture' appealed to the Victorians' passion for the seaside, regardless of class. During Queen Victoria's reign, leisure-time not only increased but also progressively commercialized. Provincial seaside towns, like Bridlington and Scarborough in Yorkshire or Torquay in the South, began to diversify their economic base by building resort facilities.[19] Frith's canvas offered countless opportunities for viewers to establish some sort of personal identification with the animated depiction of activities and characters.

The subject of his second great panorama of modern life, *Derby Day,* delighted its audience for similar reasons. The annual Derby at the Epsom race course was hugely popular and visited by all sections of society and its colourful ambiance was familiar to many. The *Art Journal* review of this painting recognized precisely this aspect: '... it matters not who approaches it, he or she can at once see a reflex of him or herself ...'[20] Ruskin also endorsed the painting, writing that it was 'quite proper and desirable that this English carnival should be painted'.

A similar cross section of Victorian society was depicted in Frith's *Railway Station.* Among the nineteenth-century technological innovations, trains had perhaps the biggest single impact on the average Victorian. Both the dealer Flatou, by commissioning and promoting this canvas, and Frith, in its execution, demonstrated their keen commercial instinct. All of the artist's visual panoramas shared this broad appeal and familiar, enjoyable, and/or exciting subject matter, executed in a manner that invited spectators to examine the pictures in the greatest detail. Like a novel, they all involved viewers in their kaleidoscope of narratives. Such large compositions involving the balanced placement of numerous figures are among the most challenging to painters. Frith handled this task with consummate skill.

While working on these pictorial enterprises, Frith still continued to paint smaller historical and sentimental subjects, quite popular with London's leading dealers, until shortly before his death in 1909.[21] Perhaps these pictures' appeal to the trade and public was more a reflection of Frith's fame than of the paintings' quality – a fame so great that it transcended the product of the artist and made his name a distinct and marketable entity that by itself lent commercial appeal to the product. The painter had become a trademark.

Frith succeeded in establishing himself as an artist who could build and maintain his reputation and financial security on no more than a half-dozen 'sensation pictures'. No other artist's paintings since the existence of the Royal Academy had to be protected, in six individual cases, by iron rails to keep admirers at bay. His reputation, or more appropriately phrased, his trademark, enabled the artist at the same time to supply the trade with a steady stream of commercial works, the production of which took much less time and effort. Frith was quite adamant about his preference for transacting business directly with dealers and was also sensitive to the 'mercantile' considerations businessmen had to take into account.[22] It would be no surprise if many of these pictures were painted for, or on the encouragement of, dealers. The difficulty in finding suitable subjects, equal to his aforementioned successes, may well have led him to return to his earlier picture type in order to satisfy demand for his work. He regularly exhibited these paintings at the Royal Academy, a fact that undoubtedly helped their marketability.

An analogy can be made with the modern fashion industry. World-famous designers annually market their commercial lines by staging glamorous, highly publicized events during which models display clothing which very few consumers can afford, much less wear in public. The accompanying sensational publicity is a vital component in marketing the everyday garments and accessories to which the designer's name is attached. Frith's 'sensation pictures' were similarly inaccessible, in terms of ownership, to all but the very rich, besides being joint enterprises, in all but the first instance, between the artist and various dealers. The masses were offered mechanical reproductions; but those who wanted to own an *original* [our emphasis] by this famous artist and had the necessary means, could still do so by visiting one of the Bond Street galleries. In today's art market, the often very high prices paid by consumers for works whose only merit consists of the fame of the responsible artist attest to the marketing superiority of the identity of certain producers over the actual quality of their products.

Different from Frith, there were instances where the identification with a successfully differentiated artistic product went so far as to become synonymous with its creator. Such was the case, for example, with William Henry Hunt (1790–1864), who became known by his nicknames 'Bird's Nest' or 'Hedgerow' Hunt.[23] The artist initially had started out as a landscape and genre painter but by the mid-1820s he hit on his signature products, bird's-nests and still lives of wildflowers and fruits (http://artmarket.tulane.edu/page23.html; http://artmarket.tulane.edu/page18.html). These subjects proved to be immensely popular with private collectors as well as dealers and Hunt began specializing in them. In addition to differentiation by subject, the artist further set his pictures apart technically by employing body colour in a decidedly individual method of hatching and stippling over white ground. The results were richly coloured, highly finished and meticulously executed works reminiscent of the fijnschilder tradition of Holland's Golden Age, and their readily apparent labour intensity and 'truth to nature' fulfilled Ruskinian demands. In slightly over a quarter of a century, Hunt showed nearly 800 of his bird's nests subjects at the Old Watercolour Society (OWS), amounting to an average production of around two such pictures every month for these public exhibitions alone.[24] Until the end of the 1870s, these and his still lives of hedgerows dominated the London auction rooms, where they were purchased almost exclusively by London's leading dealers like Agnew, Vokins and Tooth.

Hunt's career is another example of a painter creating a distinct product and actively engaging in the marketing of it while simultaneously carving out his own equally differentiated artistic identity. He made the conscious decision to promote his 'bird's nests' – precisely those works which, during Hunt's lifetime, commanded the highest prices – through the OWA and market them to the trade and ultimately the public.

Product differentiation also occurred within artist groups, as the case of Markus Stone and the St John's Wood Clique demonstrates. The group was less of an official organization than an association of like-minded artists who shared an affinity for painting historical subjects. Its main members were P. H. Calderon (1833–98), W. F. Yeames (1835–1918), H. S. Marks (1829–98), G. D. Leslie (1835–1921), J. E. Hodgson (1831–95), G. A. Storey (1834–1919), and D. W. Wynfield (1837–87). Together, these artists frequently rented Hever Castle for the summer as a setting for their historical and costume pieces. Collectively, they were known among their contemporaries, somewhat unflatteringly, as 'the School of Slashed Breeches', attesting to their successful differentiation as a group.

From the mid-1870s on, the painter Marcus Stone (1840–1921) joined the circle and soon began to change his paintings to distinguish them from the works of the other members. Before 1876, Stone painted a mixture of straight historical and literary/historical subjects, similar to those of the other painters of the Clique. They included Shakespearean themes such as his RA exhibit of 1861, *Claudio deceived by Don John, accuses Hero. 'O Hero, what A Hero hadst thou been, etc ...'*, (http://artmarket.tulane.edu/page25.html), or his previous year's contribution, *The sword of the Lord and of Gideon,* after a poem by Byron. Other RA exhibits prior to 1876 were an Elizabethan theme, a Henry VIII and Anne Boleyn subject, Edward II, Nell Gwynne, and more Shakespeare. After 1876, however, the year he was elected Associate Member of the RA, his paintings became a seemingly endless variation of the same sentimental theme: a distinctly recognizable, blandly attractive female type clad in a quasi-regency manner, painted with meticulous attention to detail, finish, and dress, placed in scenes titled *The First Love Letter,* (http://artmarket.tulane.edu/page30.html), *Waiting at the Gate* (RA, 1877), *The Time of Roses* (RA 1878), *Love at First Sight* (RA, 1891, http://artmarket.tulane.edu/page33.html), *A Stolen Kiss* (RA, 1894, http://artmarket.tulane.edu/page34.html), or *The Proposal Accepted* (RA, 1904). Henceforth, every single picture Stone selected for the prestigious annual exhibition at the RA was of this specific pictorial type.[25]

Still painting within the popular costume picture formula of the St John's Wood Clique, the artist had consciously and successfully differentiated his product and distinguished himself within the group. He was well rewarded for this financially: his new picture type sold for substantially more than his earlier works and was extremely popular among London's leading dealers.[26] Whether it was the artist who initially yielded to the demands of the market and then simply stuck with a good thing, or the market that reacted positively to Stone's newly designed product, is impossible to reconstruct. His comment reflecting on his financially highly successful career – that 'one sells one's birthright' – and his frequent diatribes against the system which forced him to 'paint such nonsense', certainly attests, however negatively, to his economic pragmatism.[27]

In the case of the immensely successful Sir Lawrence Alma-Tadema, a dealer provided skilful and professional career management early on. In 1864, while still living in Antwerp, the artist was introduced, evidently somewhat conspiratorially, to Gambart by another painter, Victor Lagye (1825–96), who was already a member of the dealer's stable. This meeting resulted in an immediate commission for Alma-Tadema for twenty-four canvases of the kind of Merovingian/medieval topics the artist had been painting for the past few years. Alma-Tadema, however, due to an earlier visit to Pompeii had become more interested in themes from classical antiquity. A compromise was struck that called for half of the commission to consist of medieval topics, while the subjects of the other twelve paintings were left up to the painter. In the 1860s, the possibilities for young painters to find their niche within the vastly expanded market for modern life subjects had shrunk to the point where it was increasingly difficult to be different than their competitors. Alma-Tadema's insistence to distinguish his work by shifting the historical context of his paintings back by nearly two millennia was a rational response to these prevailing market conditions. By 1865, Gambart was also convinced of the commercial potential of these classical themes and gave him free reign. Although the dealer experienced some initial difficulties finding buyers, he continued his patronage. For greater exposure Gambart entered thirteen of Alma-Tadema's paintings in the Exposition Universelle in Paris in 1867. Their reception occasioned him to offer the painter another, even larger, commission that same year, consisting of forty-eight pictures. In 1870, Alma-Tadema moved to London, likely on the encouragement of Gambart, and embarked on a spectacularly successful career, never once wavering from his pictorial formula.[28] Amidst the popularity of modern life paintings, the artists developed a picture type that transposed real life aspects of modern scenes into the ancient world. He portrayed Victorians in antiquity, dressed accordingly for the occasion and placed in classical settings 'as bourgeois as a Dutch kitchen'.[29] (http://artmarket.tulane.edu/page36.html; http://artmarket.tulane.edu/page37.html). Usually avoiding the monumental Aestheticism of his fellow neo-classicist, Frederic Leighton, but with great attention to archaeological accuracy, Alma-Tadema presented his public with a tangible, 'real' ancient world with which spectators could identify. The trade recognized the commercial potential of the painter's unique interpretation of classical subjects, and upon his arrival in the English capital, other leading London dealers like Agnew, Permain, Vokins and Tooth paid at auction more for Alma-Tadema's pictures than the artist had received for the latest commission from Gambart.[30] Indeed, dealers were a major factor in the demand for the painter's work: more than one third of his total output of over 400 works was painted specifically for London dealers with Gambart, Pilgeram & Lefevre and Tooth receiving the majority.[31] The display from 1869 until his death in 1912 of at least one of the painter's typical classical scenes at the annual summer exhibition at the Royal Academy helped maintain publicity.[32] His pictures, far more anecdotal and painstakingly detailed, more 'English' in fact, than those of the equally famous Frederic Leighton, appealed on a much broader level and were superbly suited for engraving, a fact that soon made the artist independent from the patronage of his first dealer.

Starting in 1872, Alma-Tadema began to assign Roman numerals to his paintings rather than the customary dates. Apparently his friend, the critic F. G. Stephens, had mentioned that dates, by differentiating between more recent and older productions, could have a negative effect on the prices of the latter.[33] Moreover, prominently placed Roman numbers further enhanced Alma-Tadema's products' identity as archeologically accurate representations of the ancient world.

The artist was also not above altering a design to accommodate a specific buyer's wishes. In 1876, after he learned that Sir William Armstrong had rejected the painting *Between Hope and Fear* because it did not depict enough marble for which Alma-Tadema was famous, the painter replied: 'Well, if he wants to have marble ... then I will reverse *The Audience* [the painting to which Armstrong had compared the rejected one] and make the same thing ... and marble will remain the main subject'.[34] This incident certainly reveals the artist's willingness to orient his products towards the market. To what extent this may have been the case with the nearly one hundred and sixty paintings Alma-Tadema produced for the trade can only be surmised.

With name and product recognition firmly established, Alma-Tadema expanded his product range to furniture, fashion and even stage designs. In all instances, he stuck to his proven formula, apparently unaffected by the emergence of Impressionism and Post-Impressionism with their entirely new aesthetics.

Contrary to Sir Lawrence's blending of mainstream Victorian bourgeois Realism with the current fashion for subjects from antiquity, Frederic Leighton embraced a nascent continental trend and exploited Classicism for its aesthetic potential. The painter was independently wealthy and throughout his life, unlike Alma-Tadema, did not have to depend on income generated by his chosen occupation. Nonetheless, Leighton was still concerned about monetary matters.

Already as a young painter in Rome in the early 1850s, he envisioned the house he planned to build 'as soon as I can earn the money to pay for it, but I must earn the money first'.[35] Therefore, just like many other painters, he too was motivated to find his niche in the market. His financial situation, however, enabled him to experiment in areas that, at least initially, stood outside the commercially more successful main trends of contemporary British painting, a fact that was evident to his contemporaries. As early as the 1850s, the painter's foreignness was already apparent when Rossetti opined that Leighton's colouring technique was the result of 'too much continental study'.[36] Attesting to the artist's successful product differentiation, F. G. Stephens wrote that it was 'rather difficult to know in what category to place Mr. Leighton's work ... They are dissimilar to any English work and we know no foreign school to which they are directly allied ... We suppose they may be taken as cosmopolitan'.[37]

Although Leighton generally was opposed to many of the narrative conventions of mid-Victorian painting, he produced for his debut at the Royal Academy's annual summer exhibition in 1855 a sensational historical epic entitled *Cimabue's Celebrated Madonna Carried in Procession through the Streets of Florence* (http://artmarket.tulane.edu/page39.html). While the theme was not contemporary, the artists still employed the same visual formula as, for example, Frith had done in his sensation picture, *At the Seaside*, the success of which Leighton had witnessed the year before: spectacular size, dozens of figures, individualized physiognomy, fanciful dress, and different anecdotal vignettes to capture viewers' imagination and 'read' the story. Leighton was not disappointed. The Queen purchased his picture for 600 guineas, and the artist became an overnight celebrity. The *Art Journal* reviewer hyperbolized: 'There has been no production of modern times more excellent than this. It is of the truest order of worth'.[38] However, with such a dazzling debut came an inherent problem: what to do for an encore? In a note to his former teacher in Frankfurt, Edward von Steinle, Leighton confessed to having much 'anxiety and apprehension; I am always thinking, "What can you exhibit next year that will fulfil the expectations of the public?"'[39] Although without major financial worry, the artist worried over popular appeal, a concern that was validated by the disappointing reception of his paintings for the next few years.

Evidently during these early years Leighton was systematically searching for his artistic identity, trying different pictorial formulas but not yet finding one that suited him and his public. The second entry for the Royal Academy summer show in 1856, for instance, his *Triumph of Music* (http://artmarket.tulane.edu/page40.html), was described by the *Athenaeum* as being 'Without doubt ... one of the worst pictures exhibited that year'.[40] Another painting, a literary subject, *The Reconciliation of the Montagues and Capulets* (1853–5, http://artmarket.tulane.edu/page41.html) received better press, but still did not find a buyer, even though Leighton had asked the dealer Colnaghi for help.[41] The artist also showed his first nude during this time, a small canvas painted during his stay in Paris that year depicting a full frontal view of a sensuously posed female figure with a little Cupid at her feet, appropriately titled *Venus and Cupid* (c.1856). Leighton was aware of the difficulty in finding a buyer for an overtly erotic picture and told his parents that there was 'not the remotest chance of selling' it when it was sent together with another painting of a mythological subject, a *Pan* (c.1856), for exhibition to the Royal Manchester Institution that year.[42] Still, he offered it for public scrutiny and was rewarded by encouraging critical response.

The artist's reasoning for sending products he deemed impossible to sell to the market is not known. Yet such a deliberate act invites conjecture. Leighton could afford financially to indulge himself. But what did he want to accomplish, particularly after the dismal failure at the Royal Academy? Had he deliberately chosen an erotic subject as a means to set himself apart and garner attention? Certainly he must have realized that, at the very least, the technically well-executed little picture would get noticed because of the subject. He may well have wanted to test-market a different product after the outright rejection of his *Triumph of Music* and Colnaghi's failure to find a buyer for the Shakespeare subject. Evidently, Leighton was considering an entire series of a dozen or so 'delicious pagan figures', of which the little *Venus* and the *Pan* may have been the first two.[43] While nothing came of this project, the positive response to his *Venus* may have led him later to return to nude subjects in numerous subsequent paintings. As Alison Smith pointed out, Leighton, indeed, was to play an instrumental role in the acceptance of the nude form as central to British painting.[44]

Even though the exhibition in Manchester offered some encouragement, Leighton appeared unsure in which direction to turn. He decided to stay out of London's public's eye, and showed nothing at the RA summer exhibition of 1857. The following year, however, he submitted two works. Both were literary topics, yet the themes were treated noticeably different from each other. The Shakespearian subject, again taken from Romeo and Juliet, was a modestly sized canvas reminiscent of Leighton's earlier Renaissance subject pictures. The second one, however, *The Fisherman and the Syren: From a Ballad by Goethe* (http://artmarket.tulane.edu/page44.html), took the eroticism of his earlier little *Venus* several steps further. The coyly posed nude goddess is transformed into a sexually predatory siren who presses her naked breasts against the bare chest of a submissive male in a fatal embrace.

Several aspects may have contributed to Leighton's deliberate decision to re-enter the public arena with these works. For one, the earlier Romeo and Juliet theme, the *Reconciliation,* that Colnaghi had been unable to sell, had been shipped to the United States as part of the first major three-city exhibition tour of contemporary British paintings in America. In early 1858, while on display in Philadelphia, the painting was acquired by a local collector, Mr. J. Harrison, whereupon Leighton replaced the sold product with another similar one. Encouraged by the sale, he also immediately replaced the *Reconciliation* with *Triumph of Music* and dispatched this soundly trounced work across the Atlantic, possibly hoping that American audiences would receive this inferior work more favourably. He also sent the as yet unsold *Pan* and the small *Venus* along.[45] The second painting, *Fisherman and Syren* must have been a follow-up on the positive critical reception of his *Venus.* Although Leighton never delved into a series of 'delicious little pagan figures', he may have thought that the sexually charged picture presented just the right kind of alternative. W. M. Rossetti agreed that while this 'passionate abandon and irresistible clinging ... may elevate some eyebrows, [it was] the right untimorous thing for the artist to have done'.[46] It was well executed, and since the picture was commissioned any concerns about the saleability of this type of risqué subject were irrelevant. Indeed, the commission sent a message to the public that there was, indeed, a market for this young artist's work.

The impression that Leighton was trying to find his artistic identity as well as generate publicity by presenting the public with different types of paintings is further underscored by his contribution to the 1859 Royal Academy exhibition. He had just learned that his *Samson and Delilah* (c.1858) had been refused by the British Institute.[47] Perhaps because of this he selected something altogether different: three works that all depicted the same woman, Nanna Risi, a professional model with whom Leighton had worked during his stay in Rome late 1858. Rather than traditional portraits, these paintings were more ambiguous. The sitter's classical Mediterranean beauty had an almost unsettling sensual quality that the painter accentuated through an equally sensual handling of surface texture and his choice of purely decorative accoutrements. Commercially, these works performed well for Leighton; the largest one, a ½ length, was bought by the noted collector, B.G. Windus, the second one was sold by the artist to George Payne, while the third one had already been acquired by Lady Hoare before the exhibition.

Although these paintings were successful, they did not seem to represent the direction Leighton envisioned for himself. For 1860, he only selected a small sunrise over Capri to represent him at the Royal Academy. Most likely, this was all he had available at the time. Leighton had just settled into his studio in London late 1859 after extensive travelling, and he had also accepted a commission for a religious subject that would keep him busy until late spring.

By 1861, the artist was ready to present himself again with a more significant assortment of works. He was frustrated about the lack of sales, writing to his father that the 'market' could be a little more 'brisk'. Consequently, Leighton carefully planned his campaign choosing six different pictures that showed his technical competence as well as his creative versatility. With the exception of garden view of an inn in Capri and the earlier mentioned religious commission,

A Vision, the dates of the remaining four works suggest that Leighton painted them specifically for the summer exhibition at the Academy. Two were portraits, one of his sister Alexandra, the other, a study, was described by Leighton as 'Aslett'; another canvas depicted the ever-popular Shakespeare theme of Paolo and Francesca; then there was his much admired *Lieder ohne Worte* (http://art-market.tulane.edu/page50.html). Prior to sending off his selection, he staged an exhibition at his studio inviting a number of friends, collectors, critics and other artists. In letters to his parents, the artist pronounced this 'little private view' a 'great success', and suggested that 'if the *Public* (Leighton's emphasis) receives my pictures as favourably as the *Private* (Leighton's emphasis) has done, I shall have no cause to complain; as far, at least, as the maintenance and increase of my reputation is concerned'. However, Leighton did not consider the hanging committee: all but the landscape were disadvantageously displayed. The painter was understandably annoyed, but he appeased himself with his belief that if his works 'have real value, public opinion will in the long run force the Academy to hang me'. Judging from the fact that Leighton had gone through the trouble to organize a prior private exhibition, he may have anticipated this unfavourable treatment. This strategy paid off: many visitors to the event were rather outspoken in their positive opinion of the artist's works.[48] The press, unfortunately, had a more mixed reaction: the *Athenaeum*, *The Times*, and *Macmillan's Magazine* were supportive, while *The Art Journal*, the *Saturday Review* and the *Critic* were less enthusiastic in their assessment of the paintings' merits.[49]

More significant than these reviews is Leighton's pronouncement that the public, not the art establishment, were the determinant of success. This conviction explains the artist's overall marketing strategy. As often as he could, the young Leighton presented his works to the public since it was with them, not the hanging committee of the Academy that, in his opinion, his fortunes rested. His first public showing was in 1850 in Frankfurt; then in 1855, in addition to the Royal Academy, he also exhibited in Paris; in 1857, one painting was sent on tour to America; in 1858, three others went to the United States, while his *Fisherman* went from the Academy to go on exhibit in Liverpool. During the same year a watercolour, *The Negro Festival,* was displayed at the Society of British Artists and then sent off to be shown at the Paris Salon the next year. Also in 1859, undeterred by the British Institution's refusal of his *Samson*, Leighton arranged for the painting to be exhibited at the Society of British Artists. In 1860, the artist displayed his drawing of a lemon tree at the Hogarth Club in London, where Ruskin much admired it; and in 1861, Leighton arranged for the *Samson* and his *Paris and Juliet* to be sent for exhibition to New York and Boston.

Regardless of his financial comfort, the painter still made rational business decisions concerning his career. In his efforts to gauge 'the expectations of the public', Leighton presented with great consistency as well as consideration, whenever and wherever possible and appropriate, one or more examples of his different types of artistic products even if they were untested. His letters discussing *Lieder ohne Worte* to his former teacher, von Steinle, in Frankfurt and to his father suggest that the painter viewed this work as experimental or even seminal. To his father he wrote that the painting was initially planned to be realistic but upon recognizing his mistake, he made it 'professedly and pointedly the reverse', and he informed von Steinle that he 'endeavoured, both by colour and by flowing delicate forms, to translate ... the pleasure the child receives through her ears'.[50] The attempt at a visual display of sound through design and colour rather than readable narrative was something rather new to Victorian audiences, a fact of which Leighton must have been aware.

This rejection of traditional Victorian tenets in favour of visual poetry and sensuous aesthetics positioned Leighton outside the conservative environment of the English art establishment. In the review of the artist's 1861 Academy selection, *The Art Journal* even accused him of introducing 'lower forms of mere decorative ornamentation' and a decidedly un-English preoccupation with 'luxuriousness' and 'sensual excess'.[51] Such categorization placed the painter in another camp, one that was receptive to different art theories that were coming to England from the Continent during this time. The buoyancy of the British art market not only exposed the Victorian public to the works of foreign painters but also to new aesthetics that were beginning to find fertile grounds. It was a challenging time for the cultural consensus that had shaped the mid-Victorian decades. The *Saturday Review* in November of 1861 opined, '[p]ainting [was] seen ... for the most part under its worst aspects – not as a fine art ennobling the artist while it instructs and delights the spectator, but as a mere manufacture and a dull routine of trade'.[52] For an artist with Continental training and familiarity with alternative art theories as well as the financial wherewithal to make immediate financial return unnecessary, it was a time of opportunity.

Although the art environment in England was becoming more receptive to different types of visual products, Leighton's struggle to find his foothold in the market continued. In 1862 he lamented to his father, who still supported him at the time, that 'no one asks about my pictures'.[53] Leighton attempted to remedy this by increasing his visibility and submitted that year his largest selected thus far to the annual summer exhibition at the Academy. Out of eight paintings he sent off, only two were rejected; the remaining six were displayed reasonably well 'on the line' or 'just above and just below'.[54]

Conditions were changing for the painter. In 1863, after one of Leighton's works was turned down by the Selection Committee, W. P. Frith, certainly a member of the old guard, wrote to the artist that the rejection was due to space considerations not quality of the work.[55] Critics also wrote more favourably. At times, their tone could be positively gushing. That year, for instance, W. M. Rossetti, described Leighton's *Girl Feeding Peacocks* (http://artmarket.tulane.edu/page53.html) and his *Girl with a Basket of Fruit* (http://artmarket.tulane.edu/page54.html) on view at the Academy as exemplifying 'that class of art in which Mr. Leighton shines – the art of luxurious exquisiteness; beauty for beauty's sake; colour, light, form, choice details, for their own sake, or for beauty's'.[56] F. G. Stephens actually wrote a prose poem describing *Girl with a Basket*.[57] Even Ruskin lavished praise. Of Leighton's contributions to the Academy, the critic wrote to the artist that they 'were the only ones that interested me ...'[58]

Finally, by 1864, Leighton had 'arrived'. One of his paintings at the Academy, *Dante in Exile* (http://artmarket.tulane.edu/page55.html), a superbly executed, eye-catching exhibition machine, was described by *The Art Journal* as '[t]he promise given by the *Cimabue* here reaches fruition'.[59] On the strength of this painting the artist was made an Associate Member of the Royal Academy that year. Gambart, who had plenty of experience in marketing this type of work, paid Leighton £1,050 for the picture. Fiscally prudent, the painter immediately invested the sum in interest bearing stocks.[60]

As the critic for *The Art Journal* already had observed, *Dante in Exile* built on the proven success formula of Leighton's debut in 1855. In that sense, the picture did not represent anything new. However, one of the other paintings exhibited at the Academy in 1864, *Golden Hours* (http://artmarket.tulane.edu/page56.html), pointed to the future and revealed the artist's 'Aesthetic' sympathies. Without distracting narrative content, the work's soft Venetian colours evoke an air of understated sensual delight shared by both viewer and protagonists. The splendid dress of the female listener, the carefully rendered inlay decorating the sides of the harpsichord, reveal a private world of luxury, while the absorbed expression on the man's face conveys the intangible beauty of this ephemeral moment. These defining features re-appeared in different forms time and time again in Leighton's paintings.

As sales went, the year 1864 was also a watershed. In addition to the business with Gambart, Leighton sold another canvas, *The Painter's Honeymoon* (http://artmarket.tulane.edu/page57.html), to a different dealer, Morby, for an undisclosed sum. These two sales coincided with Leighton's decision to ask the architect, George Aitchison, to begin designing the house the painter had envisioned many years earlier. Evidently, the demand he had imposed on himself to postpone building until he earned enough money had been fulfilled. However, it must have been more than the sale of two paintings to these dealers that occasioned this quite deliberate man to signal his 'arrival' so conspicuously. Perhaps he felt that indeed his career had reached a steady forward momentum. He had been made an Associate Member of England's still most prestigious artists' organization; critics were beginning to be responsive, and the trade was showing further interest in his work.[61]

Only one element was missing to complete the product differentiation of Leighton's paintings and his artistic identity, namely the use of classical themes as message carriers of his Aesthetic. Classicism was becoming fashionable, but for Leighton, this choice was based on more pragmatic considerations and not determined by some 'special or direct interest in the Greeks, but because they [were] the least trammelled art-subjects ...' Evidently he did not like the fact that medieval or historical themes involved questions of costume in which 'the tailor intervenes', while 'every fold in [his] drapery [was] conducive to art'.[62] Again, the painter revealed a business-like approach to designing his product. Rather than competing in the market with more conventional historical narrative subjects of the type that had made him an overnight celebrity in 1855 and an Associate Member of the Academy nine years later, Leighton began to paint works that competed under different standards. In economic terms this was a brilliant move. Staying within the conventional tradition of English painting would have meant that the artist's rising star would be judged persistently according to established standards. While the elevation to the rank of Associate Member confirmed him as a serious contender by anyone's measure, it also gave Leighton the credibility to introduce new products that competed on the merits of a different aesthetic. By thus changing the terms of competition, the painter entered a different arena, one in which he reigned supremely for the next thirty years.

Associated with the differentiation of his product was the deliberate construction of a personal identity, one apparently as elusive to stereotype as his paintings, yet as noticeably distinct. One contemporary, Vernon Lee, described Leighton as 'a mixture of the Olympian Jove and a head waiter, a superb decorator and a superb piece of decoration'.[63] To Burne-Jones, Leighton appeared always 'less as an artist than as a highly cultivated gentleman who paints'.[64] At a time when the Royal Academy was increasingly criticized for the blatant market orientation of many of its members and painting was accused of having deteriorated to 'mere manufacture and a dull routine of trade',[65] promoting an identity that set Leighton apart from the objectionable stereotype was sound public relation.

Even his private environment, Leighton House, was designed towards similar ends. Its location near the fashionable Holland Park area, where the artist's patron, Alexander Ionides, had just bought a house, clearly set it apart from the far less opulent artists' quarters around Bloomsbury. The house was designed not to project an obvious function as an artist's studio or even home, but rather to convey its owner's taste, sophistication, aesthetic sensibilities and patronage of modern art.[66] It was, in other words, an integral part of Leighton the commodity.

The image Leighton wanted to project publicly is perhaps best conveyed in his *Self portrait* of 1880 (Galleria degli Uffizi; http://artmarket.tulane.edu/

page58.html). As Paul Barlow points out, the work embodies the synthesis of the Renaissance and the Classical by which Leighton wished to be known and 'encapsulates in microcosm the complex and ambivalent character of his art'.[67] Draped in the robes of his honorary doctorate from Oxford University and posed in front of a section of the much revered Parthenon frieze, Leighton empowers the canvas with Olympian *gravitas*: the Zeus of England's artistic Pantheon. By contrast, the self portrait of his fellow classicist, Alma-Tadema (Opus CCCXLI, 1896, Galleria degli Uffizi, http://artmarket.tulane.edu/page38.html), conveys an altogether different image. The painter depicts himself with the tools of his profession, dressed in simple, orderly and unpretentious clothes engaging the viewer with kind, even slightly humorous eyes. No showmanship or artificiality is employed. Here is an everyday man who paints everyday life. Leighton, however, offers himself as an almost otherworldly creature more at home in the aesthetic world of his sensuously beautiful canvasses than in Victorian drawing rooms. His portrait represents a successfully differentiated commercial logo simultaneously aimed at the new breed of progressive collectors, like F. R. Leyland, B. G. Windus, James Knowles, Lewis Peacock or Percy Wyndham, who were also supporters of Sir Lindsay's Grosvenor Gallery stable of artists as well as the more traditional patrons of the Academy. Like the Olympian Jupiter, Leighton managed to rule over the schism within his pantheon between the forces who sought an alternative to and those who supported the artistic establishment. In that respect, the artist and his portrait are a mirror of their era. As a business approach, this strategy was quite effective. According to the records of Leighton's account at Coutts Bank, the painter's income from painting alone, once he had carved out his niche, averaged between £4,000 to £6,000 per annum.[68]

In the above cases, product differentiation among painters under conditions of an expanding market takes the form of paintings chosen by artists for public exhibitions as well as expressly pertinent primary commentary. These choices and commentaries, combined with sales and public exhibition records, point to a direct and conscious agency of artists in carving out their niche to compete in the market. The highly personal and easily recognizable visual handwriting of so many of the successful, and even less successful, Victorian painters documents the prevalence of artistic product differentiation. In some instances, the decision to create a new product may have been based on strictly aesthetic considerations, unconcerned with immediate economic consequences. However, once an artist introduced this new product to the market, an active dialectic with the exchange mechanism is established.

Even in the absence of conventional documentation, certain artists' relationship with the market can be investigated by considering their body of work in totality. One such example is the Yorkshire landscape painter, Atkinson Grimshaw (1836–93), known during his lifetime as a somewhat repetitive producer of moonlit harbour and street scenes. His easily recognizable paintings commonly feature one of Britain's famous docks, such as Liverpool, Hull, or Whitby, dramatically illuminated by moonlight reflecting off wet surfaces and the silhouettes of sailing vessels (http://artmarket.tulane.edu/page59.html). The other, related, picture type substituted a view of a street, often romantically enhanced by the inclusion of a house placed hauntingly in the background (http://artmarket.tulane.edu/page60.html). Grimshaw also experimented with the application of sand onto the canvas or board to achieve the effect of rain-wet streets. The artist was reasonably successful, but, unlike the aforementioned painters, he mainly sold to private patrons rather than working for the anonymous market or dealers. Merely three of his pictures were sold at auction during his lifetime, all purchased privately and not one depicting his trademark views. He only once, in 1885, exhibited one of his typical dock scenes, the *Salthouse Dock, Liverpool,* at the RA (no. 575, http://artmarket.tulane.edu/page61.html) together with another painting entitled *Dulce Domum* (http://artmarket.tulane.edu/page62.html). All the other works by Grimshaw exhibited there were based on mythological, historical or literary themes.

However, as this painter's works gained in popularity and price during the last three decades of the twentieth century, a body of work has emerged which reveals Grimshaw's artistic ambitions beyond the repetitive execution of the above-described views. He showed Pre-Raphaelite interests in his superbly executed interiors and in his literary works inspired by Tennyson, such as *Elaine* (1877, http://artmarket.tulane.edu/page63.html), and *The Lady of Shalott* (1874, http://artmarket.tulane.edu/page64.html). His *Summer* (1875, http://artmarket.tulane.edu/page65.html) plainly followed the footsteps of the highly successful Tissot. Yet the same painter also produced hundreds of repetitive scenes, rarely deviating from his formula, to supply a specific market of private patrons but only showed one example at the RA, the place described as crucial to keeping ones 'name before the world'.[69]

What he publicly advertised to the exhibition visitors were his other paintings, hoping to attract a following beyond the ready private purchasers of his 'commercial' work. Here another image, quite different from those of Hunt, Alma-Tadema or Leighton, emerges, one where a highly talented artist tried to change, or at least expand, qualitatively the composition of his demand and free himself from a market-initiated creative confinement. In this endeavour, Grimshaw had only limited success. Out of his slightly over 700 paintings and watercolours which sold at auction between 1970 and the end of the auction season of the year 2000, only one quarter differed from his trademark dock and street scenes even though they commanded much higher prices. This fact must have attracted, certainly over the last two decades or so during which this price appreciation occurred, most, if not all, of these paintings to the market. Several commercial exhibitions have accomplished much towards a re-assessment of Grimshaw's *oeuvre,* and there is every indication that, finally, the composition of demand for this artist's paintings may be in accordance with his own wishes.

Further evidence of artistic product differentiation can be found in Christopher Wood's *Dictionary*. The customary biographical entries in this and other such reference works emphasize a given painter's specialization in subject and/or technique. Even more informative, however, is a survey of recent auction catalogues of Victorian paintings, watercolours and drawings. Since the late 1960s, both Christie's and Sotheby's not only have conducted separate sales for works of this period, but they have created specific Victorian painting departments staffed by experts in the field. [Christopher Wood was in charge of launching the Victorian painting department and its sales at Christie's.] To that end, Sotheby's once established a separate auction facility located on Motcomb Street in Belgravia, away from the firm's Bond Street headquarters. Associated with these undertakings was an internationalization of collecting of Victorian paintings and general Victoriana, particularly in the English-speaking world, as well as substantial and still-continuing price increases. These sales' well-illustrated catalogues featuring consignments from a wide variety of sources reflect a far more accurate representation of the mix of art to which the Victorian public was exposed than standard reference works, public collections or museum exhibitions. In the first few years after the London auction houses – Sotheby's, Christie's, Phillips's and Bonham's – initially created a separate auction sales identity for Victorian paintings, [One might add that this represents simply another form of product differentiation.] the majority of consignments were private liquidity trades since prices were too low to attract speculators. As time went on and prices increased overall, some speculation began to occur but, more importantly, the higher values increased the flow of consignments from private sources as the sales of various heirlooms began to have greater utility to their owners than their ownership. Thus, in the early stages of the specialized auction market for Victorian paintings, the content of the auction catalogues represented a random cross selection of paintings of this period rather than a reflection of current consumption preferences. Over time, of course, certain paintings and painters achieved higher prices than others and, in turn, affected the market that began to mirror a distinctly late twentieth century taste for Victorian pictures. Not surprisingly, many of the artistic 'superstars' of the Victorian age have, again, become the favourites of present-day collectors. A major factor in this development is the use by today's picture merchants of the promotional potential inherent in past stardom. Of course, there are exceptions to this. Grimshaw, for instance, would have been greatly pleased to have any of his patrons part with the 1870s equivalent of £400,000 in exchange for the artist's thoroughly typical wet street scene entitled *Sixty years Ago* (1879, http://artmarket.tulane.edu/page66.html), which sold at Christie's on 10 June 1999. But, as any art dealer will confirm, there is also much profit to be derived from correcting the position of the unjustly ignored.

Although present day auction sales of Victorian paintings reflect the market context in which they occur, the catalogues still illustrate the extent to which product differentiation occurred among painters during the Victorian era. It requires no expert knowledge or trained eye to recognize after a relatively short time, for example, the characteristic colouring in the skies of the landscapes by James Burrell Smith (fl. 1850–76), the distinctive treatment of the water in the waterfall paintings of John Brandon 'Waterfall' Smith (1848–84), or the sentimental rustic scenes peopled with children and milkmaids executed with great skill by Miles Birket Foster (1825–99) using a similar hatching and stippling technique as William Henry Hunt. Equally easy to recognize is also the facial physiognomy of the female figures typical of many of the paintings of George Henry Boughton (1833–1905), as are John William Godward's (1861–1922) distinctive variations on the Alma-Tadema theme of pretty girls in flimsy, see-through robes. The same can be said of the twilights and sunsets of Albert Goodwin's (1845–1932) later watercolours, in which he experimented with sponging and stippling as well as pen-line in combination with watercolour wash, or George Armfield's (fl. 1840–75) seemingly endless variations of the same scruffy terriers chasing birds, cats, mice or rats. In today's fashion industry, where product differentiation is an all-important key to success in a highly competitive market, designers have had to resort to such unimaginative means as decorating their otherwise relatively indistinct mass products with their conspicuously printed names. Victorian painters were subtler, yet within their own field, their methods of distinguishing their products were and still remain as effective.

An examination of these auction catalogues also dispels the notion that these painters were merely formulaic. Quite to the contrary, the devices by which this product differentiation was achieved were, in the majority of cases, imaginatively incorporated into well-executed and generally appealing compositions. Particularly when compared to the works of some of the well-known artists of the twentieth and twenty-first centuries, to whom product differentiation has become even more crucial, the body of work of the Victorian painters mentioned looks refreshingly varied. To the layman it would be nearly impossible to distinguish the hundreds of slashed canvases of Lucio Fontana (1899–1968) from one another. Similarly, the drip paintings of Jackson Pollock (1912–56) would appear far more formulaic to all but the connoisseur than the neo-classical compositions of John W. Godward.

The initially controversial Pre-Raphaelite painters also fit into the differentiation model. The group's elaborate strategies to distinguish itself from the vast number of other contemporaneous and preceding art producers included not only such formal aspects as insisting on painting their compositions on white ground, but they also extended to the creation of a new theory. The intellectual dimension of the product character of paintings made such distinction possible. There is no direct evidence that the individual members of the brotherhood consciously designed a different art product with the specific intention to gain an advantage over their competitors, although this is quite possible. The veil of secrecy with which they surrounded their initial 'outing' and the use of a trademark – for that is what the use of the initials PRB constitutes – show, at the very least, an intuitive commercial sense. In a commentary written on the Royal Academy exhibition of 1854, Burne-Jones recognized the opportunity and need for product distinction, commenting that 'altogether, what with silly unmeaning subjects, and those of more questionable character, devoted to the hero-worship of traitors and robbers, or to the prettiness and romance of a heartless religion, I saw that the Pre-Raphaelites had indeed come at a time when there was need for them ...'[70] The length of time it took them to become financially successful also demonstrates that effective product differentiation does not automatically guarantee monetary rewards. As was the case with most other painters of this and subsequent periods, the involvement of professional middlemen was the main determinant.

The interdependency that existed between painters and dealers was recognized and accepted, although not always entirely welcomed, by the former. While direct transactions between artists and private patrons continued, the influence of middlemen over the consumption habits of the end consumer of art was an established fact and openly acknowledged. In his *Autobiography*, Frith remarked that 'it too often happens that until a picture has received the "hall mark" of the picture-dealer the collector is not satisfied; but after that he is often ready to pay for his ignorant incredulity in the form of a great advance on the price for which he might have acquired the work'. Frith actually preferred selling his paintings to the trade and, as a result, 'invariably escaped the tribulation that so often attends the patrons' patronage'. He explains that dealers understand art and artists, can be contractually bound, and cater to a variety of different tastes while the 'whims and fancies' and the 'ignorance' of private buyers make the life of a painter 'not a happy one'. Of course, dealers as businessmen had to consider 'mercantile' aspects[71] and, as it happened to the young Millais in 1849, could well reject works on the basis of lack of commercial appeal. Quite obviously frustrated, the artists revealed a somewhat naive strategy designed to combat the influence of middlemen: '... by putting a very high price on [my works], the dealers are entirely shut out ... When I sold my works to the dealers they were my friends ... There is, without doubt, an immense amount of underhand work, and I can scarcely regard a single professional man as my friend. I am quite settled, however, in my position, to stand a violent siege'. Not surprisingly, Millais, was unable to maintain his position and soon capitulated: '... there is no chance of my selling pictures to gentlemen – the dealers are too strong'.[72] Lamenting this condition, Hamerton proclaimed that poverty was liberty compared with work under a dealer's pressure to produce according to an established success formula.[73]

Any discussion, therefore, of the 'homely' quality to which Taylor refers, must incorporate dealers as rational, self-interested agents of distribution as well as the inherent dialectic which governed the relationships of producers and consumers of art with these institutionalized middlemen. Their economic success or failure depended on their ability to invest in the type of inventory best suited for the domestic mass consumption character of the Victorian art market – that is, homely pictures. Not surprisingly, dealers at times went as far as requesting specific subjects or suggesting changes to painters to make their works more sellable.

Gambart, for example, drew up an agreement with John Linnell which stated that the dealer

> wants subjects comprising good & well defined foreground with figures & animals & other accessories, as well & completely finished as the subjects & effect will allow – What is called sketchy to be avoided – with diversified middle distance showing an easily travel [sic] through the Landscape of an extensive country – modern English or Scotch Subjects – E.G. [Ernest Gambart] agreing [*sic*] to procure some Scotch Sketches or Caltypes for the latter.[74]

Another instance is Holman Hunt's account of the arrangement between Millais and Ralph Thomas, a Chartist barrister turned picture dealer, which called for the artist to paint daily, at a remuneration of one guinea per diem, and produce every day or two a finished picture for the employer. For the duration of the contract Millais stayed for dinner and during the meal the patron and his wife would discuss the subject of the next work. Hunt himself also often resorted to painting, mainly replicas, for dealers in order to make ends meet while working on major works intended for reproduction.[75] A further example is Thomas Agnew's commission around 1850 of James Baker Pyne to paint a series of landscapes of the Lake District.[76]

Additional such cases of the direct influence of middlemen – and, therefore, by extension, of their perception of consumer demand – on the formal appearance of Victorian paintings may well be revealed by a detailed and specific investigation of correspondence between artists and dealers. One can reasonably assume that many more such instances occurred during verbal exchanges as well. However, the examples mentioned above should suffice as an illustration of the dialectic that existed between middlemen and producers and how it left its mark on much of the art of the Victorian period. Thus, the homely quality Taylor mentioned and which the Parliamentary Committee praised was, as far as subject matter of pictures was concerned, part of a trend towards a domestication of paintings. Since one of the defining features of the modern art market is the appropriation of the consumption of paintings by the middle classes for private, domestic use, the product as well as the exchange mechanism commoditized in a variety of ways towards facilitating this domestication. The increase in 'homeliness' was but a reflection of the growth as well as the composition of middle-class demand as perceived, modified and communicated by dealers to painters.

Of course, exceptions to this model existed, and it is not our intention to dismiss the influence of other visual and social strategies in the art produced in Britain between 1700 and 1900. Indeed, many of the period's paintings reflect religious, political, social, and moral issues and pre-occupations. These concerns make up a large part of middle-class identity and, therefore, also fit within the above suggested domestication model. Associating, therefore, this appropriation of paintings for middle-class domestic use with the market's call for product differentiation provides a conceptual construct that helps explain the difference, in terms of subject matter, of Victorian paintings from their predecessors.

Generally speaking, paintings commoditized, in terms of subject matter, along two main paths. In the first instance, increasing differentiation among producers occurred; in the second instance, within each broader subject category, representations changed towards facilitating their appropriation for middle-class domestic use. Accordingly, in May, 1855, *The Times* commented 'that to private purchasers alone the English artist owes his existence ... Studies of humble life, and reminiscences of juvenile innocence divide with landscape almost the whole attention of our rising artists'.[77] Tom Taylor's comments should be understood in this context.

Another effect of domestication on the physical appearance of pictures, the responsibility for which can firmly be assigned to middle-class consumers is the earlier mentioned reduction in the average size of contemporary paintings compared to those of the preceding century. As mentioned earlier, our auction sales data and Tooth's stock books show that the majority of contemporary works sold at auction during the period under discussion were of a size commonly described by the present-day trade vernacular as 'sofa-size'. This expression, nowadays, is more often used for 'decorative' pictures and describes, as the phrase implies, painting best suited to hang above a sofa, side board or mantle. Dimensions range from 18 x 24 to 30 x 40 inches. The average size of reproductive engravings fell also within the same range of dimensions. This reduction in size of paintings to facilitate their use in domestic settings was already recognized by Richard Redgrave in the 1890s. Describing the post-Hogarth art production, he states that 'it was soon found that pictures to suit English taste must be pictures to live by; pictures to hang on the wall of that home in which the Englishman spends most of his time ... His rooms are relatively small, and he cannot spare much wall space for a single picture ... Works had at least a common likeness, in that they were of cabinet size'.[78] It is therefore no surprise that the relationship of size to price was inversely proportional: the larger the painting, the less is the price per square inch.

Several conclusions can be made from these observations. Commoditization led to changes in the average size of contemporary pictures to accommodate their decorative function within middle-class urban homes. In addition, dealer dominance of the market exerted a similar influence on size and price: the larger the selection of goods displayed, the greater the opportunities were for sales in a gallery or commercial exhibition. Similarly, the larger an individual painting, the smaller was the number of potential buyers with the financial means and sufficient space for displaying it while a smaller work could be placed easily within a domestic interior. Thus, as in the sixteenth-century Netherlands, two interlocked forces on the demand side impacted the physical appearance of contemporary paintings.

Large paintings of course continued to be produced. The market demanded of artists to paint attention-getting works in order to compete effectively. Imposing size was one of the means to do so. However, as already noted, such works, while necessary, were costly to produce, difficult to sell and required subsidy either in the form of smaller works, potboilers, or reproductive engravings.[79] Dealers also required crowd-drawing attractions of which not only reproductive engravings were sold but that also helped to sell smaller works to private consumers.

Further effects of a supply/demand relationship on the art environment can be demonstrated by associating average price with different subject categories. The results show that the traditional hierarchy of paintings, which gave pre-eminence to history, mythological and religious subjects and ranked landscapes, animal and genre paintings the lowest, was overturned and replaced by a market-oriented structure which assigned the highest monetary value to landscapes, animal subjects, genres, still lives and interiors (Table I.2). The production of paintings during the Victorian period was dominated by landscapes: nearly 45 per cent of all paintings by contemporary Victorian and almost 40 per cent of works by contemporary Continental artists listed in Graves's data belong to this category. The trade noticeably favoured this type, buying over 65 per cent of the landscapes by living painters from the Continent and 59 per cent of such pictures by Victorian artists. Landscape paintings are an easily approachable genre for the novice art consumer then and now, requiring little intellectual or theoretical background for producer, middleman and consumer. In an economic context, landscape paintings represent a highly commoditized visual product for which relative demand and supply was at a higher equilibrium than that of other genres.

The second position was taken by genre paintings with 25 per cent and 33 per cent respectively, while the third place in the market-based hierarchy was occupied by animal subjects, which accounted for 9 per cent of all contemporary Continental pictures and nearly 8 per cent of those of living British artists. By contrast, there was little demand for the previous leaders of the hierarchy. Only 2 per cent of paintings by Victorian artists listed in our data were mythologies; 3

per cent were religious subjects and 5.5 per cent history paintings. Among works by contemporary painters from the Continent, the distribution on the basis of subject was 0.6 per cent, 2.3 per cent, and 3.4 per cent respectively.[80] On average too large and intellectually too demanding, these paintings were ill-suited for domestic consumption by the typical Victorian picture buyer and were mainly bought by institutions. Contemporary accounts confirm this. Frith wrote: 'I am fully persuaded that history painting, even when practised by a master-hand, would find no support in England; few houses are large enough to contain works of the scale that history painters affect, and still fewer are the purchasers who have the desire – bred of taste and knowledge – sufficiently strong to induce them to patronize historical or sacred pictures at all'.[81] As a consequence of art institutions' preference for such works, present-day museum visitors expecting to gain a visual impression of the pictorial output of specific historical periods can conceivably get inaccurate information. A similar observation can be made with respect to art history textbooks. Therefore, any assessment of art history on the basis of art works exhibited on museum walls or illustrated in textbooks must take into account the economics involved in the process of their display or illustration.

Perhaps the most significant impact of the replacement of the centuries-old, traditional, academy-based hierarchy of paintings is the consequences this had for the avant-garde. The expansion of the market and its associated demand for product differentiation, the decline of the engravings trade, and the multifaceted, complex relationship among producers, middlemen and consumers, all paved, economically speaking, a path for product innovations of hitherto unknown degree.

Product differentiation does not imply that artists must have exclusively commercial reasons for developing their styles distinct from others. Their incentive may well be a desire to convey their own personal vision or aesthetic philosophy. Regardless of motivation, however, the result is a differentiated art product that, if it enters the market place, serves to distinguish itself and its producer from close competitors. Effective differentiation has the potential to improve marketability; it also provides art writers, art historians and curators with new impetus to sell their own products and services. Therefore, product differentiation in the arts, be that in the form of radical innovation or in the subtler ways employed during the Victorian period, is an essential fuel to the life of a vibrant arts environment. Without it, the forward momentum would cease, the arts would feed upon themselves and, ultimately implode.

Of course, economic reasons were not the only ones that facilitated the rise of an avant-garde. Other, more traditional, issues also played a significant role. However, the institutionalization of dealers as the market hub is among the primary agent responsible for the successful fundamental re-definition of the medium of painting. The resulting deconstruction of centuries-old notions of what paintings should be, that began in the last thirty years or so of the nineteenth century, expanded the commodity definition of pictures to encompass an ever increasing number of differentiated aesthetic products.

The extent to which Tom Taylor was aware of the multiple manifestations and implications of his concern regarding the 'homeliness' of paintings is unknown. Most likely, the full impact of the orientation of nineteenth-century picture production towards domestic consumption through the agency of middlemen can only be assessed retrospectively. However, choice of subject, manner of execution, stylistic innovations, size and format were all affected to varying degrees by the market-related aspects this contemporary observer of the Victorian arts milieu articulated.

10 THE END OF THE 'GOLDEN AGE'

By the mid-1870s, the supremacy of contemporary English painting was in slow decline. In economic terms, the rise and fall of this 'Golden Age' were associated in greater proportion with the history of the mass-marketed reproductive print than with any other single factor. Record demand during mid-century occasioned publishers to explore ways to speed up the production process, lower overall costs and increase the size of editions. However, this very prosperity and the resulting market expansion carried the seeds of the downfall of the reproductive print.

As the economics of the print industry changed so did the relevance of many of the related factors that had shaped the appearance of countless original works. Mass appeal, readily apparent labour intensity, high finish, and scrupulous attention to detail lost in importance. Precisely these aspects had delineated much of the style of contemporary pictures of this period. The emerging stylistic changes and new aesthetics coinciding with the decline of the reproductive print market must therefore be considered within the context of the art market's increasing economic diversification.

Not every artist benefited directly from the buoyancy of the print trade. Nonetheless, the resulting market growth spread its largesse far beyond the individual recipients of copyright revenues. The unprecedented growth in the number of professional artists was to a large extent a consequence of the print industry's immense cash infusion into the market. The profits of publishing ventures must have contributed significantly to the financial wherewithal of dealers to begin and/or continue trading in pictures by living artists. Agnew's, for example, after initially focusing on old masters, first entered publishing in the late 1840s and only then began seriously dealing in works by living artists. The scenario was similar with Gambart who also diverted profits from print publishing to dealing in contemporary paintings.[1] The reproductive print had become the 'cash cow', the *sine qua non,* of the English art economy as it functioned during its peak. This economic dependency made this segment of the art industry the Achilles heel of the contemporary art market.

The first serious challenge to this essential derivative product was issued by the new medium of photography. This novel technique was promoted as a superior reproduction of an original than engravings or mezzotints. In 1864, an article in *The Athenaeum* announced that photographic copies 'have ... great advantages over ordinary engravings, and, in some respect, far exceed in artistic value, even the possibilities of engraving of the most costly sort ...'[2] Many of the leading dealers like Agnew, the Fine Arts Society, or Colnaghi started to deal in both engravings as well as photographic reproductions, using the same rarity hierarchy as a marketing tool that was employed in selling traditional engravings. In response to the increasing acceptance and popularity of this new medium, the Art Union of Glasgow even began in 1863 to substitute the engraving that was offered annually to its subscribers with photographs.

Beyond its use as an alternative, superior reproduction method for original works, photography was also employed to pirate existing engravings. Selling inexpensive photographs of these prints became so widespread that Parliament, in 1862, amended the laws of copyright in relation to the fine arts. The trade responded with a series of test cases for deliberation, arguing that photographic piracy of famous engravings jeopardized sales of original prints. Gambart, for example, filed suits in 1863 involving his most frequently pirated print, *The Light of the World* after Holman Hunt. It had come to the dealer's attention that over the preceding two years, sales of this engraving, which had grossed around £10,000 in revenue during its first year on the market, had seriously declined, allegedly due to the availability of cheap photographic copies. Gambart stated in court that he intended 'to prosecute in every case ... I must do so, or give up my business. It is of no use for me to go on publishing engravings if the moment I publish I am knocked out of the field by piracies'.[3] After winning the case, the dealer even issued a long pamphlet entitled, *On Piracy of Artistic Copyright*. Yet despite all these efforts, Gambart was still unable to put an end to these copy-rights violations. His actions, nonetheless, did become part of legal history.

Violations continued and their harm to the print market extended beyond the immediate effects on sales. For one, declining demand due to the availability of cheap substitutes, *ceteris paribus,* lowers the price of a commodity. Since certain production costs of prints, such as cost of plates, paper and ink, were largely fixed, the downward pressure affected the market value of the copyright and the associated price of labour. Furthermore, the monopoly aspect of an edition permitted a more definitive revenue calculation, an advantage in, if not essential to, raising venture capital from outside sources as was the case with Gambart and the private investor, Gillot.[4] To what extent the use of outside venture capital was involved in other print publishing enterprises is not known; however, external capital for business projects was a commonly used resource in England, and we assume that Gambart's arrangement was not unusual.

A second factor compounded the negative pressure on the prevailing economics of the art market: by the early 1870s, the main vehicle for direct sales of engravings, the single picture exhibition, was beginning to lose its public appeal. In a 1873 letter to Stephens, the editor of the *Athenaeum*, about a planned exhibition of Hunt's *Shadow of Death*, Agnew publicly voiced concerns for the first time about the financial performance of single picture exhibitions. Evidently, the dealer had been noticing an attendance decline of such events.[5] Perhaps, like any fad, it too was beginning to lose the persuasiveness of its hyperbole. Yet earnings from entrance fees to exhibition events were a crucial source of income for dealers. In the case of Hunt's *The Finding of the Saviour in the Temple* Gambart anticipated revenues of approximately £6,000 over four years, enough to pay for the entire costs of engraving and printing and still have money left.[6] Moreover, any decline in entrance fees was a direct measure of attendance of potential buyers and thus affected sales. Single picture exhibitions provided the ideal ambiance to enthuse visitors about the dramatically displayed painting and gave dealers and their staff the opportunity to sell engraved reproductions of the featured work. In his *Autobiography*, Frith offered an amusing account of the dealer Flatou's sales techniques during the 1862 exhibition of the painter's sensational canvas *Life at the Railway Station,* allegedly seen by 83,000 visitors. 'Flatou was triumphant; coaxing, wheedling, and almost bullying, his unhappy visitors. Many of them, I verily believe, subscribed for the engraving to get rid of his importunity'.[7] However, ten years later, given the declining effectiveness of single picture exhibition as a marketing device, dealers in general must have been reluctant to invest in suitable works, persuasive talents such as Flatou's notwithstanding. Consequently, painters were discouraged from producing the type of painting that had formerly fulfilled the role of star attraction for these events.

Tangentially we should note that since the late twentieth century, this economic inter-dependency between original works and its derivative properties has led to the creation of original works of art the ownership of which, unlike the Victorian sensation pictures', is no longer transferable. Among the most widely acclaimed such creations are the wrapped objects by Christo. His original works are, by definition, ephemeral and largely financed by the sale of limited editions of reproductions of preparatory studies. Christo's business model can be traced back to late eighteenth-century England to the pictorial enterprises of J. S. Copley discussed earlier. Christo, however, took the commoditization of his artistic activities substantially further by creating original works that are freed entirely from the limitations imposed by the conventional exchange mechanisms for art and solely rely on derivatives to generate revenue. In this manner, the artist succeeded in finding an ingenious way to commoditize, that is, to make marketable, aesthetic concepts and ideas that hitherto had been impossible to translate into saleable visual products. Rather than accepting the confinements imposed by the existing economics of the contemporary art market, Christo, in a brilliant example of creative artistic entrepreneurship, exploited these conditions to produce something altogether new.

Meanwhile, however, the deconstruction of the financial potential of Victorian sensation pictures and their derivative properties continued. In addition to copyright violations and declining exhibition attendance, a third challenge to the profitability of these paintings came from another technical innovation. By the mid-1880s, the market for two or three guineas steel engravings was giving way to the chromo-lithograph, which could be reproduced by the hundreds of thousands for as little as a shilling each. The medium required neither high finish in the original painting nor particularly fine work in the reproduction. The reproductive steel engraving, despite its proclaimed artistic merit and status as messenger of art among the masses, could not compete with the purely mechanically produced chromo-lithograph for which human effort had ceased to be a measure of value. This combination of cheap price and fewer demands on artistic talent further deflated the value of an artwork's copyright. This trend was further compounded by the introduction of a profusion of other types of printed images. A review of prints published in the *Art Journal* in July 1872 gives an indication of the choice consumers faced: photosculptural views of Pompeii; mechanical wood engravings; photo-mezzotints; engravings from paintings and chromolithographs were all discussed under separate headings.[8] Without at least a modicum of knowledge of the specific characteristics of each different type of print, consumers may have been reluctant to make choices for purchase. Economic theory suggests that under such conditions increasing product differentiation and/or price competition by very close substitutes are likely to occur. In Victorian England a shift of market attention occurred, away from reproductive prints towards original print-making and a gradual replacement of the more expensive type of reproductions, like line engraving, mezzotint, or stipple, by more cheaply produced copies.

As reproduction gradually lost its potential as additional income source it developed into an advertisement for the original work.[9] Artists and dealers, therefore, could no longer consider potential earnings from the sale of reproductions in their calculations. Consequently, the 'sensation' picture, which had appeared in the modern art market a century earlier and depended for its production on the revenue potential of its copyright property, became financially even less attractive for artists to produce on speculation or for middlemen to commission.

New conditions resulting from this contracting market for reproductive steel engraving, however, spelled new opportunities for the production of etchings, both as original works as well as close substitutes for reproductive engravings. In his review of 'Fifty Years' Development of the Graphic Arts', published in *The Art Journal* in 1887, J. S. Hodson observed that line engraving was 'fast becoming a thing of the past' and that etching had 'in a degree supplanted line-engraving'.[10] Much faster and technically easier to produce, less concerned with high finish and detail, etching could be employed both to reproduce a much wider range of paintings and also supply the trend of the moment.

Original etchings underwent a 'revival' of a certain kind, and it is worth examining this issue in greater detail as another example of economics relating to artistic product differentiation. It also serves as a case in point of artists' deliberate action under changing market conditions.[11]

Artful Economics: The 'Revival' of Etching

The art of etching had never died out in England, and the term 'revival' is somewhat misleading. The phrase was purposely used as part of a product differentiation rhetoric by producers/promoters of a medium that had been sidelined by reproductive engravings and demoted to a more or less amateur status with a distinctly 'feminine' aura.[12] Labelling pre-'revival' etchings as feminine leisure pursuits was an easy way of marginalizing both products and their producers. As a commercial strategy this served two purposes. For publishers of reproductive prints it constructed a superior image for their own products, while 'revival' etchers found such pejorative terms useful in their efforts to differentiate their products from those of their immediate predecessors.

Indeed, the practice of etching was by no means limited to amateurs and women, but had been seriously pursued and even institutionalized during the 'dead' period suggested by the use of the term 'revival'. During the early decades of the nineteenth century, for example, the landscape painters of the Norwich School with such notable members as John Crome (1768–1821) and John Sell Cotman (1782–1842), produced topographical etchings that, in terms of spontaneity, fulfilled the aesthetic demands of the revival group members and their own landscapes.[13] Furthermore, etchers, amateur and professional artists alike, had formed their own organizations. The longest-lived, the Old Etching Club, functioned between 1838 and 1885; others, like the Junior Etching Club, the Painters' Etching Society and the Antiquarian Etching Club, all operated before 1850, the year that, according to one of new etching movement's principal spokesmen, Seymour Haden, marked the official commencement of the revival.[14]

Another aspect of this campaign to differentiate 'revival' etchings and etchers intended to provide the medium with a legitimizing provenance that defined it within a history going back to Rembrandt and his contemporaries, echoing a tactic that had already been employed successfully by painters in the preceding century. They, too, had placed their art into a sweeping historical context and effectively raised their occupation's status. In the case of etchers, the public was presented with an image of contemporary practitioners as the 'disciples of Rembrandt', the 'great representative of etchers of all time'.[15] With such pedigree, modern etchers could promote themselves as custodians of an ancient tradition that somehow had fallen into misuse. Adopting Rembrandt as the profession's patron saint was particularly effective and well timed since this artist's name and particularly his work as an etcher had received a tremendous publicity boost from the 1867 auction sale of his *Hundred Guilder Print Christ Healing the Sick* (http://artmarket.tulane.edu/page106.html) for the astounding sum of £1,180. Even Rembrandt's own image commoditized towards a more suitable artistic role model. The earlier characterization of him as an artist who prostituted his art for a life of lust and lucre,[16] changed into one of an enlightened, yet misunderstood, noble professional.[17]

Other commercial strategies of this 'revival' included the medium's promotion as a highly original and intellectual art, created and consumed by a refined elite, distinct from common consumers of mass-produced reproductive prints. A deliberate rhetoric was employed to advance a specific set of associations in potential consumers of original etchings. P. G. Hamerton, among the most influential advocates of this product re-definition, made his initial appearance as a spokesperson for the medium with a long essay on French etching published in *The Fine Arts Quarterly Review* in 1864.[18] Already in his first article, the 'revival' agenda became apparent. The author, himself an artist, avowed that etching was an art which 'to the ordinary spectator ... is uninteresting, because unintelligible ... very great knowledge is required in the spectator to read them at all ...'[19] In his seminal work, *Etching and Etchers*, he continued along those lines, shifting emphasis from intellectual to cultural elite. He argued that 'indifference to etching is wholly incompatible with high culture', and that it was 'a matter less for regret than congratulation that an art should exist safe from the baneful influence of vulgar patronage'.[20] The notion of 'revival' also allowed him to sweep aside the label of 'femininity' by pronouncing that now 'a treatise on etching is necessarily a treatise on the mental powers of great men'.[21] Frederick Wedmore even likened the appreciation of original etchings to the enjoyment of great wines: 'The true print lover can talk about different paper...as the connoisseur of clarets talks of Pontet Canets and Pichon Longuevilles'.[22] The writer presented his readers an image of intimate, refined, even sensual leisure, the pursuit of which was, naturally, expensive.[23]

This aura of exclusivity was further intensified by emphasizing the rarity of original prints. The very manner in which many of these works were executed coupled with certain physical limitations imposed by the medium itself lent credence to this claim of scarcity. Unlike reproductive engravings, etchings of the revival movement were often printed by artists personally or under their immediate supervision. Both Haden and Frederick Goulding, the leading printer of the movement, advocated the direct participation of etchers in the printing process. The resulting artist-printed proofs were promoted as the rarest of the rare, the unspoiled and purest manifestation of the entire creative process. In Goulding's opinion,

> no printer, be he as good a craftsman as may be, could print an etcher's etching the same as he can do it himself...he [the artist] may not 'pull' two proofs alike, but in each and every one he will have his own feeling tricking down his arm to his finger's end, and put on or wipe off his plate those art feelings which are passing through his mind, and in each proof there will be an individuality no craftsman could exactly imitate.[24]

Haden felt no differently, explaining that while a commercial printer had been 'educated to handle everything with roughness', the printer of etchings must have the delicacy of the 'palm of a duchess'.[25] This emphasis of the direct engagement of artists with the production of their prints coupled aristocratic refinement with a sense of intimacy between producers and consumers.[26] Unlike the mass-produced and mass-consumed reproductive engraving, each original etching, and by extension, its owner was special.

However, not every aspect of the reproductive print industry was outright rejected. Indeed, the revival movement embraced, in an appropriately refined form, one of the principle marketing devices of the engraving industry: the issuing of limited editions. Unlike reproductive prints the limited editions of which, even the rarest 'artist's proofs', usually numbered five hundred or more impressions, editions of original etchings typically contained well below a hundred sheets. Moreover, it was recommended that after a certain number of pulls, the plate be 'destroyed whilst the work is in a perfectly sound condition'.[27]

While rarity as a marketing tool was nothing new, the etching movement employed it particularly emphatically. In an article on Whistler, *The Pall Mall Gazette* observed that the collector 'hates the common crowd, and will only have etchings that are rare. It is easy to gratify him by keeping the supply down'.[28] This was nothing new to Whistler. Already in 1868, Hamerton remarked on the American artist's awareness 'that etchings are usually sought as much for their rarity as their excellence', and his commercial strategy 'to have determined that his own plates be exceedingly rare'.[29]

To create this aura of rarity and masculine exclusivity, etchers differed from their artistic brethrens of the eighteenth century who had broadened the consumer base for their products by deliberately expanding the appreciation and consumption of painting beyond the exclusive domain of the enlightened few to include the 'vulgar patronage' objected to by Hamerton. However, under conditions of increasing competition for a fairly inelastic consumer base – one must not forget the unfavourable market conditions for luxury goods as a result of the agricultural depression between the 1870s and early 1890s – the paths taken by etchers to re-design their products' identity was a sound economic strategy. Markus Borne Huish's observation in 1878, that 'there is no branch of art which is more rapidly forcing its way into the notice of the English art-loving world, than etching' attests to their success.[30]

Differentiation did not stop here. Constructing a new artistic lineage and promoting product scarcity and consumer elitism was coupled with the creation of a new aesthetic, one that ran counter to the market value Victorian art consumers placed on high finish, detail, realistic rendering, easily discernable narrative content, and clear evidence of time-consuming labour. Already in his first essay on this topic, Hamerton portrayed these aspects in a negative light, postulating that 'the uninformed spectator admires execution for itself, as handicraft, with little reference to its meaning; the true judge calls that the best execution which expresses the most'.[31] Visible evidence of physical effort, another cornerstone of the prevailing aesthetic, was also dismissed: 'Whatever there is of toil and trouble in art should be kept as much as possible out of sight, and conquered in the preliminary and preparatory drawing'.[32] Haden, too, argued that 'too minute renderings in matters of art is bad' because it tended 'to weaken the primary ideas and conceptions of the artist'.[33] For these 'primary ideas and conceptions' to develop into visual expression, unspoiled by distractingly apparent laborious 'toil and trouble', speed of execution was essential. Such skill, however, could only be attained by 'spend[ing] a great deal of time in looking, and having decided upon the strokes to be laid, lay[ing] them at once and leav[ing] them'. Confident speed of execution was given market value by describing it as the masterful result of time-consuming observation and the very means through which artistic ideas must be expressed in order to appear in their purest, most 'honest' form.[34]

Rather than attacking the Victorian credo of labour/exchange value, the rhetoric of this brilliant campaign instead fully embraced it simply by relegating labour, as far as the consumer was concerned, into the realm of the intangible, made visible to the cultured connoisseur only by the obvious absence of laboured effort. This tactic was not altogether without precedent. It echoes the earlier discussed views expressed by Sir Reynolds in his *Discourse IX*, delivered at the opening of the Royal Academy, October 1780. ' ... the beauty of which we are in quest is general and intellectual; it is an idea that subsists only in the mind; the sight never beheld it: it is an idea residing in the breast of the artist ...'[35] This abstract nature of beauty advocated by this artists; its intellectual, non-descriptive or non-imitative dimension; the notion of the artist as the proprietor of this beauty, were all concepts that removed art works from the more readily measurable standards of labour, detail, realistic depiction or clarity of content. Precisely that was part of the overall strategy of the theorists of the etching revival.

Their efforts towards designing a new product 'biography' for their prints were an undisguised attack on the entire market on which reproductive engravings was built. The financial importance to the art market of these products had become, on one level, a barrier to the continuing economic emancipation of artists. To appeal to a mass market, an easily quantifiable system of exchange value had to be constructed for reproductive engravings and, by extension, for paintings as well. The value-determining components needed to be readily apparent, easily communicated visually and in writing and in agreement with prevailing value systems applicable to other luxury goods. There was, however, the inherent danger that consumers would place painters on the same level as, for example, clock or furniture makers and thus reverse the tedious process painters had laboured through for well over two centuries to distinguish their profession. The reputation of typical mid-Victorian painting in general was beginning to suffer from precisely such image problems, namely 'mere manufacture and a dull routine trade'.[36] The weakness in the market for reproductive engravings provided the opportunity to shed these stifling standards and offer instead an alternative aesthetic that obfuscated measurable input of labour and put far greater control over the design of their product back into the hands of the artist. By doing so, the members of the revival movement succeeded in creating a clearly distinct and marketable commodity character for their product.

The language they employed in the promotion of their products also differentiated the revival movement from older etching practices and organizations. Prints produced by The Etching Club, for instance, were, by agreement of its members, priced according to the amount of labour, that is, the more lines were visible on the plate, the higher was the price of the print. Such practices ran counter to the aims pursued by Haden or Hamerton. One of the purposes of the term 'revival' was to draw a clear separation between them and earlier etchers whose 'productions were for the most part fidgety, prim, at best desperately pretty and ridiculously elaborated ...'[37]

Another dimension of this campaign was a vast outpouring of books, articles and even the publication of a magazine primarily devoted to the field of etching. Haden's 1866 article 'About Etching', in *The Fine Arts Quarterly Review*[38] was but the first such commentary. Hamerton established himself as an authority on the topic with his book *Etching and Etchers* published in 1868. Two years later he founded *The Portfolio*, a journal principally committed to the promotion of original etching. Other magazines were *The Etcher* and *English Etchings* established in 1879 and 1881 respectively.[39]

The last step taken by the advocates of the revival movement in this strategic commoditization of original etchings was the establishment of an institutional representation of their interests. In 1850, Haden had attempted to have etching included as a profession within the fine arts and submitted a selection of works to the Royal Academy. Although the campaign was unsuccessful, the rejection prompted Haden to launch a crusade to establish etchers' professional status within the fine arts. His efforts ultimately led to the formation of the Society of Painter-Etchers, founded in 1880, establishing producers of original etchings as a separate and distinct professional group.

This last phase of the etching revival campaign, the formation of a Society, is echoed elsewhere in the arts environment. Organizations are by definition exclusionary, and membership in an artists' Society helps legitimize specific activities or interests of its members as well as sets them apart from non-members competing in the same market. Forming such groups had enjoyed great popularity among artists for some time, a fact that attests to such organizations' perceived effectiveness. In addition to those earlier mentioned as established before 1850, the last two decades of the century witnessed the formations of the Society of Portrait Painters in 1891; the Society of Medallists in the same year; two societies of miniaturists in 1895; the Society of Oil Painters in 1898; and the Society of Pastellists in 1899. Again, the increase in numbers of such groups was, as it had been in the earlier part of the century, a direct consequence of an expanding art market.

Regardless of institutional framework, no product can succeed in the market without some means of disseminating it among the public. Undoubtedly, the establishment of a professional Society had a positive impact on marketing the newly constructed etchers' product. However, in an art market that was fuelled by middlemen, revival etchings needed dealer support to attain economic sustainability. Certainly, personal efforts of the artists themselves played a role in creating a market. Haden even embarked on an extensive lecture tour to the United States in 1882 to promote the new etchings.[40] He also frequently used the press to declare publications of his work rather than going through middlemen. One such notice, placed in *The Athenaeum* in February 1878, showed the artist's intention to differentiate himself and his product from the reproductive print trade. It read that the publications of his etchings 'will adhere to the traditions and practices of the old painter-etchers, which are founded on reason and experience and have nothing in common with the practices and trade arrangements of the steel engraving ...'[41]

However, such personal efforts notwithstanding, it is doubtful that Huish could have made his earlier observation concerning the rapidly rising popularity of etchings among the English art collecting public without the involvement of several of the prominent dealers in London. Leading houses like Colnaghi, Agnew, and particularly The Fine Arts Society dealt, in addition to paintings, drawings and reproductive engravings, also in original etchings. There existed compelling economic reasons for these dealers to re-direct some of their resources away from their core commercial activities and allocate them to the as yet tenuous business in original etchings. Already in 1873, Agnew had begun to notice a change in the market and voiced concerns about the drop in attendance of single picture exhibitions. Hedging positions by expanding one's product range to include commercially comparatively untested works reflected a sound policy of diversification. Furthermore, in order to gain a foothold with dealers and the resulting needed visibility, revival etchers likely offered terms advantageous to dealers. Compared to the costly publications of reproductive engravings involving original work, its copyrights, the actual cost of engraving and printing, as well as exhibition and marketing, a set of original etchings consigned to, or even produced for, the gallery by the artist was a relatively low- risk addition to the sellable inventory. The small size of the works required little wall space for display, while their presence expanded the product range at negligible overall cost to the gallery. Competition among the trade thus facilitated the introduction and dissemination of new cultural products and their associated aesthetics among consumers.

By 1881, perhaps encouraged by the founding of the Society of Painter-Etchers the year before, Robert Dunthorne started the first gallery almost exclusively dedicated to the support of original etchings. The head of Rembrandt was appropriately featured on its big shop sign.

The commercial history of the etching revival in late Victorian England is a textbook illustration of producer agency in the face of economic competition. The artists involved were engaged in what modern business vernacular describes as niche marketing. They embarked on a multi-faceted campaign to design a new identity for their product to optimize its competitive advantage in a specifically targeted market. Rather than simply continuing with certain practices, well established in their particular medium, the members of the new etching movement consciously set out to differentiate themselves as well as their products. Since this action involved cultural products, it also had to include a radical deconstruction of prevailing aesthetics and the creation of new more suitable ones. The labour based value system of the Old Etching Club left the revivalists with no other option but to oppose it diametrically and promote an aesthetic that, in practical terms, was faster to turn into a marketable product and thus substantially more cost-effective. It also gave much greater control to the producer.

Within less than two decades after the revival etching movement had reached economic viability, one of the cornerstones of the foundation of the mid-Victorian art boom entirely crumbled. In 1897 the Copyright Commission legislated that owners of a work of art also owned its copyright. With this ruling, copyrights of paintings legally ceased to be a property independent of the original work and the division of a painting into three separately marketable entities – the major, if not essential, revenue-generating feature of the Victorian art boom – officially came to an end.

Increasing differentiation was not limited to prints but also occurred in the production of paintings. With the collapse of the whole system on which the market for mass-produced reproductive engravings was based, the economic incentive to create the necessarily labour-intensive original paintings also crumbled. Therefore, instead of investing all their resources to produce time-consuming, highly detailed pictures for their derivatives' income properties, artists altered their products to compete more effectively within the changing economics of the market. One of the consequences of this process was, among many artists, a trend away from highly finished pictures towards a painterly and thus less labour intensive palette to maximize the returns from their labour. The construction of aesthetics to go with the redesigned product was just part of the same package. This move was among the few options available to painters to replace the income previously generated by mass-marketed derivative products. As mentioned earlier, the Whistler vs. Ruskin trial concerning the latter's allegation that the American artist's painting was unfinished, symbolized the conflict between the old value system and a new one not based on input of labour. Likewise, the contemporaneous emergence of Aestheticism was part of the search for, and testing of, alternative standards with which to assess the merits of paintings under changing market conditions. Moreover, the explosive expansion of styles that characterized the international arts environment from this point forward is but a manifestation of this increasing demand for clearly differentiated cultural products. It called for 'novelty at all costs', to repeat Elizabeth Pennell astute observation.[42] Similarly, the rise in portraiture production – the traditional safe haven of painters – that occurred during the last decades of the nineteenth century is but another manifestation of this uncertainty and state of flux in the market.[43]

When engravings as reproductions of original paintings gave way to technically superior photo-mechanical products, art consumers must have become more sensitive to the unique physical aspects of original works. This trend further expanded the range of competition for painters. Artistic product differentiation henceforth was no longer restricted to subject matter and the types of conventional style variations suitable for traditional reproduction by steel engraving. Since Victorian painters had already explored an extraordinarily wide array of themes in their pictures, the emphasis shifted to stylistic and technical distinctiveness. Indeed, the collapse of the mass market for reproductive engravings liberated painters from the need to fashion their works, to whatever extent, to suit such purpose. At the same time, it also challenged them to explore other markedly different and unconventional means of visual articulation. It is no coincidence that the increasing experimentation in styles and techniques during the last quarter of the nineteenth century and beyond stood in a negative correlation to the changing role of reproduction from a potentially lucrative independent property to mere information bearer. The economic causes behind these changes and their associated aesthetics do not invalidate their social, intellectual and emotional foundations or attempt to disqualify the complex personal experiences that shape an individual's notions of beauty, sincerity and honesty in art. They simply explain how such concepts enter the public domain as tangible consumer products through the exchange mechanism.

It was not only the decline of the mass-produced reproductive engraving industry that put pressure on the market to continue to adapt and evolve. The growing number of painters and the overall market expansion, not just in England, but also on the Continent, further fuelled the demand for increasing differentiation. This trend inevitably brought some artists onto a collision course with the Royal Academy. Ever since it was founded, the exclusivity of this organization, its doctrinaire rules and discriminatory hanging practices had represented an entry barrier to certain producers. Moreover, the equally restrictive cultural consensus that marked the mid-Victorian art market boom, during which the hegemony of the Academy had remained largely unchallenged, was beginning to crumble under the pressure of new aesthetic ideas expressed by painters and critics as a means to distinguish both paintings and accompanying theories. These artists needed venues not only to present their work to a public audience but, if possible, also to attract the attention of art writers. Thus, the last third of the century witnessed again the birth of alternative exhibition facilities. One such facility was the Dudley Gallery (1865–1918?), which occupied a small room inside the Egyptian Hall and staged, among others, spring watercolour exhibitions, a winter show of oil paintings, as well as an event featuring prints and drawings. There was also the New British Institution (1870–76), focusing on showing non-Academicians and the Supplementary Exhibition (1869–71), which largely displayed Academy rejects. In addition to these establishments, there were by the 1880s around 40 different smaller exhibition societies and art clubs in London.[44] Of course, these exhibition facilities did not topple the authority of the Royal Academy or even threaten it. They were hardly the environment in which to dazzle an audience that had been spoiled by the pictorial sensationalism of the age. A critical challenge, however, was presented by the Grosvenor Gallery, unquestionably the most important of these new exhibition venues. Founded in 1877 by the wealthy aristocratic couple, Sir Coutts and Lady Lindsay, the Grosvenor Gallery set itself apart from its competitors, including the Royal Academy and London's top dealers, by aiming to become a trade mark itself. Its story not only provides a model of redesigning a marketing method that had gone stale but also an example of differentiation that is as much symptom as agent of a changing arts environment.

Agents of Change: The Grosvenor Gallery

The Grosvenor Gallery was established for the explicit purpose of providing those artists who were not accommodated by the conservative official bodies with an outlet for their works, although on principle paintings by leading Academicians were not excluded. The gallery gained almost instant notoriety as a result of the publicity surrounding the famous Whistler vs. Ruskin trial: it was there at the inaugural summer exhibition in 1877 that Whistler showed his *Nocturne in Black and Gold: The Falling Rocket* that so offended Ruskin. Until 1890, when Sir Coutts had to close the Grosvenor Gallery due to financial reasons, it remained the most fashionable place for progressive artists to show their works. As Lord Henry Wotton pointed out to the painter, Basil Hallward, in Oscar Wilde's *Picture of Dorian Gray* (1890), 'The Grosvenor is really the only place'.[45] Furthermore, because of Lady Lindsay, herself a talented amateur, the exhibition facility became also an important venue for the promotion of women artists.[46]

The history of the gallery is a remarkable model of differentiation on several levels. In many respects the character of the Grosvenor was shaped by the need to distinguish itself from the Royal Academy. Perhaps the most noticeable difference that would have impressed a visitor to the gallery was the manner in which paintings were presented. The Academy's chief attraction for artists was the potential for sales. To that end, the institution's hanging committee used every inch of available space to install as many art works as possible, a practice widely adopted by middle-class households and, unquestionably, of great benefit to the art market. Yet this department store-type practice of displaying as much merchandize as space allowed paid little heed to the harmonious relationship of individual works to each other and to the exhibition as a whole, or to the general quality of the overall visual impact. Wilde's Lord Wotton bitterly complained that there were 'so many pictures that I have not been able to see the people ...'[47] Such overcrowded conditions also suggested that art works thusly displayed were nothing but another commodity hawked to the public.

By contrast, at the Grosvenor, each artwork was regarded independently. Paintings and sculptures were displayed to highlight their distinctiveness and with regard to their interaction with the audience as well as their coherence with other works. Moreover, individual painter's work was grouped together and, whenever possible, visually separated from other artists' pictures, thus emphasizing the individuality and originality of each artist.[48] In addition to such novel hanging practices, the Lindsays further set off the exhibition space through the use of skylights similar to those of the recently completed E. M. Barry wing at the National Gallery. As a result, the manner in which the art works were displayed evoked an association with a museum rather than a dealer's gallery or the Academy. This distinction further underscored the differentiation of the exhibited art from that seen in other more conventional venues. Another later innovation was the installation of electric lighting in 1882.

Due to their aristocratic and moneyed background, Sir Coutts and his wife were in the position to target and accommodate an elite clientele.[49] The Royal Academy, as far as the social composition of its visitors was concerned, had long lost any aura of exclusivity and become 'too vulgar'.[50] Moreover, since London had thus far no gallery specifically catering to the upper classes, that niche was vacant. In fact, the very design of the Grosvenor gallery's exterior and interior suggests that filling this function must have been a key component of Sir Coutts's business plan. From New Bond Street, the site of numerous other commercial galleries, the visitor entered through an imposing original Palladian portal that once graced one of the entrances of the Church of Santa Lucia in Venice.[51] The palatial dimensions of the doorway as well as its Manneristic style harmonized with the neo-Renaissance façade of the building. Inside, a richly decorated columned hallway, divided into nave and aisles, guided the patrons towards a wide set of steps flanked by pedestals for statues and from there to the other spaces of the gallery's vast interior. The overall impression was one of entering a palatial English country house, an Italian *palazzo* or Parisian *hôtel*.[52] Within just two months after the Grosvenor Gallery's opening on 1 May 1877, the press acknowledged the persuasiveness of Lindsay's effectively differentiated exhibition design concept by describing his undertaking in a poem entitled 'The palace of Art (New Version), Part I.' and likening Sir Coutts to one of the greatest aristocratic patrons, the Medici Pope Leo X.[53] The aura of upper class surroundings was further emphasized by the inclusion of several smoking rooms and one for billiard. The latter, by the 1870s, had become almost a standard feature in an English country home.[54] Moreover, one of the leading supporters of the gallery, the Prince of Wales, was a noted cigars aficionado, and his passion for a good smoke was quite contagious among fashionable men.[55] Other amenities included a restaurant with a license to serve alcoholic beverages – rare in London at the time and of particular appeal to upper class ladies – as well as a circulating library. While the latter two facilities were not among those one would expect to find in an aristocratic private home, such services were nevertheless part of the marketing strategy designed to attract elite visitors to the gallery. They were also potentially lucrative sources of additional revenue. Sir Coutts claimed that the restaurant served on average between three hundred to four hundred people a day.[56] During the 1880s, again imitating fashionable society's customs and continuing the policy of augmenting marketing via extra-curricular attractions, the gallery also staged regular musical concerts and in 1885 even hosted one such event with Franz Liszt.[57]

Another important distinction was the de-emphasis of anything that might be reminiscent of the commercial art trade. Most likely, the type of clientele targeted by the organization would have taken offense at the more aggressive sales pitches of a Flatou or Gambart, and it is further testimony of Sir Coutts's marketing savvy, that he adjusted his business accordingly. One had to refer to the catalogues to determine which paintings were available for purchase, and only an inquiry with the secretary of the gallery disclosed the price.

The general aura of upper class exclusivity that was part of Lindsay's image strategy brought about another novel institution within the gallery, the establishment of a numerically restricted circle of supporting members. In addition to the real benefit of special seasonal tickets that granted admission at any time, including Sundays, this group, limited to no more than five hundred individuals, could enjoy the prestige of refined and exclusive cultural patronage surrounded by their peers. Furthermore, each member of this set was a potential sales representative who could invite others from her or his social circle to patronize the gallery and its other facilities.

The type of art that was promoted through this superbly constructed marketing venue was an equally well-considered selection of works by celebrity artists from both within and outside the establishment mixed with examples of the emerging avant-garde. This heterogeneous mixture effectively helped to legitimize the fringe by association with the establishment. Unlike the RA, the Lindsays actively solicited artists to exhibit at the Grosvenor. This practice not only gave them greater control over the type of art they wanted to display, but it also avoided the pitfalls connected with the rejection of an artist's work. Furthermore, being able to possess artworks personally chosen by the 'modern day Lorenzo', as Walter Crane called Sir Coutts, was far more prestigious than owning one which only criteria was that it had not been rejected by a committee.[58]

Visitors to the Grosvenor could admire paintings by celebrated Academicians like Millais, Leighton or Hunt juxtaposed with decidedly anti-establishment canvases by Whistler and others of the Aesthetic circle around him. At the same time, commercial successes like Alma-Tadema and Tissot were also invited to exhibit. So were relatively unknown artists from the Continent, such as the German Karl Schloesser (1811–86) or the distinctly unique French painter, Gustave Moreau (1826–98). Auguste Rodin (1840–1917) showed a bronze mask in 1882, and some of Fantin-Latour's (1836–1904) exquisite florals could also be found there. In the later years, even works by the Irish and London Impressionist circles as well as the Glasgow Boys were offered for sale at the gallery. The one artist whose career was perhaps most closely identified with the gallery was Burne-Jones (1833–98). Strongly anti-Academy in his attitude, he contributed not only his name recognition but also his group of followers of second generation Pre-Raphaelites, like Rodham Spencer Stanhope (1829–1908), Melhuish Strudwick (1849–1935), or Evelyn Pickering De Morgan (1850–1919) and Marie Stillman (1844–1927).

While there was an obvious and close association of the Grosvenor with the Aesthetic set, Sir Coutts once again demonstrated his remarkable understanding of modern public relations and marketing with his decision to include distinctly mainstream painters chosen from the ranks of the Academy as well as works by artists outside of either circle. Rather than limiting his enterprise to promoting one style, he created an umbrella business with which to market a broad range of paintings from old masters during the annual winter exhibitions to decidedly advanced contemporary works from the Continent. All these works had in common Sir Linday's and the Grosvenor Gallery's hallmark of approval, the principle product his enterprise sold.

Although many of the innovative practices instituted by his gallery indeed resembled those used by present day contemporary art museums, they do so because of certain shared underlying economics rather than due to a kinship of cultural mission.

There is no doubt that the Grosvenor Gallery was a business, not a museum. Sir Coutts, heir to a landed fortune and related to two banking houses – the Rothschild through marriage and Coutts Bank by blood – was quite clear about this issue. In an interview he gave to the *Pall Mall Gazette* in response to his former associates' Carr and Halle letter to *The Times* in which they addressed certain grievances, the Grosvenor's owner stated 'I wanted no profit; but I did look to some interest for my capital – some rental, at least from the building. It is all very well to say, "what has money got to do with art?" but you cannot keep a gallery going nor buy pictures without it'.[59]

Several aspects of the above statement warrant a closer look. His rejection of profit, in the making of which no member of the upper class should be involved, was part of the same image maintenance Lindsay consistently employed since the inception of this enterprise. How else to distinguish it, and by extension his clientele, from the profit-making picture merchants and their common country-accented customers? Interest on capital, however, particularly in the form of rent, was the accepted form of income for the aristocracy. Of course, no mention of an amount of this rent is made, but he does state that his overall financial outlay since the beginning totalled 'something like £200,000'.[60] With average annual revenues of £7,000 from commissions on pictures and catalogue sales and 50 per cent of this sum going to expenses, the remaining amount represents a less than 2 per cent return on Sir Coutts's capital investment.[61] If one assumes that he, as a landowner, had to borrow all or part of this amount at interest rates exceeding the return he received, the revenue-augmenting, extra-curricular activities for which he was criticized take on a different light: they were, in fact, necessary subsidies to keep the nascent enterprise financially afloat.

Therefore, to understand this gallery and its role in the arts environment of the era, it must be analyzed as a commercial undertaking, not as a museum. Sir Coutts was in the process of building an enterprise similar to today's luxury goods houses, such as Tiffany, Cartier or Gucci, whose trademark names validate, and even create demand for, a wide variety of products regardless of 'style'. Like these businesses, Sir Coutts aimed to establish a trade name, the association with which, be that as a producer, product, or as a consumer, would be synonymous with quality, class, refinement, taste, etc., in other words, all those things that promote the consumption of luxury goods.

This type of art enterprise was quite new. The Lindsays were in the unique position to target the most affluent circles of English society. To do so, they created physical surroundings designed not just to set the business apart visually from other competing galleries, but to cater to, and attract, a specific market. From this 'Palace of Art', England's 'modern day Lorenzo', assisted by his wife, sold cultural luxury goods sanctioned by his approval to those who were, or desired to be, part of his elite circle.

For the art historian, the Grosvenor Gallery was England's first exhibition facility through which many of the new ideas concerning art were disseminated. In these prestigious surroundings in the centre of the commercial art world many of the English and a number of foreign painters whose works reflected the growing influence of Continental ideas were first able to exhibit. Credit must also be given to the Grosvenor for building an international reputation for several of its artists. Particularly Burne-Jones benefited from the worldwide scope of Sir Coutts's marketing. To that end, it was most fortuitous that the Prince of Wales, an avid supporter and personal friend of Sir Coutts, asked him to serve on the jury that selected the painters to represent England at the Exposition Universelle in Paris in 1877, just one year after the Grosvenor's inaugural exhibition. Moreover, Sir Coutts's assistant, Comyns Carr, functioned as the English editor of the popular French periodical *L'Art* from 1877 to 1883 to promote the very artists who exhibited at the Grosvenor.[62] In his first article for the magazine, he informed his readers that the gallery was established because the Royal Academy did not provide an accurate representation of the present state of contemporary English painting.[63] This juxtaposition of the Grosvenor Gallery with the official institution suggested to the readers that the new enterprise was indeed not only an equal of the over one hundred year old Academy but, in fact, the true showcase – as well as commercial outlet – of present-day English art.

Promoting English painters in general in France was much needed. After Arrowsmith and Schroth discontinued their patronage of Constable, French dealer support for English painting, essential to building international demand, virtually collapsed. The occasional presence at the Salon of a few works from across the Channel was insufficient to maintain a market.

In these respects, The Grosvenor Gallery's ambitions towards establishing a foothold in the French art market were an example of missed business opportunities. The gallery's reasons for not following through with concrete action after having established a presence and name-recognition in France through the editorship of Carr are impossible to reconstruct. After the broad exposure in France of English art as a result of the 1878 Exposition Universelle, Sir Coutts could have established a commercial liaison with a French dealer to continue promoting and selling the Grosvenor's stable of artists. Of course, such arrangements would have been accompanied by financial and logistical challenges that may have dissuaded Sir Coutts from launching such a complex undertaking. However, the fact that in 1888, the year after Carr's and Halle's resignation from the Grosvenor, he hired the ex-Parisian, Charles W. Deschamps, who, as the former manager of Durand-Ruel's London branch, was well-connected in France, might well reflect a renewed interest on Sir Coutts's part in establishing a commercial connection in Paris. Why this never came to fruition, or if it was ever even considered, remains conjecture. Had such plans materialized, they may well have changed the international reputation of many of the painters who have come to be identified with the Grosvenor.

The ultimate failure of this business was not due to a flaw in Sir Coutts's plan, but was instead due to the inability of key managers and several popular artists to appreciate the necessary link between sound economics and art. As a result, they did not support him in the crucial task of developing the revenues necessary to subsidize the enterprise's art dealing side until the latter could stand on its own. Even in the absence of detailed business accounts, the above mere cursory look at the financial side of this undertaking shows that subsidy at this stage was essential. Furthermore, as Halle mentioned, around 1884, Sir Coutts experienced some personal monetary difficulties due to 'domestic differences'.[64] Most likely, he was referring to the fact that Lady Lindsay who, after separating from her husband in 1882, had withdrawn her investment in the gallery shortly thereafter. This must have put additional strain on Sir Coutt's financial resources. Halle, Carr, Burne-Jones, accompanied by his group of Pre-Raphaelites, and together with the commercially successful Classicists left the Grosvenor in 1887 strongly objecting to the evidently increasing extra-curricular activities Sir Coutts undertook to generate revenues needed to keep the art dealing division financially afloat.[65] Lindsay had 'found it imperative to place the Grosvenor in the hands of businessmen ... since the gallery no longer paid its way and was in danger of a collapse'.[66] Since the gallery was a business with a substantial amount of his personal capital at stake, Sir Coutts's decision seems prudent. Nonetheless, neither his associates nor the disgruntled painters were convinced by such financial reasoning and departed to launch their own venture, the New Gallery. By 1890, Sir Coutts was no longer in the position to subsidize his enterprise, and the Grosvenor Gallery closed its doors permanently.

For the business historian, the Grosvenor Gallery represents not just a prototype of the earlier mentioned luxury goods houses but also a further illustration of niche marketing facilitated by changes in the art market. Moreover, the gallery exemplifies another new product in the market of exhibition venues. The earlier mentioned barriers that kept certain producers of art from unrestricted participation in the exchange mechanism had to yield under the pressure of the market's continuing commoditization. In the case of the Grosvenor, this led to the introduction and dissemination of new ideas that radically changed our concepts of art.

Even among the relatively progressive group of painters who exhibited at the Grosvenor, evidence could be found for the economic decline of the more traditional artists and the advance of those who heralded the future. A statistical comparison between Burne-Jones who, as the leader of the second generation Pre-Raphaelite, represented the old guard, and Whistler as an envoy of the new direction, corroborates the anecdotal accounts of change. During the decade from 1886 to 1896, the average auction price of Burne-Jones's paintings was £1,210; then between 1897 and 1910, the figure dropped to £551. Whistler, however, saw his average price increase from £116 to £373 respectively. Clearly, Burne-Jones was falling out of favour, although he apparently still commanded prices substantially higher than Whistler. Yet Burne Jones's paintings tended to be larger than Whistlers: the former's average size was around 2,000 square inches while the latter's works averaged only 195 square inches. This large difference in average size calls for an analysis that examines the two artists' paintings under the common denominator of average price per square inch. The yield of Burne-Jones's labour declined from £1.04/square inch to £0.5 during the above outlined time periods. In the case of Whistler, however, the figure increases from £0.6/square inch to £1.9 – nearly four times as much as Burne-Jones.

Applying this price per square inch comparison outside the Grosvenor circle to an even more typical representative of high Victorian art makes the decline even more evident. Edwin Long (1829–91), whose monumental *Babylonian Marriage Market*, measuring 68 x 120 inches (http://artmarket.tulane.edu/page107.html) was bought from the walls of the RA in 1875 for £7,350, typified the High Victorian period. His imitation of the success formula of his celebrated competitor, Alma-Tadema, was commercially very effective: Long refused an offer of £5,250 for his *Parable of the Sower* (1891) just before he died in his luxurious home on Fitzjohn's Avenue.[67] Whistler, on the other hand, was told during the famous trial of 1878 that his impressionistic *Nocturne in Black and Blue*, exhibited in the same year, was not worth the asking price of £200. But the tide was turning. Edwin Long's works were typically quite large and highly detailed, suitable for traditional reproduction; his average canvas size was around 50 x 62 inches, or 3,100 square inches, while his overall average auction price was £724, or £0.23/square inch. Whistler's much more painterly works were substantially smaller and also much less expensive. In this case as well, average prices over time show that Long's prices were in decline while Whistler's were increasing. The former's highest sums were realized between 1880 and 1885, when his average prices hit a high of £1,180 or £0.38/square inch; from 1886 to 1889 this figure plummeted to £373 or £0.12/square inch, and it further declined to £198 or

£0.06/square inch during the first decade of the new century, a time when Whistler commanded £1.91/square inch.

Several observations can be made from the above data. Firstly, they confirm that size and direct monetary return of artistic labour were indirectly proportional: the larger a painting, the less was the price per unit of size. Yet the exhibition system, as it functioned during the High Victorian period, still demanded that painters create works of monumental size. However, once the structure of the market changed and mass-marketing of reproductive engravings stopped being a reliable source of income for painters and/or profitable for middlemen, the main economic *raison d'être* of the High Victorian 'sensation' pictures disappeared and, as the example of Long shows, their value plummeted. Secondly, the deterioration of the economic foundation of the engraving market provided impetus for the production of works intended to replace the lost income from derivatives. On average smaller in size, more painterly and quicker to execute, such paintings, while much less expensive to middlemen and end consumers, had for the artists the potential of yielding greater financial returns per input unit of labour than the time-consuming 'sensation' piece. In this manner as well, the decline of the 'cash cow' of the mid-Victorian art boom translated into new opportunities for producers and dealers and paved the way for the introduction of altogether new aesthetics.

Several caveats should be offered here. The market for typical High Victorian pictures did not collapse overnight and economic theory does not provide all the answers. Alma-Tadema, for example, still occasionally commanded high prices as late as 1912. Purchases by the Chantrey Bequest, which were chosen exclusively from the walls of the Royal Academy, also subsidized the old school.[68] However, the last two decades of the nineteenth century witnessed the wholesale decline of the kind of paintings that had characterized the preceding half-century and the emergence of a new type. The juxtaposition of Long and Whistler is but one illustration. Similar observations could be made by comparing, for example, the price histories of Degas and Frith, or Millet and Landseer.

The Long-Whistler comparison also illustrates the effects of a trend that had started in the early years of the century when Léthiere and Gericault first sought fame and fortune in England through public exhibitions of their paintings. French artists found the economics of the English art market with its relative independence from the traditional patronage of church and state sources appealing. By the late 1860s, there existed a sizeable and growing community of Continental artists who had followed Whistler's footsteps from Paris to London where many of the leading London dealers like Agnew, Wallis, the new owner of the French Gallery, Tooth or McLean had an established trade in pictures from the Continent. The French dealers Goupil and Durand-Ruel joined these painters and attempted with mixed success to sell their own stable of artists to the

London audience.[69] While the haphazard exposure of such radically different paintings in London was not an immediate economic threat to native English artists, it must have stimulated greater awareness among the art consuming public of alternative pictorial modes and thus contributed to the gradual erosion of the general consensus on taste. The Whistler – Long evaluation quantifies this development. Had Durand-Ruel had the benefit of the kind of well-oiled marketing machine that Tooth and his network offered, the history of French Impressionism, not just in England, might well have turned out differently.

In addition to new aesthetic concepts introduced by native English and Continental artist, the demise of the reproductive engraving industry and its chief marketing tool, the sensation picture exhibition, London's contemporary painting market was also affected by a substitution effect that redirected the attention of dealers and consumers to the detriment of the financial fate of contemporary painters. Our data show that, while the old master market had also undergone an increase in average prices since the 1840s, it was far less dramatic than the appreciation experienced by contemporary paintings. Old master paintings had never entirely disappeared from the public's eye during the 'Golden Age' of contemporary painters. Recurring exhibitions of such works were, for instance, held at the British Institute. Furthermore, the 1857 exhibition in Manchester featured some of the greatest examples of old masters in English collections as did the 1868 exhibition in Leeds. In London, the Burlington Art Club staged a showing of old masters in 1871, and the Royal Academy began regular exhibitions of such works in 1870. Yet in spite of such exposure, prices were depressed. During the 1850s, the same decade when Hunt and Frith commanded prices between £5,000 and £10,000 for their major works, the National Gallery paid £210 for Rubens's *Horrors of War.* Rembrandt's average price was around £350,[70] while Reynolds's and Gainsborough's paintings fetched an average for the decade of £125 and £58, respectively. The market underwent, in this respect, a correction between 1875 and 1885. The disastrous sale at Christie's in June 1883 of the contemporary painting collection owned by the Catalan banker Jose Murietta, the Marquis de Santurce, can serve as a symbolic turning point. Over 70 per cent of the works by a representative roster of artistic stars of the period, failed to reach their reserves. The dealers Agnew, Foster, Vokins and McLean were the only buyers of note. Although the complete collapse of this market was still several decades away, the inevitable decline had begun. Old masters were cheap in comparison, chiefly due to the price-depressing effect of the *Art Journal's* earlier-described persistent campaign against fraudulent old master dealers and the inflationary aspects inherent in the boom in contemporary paintings. Furthermore, the necessary investments middlemen had to make to remain profitable in the contemporary market had spiralled to such heights that together with the aforementioned changes in the print market and their effects on exhibition revenues, the risk/earnings ratio had ceased to be attractive. The passage of the Settled Lands Act in 1882, which permitted the disposal of land and chattels free of tax, provided that the proceeds remained in trust, added further pressures on this market. The Act allowed heirs of the great landed estates of England to pay taxes and other expenses related to the maintenance of their inherited properties from revenues generated through sales of suitably liquid assets of these estates. As a result, a great number of old master works with impeccable provenances came onto the market and attracted the attention of powerful dealers like Agnew and the colourful newcomer, Joseph Duveen.[71] Comparatively undervalued and relatively ignored during the boom years of contemporary art, these paintings had excellent earning potential and were profitably sold to a new type of pedigree-hungry collector, the American industrial millionaire.

Dealer patronage of living artists continued but the Golden Age, the economic boom, of High Victorian painting had run its course. The new economics of the market asked for different products and different ways of marketing.

In an emotional diatribe against this new art, Holman Hunt wrote in 1905:

> Of late years continental taste has been asserting itself injuriously amongst us making familiar and commonplace what else was outlandish and abhorrent to the inheritors of healthy and sturdy English tradition ... man is told by dealers in modern materialistic fantasy that ... virtuous effort on his part is simply futile ... Wild revolt shows itself in the art of our day ... Undoubtedly many of the works ... have no evidence of sober common-sense; they are without perspective, correct form, or any signs of patient drilling and scholarship ... the hideous canvases often appearing in exhibitions in recent days, chaotic in form, of sullied pigment plastered on offensively ... their makers are now the nucleus of an obtrusive party in the art world, and being a standing peril to honest and honourable art ... The critics trained under the same libertinage naturally ridicule the creed that art should perform a wholesome and divine service to humanity.[72]

These few sentences contain the obituary of his age. Collectors, dealers, artists and critics collectively rejected and replaced all that Holman Hunt and his art stood for.[73]

11 POSTSCRIPT: A PERPETUAL INNOVATIVE WHIRL

Oh, the days which we sold pictures in
Are still to mem'ry dear.
Though they have vanished into space
For many a weary year.
We ne'er shall see their like again,
Nor prices get like those
With which the eager buyer would
Incontinently close.
Now feel we hardness of the times,
Our debts still daily grow;
Ah, the days which we sold pictures in,
A long time ago!

Henry Stacy Marks, *Pen and Pencil Sketches*

Unlike Holman Hunt's bitter attack on the new art scene cited at the end of the preceding chapter, the painter Henry Stacy Marks (1829–98), in his typically humorous fashion, looked back and eulogized the heady days of the 'Golden Age of Living Painters'. Indeed, an era had passed which had taken the production of painting to an unprecedented level. The confluence of the diverse interests of which the arts environment is composed and which lies at the root of the mid-Victorian boom was inherently unstable. This coming of age of the market for contemporary paintings brought artists, dealers, press and consumers together for a several-decade long celebration of art production and consumption. When the party was over, the guests left alone or in groups, but much richer for the experience. The now mature market continued to adapt, applying and refining the lessons of its youth. As it continued to expand with all its components now firmly in place, the exchange mechanism for art became more complex and diverse.

The modern discussion on the benefits of art to society in general that started with Shaftesbury and the related concerns of civic humanism in the eighteenth century has reached a consensus, certainly among economists, that art is a 'good' thing for society. As a result, taxpayer subsidized art events are being recognized as expenditures that yield greater economic benefit than cost.

The seeds for these phenomena were planted by native English painters at the beginning of the eighteenth century when the combination of declining traditional patronage and the emergence of an affluent urban commercial class challenged them to explore alternative means to gain financial returns from their labour. In many ways, the preceding discussion tells the story of the agency of artists in a new and modern commercial world. In a larger context, however, it is also the story of the economic emancipation of the individual in an emerging consumer society under free market conditions. The tenacity and ingenuity with which these producers of cultural luxury goods established themselves in social and economic terms, dispels the notion that artistic temper and sound business thinking are incompatible or worse, mutually destructive. Moreover, the paintings produced for the market, that is, with the specific intention to sell, were by no means qualitatively inferior. Quite to the contrary, the great richness of varieties in style, aesthetic persuasions, and content – in short, the great kaleidoscope in the visual arts which emerged during the nineteenth century – must be, to varying degrees, credited to the economic conditions under which these paintings were created. Along the path towards the realization of their economic opportunities, painters reinvented their occupation as well as their product. Unable to continue to exist under the relative security of the earlier system of direct patronal support, they became free agents responsible, not just for all phases of design and production, but also initially for the distribution of a luxury good in an anonymous and highly competitive market. To this freedom, with all its inherent challenges, we owe much of the diversity of creative expression then and now.

At the same time, a new player emerged in the arts environment, the dealer in contemporary art, whose very existence was a direct consequence of the success painters had in establishing themselves as independent entrepreneurs. Ever since this specialized trade came about in England in the early years of the nineteenth century, it has grown, as the new dispenser of patronage, to ever increasing importance. The influence and power of middlemen as agents in the arts environment was, and still is, equally praised and condemned. However, without the institutionalization of the dealer in contemporary art, and the economic function played by the trade in promoting and disseminating cultural products, the expansion of the market, both in terms of diversity and quality, would have been less.

As one of the consequences, theories of art have vastly multiplied to a dizzying number of 'isms' and now embrace works that are no longer physically made by the artists who claim authorship. Art and corresponding theory have become inseparable and essential to each other to the point where certain art products' distinction becomes manifest only through its associated theory. Countless artist groups, exhibition societies and art schools compete for attention, each trying to express and market its distinct identity. The demand for innovation that accelerated as a consequence of the institutionalization and rapid expansion of fixed location retail galleries has even measurably changed artists' age-price profiles.[1] Now 'masterpieces' are created by artists in their twenties, and the notion of youthful and radically innovative genius has become standard sales talk.

The all important 'sensation' pictures concept is mirrored in the 1997 'Sensation' show of Young British Artists from the Saatchi collection that included Damien Hirst's shark in formaldehyde and Chris Ofili's infamous elephant dung Madonna. Moreover, Giclee technology has created a renaissance of the sensation picture/publishing enterprise. Painters are again able to create time-consuming oversized attention-getters and then sell near perfect computer-generated reproductions that are marketed under the same artificial scarcity concept used by London's Print Seller Association in the nineteenth century. The pictorial showmanship pioneered by Copley came back in another form as Christo's vast enterprises, which are entirely financed by derivative products. 'Blockbuster' museum shows rely heavily on sales of related merchandize, and their promotional and public relations efforts take the lessons of Edward Bernays fully into account.[2] Similarly, Hogarth's recognition of the merits of coupling humanitarianism with art is echoed in actor Brad Pitt's Pink Project (2007) in the flood-ravaged Ninth Ward of New Orleans.

The near monopoly status of Christie's gave way to a near duopoly of Christie's and Sotheby's working in tandem bordering on collusion. Market-making and regulatory measures are employed by dealers and auction houses to manage the flood of second rate Impressionists resulting from the collapse of the Japanese real estate bubble in the 1980s or the forced sales of contemporary art resulting from the financial crisis of 2008–10. Dealers and auction firms are well aware of the publicity element inherent to auction sales and employ it to their advantage in a manner similar to that of their Victorian predecessors. Auction firms again compete for consignments by offering advances on certain works of art if sold through them, a scheme that not only is fraught with potential pitfalls, but also jeopardizes their impartiality.

Furthermore, the securitization of art is well underway. Indexes are compiled, complex analyses are published and the results are used to devise collecting strategies. A new breed of art advisors professionally manage collections and lend specific works to appropriate exhibitions to add much prized provenance. Promoting a carefully cultivated exclusivity, the leading such firms screen potential clients before accepting them and will also sever their relationship if clients do not follow the outlined collecting strategy. Dealers now sell 'programmes' rather than simply works from their stable of artists.[3] In the financial industry, specialized lending institutions now finance new purchases and make loans collateralized by works of art. Efforts are in progress to create trading platforms for art financed by venture capital in order to compete with the auction industry.

It was our intention to introduce a methodologically different way to search for plausible answers to a few of the questions we face as historians in our efforts to seek some sort of order in the apparent disarray of our past. This method – the use of models and quantifications to facilitate analyses – has been successfully applied in the field of social history, anthropology, and economics and by now has become a conventional tool of analytical investigation. The application of conceptual models can easily raise the spectre of economic or social determinism. Such criticism, however, is misplaced because, rather than seeking answers in large, abstract, social, political, or philosophical trends, the very nucleus of our inquiries is the individual and the assumption that most of us have a common desire to survive, to better ourselves, to improve our economic and, often, our social status, to gain recognition and acceptance among our peers and to be in charge of our own fate. In spite of the overused term 'market forces', economies are not driven by abstract powers. These mysterious 'market forces' are merely the compounded effects of choices made by individuals when faced with specific circumstances. The assumption that inherent to the exchange function of every economy is a built-in force driving the exchange system towards increasing commoditization is simply another way of stating that those of us involved in the exchange of goods and/or services in a free market generally endeavour to facilitate that exchange and modify our actions or products to that end. Similarly, the search for new opportunities, whatever form it may take, is not due to some *abstract* (our emphasis) internal logic of exchange, but the result of human agency without which no voluntary exchange takes place.

In view of the apparent disorder of human action and contrary social and ideological forces, the application of diverse theoretical constructs taken from different academic fields and adapted for art history thus helped us bring some degree of coherence to our attempt to investigate the genesis of the modern British art market as an historical phenomenon. It also gave us new insight into many of the pictures and picture types characteristic as well as atypical of this era. Beyond that, it suggested a framework under which to examine the art produced in other periods, past and present. Moreover, the association of these models with statistical and micro-econometric information contained in our data, revealed on-going trends, cyclical tendencies and structural changes, which have relevance today. Most importantly, however, our economic approach confirms the market for art to be a 'perpetual innovative whirl' capable of stimulating extraordinary levels of human creativity.

NOTES

Introduction

1. H. Floerke, *Studien zur Niederlandischen Kunstgeschichte* (Munchen and Leipzig: Georg Muller, 1905), pp. 6, 67 mentions art dealing activities in Bruges as early as 1450. Also De Marchi and Van Miegroet, 'Rules Versus Play in Early Modern Art Markets', *Louvain Economic Review* 66 (2000), pp. 146–8. In 1508, the Antwerp St Lucas Guild was granted the right to conduct periodic public auctions. Floerke, pp. 38, 42, 44; also G. F. Koch, *Die Kunstausstellung* (Berlin: Walter de Gruyter & Co., 1967), p. 67. By 1540, the city of Antwerp provided artists and art dealers with a permanent facility for the sale of paintings on the upper gallery of the Antwerp stock exchange. Floerke, pp. 8–9. N. De Marchi and H. J. van Miegroet, in V. Ginsburgh (ed.), 'The History of Art Markets', *Handbook of the Economics of Art and Culture* (Amsterdam: Elsevier, 2006), vol. 1, pp. 69–122, pp. 73–7, suggest similar dates for Florence.
2. F. Haskell, *Patrons and Painters* (New Haven, CT and London: Yale University Press, 1980). This book represents the first systematic attempt to relate the art of a particular period to the patronal environment in which it was produced. Haskell emphasizes that he deliberately avoided any attempt to 'explain art in terms of patronage' (p. viii) and stresses the risk in writing about a subject which 'falls half way between History and Art History' (p. ix).
3. C. and H. White, *Canvases and Careers: Institutional Changes in the French Painting World* (Chicago, IL: University of Chicago Press, 1965); N. Green, 'Dealing in Temperaments: Economic Transformation of the Artistic Field in France during the Second Half of the Nineteenth Century', *Art History*, 10:1 (March 1987), pp. 59–76; R. Goldthwaite, *Wealth and the Demand for Art in Italy, 1300–1600* (Baltimore, MD: The Johns Hopkins University Press, 1993); M. Montias, *Artists and Artisans in Delft: a Socio-Economic Study of the Seventeenth Century* (New York: Princeton University Press, 1983), his 'Art Dealers in the Seventeenth Century Netherlands', *Simiolus* 18:4; N. De Marchi and H. J. Van Miegroet (eds), *Mapping Markets for Paintings in Europe, 1450–1750* (Turnhout, Belgium: Brepols Publishers n.v., 2006); D. Galenson, *Painting outside the Line* (Cambridge, MA.: Harvard University Press, 2001); D. Galenson and R. Jensen, 'Careers and Canvases; the Rise of the Market for Modern Art in Nineteenth-Century France', *Current Issues in 19th-Century Art*, Van Gogh Studies 1 (2007), pp. 137–66. R. Jansen, *Marketing Modernism in Fin-de-Siecle Europe* (Princeton, NJ: Princeton University Press, 1994). This list is by no means complete.

4. For example, J. Warren and A. Turpin (eds), *Auctions, Agents and Dealers* (Oxford and London: The Beazley Archive and Archaeopress in association with The Wallace Collection, 2008).
5. S. N. Behrman, *Duveen* (New York: Random House, 1952), pp. 30–1.
6. J. Schumpeter, *Capitalism, Socialism and Democracy*, 3rd edn (New York: Harper, 1950), p. 95.
7. A. Graves, *Art Sales from early in the Eighteenth Century to early in the Twentieth Century*, 3vols (New York: Burt Franklin, 1970); G. Redford, *Art Sales: A History of Sales of Pictures & Other Works of Art* (London: 1888).
8. Thanks go to Jeremy Rex-Parkes and Lynda Mcleod. Their warm welcome at Christie's archives, their supportive attitude and superb English wit was as helpful as the unimpeded access to the archive's collection of catalogues.
9. A. Bredius, *Künstler-Inventare; Urkunden zur Geschichte der Holländischen Kunst des XVIten, XVIIten und XVIIIten Jahrhunderts* (The Hague: M. Nijhoff, 1915–1922), 7 volumes and index; also above, p. 2, n. 3 and A. Chong, 'The Market for Landscape Painting in Seventeenth-Century Holland', P. Sutton (ed.), *Masters of the Seventeenth Century Dutch Landscape Painting* (Boston, MA: Boston Museum of Fine Art, 1987).
10. The regressions used the log of the transaction prices to improve the statistical results. The coefficients are therefore difficult to interpret. Our primary interest here was the statistical differences between groups.

1 The Early Stages: From the Netherlands to Great Britain

1. D. Wolfthal, *The Beginning of Netherlandish Canvas Painting: 1400–1530* (Cambridge: Cambridge University Press, 1989), pp. 12–13.
2. Floerke, *Studien zur Niederländischen Kunstgeschichte,* pp. 129–34, 154–5, 158; K. van Mander, *Dutch and Flemish Painters* (New York: MacFarlane, Warde, MacFarlane, 1936), pp. 158–60.
3. Chong, 'The Market for Landscape Painting in Seventeenth-Century Holland', pp. 104–20.
4. P. Stabel, 'Selling Paintings in Late Medieval Bruges: Marketing Customs and Guild Regulations Compared', in De Marchi and Miegroet (eds), *Mapping Markets for Paintings in Europe, 1450–1750*, pp. 90–3. De Marchi and Miegroet, 'The History of Art Markets', pp. 69–122, pp. 86–90.
5. L. Campbell, 'The Art Market in the Southern Netherlands in the Fifteenth Century', *Burlington Magazine*, 118 (March 1976), pp. 188–98 and J. C. Wilson, 'The Participation of Painters in the Bruges' "Pandt" Market, 1512–1550', *Burlington Magazine* 125 (August 1983), pp. 476–9; on export trade of dealers, J. M. Montias, 'Flemish and Dutch Trade in Works of Art in the 16th and 17th Centuries', *Institution for Social and Policy Studies* (Cambridge: Yale University Press, 1985), working paper no. 1022; on art dealers in the seventeenth-century see, Montias, 'Art Dealers in the Seventeenth-Century Netherlands', *Simiolus*, 18:4, pp. 244–56.
6. I. Kopytoff, 'The Cultural Biography of Things: Commoditization as Process', in A. Appadurai (ed.), *The Social Life of Things: Commodities in Cultural Perspective* (Cambridge, MA: Yale University Press, 1986), pp. 64–91; quote, p. 87.
7. On commodity and commoditization in art see P. Wood, 'Commodity', in R. S. Nelson and R. Shiff (eds), *Critical Terms for Art History* (Chicago, IL: University of Chicago Press, 1966), pp. 257–80.
8. E. Romein and G. Korevaar, 'Dutch Guilds and the Threat of Public Sales' in De Marchi and Miegroet (eds), *Mapping Markets for Paintings in Europe, 1450–1750*, pp. 165–84.

9. Montias, *Artists and Artisans in Delft*, pp. 263–4, and 'Art Dealers in the Seventeenth Century Netherlands', p. 245. More recently, F. Vermeylen, *Painting for the Market: Commercialization of Art in Antwerp's Golden Age* (Turnhout, Belgium: Brepols, n.v., 2003), pp. 15–109.
10. Stabel, 'Selling Paintings in Late Medieval Bruges: Marketing Customs and Guild Regulations Compared', especially p. 94.
11. Ormrod, 'The Art Trade and its Urban Context: England and the Netherlands compared, 1550–1750', in J. Warren and A. Turpin (eds), *Auctions, Agents and Dealers*, pp. 11–19, p. 13 and n. 21.
12. Campbell, 'The Art Market in the Southern Netherlands in the Fifteenth Century', p. 191, referring to van Mander who mentions frequent challenges to these regulations and to the guild system as a whole. Recent research suggests that guilds tried to control the new marketing system of paintings and ultimately adopted them. Romein and Korevaar, 'Dutch Guilds and the Threat of Public Sales', pp. 177–83.
13. N. de Marchi and H. Van Miegroet, 'Art, Value and Market Price in the Netherlands in the Seventeenth Century', *Art Bulletin*, 76 (1994), pp. 451–64, p. 452.
14. Ormrod, 'The Art Trade and its Urban Context', pp. 11–12 and n. 9.
15. J. M. Montias, Cost and Value in Seventeenth-Century Dutch Art', *Art History*, 10 (December 1987), pp. 455–66, on pp. 463–4.
16. J. van Gool, *De Nieuwe Schouburgh der Nederlantische Kunstschilders en Schilderessen*, 2 vols (The Hague: 1750), vol. 1, pp. 105, 360–1, vol. 2, pp. 112–13.
17. H. Walpole, *Anecdotes of Painting in England*, 3 vols (London: Henry G. Bohn, 1849), vol. 1, ix, commenting that 'Flanders and Holland have sent us the greatest men that we can boast'.
18. J. Evelyn, *Diary & Correspondence of John Evelyn, Frs.*, ed. W. Bray (London: G. Bell and Sons, 1883–7), p. 15.
19. As late as 1645, Parliament ordered the destruction of religious paintings and sculptures. R. Redgrave, *A Century of Painters of the English School* (London: Sampson Low, Marston & Company, Ltd., 1890), p. 7. Walpole, *Anecdotes of Painting in England*, vol. 2, p. 426, on the iconoclastic environment in England during the reign of Charles II (1660–85): 'The arts were, in a manner, expelled with the royal family from Britain ... Painting became idolatry ... What the fury of Henri VIII had spared, was condemned by the Puritans: ruin was their harvest ...'
20. Walpole, *Anecdotes of Painting in England*, vol. 2, p. 9: 'While many works of art in England have suffered so greatly from neglect, ignorance, and fanaticism, added to accidental damage and natural decay, the names of our countrymen, to whom many of these works must be assigned, perished with them'. Walpol (in vol. 1, p. ix), further observes that 'this country, which does not always err in vaunting its own production, has not a single volume to show on the works of its painters. In truth, it had rarely given birth to a genius in that profession'.
21. F. Hermann, *The English as Collectors* (New York: W. W. Norton & Co., 1972), p. 9, and n. 1; Redgrave, *A Century of Painters of the English School*, p. 11.
22. Redgrave, *A Century of Painters of the English School*, p. 12, writing that 'Charles II had neither the love for art nor the judgment of his unfortunate parents. He took some pains, however, to secure and collect such of the scattered works of his father's collections as came to his knowledge'.
23. The Navigation Act of 1660 was one of six such acts during the seventeenth century aimed against the Dutch and intended to increase revenues from colonial trade. (The

others were in 1650, 1651, 1663, 1672, and 1696, respectively.) The 1660 Act required that certain colonial goods were to be shipped only to England regardless of the nationality of the carrying vessel. This system of mercantilism ultimately proved too difficult to enforce and the Acts were repealed in 1849 and 1854 in a political climate that favoured free trade.

24. M. Foss, *The Age of Patronage* (Ithaca, NY: Cornell University Press, 1971), pp. 67–9. Redgrave, *A Century of Painters of the English School*, p. 7, mentions the fire of London's destruction of works of art. Viewed under a supply/demand model, the destruction of a limited inventory of art goods signals the market to replace them.
25. Foss, *The Age of Patronage*, p. 74.
26. L. Lippincott, *Selling Art in Georgian London* (New Haven, CT: Yale University Press, 1983), p. 102; I. Pears, *The Discovery of Painting* (New Haven & London: Yale University Press, 1988), pp. 51–5 and n. 20; Redgrave, *A Century of Painters of the English School*, pp. 5–6. W. T. Whitley, *Artists and Their Friends in England 1700–1790* (London & Boston, MA: The Medici Society, 1938), vol. 1, p. 309.
27. Ormrod, 'The Art Trade and its Urban Context', p. 16.
28. S. Hutchison, *The History of the Royal Academy 1768–1968* (London: Robert Royce, Ltd, 1968), pp. 13–14; Lippincott, *Selling Art in Georgian London*, p. 108, mentions the practice of Arthur Pond, painter, dealer and publisher, of providing a written guarantee of authenticity; R. Paulson, *Hogarth: His Life, Art, and Times* (New Haven, CT and London: Yale University Press, 1971), vol. 1, p. 372; vol. 2, p. 330; Pears, *The Discovery of Painting*, p. 100; J. Pye, *Patronage of British Art, A Historical Sketch* (London: Longman, Brown, Green and Longmans, 1845), p. 43, and n. 43, p. 242; D. Solkin, *Painting for Money* (New Haven & London: Yale University Press, 1993), pp. 251, 254–5; J. Steegmann, *The Role of Taste from George I to George IV* (London: MacMillan and Co. Ltd., 1936), p. 27; Walpole, *Anecdotes of Painting in England*, vol. 3, p. 730; Whitley, *Artists and Their Friends in England 1700–1790*, vol. 1, pp. 110, 156, 210.
29. Pye, *Patronage of British Art*, p. 30, and n. 18 and n. 20; Walpole, *Anecdotes of Painting in England*, vol. 2, pp. 643–5; vol. 3, p. 989; Whitley, *Artists and Their Friends in England 1700–1790*, vol. 1, p. 3; Paulson, *Hogarth: His Life, Art, and Time*, vol. 2, pp. 212–13, referring to J. A. Rouquet, *The State of the Arts in England* (London: J. Nourse, 1755).
30. Walpole, *Anecdotes of Painting in England*, vol. 2, pp. 585, 627.
31. Pye, *Patronage of British Art, A Historical Sketch*, p. 44, n. 44.
32. Rouquet, *The State of the Arts in England*, p. 14.
33. Ormrod, 'The Art Trade and its Urban Context', p. 16, table 1; p. 17, n. 41; pp. 18–19.
34. N. De Marchi and H. Van Miegroet, 'Rules Versus Play in Early Modern Art Markets', *Louvain Economic Review*, 66 (2000), pp. 151–2.
35. Pye, *Patronage of British Art, A Historical Sketch*, p. 44, n. 46.
36. Whitley, *Artists and Their Friends in England 1700–1790*, vol. 1, p. 309. Redgrave, *A Century of Painters of the English School*, p. 5, on the frequency at which such works sold at Langford's auction house. Their numbers increased when, by 1721, the regulation, which had previously assessed the duty on art on an ad valorem basis, changed to an evaluation based on size. Also Pears, *The Discovery of Painting*, pp. 51–5, and n. 20; Lippincott, *Selling Art in Georgian London*, p. 102. However, the extent of the impact of tariffs on imported paintings is difficult to assess. See also Rouquet's observation that dealers 'amuse those whom they have access to, with the absurd notion, that a picture becomes more valuable in proportion to its antiquity'. Rouquet, *The State of the Arts in England*, p. 23.

37. Rouquet, *The State of the Arts in England*, pp. 22–3. On imports Rouquet comments that '... the cabinets of the virtuosi contain nothing but foreign pictures, which are generally more considerable for their number than for their excellence'. Pye, *Patronage of British Art, A Historical Sketch*, p. 27, n. 14, cites an article in the *London Magazine* (1737) attributed to Hogarth: 'The picture-jobbers from abroad are always ready to raise a cry in the public prints, whenever they think their craft is in danger; and indeed, it is their interest to depreciate every English work as hurtful to their trade of importing ...'
38. B. Denvir, *The Eighteenth Century* (London and New York: Longman, 1983), pp. 167–9 mentions Rouquet's emphasis of the spectacular growth of the art trade in London.
39. Pye, *Patronage of British Art, A Historical Sketch*, p. 28. Hogarth opined that the British, as a commercial people, were more interested in the trade in art than painting itself. J. Ireland and J. Nichols, *Hogarth's Work* (Edinburgh and London: Oliphant, Anderson & Ferrier, 1874), vol. 3, pp. 64 ff.
40. S. H. A. Bruntjen, *John Boydell (1719–1804) A Study of Art Patronage and Publishing in Georgian London* (New York: Garland Publishing, Inc., 1985), p. 148, and n. 98; Whitley, *Artists and Their Friends in England 1700–1790*, vol. 2, p. 241, mentions that the first raffle of art in England was organized by members of the 'St. Luke's Club', sometimes also called 'Society of Virtuosi' in 1689.
41. Ormrod, 'The Art Trade and its Urban Context', p. 12.
42. Goldthwaite, *Wealth and the Demand for Art in Italy, 1300–1600*, p. 45.
43. N. McKendrick, J. Brewer and J. H. Plumb, *The Birth of a Consumer Society* (London: Europa Publications Limited, 1982).
44. P. Borsay, *The English Urban Renaissance, Culture and Society in the Provincial Town 1660–1770* (Oxford: Clarendon Press, 1989).
45. D. Cressy, 'Literacy in Context: Meaning and Measurement in Early Modern England', in Brewer and Porter (eds), *Consumption and the World of Goods* (London: Routledge, 1993), pp. 305–19.
46. C. Y. Ferdinand, 'Selling it to the Provinces: News and commerce around eighteenth-century Salisbury', in Brewer and Porter (eds), *Consumption and the World of Goods*, p. 397 places the exact amount at 30 per cent. He also records a general growth of ads in newspapers in eighteenth-century Salisbury of 340 per cent between 1752 and 1770, by itself a convincing indicator of the presence of something like Brewer's 'consumer revolution'. I. Rivers (ed.), *Books and Their Readers in Eighteenth-Century England* (New York: St Martin's Press, 1982), ch. 1, suggests that, while the population of England doubled in the eighteenth century, readers more than doubled and she partly credits growth of schools and improved transportation leading to better distribution for that fact.
47. For additional statistics on the English book trade see M. Plant, *The English Book Trade* (New York: P. P. Bowker, 1939), ch. 4.
48. R. M. Wiles, 'Provincial Culture in Early Georgian England', Fritz and William (eds), *The Triumph of Culture: Eighteenth Century Perspectives* (Toronto: A. M. Hakkert Ltd., 1972), pp. 36, 50–2 and M. Harris, *London Newspapers in the Age of Walpole* (London: Associated University Presses, 1987), pp. 176–9.
49. *Spectator*, 10 (12 March 1710–11). Also Harris, *London Newspapers in the Age of Walpole*, p. 190.
50. J. H. Plumb, 'The Public, Literature and the Arts in the Eighteenth Century', in P. Fritz and D. Williams (eds), *The Triumph of Culture: Eighteenth Century Perspectives* (Toronto: A. M. Hakkert, Ltd., 1972), pp. 27–48, p. 33.

51. For example the following issues of the *Spectator* during its first year of publication: 67 (17 May 1711); 83 (5 June 1711); 215 (6 November 1711); 226 (19 November 1711); and 244 (10 December 1711).
52. For Byron see S. Smiles, *Memoir and Correspondence of the late John Murray* (London: Murray, 1891), vol. 2, p. 187; for Moore, see Plant, *The English Book Trade*, p. 410 and n. 41.
53. A. S. Collins, *Authorship in the Days of Johnson* (London: R. Holden and Co., Ltd, 1927), p. 241.
54. The commodity characteristics of paintings in relation to households' consumption of other luxury goods are discussed by Montias, 'Works of Art Competing with Other Goods in Seventeenth-Century Dutch Inventories', in De Marchi and Miegroet (eds), *Mapping Markets for Paintings in Europe, 1450–1750*, pp. 55–64. Unfortunately, no similar investigation of English inventories exists.
55. E. A. Wrigley, 'Urban Growth and Agricultural Change: England and the Continent in the Early Modern Period', *Journal of Interdisciplinary History*, 15, pp. 683–728.
56. N. Crafts, 'The Industrial Revolution', in F. Floud and D. McCloskey (eds.), *The Economic History of Britain since 1700* (Cambridge: Cambridge University Press, 1981), vol. 1, p. 44.
57. P. Mathias, *The First Industrial Nation*, 2nd edn (New York: Methuen, 1983), p. 2. This process continued beyond 1840.
58. Crafts, 'The Industrial Revolution', pp. 45, 46, table 3.2, 47, table 3.3, and vol. 2, pp. 2, 7, table 1.1.
59. P. G. M. Dickson, *The Financial Revolution in England* (London: Macmillan, 1967), p. 17.
60. L. Neal, *The Rise of Financial Capitalism* (Cambridge: Cambridge University Press, 1990), pp. 5–19.
61. De Marchi and Van Miegroet, 'Rules Versus Play in Early Modern Art Markets', 153–5 and n. 16.
62. P. Mathias, *The Transformation of England* (London: Methuen, 1979). The most important development in the financial environment was, according to Mathias, the progressive efficiency and expansion of conduits and institutions serving the short-term money market.
63. Rouquet, *The State of the Arts in England*, p. 33 remarking that 'Portraiture is the kind of painting the most encouraged, and consequently the most followed in England'. Also Lippincott, *Selling Art in Georgian London*, p. 64.
64. L. Lipking, *The Ordering of the Arts in Eighteenth-Century England* (Princeton, NJ: Princeton University Press, 1970).
65. J. Barrell, *The Political Theory of Painting from Reynolds to Hazlitt* (New Haven, CT and London: Yale University Press, 1986).

2 The Commoditization of Theories of Art

1. *The Painting of the Ancients* (London: 1638). This summary on Franciscus Junius the Younger is taken from Lipking, *The Ordering of the Arts in Eighteenth-Century England*, pp. 23–31.

2. *The Letters of Peter Paul Rubens*, trans. R. S. Magurn (Cambridge, MA: Yale University Press, 1955), p. 407.
3. C. Ward, *The Life of John Dryden* (Chapel Hill, NC: University of North Carolina, 1961), pp. 272, 367. J. Dryden (trans.), *De Arte Graphica. The Art of Painting*, 2nd edn (London: Bernard Lintott, 1716), i/ii. De Fresnoy, a painter himself, addressed those aspects which Rubens found lacking in Franciscus Junius's work.
4. Dryden (trans.), *De Arte Graphica. The Art of Painting*, ixiii, ixiv, ixv. The wide range of topics constitutes a 'how to' make and view approach to painting based on judgements wrought from experience. This empirical quality – de Piles makes a point to advertise that the book is the result of extensive empirical investigation – must have helped its popularity.
5. W. Mason, in the preface to his 1783 translation describes it as 'one of the principal tests of picturesque excellence'. W. Mason (trans.), 'The Art of Painting', *The Works of William Mason, M.A.* (London: 1811), vol. 3, p. 8. Lipking, *The Ordering of the Arts in Eighteenth-Century England*, pp. 46–8, n. 21 mentions, in addition to Dryden's and Mason's, also other versions authored by D. Defoe (1720), J. Wills (1754), and W. Churchey (1789), as well as other writers like W. Aglionby, T.. Page and J. Richardson who were all influenced by this book.
6. Quote from Mason, 'The Art of Painting', vol. 3, p. 6. By the 1780s the Royal Academy was firmly established and besides the public exhibitions at Vauxhall Gardens and the Foundling Hospital numerous smaller, private exhibitions, as well as a growing auction market had helped facilitate the public's familiarity with paintings.
7. An exhaustive discussion of the relevant literature of the period can be found in J. Dobai, *Kunstliteratur des Klassizismus und der Romantik in England* (Bern: Bentelli Verlag, 1974), 3 vols.
8. In this context it is useful to consider the Durkheimian notion that cultural systems of classification reflect the structure of the societies in question. E. Durkheim and M. Mauss, *Primitive Classification*, trans. R. Needham (Chicago, IL: The University of Chicago Press, 1963), pp. 81–8.
9. Walpole, *Anecdotes of Paintings*, vol. 1, p. 657. On Richardson's success as a portraitist see p. 658; on the economic opportunities offered by portrait painting see Pye, *Patronage of British Art, A Historical Sketch*, pp. 26–7; Rouquet, *The State of the Arts in England*, pp. 33–49.
10. A. A. Cooper, third Earl of Shaftesbury, *Characteristics of Men, Manners, Opinions, Times* (1711), ed. J. M. Robertson, 2 vols (Indianapolis, IN and New York: University of Indiana Press, 1964), vol. 1, p. 96; and his, *Second Characters, or the Language of Forms*, ed. B. Rand (Cambridge, MA: Harvard University Press, 1914), p. 135, where the Earl described portrait painting as 'not so much a liberal art not to be so esteemed, as requiring no liberal knowledge, genius, education, converse, manners, moral-science, mathematics, optics, but merely practical and vulgar'.
11. J. Richardson, *Essays on the whole Art of Criticism as it relates to Painting* (London: 1719), pp. 15–16.
12. Richardson, *Essays on the whole Art of Criticism as it relates to Painting*, pp. 15–16, 26–8.
13. Rouquet, *The Present State of the Arts in England*, p. 21, mentions that 'it is not the spirit of avarice that excites the English to the pursuit of wealth, but the desire of enjoying it'.
14. B. Mandeville, *The Fable of the Bees: or Private Vices, Publick Benefits*, ed. F. B. Kaye, 2 vols (Oxford: Clarendon Press, 1924). All subsequent references to the *Fable* are to this edition.

15. Solkin, *Painting for Money*, p. 90, for a reprint of G. Berkeley, 'An Essay Towards Preventing the Ruin of Great Britain' (1721). For a discussion on various interpretations of 'luxury', see J. Sekora, *Luxury: The Concept in Western Thought, Eden to Smollett* (Baltimore, MD: Johns Hopkins University Press, 1977).
16. Mandeville, *The Fable of the Bees: or Private Vices, Publick Benefits*, vol. 2, pp. 29–41; quote, vol. 2, p. 36.
17. R. Williams, *Culture and Society 1780–1950* (New York: Columbia University Press, 1983), pp. 30–48.
18. S. Copley, *Literature and the Social Order in Eighteenth-Century England*, pp. 106, 110, citing D. Hume, 'Of Commerce' (1742), reprinted from D. Hume, 'Of Refinement in the Arts' (1742) and p. 113 citing J. Tucker, *The Elements of Commerce and Theory of Taxes* (1755). On Hume, see also C. Goodwin, 'Art and Culture in the History of Economic Thought', *Handbook of the Economics of Art and Culture* (Amsterdam: Elsevier, 2006), vol. 1, pp. 33–4.
19. J. Steuart, *Principles of Political Oeconomy* (London: A. Millar and Cadell, 1767; reprinted New York: Augustus M. Kelley), book 2, p. 218.
20. A. Smith, *An Inquiry into the Nature and Causes of the Wealth of Nations* (Edinburgh: A. and B. Black, 1872), p. 6.
21. Ibid., p. 7.
22. G. Turnbull, *Treatise on Ancient Painting*, pp. 78–9 (quote), 141–2.
23. Solkin, *Painting for Money*, p. 171.
24. *Tatler*, 209, (8–10 August), cited by Paulson, *Hogarth: His Life, Art, and Times*, vol. 1, pp. 144–5. For quote, *Spectator*, no. 226, cited by Paulson, *Hogarth: His Life, Art, and Time,* vol. 1, pp. 144–5. Paulson does not provide a date for this letter.
25. Paulson, *Hogarth: His Life, Art, and Times*, vol. 1, p. 145.
26. M. Eisenberg, 'Watteau Paintings in England in the Early Eighteenth Century', *Burlington Magazine*, 107 (Sept. 1975), pp. 576–82; R. Raines, 'Watteaus and "Watteaus" in England before 1760', *Gazette des Beaux Arts*, 89 (February 1977), pp. 51–64.
27. Solkin, *Painting for Money*, p. 78.
28. Walpole, *Anecdotes of Paintings* vol. 3, p. 722 assigns Hogarth a place 'between the Italians ... and the Flemish painters'. Volume 2, p. 703 describes the painter Philip Mercier (1689–1760) as an artist who painted 'pictures of familiar life in a genteel style of his own, and with a little of Watteau ...'
29. Rouquet, *The State of the Arts in England,* p. 27 credits Hogarth with furnishing 'England with a new kind of pictures ...' Vertue, *Notebooks*, vol. 22, p. 40, describes Hogarth as an painter rewarded with 'daily success ... in painting small family pieces & Conversations with so much Air & agreeableness [which] causes him to be much followd, & esteemed'.
30. J. Ireland, *Hogarth Illustrated* (London: J. & J. Boydell, 1791–8), 1805 edition, vol. 3, p. 31.
31. Rouquet, *The State of the Arts in England*, p. 29. Also Walpole, *Anecdotes of Paintings*, vol. 3, p. 730 for a brief discussion of Hogarth's writing.
32. Walpole, *Anecdotes of Paintings*, vol. 3, p. 721. Walpole also refers to Hogarth as 'compos[ing] comedy as much as Moliere'.
33. Sir J. Reynolds, *Discourses on Art*, ed. R. R. Wark (New Haven, CT and London: Yale University Press, 1959), p. 171.
34. The painter sent copies of his writings to people of prominence, and during many of his later lectures, visitors outnumbered students. For more on Reynolds's pursuit of a

wider audience see, Lipking, *The Ordering of the Arts in Eighteenth-century England*, pp. 186–7; Whitley, *Artists and Their Friends in England 1700–1790*, vol. 2, pp. 134–5; F. W. Hilles, *Literary Career of Sir Joshua Reynolds* (New York: The Macmillan Co., Cambridge, England: The University Press, 1936), pp. 144–5.

35. Reynolds, *Discourses on Art*, pp. 70–1.
36. W. Hazlitt, *Complete Works*, ed. P. P. Howe, 21 vol, after the edition of A. P. Waller and A. Glover (London, Toronto: J. M. Dent & Sons, Ltd., 1930–4), vol. 18, pp. 70–7. Also W. Hazlitt, *Criticism on Art and Sketches of the Picture Galleries of England* (London: J. Templeman, 1843; 2nd edn, 1846), p. 207. Also E. C. Elliott, 'Reynolds and Hazlitt', *Journal of Aesthetics and Art Criticism*, 21 (1962), pp. 73–9, and L. M. Trawick, 'Hazlitt, Reynolds, and the Ideal', *Studies in Romanticism*, 4 (1965), pp. 240–7.
37. Hazlitt, *Criticism on Art*, p. 176.
38. Barrell, *The Political Theory of Painting from Reynolds to Hazlitt*, p. 320.
39. Hazlitt, *Criticism on Art*, p. 226.
40. Ibid., pp. 233, 235–7.
41. *The Life and Writing of Henry Fuseli*, ed. J. Knowles (London: Templeman, 1831), vol. 2, pp. 214–16; vol.3, pp. 43–5, 49, 53–4.
42. *The Complete Writings of William Blake*, ed. G. Keynes (London, New York: Oxford University Press, 1972), pp. 452, 573, 591, 600, 1(quote).
43. A. Pasquin, *Memoirs of the Royal Academicians; being an attempt to improve the national taste* (London, 1796), p. 148.
44. Barrell, *The Political Theory of Painting from Reynolds to Hazlitt*, p. 339.

3 The Painter as *Homo Economicus*

1. Rouquet, *The State of the Arts in England*, pp. 22–4.
2. Walpole, *Anecdotes of Paintings*, vol. 3, p. 730.
3. J. Barry, *Inquiry into the Real and Imaginary Obstructions to the Acquisition of the Arts* (New York: Garland Publishing, 1972), pp. 75–6.
4. J. Okley, *St. James Chronicle* (2 April 1761), pp. 3–4.
5. See above, p. 43, ns 1 and 2.
6. N. de Marchi, 'The Role of Dutch Auctions and Lotteries in Shaping the Art Market(s) of 17th Century Holland', *Journal of Economic Behavior and Organization*, 28 (1995), pp. 203–21.
7. G. Reitlinger, *The Economics of Taste. The Rise and Fall of Picture Prices 1760–1960* (New York: Hacker Boos, 1982), vol. 1, title of chapter 6.
8. Walpole, *Anecdotes of Paintings*, vol. 2, pp. 586, 643.
9. Pye, *Patronage of British Art, A Historical Sketch*, p. 34, n. 24 and Ireland, *Hogarth*, vol. 3, supplement, pp. 35 and 190.
10. Pye, *Patronage of British Art, A Historical Sketch*, p. 26 and n. 13; p. 66, n. 25.
11. C. Gibson-Wood, 'Picture Consumption in London at the end of the Seventeenth Century', *The Art Bulletin*, 84:3 (September 2002), pp. 491–500, p. 495.
12. W. Buchanan, *Memoirs of Painting*, ed. J. Greig (London: Ackermann, 1824), vol. 1, p. 96, discussing J. Irving, J. Campbell, G. A. Wallis, and J. More. J. Farington, *The Farington Diary* (London: Hutchinson & Co., 1923), vol. I, p. 12, also mentioned that More had become rich partly by buying and selling pictures.
13. Walpole, *Anecdotes of Paintings*, vol. 2, p. 479.
14. Lippincott, *Selling Art in Georgian London*, pp. 60–1.

15. S. Bennett, *Thomas Stothard* (Columbia, MO: University of Missouri Press, 1988), pp. 7, 36, 44; Hermann, *The English as Collectors*, p. 23; Lippincott, *Selling Art in Georgian London*, pp. 59–60, 75, 92–5, 112, 148 ff; Walpole, *Anecdotes of Paintings*, vol. 1, p. 715; vol. 2, pp. 632, 702; vol. 3, pp. 723, 733, 748, 978; Whitley, *Artists and Their Friends in England 1700–1790*, vol. 1, pp. 53–5.
16. Ormrod, 'The Art Trade and its Urban Context', p. 16, table 1, pp. 17–18.
17. Walpole, *Anecdotes of Paintings*, vols 2 and 3 under respective listings.
18. For Vertue see W. Sandby, *The History of The Royal Academy of Arts* (London: Longman, 1862), vol. 1, p. 18; Further references to this and the other mentioned organizations can be found in N. Pevsner, *Academies of Art, Past and Present* (Cambridge: Cambridge University Press, 1940), pp. 15, 124; Hutchison, *The History of the Royal Academy 1768–1968*, p. 5. Whitley, *Artists and Their Friends in England 1700–1790*, vol. 1, pp. 7, 74. R. Paulson, *Hogarth: His Life, Art, and Times*, vol. 1, p. 347; vol. 2, p. 43. Lippincott, *Selling Art in Georgian London*, p. 30, lists the 'Rose and Crown' as having been founded in 1720, making Vertue's membership in 1704 impossible. Neither Whitley nor Lippincott gives sources for their statements.
19. Lippincott, *Selling Art in Georgian London*, p. 15.
20. Whitley, *Artists and Their Friends in England 1700–1790*, vol. 1, p. 17 and 2, pp. 7–8.
21. Pye, *Patronage of British Art, A Historical Sketch*, p. 44 and n. 44.
22. For more information on Kneller's, Thornhill's and Vanderbank's academies see Hutchison, *The History of the Royal Academy 1768–1968*, pp. 7–10; Koch, *Die Kunstausstellung*, pp. 200–1; Paulson, *Hogarth: His Life and Art, and Times*, vol. 1, pp. 92–9, 108; Pevsner, *Academies of Art, Past and Present*, pp. 124–5; Pye, *Patronage of British Art, A Historical Sketch*, pp. 19–21, 73–4; Walpole, *Anecdotes of Paintings*, vol. 2, p. 647, vol. 3, p. 727; Whitley, *Artists and Their Friends in England 1700–1790*, vol. 1, pp. 7–16; R. Wittkower, 'The Artist', in J. Clifford (ed.), *Man versus Society in Eighteenth-Century Britain* (Cambridge: Cambridge University Press 1968), pp. 77–8.
23. Paulson, *Hogarth: His Life, Art, and Times*, vol. 1, p. 369–75; quote (p. 347) is attributed to Vertue without providing a source. For additional information on Hogarth's St Martin's Lane Academy see Hutchison, *The History of the Royal Academy 1768–1968*, pp. 10–13; Pears, *The Discovery of Painting*, p. 124; Pevsner, *Academies of Art, Past and Present*, pp. 125–6; Pye, *Patronage of British Art, A Historical Sketch*, pp. 22/3; Whitley, *Artists and Their Friends in England 1700–1790*, vol. 1, p. 27.
24. Pye, *Patronage of British Art, A Historical Sketch*, pp. 43–4 and n. 44 and n. 45.
25. Denvir, *The Eighteenth Century*, p. 182.
26. Hutchison, *The History of the Royal Academy 1768–1968*, p. 10; Whitley, *Artists and Their Friends in England 1700–1790*, vol. 1, pp. 29–30. On Moser, also Koch, *Die Kunstaustellung*, p. 201; Paulson, *Hogarth: His Life, Art, and Times*, vol. 2, p. 140; Whitley, *Artists and Their Friends in England 1700–1790*, vol. 1, p. 27. On Gwynn see Hutchison, *The History of the Royal Academy 1768–1968*, p. 13, and Paulson, *Hogarth: His Life, Art, and Times*, vol. 2, pp. 137–8; on Vertue's and others' plans see Vertue, *Notebooks*, vol. 2, p. 150 ff. On the Duke of Richmond, see Hutchison, *The History of the Royal Academy 1768–1968*, p. 10 and Pevsner, *Academies of Art, Past and Present*, p. 125.
27. Pye, *Patronage of British Art, A Historical Sketch*, pp. 73–4; Denvir, *The Eighteenth Century*, p. 183. For quote and a contemporary description of Kneller's methods, see Whitley, *Artists and Their Friends in England 1700–1790*, vol. 1, pp. 4–5, without providing a source. As yet little research has been done on artists' organizations outside London. Cooper's school is mentioned in R. Strange, *Memoirs* (London: E. and C. Dilly,

1775), vol. 1, p. 26; Liverpool is discussed in E. R. Dibdin, 'Liverpool Art and Artists in the Eighteenth Century', *Walpole Society* (Oxford: Oxford University, 1917–18), 6, pp. 65–6; the Foulis Academy is described in D. and F. Irwin, *Scottish Painters at Home and Abroad 1700–1900* (London: Faber, 1975), pp. 83–97. Also Koch, *Die Kunstaustellung*, p. 215; Pears, *The Discovery of Painting*, pp. 120–3; Pevsner, *Academies of Art, Past and Present*, p. 140; Whitley, *Artists and Their Friends in England 1700–1790*, vol. 2, p. 69.

28. W. O. Englefield, *History of the Painter-Stainer Company* (London: Chapman and Dodd, Ltd., 1923).
29. Pye, *Patronage of British Art, A Historical Sketch*, pp. 43–4 and n. 44 and n. 45; also Whitley, *Artists and Their Friends in England 1700–1790*, vol. 1, p. 15.
30. G. A. Akerlof, 'The Market for "Lemons": Quality Uncertainty and the Market Mechanisms', *An economic theorist's book of tales* (Cambridge University Press, 1970), pp. 7–22.
31. L. Cust, *The History of the Society of Dilettanti* (London: Seeley & Co., 1898), p. 58; Hutchison, *The History of the Royal Academy 1768–1968*, pp. 12–13; Pye, *Patronage of British Art, A Historical Sketch*, pp. 75–6; Paulson, *Hogarth: His Life, Art, and Time*, vol. 2, p. 142; Sandby, *The History of the Royal Academy of Arts from its Foundation in 1768 to the Present Time*, vol. 1, pp. 26–7; Whitley, *Artists and Their Friends in England 1700–1790*, vol. 1, p. 157.
32. Cust, *The History of the Society of Dilettanti*, pp. 52–5; Hutchison, *The History of the Royal Academy 1768–1968*, p. 12; Koch, *Die Kunstaustellung*, p. 201; Whitley, *Artists and Their Friends in England 1700–1790*, vol. 1, p. 157.
33. *Gentleman's Magazine*, 84 (1756), p. 61.
34. This organization which connected art, business and technology, was the prototype for the great industrial exhibitions of the nineteenth century. K. Luckhurst, *The Story of Exhibitions* (London, New York: Studio Publications, 1951), p. 63 ff.
35. Hutchison, *The History of the Royal Academy 1768–1968*, p. 10; and Pears, *The Discovery of Painting*, p. 129.
36. Graves under Wotton and Monamy respectively.
37. For more on the genesis of the RA, see Hutchison, *The History of the Royal Academy 1768–1968*, pp. 18–23; Koch, *Die Kunstaustellung*, pp. 203–6; Paulson, *Hogarth: His Life, Art, and Time*, vol. 2, pp. 322–3, 339, 352, 384; Pevsner, *Academies of Art, Past and Present*, p. 185; Pye, *Patronage of British Art, A Historical Sketch*, pp. 103–29, 132, 163–74; Solkin, *Painting for Money*, pp. 176–9; Whitley, *Artists and Their Friends in England 1700–1790*, vol. 1, pp. 171–92.
38. Whitley, *Artists and Their Friends in England 1700–1790*, vol. 1, p. 7.
39. Solkin, *Painting for Money*, pp. 27–47, and n. 8 and n. 9.
40. Lippincott, *Selling Art in Georgian London*, p. 30.
41. For an account of London clubs during this period, see R. J. Allen, *The Clubs of Augustan London* (Cambridge, MA: Harvard University Press, 1933); Lippincott, *Selling Art in Georgian London*, pp. 44–8 on Pond's use of clubs to further his business.
42. Lippincott, *Selling Art in Georgian London*, pp. 48/9.
43. Paulson, *Hogarth: His Life, Art, and Time*, vol. 1, pp. 213–14, 372; vol. 2, p. 344. On other artists advertising to invite the public to their houses, see Whitley, *Artists and Their Friends in England 1700–1790*, vol. 1, p. 115; Lippincott, *Selling Art in Georgian London*, p. 32 ff. M. Foss, *Man of Wit to Man of Business* (Bristol: Bristol Classical Press, 1988), pp. 177–8.
44. Ireland, *Hogarth*, vol. 3, supplement, p. 24.
45. Lippincott, *Selling Art in Georgian London*, pp. 32–54.

46. On 'aura', see W. Benjamin, *Das Kunstwerk im Zeitalterseiner Reproduzierbarkeit* (Frankfurt: Surkamp Verlag, 1977).
47. For more on Saltero see B. Lillywhite, *London Coffee Houses* (London: G. Allen and Unwin, 1963), pp. 194–5; also A. Ellis, *The Penny Universities, A History of the Coffee-Houses* (London: Secker & Warburg, 1956), pp. 154–8.
48. *A Brief Historical and Descriptive account of the Royal Gardens, Vauxhall* (London, 1822), p. 7. For a detailed history of the Gardens, see W. Wroth, F.S.A., *The London Pleasure Gardens of the Eighteenth Century* (London: MacMillan and Co., Ltd., 1896), pp. 287–326.
49. B. Weinreb and C. Hibbert (eds), *London Encyclopedia* (New York: St. Martin's Press, 1983), p. 910.
50. Solkin, *Painting for Money*, pp. 137–56.
51. Paulson, *Hogarth: His Art, Life, and Time*, vol. 1, p. 347.
52. Ibid., vol. 2, pp. 70–1 and n. 73.
53. Walpole, *Anecdotes of Paintings*, vol. 3, p. 758.
54. Solkin, *Painting for Money*, p. 179.
55. Paulson, *Hogarth: His Art, Life, and Time*, vol. 2, pp. 35–7, 49; Solkin, *Painting for Money*, p. 165; Rouquet, *The State of the Arts in England*, pp. 25–7; Whitley, *Artists and Their Friends in England 1700–1790*, vol. 1, p. 163; Pye, *Patronage of British Art, A Historical Sketch*, pp. 87–90. The exact date is difficult to establish. Whitley mentions a remark made by Vertue in 1745, concerning the painter Hardin who 'has lately painted some pieces of landscape in rounds, which he has presented to the Foundling Hospital to adorn their room'. Paulson, *Hogarth: His Art, Life, and Time*, vol. 2, p. 49 describes a dinner held on 1 April 1747 at the Foundling Hospital where four paintings by Hayman, Hogarth, Hymore and Wills were displayed.
56. Pye, *Patronage of British Art, A Historical Sketch*, p. 25; For a detailed history of the Foundling Hospital see R. H. Nichols and F. A. Wray, *The History of the Foundling Hospital* (London: Oxford University Press, 1935).
57. Rouquet, *The State of the Arts in England*, p. 27.
58. R. D. Altick, *The Shows of London* (Cambridge: Harvard University Press, 1978), p. 101; Paulson, *Hogarth: His Art, Life, and Time*, vol. 2, p. 50.
59. Rouquet, *The State of the Arts in England*, p. 252.
60. Whitley, *Artists and Their Friends in England 1700–1790*, vol. 1, p. 165.
61. Anon., *The Conduct of the Royal Academician with Members of the Incorporated Society of Artists of Great Britain* (London, 1771), p. 8; also Hutchison, *The History of the Royal Academy 1768–1968*, p. 16; Pye, *Patronage of British Art, A Historical Sketch*, pp. 91–4 and n. 8 (Pye records the date as 12 November.); Solkin, *Painting for Money*, p. 174.
62. For additional information on the 'Society of Arts' see D. Hudson and K. W. Luckhurst, *The Royal Society of Arts, 1754–1954* (London: Murray, 1954); Koch, *Die Kunstaustellung*, pp. 201–2; Luckhurst, *The Story of Exhibitions*, p. 63 ff.; Pye, *Patronage of British Art, A Historical Sketch*, pp. 60–1.
63. Pye, *Patronage of British Art, A Historical Sketch*, p. 92, citing the original letter.
64. *The London Chronicle*, 3–5 April 1760, p. 1; *London Evening Post*, 3–5 April 1760, p. 1; the *Whitehall Evening Post*, 5 April 1760, p. 1; *Public Advertiser*, 18 April 1760, p. 2; *The London Chronicle*, 12 April, p. 362, and April 17, p. 378.
65. For this quote and data on the event see Pye, *Patronage of British Art, A Historical Sketch*, pp. 91–5; Solkin, *Painting for Money*, pp. 174–5; Whitley, *Artists and Their Friends in England 1700–1790*, vol. 1, pp. 165–7.

66. Pye, *Patronage of British Art, A Historical Sketch*, p. 94, and n. 12; p. 91 and n. 8, referring to the Minutes of the meeting at Turk's Head, citing *The Literary Panorama* for 1808, vol. 3, pp. 1013–14, 1226–8;1295 and n. 13 referring to the *Literary Panorama* for 1808, vol. 3, p. 1226.
67. Pye, *Patronage of British Art, A Historical Sketch*, pp. 96–9.
68. *St. James Chronicle*, 2 May 1761, p. 4; *Public Advertiser*, 6 May 1761, p. 4.
69. *Public Advertiser*, 6 May 1761, pp. 3 and 1, respectively.
70. For example: 'The powers of Mr. Reynolds are perfect', or 'Mr. Ramsey is exact in his imitations', or 'Mr. Hudson is extremely just in his representations', *London Chronicle*, May 12 to 14, pp. 460–1.
71. *Public Advertiser*, 6 May 1761, p. 2.
72. Thanks to Emma Lloyd-Jacobs at the Mellon Centre in London for assembling the countless English news clippings pertaining to the arts in Britain. Below is a chronological listing of publications that make reference to the above-discussed events. *London Chronicle*, 3–5 April 1760, p. 1; *London Evening Post*, 3–5 April 1760, p. 1; *Whitehall Evening Post*, 5 April 1760, p. 1; *London Chronicle*, 12 April 1760, p. 362 and 17 April 1760, p. 378; *Public Advertiser*, 18 April 1760, p. 2; *London Chronicle*, 16–18 April 1761, p. 375; *Whitehall Evening Post*, 16–18 April 1761, p. 1; *Public Advertiser*, 17 April 1761, p. 1; *London Chronicle*, 18 April 1761, p. 400; *London Chronicle*, 23–5 April 1761, pp. 394–5; *London Chronicle*, 23–5 April 1761, p. 393–4; *London Evening Post*, 23–5 April 1761, p. 1; *St. James Chronicle*, 23–5 April 1761, p. 3; *St James Chronicle*, 25–8 April 1761, p. 3; *Whitehall Evening Post*, 25–6 April 1761, p. 2; *Public Advertiser*, 27 April 1761, p. 3; *London Chronicle*, 28–30 April 1761, p. 2; *St James Chronicle*, 30 April-2 May 1761, p. 2 and 2–5 May 1761, pp. 2, 4; *Public Advertiser*, 5 May 1761, p. 4 and 6 May 1761, p. 4; *St James Chronicle*, 5–7 May 1761, p. 2 and 7–9 May 1761, pp. 2–3 and 9–12 May 1761, p. 2; *Public Advertiser*, 11 May 1761, p. 4; *Public Ledger*, 11 May 1761, p. 1; *London Chronicle*, 11 May 1761, pp. 460–1; *St James Chronicle*, 14–16 May 1761, pp. 2, 4; *London Evening Post*, 14–16 May 1761, p. 1; *St James Chronicle*, 23–6 May 1761, p. 2; *London Evening Post*, 27–9 May 1761, pp. 504–5; *St. James Chronicle*, 28–30 May 1761, p. 3 and 2–4 June 1761, p. 2; *General Evening Post*, 4–6 June 1761, p. 1.
73. Pye, *Patronage of British Art, A Historical Sketch*, pp. 94–5.
74. Whitley, *Artists and Their Friends in England 1700–1790*, vol. 1, p. 179.
75. Ibid., vol. 1, pp. 114–16; Walpole, *Anecdotes of Paintings*, vol. 2, pp. 716–17 and n. 1.
76. Whitley, *Artists and Their Friends in England 1700–1790*, vol. 1, p. 269, and our own sales data.
77. Walpole, *Anecdotes of Paintings*, vol. 2, p. 716, n. 1.
78. Graves, *Art Sales*, vol. 2, p. 178. See Christie's catalogue of this sale in conjunction with our own data.
79. Whitley, *Artists and Their Friends in England 1700–1790*, vol. 1, p. 122, quoting Vertue.
80. Reviews of these exhibitions can be found in *Lloyd's Evening Post, and British Chronicle*, 1–3 May 1769, p. 427 and 3–5 May 1769, p. 4. For a history of the early years of the Royal Academy, see Hutchison, *The History of the Royal Academy 1768–1968*, pp. 23–44. Other texts on this topic include C. Holme, *The Royal Academy from Reynolds to Millais* (London, New York: The Studio, 1904); W. R. M. Lamb, *The Royal Academy* (London: A. Maclehose & Co., 1935); D. Solkin (ed.), *Art on the Line* (London and New Haven, CT: Yale University Press, 2001); Sandby, *The History of the Royal Academy of Arts*.

81. M. Butlin, 'An Eighteenth Century Scandal: Nathaniel Hone's "The Conjurer"', *Connoisseur*, 174 (1970), pp. 1–9; also Altick, *The Shows of London*, p. 104; Koch, *Die Kunstaustellung*, p. 215; Whitley, *Artists and Their Friends in England 1700–1790*, vol. 2, p. 266.
82. We found over twenty individual mentions in London papers dating from 1 May to 21 June 1781 of this event in the collection of art-related press clippings at the Mellon Centre in London.
83. Using the retail price index. Applying an average earnings conversion, the amount increases to £ 6.4 million. E. H. net.
84. On Copley's enterprises see Farington, *The Farington Diaries, 1793–1817*, vol. 1, p. 48, vol. 2, p. 76; M. B. Amory, *John Singleton Copley, R.A.* (New York: Houghton, Mifflin and Co., 1982), ch. 5; Altick, *The Shows of London*, p. 105; Koch, *Die Kunstaustellung*, pp. 215–16; Whitley, *Artists and Their Friends in England 1700–1790*, vol. 2, pp. 137–40; on the involvement of Boydell in the second project see Bruntjen, *John Boydell*, p. 207.
85. Paulson, *Hogarth: His Life, Art, and Times*, vol. 2, p. 323.
86. Koch, *Die Kunstaustellung*, p. 215; E. Waterhouse, *Painting in England 1530–1790* (London and Baltimore, MD: Penguin Books, Ltd., 1953), p. 257; Whitley, *Artists and Their Friends in England 1700–1790*, vol. 1, pp. 400–1.
87. Altick, *The Shows of London*, pp. 105–6; Koch, *Die Kunstaustellung*, p. 216; C. Mitchell, 'Benjamin West's "Death of General Wolf" and the popular History Piece', *Journal of the Warburg and Courtauld Institute*, 7 (1944), pp. 20–3; E. Wind, 'The Revolution of History Painting', *Journal of the Warburg and Courtauld Institute*, 2 (1938–9), pp. 116–27.
88. E. Holt, *From the Classicists to the Impressionists* (New Haven, CT and London: Yale University Press, 1986), pp. 4–6 and her *Triumph of Art for the Public* (Washington, DC: Decatur House Press, 1980), pp. 6, 121.
89. Farington responding to Lawrence's doubt about exhibiting at the RA in 1803. Farington, *Diaries*, vol. 2, p. 86.
90. Solkin (ed.), *Art on the Line*, p. xi.
91. Farington, *Diaries*, vol. 3, p. 70 and vol. 2, p. 95.
92. Anon., 'Our Royal Academical Lounge', *Fraser's Magazine*, 5 (July 1832), pp. 710–11, cited, Farington, *Diaries*, vol. 2, p. 5.
93. BL Add. MSS 47,792, fol. 14 verso, cited by M. Myrone, in Solkin (ed.), *Art on the Line*, p. 82.
94. The term 'fusilesque' was first used by J. Dallaway, *Anecdotes of the Arts in England* (London: 1800), p. 524, cited by Myrone, *Art on the Line*, p. 83.
95. A. Bermingham, 'Landscape-O-Rama: The Exhibition Landscape at Somerset House and the Rise of Popular Landscape Entertainment', in Solkin (ed.), *Art on the Line*, pp. 127–43; quote 142.
96. M. Rosenthal, 'Turner Fires a Gun', in Solkin (ed.), *Art on the Line*, pp. 145–55.
97. Farington, *Diaries*, vol. 3, p. 227.
98. Quoted by R. Redgrave, *A Century of British Painters* (New York: Cornell University Press, 1981), p. 2.

4 Critics and Auctions

1. P. Trolander and Z. Tenger, *Sociable Criticism in England 1625–1725* (Newark, DE: University of Delaware Press, 2007), p. 20.

2. Solkin, *Painting for Money*, ch. 7 and notes. Paulson, *Hogarth: His Art, Life, and Time*, vol. 2, p. 307; Whitley, *Artists and Their Friends in England 1700–1790*, vol. 1, pp. 167–8 and vol. 2, p. 271 for names of several of the early art critics and the publications for which they wrote. See also the art-related materials from the London press from the 1760s in the Paul Mellon Center for Studies in British Art, Yale University, assembled by Claire Lloyd-Jacob.
3. Whitley, *Artists and Their Friends in England 1700–1790*, vol. 1, p. 167.
4. *Gazetteer and New Daily Advertiser*, 21 May 1765, p. 4.
5. Farington, *Diaries*, vol. 3, p. 276.
6. Exhibition label, Tate Gallery, London, 2003. 2003–1600. Also, A. Earland, *John Opie and his Circle* (London: Hutchinson & Co., 1911), p. 25.
7. Kopytoff, 'The Cultural Biography of Things: Commoditization as Process', p. 87.
8. For example the General W. Stuart sale on 14 April 1730 at which articles of furniture were offered at fixed prices while the paintings were auctioned off. *Catalogue of the dwelling House of the Rt. Hon. General (Wm.) Stuart (deceased)* (14 April 1730) in the Bodleian Library Johnson collection d778.
9. D. Ormrod, 'The Origins of the London Art Market 1660–1730', in M. North and D. Ormrod (eds), *Art Markets in Europe 1400–1800* (Aldershot, Great Britain: Ashgate Publishing, 1998), pp. 167–86. These early auctions also often contained common household goods.
10. B. Cowan, 'Art and Connoisseurship in the Auction Market of Later Seventeenth-Century London', in N. De Marchi and Hans Miegroet (eds), *Mapping Markets for Paintings in Europe, 1450–1750* (Turnhout, Belgium: Brepols 2006), p. 264 and n. 5, p. 271, table 16, p. 275. Cowan mentions that there must have been many more auctions than were advertised. Ormrod, 'The Origins of the London Art Market 1660–1730', p. 169 mentions that between 1688–91 the number of annual picture auctions rose from fourteen to ninety-two.
11. N. De Marchi, 'Auctioning Paintings in Late Seventeenth-Century London: Rules, Segmentation and Prices in an Emergent Market', in V. A. Ginsburgh (ed.), *Economics of Art and Culture* (Amsterdam: Elsevier, 2004), pp. 97–128, p. 122, referring to a group of 131 printed catalogues in the British library (shelf mark 1402.g.1).
12. Ormrod, 'The Origins of the London Art Market 1660–1730', p. 179, table 13.3 and p. 18, n. 63. The earliest record dates from 1697–1701 and lists an annual average of 457 paintings. Most likely the preceding fifteen years had not experienced a dramatic difference. The mean declared value was £1.29 and the median value £0.88.
13. Gibson-Wood, 'Picture Consumption in London at the End of the Seventeenth Century', p. 496.
14. Cowan, 'Art and Connoisseurship in the Auction Market of Later Seventeenth-Century London', p. 274.
15. B. Cowan, 'Arenas of Connoisseurship: Auctioning Art in Later Stuart England, in M. North and D. Ormrod (eds), *Art Markets in Europe, 1400–1800*, p. 154. For auctions in general, p. 163, n.1 , citing *Historical Manuscripts Commission* (1891), p. 65; H. V. S. and M. S. Ogden, *English Taste in Landscape in the 17th Century* (Ann Arbor, MI: University of Michigan Press, 1955), pp. 86–92; Walpole, *Anecdotes of Paintings*, vol. 2, p. 433, n. 4.
16. D. Ormrod, 'The Rise of the London Art Market, 1660–1760', in S. Cavaciocchi (ed.), *Economica e Arte, Secc. XIII-XVIII: Atti Della 'Trentatreesima Settimana Di Studio' 30 Aprile–4 Maggio 2000* (Florence: Le Monnier, 2002), pp. 305–21, p. 316.

17. Cowan, 'Art and Connoisseurship in the Auction Market of Later Seventeenth-Century London', p. 274 and n. 44, p. 275 and n. 48.
18. De Marchi, 'Auctioning Paintings in Late Seventeenth-Century London', pp. 120–4. We disagree with De Marchi's contention that these works had no asset value.
19. De Marchi, 'Auctioning Paintings in Late Seventeenth-Century London', pp. 102–7 for this and a detailed discussion of these regulations. Also De Marchi and Van Miegroet, 'The History of Art Markets', pp. 106–7.
20. Redford, *Art Sales: A History of Sales of Pictures & Other Works of Art*, pp. 23–7 referring to the *London Gazette* (29 February to 3 March 1692), for an advertisement of such a pamphlet. Also, Cowan, 'Art and Connoisseurship in the Auction Market of Later Seventeenth-Century London', p. 277 and n. 57.
21. Rouquet, *The State of the Arts in England*, p. 125.
22. R. North, *The Lives of the Norths*, ed. A. Jessop (London: G. Bell and Sons, 1890), vol. 3, p. 193 in connection with the Lely sale of April 1688. Also Graves, *Art Sales*.
23. Cowan, 'Arenas of Connoisseurship: Auctioning Art in Later Stuart England', in M. North and D. Ormrod (eds.), p. 155 and n. 17 referring to advertisements in the *London Gazette* for the years 1689–92 and the collection of sales catalogues in the British Library, shelf number 1402.g.1.
24. Rouquet, *The State of the Arts in England*, pp. 121–6.
25. Hermann, *The English as Collectors*, p. 28 referring to Redford, *Art Sales*, vol. 2, without providing a page number. Also, Cowan, 'Art and Connoisseurship in the Auction Market of Later Seventeenth-Century London', p. 279.
26. Paulson, *Hogarth: His Art, Life, and Time*, vol. 2, p. 60, and n. 10.
27. Cowan, 'Art and Connoisseurship in the Auction Market of Later Seventeenth-Century London', p. 282.
28. Rouquet, *The State of the Arts in England*, pp. 124–5.
29. Hermann, *The English as Collectors*, p. 28.
30. Walpole, *Anecdotes of Paintings*, vol. 2, p. 651; Rouquet, *The State of the Arts in England*, p. 126.
31. Cowan, 'Art and Connoisseurship in the Auction Market of Later Seventeenth-Century London', p. 266, table 15: Auctions advertised in England by location; also Redford, *Art Sales: A History of Sales of Pictures & Other Works of Art*, p. xv.
32. E. W. Manwaring, *Italian Landscape in Eighteenth-century England*, 2nd edn (London: F. Cass, 1965), p. 64.
33. Rouquet, *The State of the Arts in England*, pp. 123, 126.
34. *London Gazette* (January 1690), pp. 27–30; (January 1692), pp. 18–21.
35. For example the 263 guineas paid at Cock's on 12 March 1726 for a depiction of William III on his yacht by William Vandevelde; or 483 guineas for a landscape by Claude Lorraine at Prestage's on 16 November 1763.
36. Lippincott, *Selling Art in Georgian London*, pp. 63–4 based on an examination of a collection of annotated sales catalogues compiled by R. Houlditch of Great Queen Street located in the manuscript collection of the Victoria and Albert Museum, London (MS 86.008–19).
37. Graves's data sorted by auctioneer, date of sale and artist category.
38. Lord Halifax's property was sold in 1840 as was the collection of the painter Charles Jervas; Cock's auctioned off works owned by the Earl of Suffolk in 1741; 1742 witnessed the Earl of Oxford sale; Mary Edward's auction took place in 1746; and in 1747 the collections of the Duke of Chandos and the painter Jonathan Richardson went on the

block. See Ormrod, The Rise of the London Art Market, 1660–1760', pp. 318–19. Also Graves's data sorted by sales date.

39. For example the dealer Greenwood's sale at Christie's, February 1773; Count Schulenburg's sale at Christie's, April 1775; property from Paris sold at Walsh's, May 1775; the de Grote sale at Christie's, March 1776; Signor Biondi's sale at Christie's, February 1777. For these and others see Graves sorted by sales dates.
40. For example, the Duke of Argyle sale at Langford's, March 1771; Robert Ansell's sale at Walsh's in March 1775; John Bertel's sale at Walsh's in April 1775; Gilbert Marshall's sale at Walsh's in April 1776; 'noblemen's' collections at Squibb's in March and at Walsh's in April 1777. Graves's data sorted by sales dates for these and others.
41. For example, Joseph Salvador's sale at Christie's, January 1773. The seller was one of the directors of the East India Company.
42. Christie's sale of 16 and 25 April 1777 including the property of Rev. D. Friend; or the sale of the dealer N. Desenfans at Christie's on 8 April 1786; similarly, the dealer Vandergucht's sale held there on 14 March 1788 and Dr Newton's sale of 8 April 1788, also at Christie's. Exceptions to this include the above mentioned Earl of Oxford sale on 7–11 March 1741 at Cock.
43. Christie's sales' catalogues as well as Graves's entries for these artists. The same information can be obtained by sorting Graves's data by auction date and artists' date of death. Also Langford's sale of J. Richardson's paintings on 18 February 1772 and S. Scott's sale at the same house on 13 January 1772.
44. For example, Gambarini sale at Cock, 10 March 1725; Geminiani sale at the same house on 21 April of the same year; the Greenwood sale at Christie's on 22 February 1773; the Vandergucht sale at Christie's on 6 March 1777 or the Desanfans sale of 8 April 1786.
45. Pears, *The Discovery of Painting*, p. 102, estimates that dealer-organized sales account for some 35 to 40 per cent of all surviving records of auctions between 1711 and 1760, amounting to approximately 10,000 pictures out of a total of about 25,000. He does not provide any observations over time which might indicate certain trends. Graves's records are too sparse in this early period to permit any conclusions. However, Pears's estimate amounting to a total of no more than 500 pictures per year seems too low in light of the significantly higher turnover figures during the late 1680s and early 90s.
46. Who the painters of these works were is difficult to determine.
47. De Marchi, 'Auctioning Paintings in Late Seventeenth-Century London', V. A. Ginsburgh (ed.), p. 111 and n. 43.
48. Farrington, *Diaries*, vol. 1, p. 36.
49. For appraisers see R. Campbell, *The London Tradesman* (London: T. Gardner, 1747), p. 175.
50. Law Geo.III cap. 50, of September 1777 and 19 Geo. III cap. 56 in 1779. With some modification.
51. J. Bateman, *The Law of Auctions* (London, 1838), p. 341. This opinion is still used today by auction houses in the glossary describing the hierarchical ranking of attribution.

Chapter Five: The Evolution of Picture-Dealing

1. Pears, *The Discovery of Painting*, p. 102.
2. Paulson, *Hogarth: His Life, Art, and Times*, vol. 1, p. 372, sees Hogarth's contempt for dealers as the main reason for the artist's business methods. He even specifically excluded them from attending his studio sales for fear that they would form a ring.

3. Pears, *The Discovery of Painting*, p. 102.
4. Gibson-Wood, 'Picture Consumption in London at the End of the Seventeenth Century', see above ch 4, n. 13.
5. Pears, *The Discovery of Painting*, p. 166. The average price for the entire century is £80.50 with a median of £31.60. However, since Graves lists only paintings by artists whose works have sold over £100 during the 200 years he records, the actual average was, most likely, lower.
6. Pears, *The Discovery of Painting*, pp. 72–3, 77–92 for the costs involved in operating as an international dealer.
7. Lippincott., *Selling Art in Georgian London*, pp. 77–96 and notes offer accounts of several of these and other subsequently mentioned dealers' lives and professional activities. F. Simpson, 'Dutch Paintings in England before 1760', *Burlington Magazine*, 95 (February 1953), pp. 39–42, mentions Peter A. Mottaux, Samuel Paris and Robert Bragge. Also, Bruntjen, *John Boydell*, p. 89, and Whitley, *Artists and Their Friends in England 1700–1790*, vol. 1, p. 338, vol. 2, pp. 76, 84, 87, 133. Noel Desanfans is mentioned by Hermann, *The English as Collectors*, pp. 171–2 and Whitley, *Artists and Their Friends in England 1700–1790*, vol. 1, pp. 109, 283; vol. 2, pp. 10, 13, 32, 77, 88, 142, 190 and W. T. Whitley, *Art in England* (New York: Hacker Art Books, 1973), 2 vols, vol. 1, pp. 30–4. This dealer published a pamphlet in 1799 promoting 'A Plan for improving the Arts in Britain'. Farington, *Diaries*, vol. 4, pp. 1132–3, entries for Jan. 11/12, 1799. Lippincott, *Selling Art in Georgian London*, discusses Pond and also mentions Hay, as does Vertue, *Note Books*, vol. 3, pp. 13–14, 125. Whitley, *Artists and Their Friends in England 1700–1790*, vol. 1, pp. 75, 98, 109, 243 discusses Hay, vol. 1, pp. 18, 29, 31, 64, 124, 332, Arthur Pond, and vol. 2, p. 190, Michael Bryan; vol. l, p. 261 describes briefly the activities of the dealer Goodall. Bryan is discussed in J. Armstrong-Totten, 'The Rise and Fall of a British Connoisseur: the Career of Michael Bryan (1757–1821), Picture Dealer *extraordinaire*', Warren and Turpin (eds), *Auctions, Agents and Dealers*, pp. 141–50.
8. J. T. Smith, *Nollekens and His Times*, ed. W. Whitten (London and New York: 1917), 2 vols., vol. 1, pp. 381–3, as cited by Lippincott, *Selling Art in Georgian London*, p. 108, n. 19.
9. Graves data sorted by sellers.
10. Buchanan, *Memoirs of Painting*, vol. 2, p. 96. Whitley, *Artists and Their Friends in England 1700–1790*, vol. 2, pp. 200, 203, 325, 344 mentions an artist/picture dealer named James Irvine, most likely identical to the above James Irving. Jacob More is discussed in vol. 1, pp. 350, and vol. 2, pp. 199–203.
11. Whitley, *Artists and Their Friends in England 1700–1790*, vol. 1, p. 262 and vol. 2, pp. 31, 160, 191, 192, 194.
12. Ormrod, 'The Rise of the London Art Market', *Economia e arte, see. XIII-XVIII*, p. 315.
13. Hermann, *The English as Collectors*, p. 30, and Lippincott, *Selling Art in Georgian London*, pp. 99–100.
14. I. Pears, 'Patronage and Learning in the Virtuoso Republic: John Talman in Italy 1709–12', *Oxford Art Journal*, 5, no 1 (1982), pp. 24–30.
15. British Museum, Add. MS 23724, ff. 14, 40, 60, 61, 62, 74, on Dr. Hickman, and 98, 103, 112, 129, 130, on Selwin, as cited by Lippincott, *Selling Art in Georgian London*, p. 114, ns 32 and 33.
16. L. Lewis, *Connoisseurs and Secret Agents in 18th Century Rome* (London: Chatto & Windus, 1961).

17. This commercial alliance is discussed in the *Art Journal* (Feb. 1851), p. 63. For dealers' use of auctions, see *Art Journal* (August 1851), p. 246.
18. R. Godfrey, *Printmaking in Britain* (New York: New York University Press, 1978), pp. 10, 43.
19. Hogarth is cited in *Artists on Art* (New York: Pantheon Books, 1945), R. Goldwater and M. Treves (eds), p. 179; Walpole, *Anecdotes of Painting in England*, vol. 3, p. 986, and W. Graves, *Sculptura-Historica-Technica; or the History and Art of Engraving* (London, 1747), p. iv.
20. Godfrey, *Printmaking in Britain*, pp. 28–30; also Vertue, *Notebooks*, vol. 3, p. 14; Rouquet, *The State of the Arts in England*, p. 82.
21. Vertue, *Notebooks*, vol. 6, p. 187.
22. For an early history of engraving in England see Vertue, *Notebooks*, vol. 6, pp. 13–30; also Walpole, vol. 3, pp. 839–963, for a description of the principal engravers active in England prior to the reign of Queen Anne. On Dorigny, see Walpole, *Anecdotes of Painting in England*, vol. 3, pp. 965–7; on Dubosc, p. 968.
23. The changes of the engraving industry during this time can be pieced together from Vertue's *Notebooks*. Also Godfrey, *Printmaking in Britain*, ch. 3; Paulson, *Hogarth: His Art, Life, and Time*, vol. 1, pp. 55, 61; Pye, *Patronage of British Art, A Historical Sketch*, pp. 47–58, for further accounts of the history of the engraving industry during the early decades of the eighteenth century.
24. Vertue, *Notebooks*, vol. 3, pp. 146–7.
25. Ibid., pp. 281–3; Walpole, *Anecdotes of Painting in England*, vol. 3, p. 728.
26. W. Hogarth, *The Analysis of Beauty with the Rejected Passages from the Manuscript Drafts and Autobiographical Notes*, ed. J. Burke (Oxford: Clarendon Press, 1955), p. 226.
27. Rouquet, *The State of the Arts in England*, p. 28 and Pye, *Patronage of British Art, A Historical Sketch*, p. 243.
28. Godfrey, *Printmaking in Britain*, p. 61.
29. Raven, 'The Book Trades', in Rivers (ed.), *Books and Their Readers in Eighteenth-century England: New Essays*, 1–34. Paulson, *Hogarth: His Life, Art, and Times*, vol. 1, p. 280, for data on seventeenth-century book publications by subscription. On the same topic see A. Beljame, *Men of Letters and the English Public in the 18th Century* (London: K. Paul, Trench, Truber, 1948), p. 363. For some profit figures of books published by subscription see G. Sherburn, *The Early Career of Alexander Pope* (Oxford: Clarendon Press, 1934), pp. 188, 253–9.
30. L. Cale, *Fuseli's Milton Gallery 'Turning Readers into Spectators* (Oxford: Clarendon Press, 2006), addresses this topic.
31. £3,000 pounds translate into £165,000 in 2008 values using the retail price index and £2.4 million using the Average Earnings index while £6,000 amount to £330,000 or £4.8 million respective to the index used. EH.net.
32. Pye, *Patronage of British Art, A Historical Sketch*, pp. 243–4 and ns 52–4; for the Earl of Suffolk's speech, see Hansard, *Parliamentary Debates*, 1 (1803–4), p. 849. In 2008 values, this amounts to around £1.1 million using the Retail Price index, or £160 million using the Average Earnings index.
33. See below ch. 7 for explanations of these terms. On product differentiation in relation to prints see Godfrey, *Printmaking in Britain*, pp. 38, 53.
34. *Memoirs and Recollections of the Late Abraham Rainbach* (London, 1843), pp. 143–4. On limited editions and implied investment potential see p. 56 and Paulson, *Hogarth: His Life, Art, and Times*, vol. 1, pp. 286, 305–7, 366.

35. Foss, *Man of Wit to Man of Business*, pp. 180–1; Paulson, *Hogarth: His Life, Art, and Times*, vol. 1, pp. 360–6. On Hogarth's specific troubles with artistic piracy see his comments cited by Paulson, *Hogarth: His Life, Art, and Times*, vol. 1, p. 119.
36. Lippincott, *Selling Art in Georgian London*, pp. 132, 148. Also Public Record Office, London, cust 3 register of imports and exports 1693–1774.
37. Whitley, *Artists and Their Friends in England 1700–1790*, p. 72.
38. J. Landseer before the Select Committee of the House of Commons on the Arts, cited by Pye, *Patronage of British Art, A Historical Sketch*, p. 211, without providing a date.
39. Waterhouse, *Painting in England*, p. 72.
40. Godfrey, *Printmaking in Britain*, p. 65.
41. Quoted by Paulson, *Hogarth: His Life, Art, and Times*, vol. 1, p. 282 (no date provided). An account of the struggle of engravers to gain full membership in the Royal Academy can be found in Pye, *Patronage of British Art, A Historical Sketch*, pp. 185–214.
42. Godfrey, *Printmaking in Britain*, p. 43.
43. Cited by Pye, *Patronage of British Art, A Historical Sketch*, p. 211, without providing a date.
44. Fuseli's enterprise is discussed in detail by G. Schiff, *Johann Heinrich Fuesslis Milton Galerie* (Zurich: Fretz & Wasmuth, 1963); also, Cale, *Fuseli's Milton Gallery*.
45. Pye, *Patronage of British Art, A Historical Sketch*, pp. 174, 291.
46. Farington, *Diaries*, vol. 2, p. 86, entry for 24 February 1803, referring to a conversation with the portrait painter, T. Lawrence.
47. S. C. Hall, *Retrospective of A Long Life from 1815–1883* (New York: D. Appleton and Company, 1883), pp. 195, 199.
48. W. Collins, *A Rogue's Life* (London: Richard Benley and Son, 1879), pp. 43–5.
49. Buchanan, *Memoirs of Painting*, vol. 1, xiii.
50. T. Winstanley, *Observations on the Arts* (Liverpool: W. Wales, 1828), pp. 3–6.
51. Ibid., pp. 3–6.
52. Pye, *Patronage of British Art, A Historical Sketch*, p. 279.
53. Ormrod, 'The Rise of the London Art Market, 1660–1760', p. 313, table 2.
54. Sorting Graves's data by auction house and sale date as well as by sellers' names and sale date. Further examples can be found in Christie's auction catalogues of this period.
55. Arguably foremost among these collections was the one assembled by the Duke of Orleans and sold through the dealer Michael Bryan both privately as well as at auction. Others included an anonymous collection sold at Christie's in 1790; the Isaac Jermineau sale at the same house in the same year; the Calonne collection sold by Skinner in 1795, the Parma collection at Christie's in 1800 or the dealer Delahante's sale at Phillips in 1814.
56. Winstanley, *Observations on the Arts*, p. 38.
57. Farington, *Diaries*, vol. 4, p. 177, entry for 15 July 1807 and vol. 1, p. 99, entry for 17 May 1795, respectively.
58. Winstanley, *Observations on the Arts*, p. 8.
59. Farington, *Diaries*, vol. 5, p. 172, entry for 24 May 1809; vol. 1, p. 15, entry for 13 November 1793; p. 201, entry for 3 July 1809, respectively.
60. For more on this topic see P. Noon, *Crossing the Channel, British and French Painting in the Age of Romanticism* with contributions by S. Bann, D. B. Brown, R. Meredith, C. Riding and M. Watteau (New York and London: The Metropolitan Museum of Art in association with Tate Publishing, 2003).
61. Noon, 'Colour and Effect, Anglo-French Painting in London and Paris', p. 27.

62. Farington, *Diaries*, vol. 1, p. 344; vol. 4, entry for 4 January 1808; vol. 2, p. 175, entry for 19 December 1803 (Opie); p. 245, entry for 1 June 1804 (Constable), respectively.
63. Pye, *Patronage of British Art, A Historical Sketch*, p. 253.
64. Godfrey, *Printmaking in Britain*, pp. 47–8.
65. Pye, *Patronage of British Art, A Historical Sketch*, p. 253, n. 62. £300,000 in 2008 values equal £16.5 million using the Retail Price index or £240 million using the Average Earning index. £46,000 pounds amount to £2.5 million or £36 million respective of the conversion method.
66. For a discussion of this collection see Reist, 'The Fate of the Palais Royal Collection: 1791–1800'.
67. J. Armstrong-Totten, 'Expand the Audience, Increase the Profits: Motivations Behind the Private Contract Sale', in R. Panzanelli and M. Preti-Hamard (eds), *La Circulation des Oeuvres d'Art, 1789–1848* (Rennes: Presses Universitaire de Rennes Institut National d' Histoire de l' Art, Getty Research Institute, 2007), pp. 45–55.
68. Buchanan, *Memoirs of Painting*, vol. 1, pp. 1–219 and pp. 18–19.
69. Farington, *Diaries*, vol. 1, p. 250, entry of 2 December 1798, recording a comment made by the Duke of Bridgwater.
70. Winstanley, *Observations on the Arts*, pp. 5–6.
71. Hall, *Retrospective of A Long Life from 1815–1883*, pp. 199, 197 for related comments.
72. *Art Union* 1:6 (July 1839), p. 104.
73. Hall, *Retrospective of A Long Life from 1815–1883*, p. 197.
74. Ibid., p. 200. Hall provides no source.
75. Hall, *Retrospective of A Long Life from 1815–1883*, pp. 199–200; *Art Union*, 7 (1845), pp. 121–2 and *Art Journal*, May 1 (1852), pp. 151–2. For an account of some of these practices and the individuals involved, see Collins, *A Rogue's Life*, pp. 39–41ff.
76. Collins, *A Roguess's Life*, p. 40.
77. *The Times*, 2 June 1828, front page. We are also indebted to W. Hobday's descendant, Roger Hobday, for sharing information contained in the family archives.
78. F. Haskell, *The Ephemeral Museum: Old Master Paintings and the Rise of the Art Exhibition* (New Haven, CT: Yale University Press, 2000). I. Reist, 'The Fate of the Palais Royal Collection: 1791–1800', in Panzanelli and Preti-Hamard (eds), *La Circulation des Oeuvres d'Art 1789–1848*, pp 27–44, pp. 36–8 and n. 47. Also D. Bindman, 'The Orleans Collection and its Impact on British Art', Panzanelli and Preti-Hamard (eds), *La Circulation des Oeuvres d'Art 1789–1848*, pp. 57–66.
79. Our records identify at least twenty such artists' estate sales between 1770 and 1830. The former head archivist of Christie's, J. Rex-Parkes, has identified many more in an as yet unpublished manuscript on studio sales that he kindly shared.

6 The Victorian Era

1. Christie's auction catalogues from his period and Graves data sorted by individual sellers and buyers.
2. Collins, *A Rogue's Life*, pp. 46–7.
3. *Autobiographical Recollections by the Late Charles Robert Leslie, R.A*, ed. T. Taylor (Boston, MA: Ticknor and Fields, 1860), vol. 1, p. 346.
4. Hall, *Retrospective of A Long Life from 1815–1883*, pp. 194–209. On Hall's editorship of this publication, see D. N. Mancoff, 'Samuel Carter Hall: Publisher as Promoter of the High Arts', *Victorian Periodicals Review* (Victorian Art and the Press I), 24 (Spring

1991), pp. 11–21; J. Maas, 'S. C. Hall and *The Art Journal*', *Connoisseur*, 191 (March 1976), pp. 206–9.

5. Hall, *Retrospective of A Long Life from 1815–1883*, pp. 197, 199–204.
6. Ibid., p. 202.
7. The report for 1877 of the Art Union of London credits Hall with having succeeded, 'by persevering attacks ... in driving from the market those spurious imitations of old masters which alone found purchasers among our Art collectors thirty years ago; in place of which fabulous prices are now paid for the works of British artists ...' Hall, *Retrospective of A Long Life from 1815–1883*, p. 203.
8. A. Dyson, *From Pictures to Print: the Nineteenth-Century Engraving Trade*, pp. 6–7. Cash prizes were awarded to members with the stipulation that the money be used for the purchase of modern paintings from specified exhibitions.
9. The above mentioned figure of 7 per cent relates the trade as a group to the number of different buyers for the entire period, while the aforementioned average of 12.6 per cent describes the percentage relationship broken down by decade. The difference of the two percentage figures derives from the fact that some dealers dropped out of the market in each decade while a steadily growing number of dealers entered the market at approximately the same rate of increase experienced by the overall number of different buyers.
10. Most likely, there were more dealers than we were able to identify. We extracted names from artists' writings, Maas's earlier mentioned book, contemporary newspapers, the London Post Office Directory, artists' biographies and diaries, contemporary periodicals, catalogues from this period kept in Christie's archives and the University of Glasgow, 'Exhibition Culture in London 1878–1908', www.exhibitionculture.arts.gla.ac.uk (Spring 2009). Our list should by no means be considered comprehensive and may contain some errors and omissions.
11. R. Floud and D. McCloskey, *The Economic History of Great Britain since 1700*, vol. 2, pp. 4–8.
12. Collins, *A Rogue's Life*, p. 47.
13. J. Maas, *Gambart* (London: Barrie & Jenkins, 1975), p. 43 quoting this letter written on 4 July 1850 by Rought without providing a source. According to Rupert Maas, this letter may have been part of his father's extensive collection of art-related correspondence from the Victorian period.
14. P. Fletcher, 'Creating the French Gallery: Ernest Gambart and the Rise of the Commercial Art Gallery in Mid-Victorian London', http://www.19thc-artworldwide.org/index.php?option=com_content&view=article&id=143:creating-the-french-gallery-ernest-gambart-and-the-rise-of-the-commercial-art-gallery-in-mid-victorian-london&catid=46:spring07article&Itemid=68.
15. Hall, *Retrospective of A Long Life from 1815–1883*, p. 205.
16. *Art Union*, March 1848, p. 95.
17. *Art Journal*, February 1851, p. 63.
18. H. Hunt, *Pre-Raphaelitism and the Pre-Raphaelite Brotherhood* (London: MacMillan, 1905), vol. 1, p. 217.
19. *Illustrated London News*, October 11 (1862), p. 7.
20. *Art Journal*, March 1 (1864), p. 80.
21. P. G. Hamerton, *Etchers and Etching* (London: MacMillan, 1868), p. 74.
22. Ibid., p. 74.
23. *Art Journal*, December 1871, p. 280.
24. *Art Journal*, August 1852, p. 246.

25. Agnew emphasized works by living British painters with over 66 per cent of the gallery's recorded purchases belonging to this group while this firm was least interested in contemporary paintings from the Continent. Colnaghi focused on English and Continental Old Masters in over 90 per cent of acquisitions; their purchases of works by E. W. Cooke, T. S. Cooper, Lord Leighton or J. A. Whistler were exceptions and may possibly have even been commissioned bids. Gooden concentrated on contemporary English paintings, as did Vokins. Wallis purchases were fairly evenly divided between contemporary Continental and British works. In fact, Wallis and Tooth showed the greatest emphasis, over 30 per cent of their buying activity, on contemporary works. Agnew purchased numerically more works of this category, but it amounted to just 8 per cent of overall purchases. Of the remaining sixty-one dealers, only McLean, Permain, Shepherd, Smith and Tooth were buyers of works belonging to any of three of the above mentioned four categories.
26. Hall, *Retrospective of A Long Life from 1815–1883*, pp. 197–8.
27. *Art Journal*, June 1863, pp. 121–2.
28. Christie's sale of 25 and 29 April, 1863, Christie's sale of 26 April 1845 and Christie's sale of 13 June 1851. More on Bicknell can be found in D. S. Macleod, *Art and the Victorian Middle Class* (Cambridge: Cambridge University Press, 1996), pp. 21–2, 30, 43–5, 163, 223, 229, 348, 384–5, 392, 393–4, 433, 438.
29. Frith, *My Autobiography and Reminiscences*, vol. 1, p. 30; vol. 2, p. 143.
30. See above, p. 105, n. 24.
31. J. Cooper, *Under the Hammer* (London: Constable, 1977), pp. 35–7, 88.
32. Letter to Effie of 27 June 1861. Pierpont Morgan Library, New York. Accession number: MA1485D, record identification: 132647.
33. In its 15 June 1829 review of the George Hibbert sale at Christie's on 13 June 1829, the *Morning Chronicle* reported that J. W. M. Turner's *Abingdon* (National Gallery #485) was bought by the artists himself, 'who, very prudently ... always attends sales to keep up the price of his work'. Whiteley, *Art of England 1821–1837*, p. 167.
34. The issue of 'toehold' and bidding strategy in corporate take-over has been discussed by J. Bulow, M. Huang, and P. Klemperer, 'Toeholds and Takeovers', *Journal of Political Economy*, vol. 107 (1999), pp. 427–54; also M. Burkart, 'Overbidding in takeover contests', *Journal of Finance*, 50 (1995), pp. 1491–1515; and R. Singh, 'Takeover Bidding with Toeholds: The Case of the Owner's Curse', *Review of Financial Studies*, 11(1998), pp. 679–709.
35. The original of the first letter is in the Beinecke rare Books and Manuscript Library, Yale University Library. The second letter is reprinted in D. G. Rossetti, *Letters*, ed. O. Doughty and J. R. Wahls (Oxford: Clarendon Press, 1965–7), letter no. 651, as well as in V. Surtees, *Dante Gabriel Rossetti: A Catalogue Raisonne* (Oxford: Clarendon Press, 1971), vol. 1, p. 5.
36. Macleod, *Art and the Victorian Middle Class*, p. 119, offers the events surrounding the sale of the Birch collection in 1855, 1856 and 1857 as possible evidence for insider bidding. See also R. Cassady, *Auctions and Auctioneering* (Berkeley, CA: University of California Press, 1967), chapter 12, 'On manipulating Auctions by Buyers and Sellers'.
37. See above, p. 105, n. 24.
38. We have fairly comprehensive accounts of two of the major dealers' activities, that of Agnew and Gambart. For the history of Agnew see, G. Agnew, *Agnew's, 1817–1967* (London: Bradbury Press, Ltd, 1967); for Gambart see Maas, *Gambart*.

39. *The Life and Letters of Frederic Shields* (London: Longmans, Green and Co., 1912), E. Mills(ed), p. 74.
40. C. Wood, *Dictionary of Victorian Painters* (Woodbridge, Suffolk: The Antique Collectors' Club, 1995). By comparison, for the eighteenth century, E. Waterhouse features less than one fifth of the number of active painters than Wood. E. Waterhouse, *Dictionary of British 18th Century Painters in Oils and Crayons* (Woodbridge, Suffolk: Antique Collectors' Club, Ltd., 1981).
41. Christie's catalogues of 24–5 March 1871 for Wallis and 31 March and 1 April 1871 for Gambart.
42. Maas, *Gambart*, pp. 97–8.
43. For detailed analyses see T. Bayer and J. Page, 'Arthur Tooth: A London Art Dealer in the Spotlight, 1870–71', *Nineteenth Century Art Worldwide*, http://www.19thc-artworldwide.org/.
44. The gallery's extensive handwritten business ledgers are stored at the Getty Research Center in Los Angeles.
45. Without information on the gallery's overhead, net profit is impossible to determine. Nonetheless, using the retail price index conversion, his gross profit amounts to approximately $310,000. However, when using the average earning conversion model, this figure swells to over $2.5 million. EH.net.
46. Using retail price index, £10,510 amounts to £750,000 or £6.2 million related to average earning; £300 translates into £21, 400 or £177,000 respectively. EH.net.
47. See above, p. 105, n. 24.
48. A cursory examination of a ten-year period (1870–80) of the stock books of the firm of Agnew, also held at the Getty Research Center, shows similar features.
49. Jansen, *Marketing Modernism in Fin-de-Siècle Europe*, ch. 6.
50. D. P. Corbett, *The World in Paint* (University Park, PA: The Pennsylvania State University Press), p. 131.
51. T. Barringer, *Men at Work* (New Haven, CT and London: Yale University Press, 2005), pp. 313–21, discusses the tension surrounding the issue of artistic labour during this period that came to a head in the *Whistler vs Ruskin* trial in 1878.
52. Examples are the sale in 1871 of the Bullock collection or the sales of the inventory of the dealers Gambart, Wallis and Agnew. Dealers were the biggest buyers at these sales. *Art Journal* (1871), pp. 140, 167, 226. The data do not explicitly show when Tooth individually performed this function except in the case of re-purchasing a picture by Frith from Murietta that the dealer had sold only 8 months earlier. The collector incurred a loss of around 10 per cent but had a ready market; Tooth, however, still made a small overall profit.
53. See above, p. 105, n. 24; p. 108, ns. 30, 31.
54. Copley's *Death of Chatham* (1781, 90 x 121 in.) is but one example of this trend towards attention-grabbing pictorial sensations.
55. Concerning the propensity among artists to make rational business decisions, see T. Bayer, J. Page, Y. Raviv and J. Rosett, 'Age, Human Capital and the Quality of Work: New Evidence from Old Masters'. Abstract, http://ssrn.com/abstract=1364417.
56. Graves's data sorted by size and date of painting.
57. We ran a test to calculate the most profitable picture size. The result supports Tooth's choice: the most profitable size range, 20 x 30 inches, was the most common one in his inventory and matches the average size of landscapes, his most frequently traded picture category.

58. The dealer Morby operated in Scotland while Grindley was located in Liverpool. We suspect that there were more individuals listed in the ledger who sold paintings in other urban centres that we could identify.

7 'Working the Oracle': The Tools of the Trade

1. Reitlinger, *Economics of Taste*, p. 143 and Maas, *Gambart*, p. 28.
2. *Art Journal*, November (1853), p. 308.
3. Dyson, *From Pictures to Print: the Nineteenth Century Engraving Trade*, preface.
4. A copy of this pamphlet was made available to us in London by Jeremy Maas.
5. Gillott papers as quoted by Maas, *Gambart*, pp. 131–2. 5,500 guineas amount to around £400,000 in 2010 values based on a retail price index conversion and approximately £3.7 million using a conversion based on average earnings; 3,000 guineas translate into £250,000 or £2 million depending on the conversion method; 88,000 guineas translate into £6.2 million or £60 million respectively.
6. *Art Journal*, (1 January 1850), p. 30.
7. Agnew, *Agnew's 1817–1967*, p. 65.
8. Dyson, *From Pictures to Prints: the Nineteenth-Century Engraving Trade*, p. 3.
9. Ibid., p. 78.
10. Hunt, *Pre-Raphaelitism and the Pre-Raphaelite Brotherhood*, vol. 2, p. 189–90.
11. British Museum, Department of Manuscripts, 46140, pp. 55, 68, 74, 122, 123, 160.
12. R. Treble, *Great Victorian Pictures* (London: Arts Council, 1978), p. 80.
13. Fine Art Society, London, Minute Book, 24 May 1876.
14. W. P. Frith, *A Victorian Canvas: The Memoirs of W.P. Frith, R.A*, ed. N. Wallis (London: Geoffrey Bles, 1957), pp. 85, 89. Also Godfrey, *Printmaking in Britain*, ch. 5 and 6.
15. Dyson, *From Pictures to Prints: the Nineteenth-Century Engraving Trade*, p. 3. The letter concerned the sold-out subscription of Landseer's *Ptarmigan Hill.*
16. M. T. S. Raimbach, *Memoirs and Recollections of Abraham Raimbach* (London, 1845), pp. 22–3.
17. By 1865, The Newspaper Press Directory listed 554 different periodicals.
18. Hunt, *Pre-Raphaelitism and the Pre-Raphaelite Brotherhood*, vol. 2, p. 461.
19. Godfrey, *Printmaking in Britain*, p. 102.
20. Redford, *Art Sales: A History of Sales of Pictures & Other Works of Art*, p. 288.
21. London Post Office Directories.
22. J. Burnett, 'Autobiography of John Burnett', *Art Journal* (August 1850), pp. 275–7, quote 276.
23. Maas, *Gambart*, p. 18.
24. *Art Union*, October 1845, p. 325.
25. Agnew, *Agnew's*, p. 11.
26. Ibid., p. 65.
27. J. Bass, 'Reconsidering Walter Benjamin', in G. Weisberg and L. Dixon (eds), *The Documented Image* (Syracuse, NY: Syracuse University Press, 1987), pp. 39–40.
28. *The Times* featured such announcements usually on its front page, column 4.
29. *Art Union* (October 1845), p. 318.
30. For example, the description of the mezzotint after Ansdell's *Death of a Stag* in the *Art Union*, on 1 May 1847, p. 183, or the review of Blanchard's engraving of Hunt's *Isabella* in the *Art Journal* of 1 May (1871), p. 148.
31. *Athenaeum* (January 1847), p. 49.

32. Maas, *Gambart*, p. 39.
33. Agnew, *Agnew's*, p. 64; Dyson, *From Pictures to Prints: the Nineteenth-Century Engraving Trade*, p. 220–2. Rupert Maas of the Maas Gallery in London advised us that the above regulations were not always strictly adhered to. To that end he provided us with M. B. Huish, *The Year's Art 1891: A Concise Epitome of all Matters Relating to the Arts of Painting, Sculpture, And Architecture which have occurred During the year 1890 together with Information respecting the Events of the Year 1891* (London: J. S. Virtue & Co., Ltd, 1891), pp. 223–4, which indicates that the publication line could appear on the bottom or the top margin.
34. *Illustrated London News* (27 October 1855), p. 495.
35. L. Johnson, 'The Raft of Medusa in Great Britain', *Burlington Magazine*, 96 (August 1954), pp. 249–54; S. Lodge, 'Géricault in England', *Burlington Magazine*, 107 (December 1965), pp. 616–27; L. Eitner, *Géricault's Raft of Medusa* (London: Phaidon, 1972), and his *Géricault, his Life and Work* (London: Orbis Publishing, 1983), pp. 209–21; Holt, *Triumph of Art for the Public*, pp. 206–10; a review of the event can be found in the *London Literary Gazette and Journal of better Letters*, 180 (1 July 1820), p. 427.
36. Maas, *Gambart*, p. 48 (quote), 91. For a discussion of Gambart in the context of the emerging commercial art gallery industry, see Fletcher, 'Creating the French Gallery: Ernest Gambart and the Rise of the Commercial Art Gallery in Mid-Victorian London'.
37. Hunt, *Pre-Raphaelitism and the Pre-Raphaelite Brotherhood*, vol. 1, p. 351 and Maas, *Gambart*, p. 161.
38. Hunt, *Pre-Raphaelitism and the Pre-Raphaelite Brotherhood*, vol. 2, pp. 187–97.
39. Ibid., vol. 2, p. 96.
40. M. Clive, *The Days of Reckoning* (London: Macmillan, 1964), p. 10, provides an account of the production cost of S. E. Waller's (1850–1903) painting *One and Twenty*.
41. *Athenaeum* (11 August 1860), p. 201.
42. W. B. Scott, *Autobiographical Notes* (New York: Harper, 1892), vol. 2, p. 58.
43. Holman Hunt papers as cited by Maas, *Gambart*, p. 217.
44. M. Pointon (ed.), *Pre-Raphaelites Reviewed* (Manchester and New York: Manchester University Press, 1988), p. 37.
45. J. G. Millais, *The Life and Letters of Sir John Everett Millais* (New York: Frederick A. Stokes Company, 1899), p. 78.
46. This was pointed out to us by the film director, Peter O'Fallon.
47. Gambart's relationship with S. C. Hall, editor of the *Art Journal*, F. G. Stephens of the *Athenaeum*, and Tom Taylor of *The Times* is mentioned by Maas, *Gambart*, pp. 36–7, 65, 72.
48. *Illustrated London News* (8 December, 1860), p. 545; (22 December, 1860), p. 584; (20 September 1862), p. 310.
49. *Athenaeum* (13 February 1858), p. 214; (13 March 1858), p. 344; *Art Journal* (1 April 1858), p. 126; and Hunt, *Pre-Raphaelitism and the Pre-Raphaelite Brotherhood*, vol. 1, p. 191.
50. *Athenaeum* (25 February 1860), p. 274.
51. *Athenaeum* (21 April 1860), p. 549.
52. Maas, *Gambart*, p. 212 and Holman Hunt Papers, cited by Maas, p. 221, n. 7.
53. Agnew, *Agnew's*, p. 65.
54. Maas, *Gambart*, pp. 75–6, 79, 92–3, 158.
55. Maas, *Gambart*, p. 75, n. 14, referencing a letter from W. B. Scott to J. Leathart of 21 March 1870. Leathart papers, University of British Columbia. http://resolve.library.ubc.ca/cgi-bin/catsearch?bid=3156975
56. See above, p. 121, n. 15.

57. T. M. Bayer, 'Degas and the English Connection 1872–1876', *Athanor*, 16 (1998), pp. 31–8; M. Guerin (ed.), *Degas Letters* (Oxford: Cassirer, 1947) pp. 11–12, 19, 34; T. Reff, 'Some unpublished letters of Degas', *Art Bulletin* LI (March 1968), p. 8. The history of this canvas is discussed in M. Brown's *Degas and the Business of Art: A Cotton Office in New Orleans* (University Park, Pa.: Pennsylvania State University Press, 1994).
58. M. Bennett, 'The Price of "Work": The Background to its First Exhibition, 1865', L. Parris (ed.), *Pre-Raphaelite Papers* (London: Tate Gallery, 1985), pp. 143–52. Also Graves under F. M. Brown.
59. S. Casteras, 'The 1857–58 Exhibition of English Art in America and Critical Responses to Pre-Raphaelitism', in Linda Ferber and William Gerdts (eds), *The New Path, Ruskin and the American Pre-Raphaelites* (New York: Schocken Books, Inc, 1985), pp. 109–33; The analysis of sales figures was undertaken by T. Bayer in an unpublished paper entitled 'The American Exhibition of British Art, 1857–58'.
60. Holt, *The Triumph of Art for the Public*, p. 134.
61. *Art Union* (March 1848), p. 95.
62. *Art Union* (September 1848), p. 285.
63. Hunt, *Pre-Raphaelitism and the Pre-Raphaelite Brotherhood*, vol. 1, p. 176.
64. Maas, *Gambart*, p. 53.
65. R. Fry, *Art and Socialism, Vision and Design* (London: Phoenix, 1928), p. 58.
66. *Englishwoman's Review*, 8 (April, 1868), p. 468.
67. C. Yeldham, *Women Artist in Nineteenth-Century France and England* (New York: Garland: 1984), vol. 2, p. 199; Gillett, *The Victorian Painter's World*, p. 205.
68. P. Fletcher and A. Helmreich, 'The Periodical Press and the Art Market: Investigating the "Dealer-Critic System" in Victorian England', *Victorian Periodicals Review*, 41:4 (Winter 2008), p. 323; also A. Burton, 'Nineteenth Century Periodicals', in T. Fawcett and C. Phillpot (eds), *The Art Press: Two Centuries of Art Magazines* (London: The Art Book Company, 1976), p. 4.
69. H. E. Roberts, 'Art Reviewing in the Early Nineteenth-Century Art Periodicals', *Victorian Periodicals Newsletter*, 19 (March 1973), pp. 9–20, pp. 9–10 and ff for a discussion of several of the leading periodicals of the period.
70. Roberts, 'Art Reviewing in the Early Nineteenth-Century Art Periodicals', p. 11 and n. 7. Roberts also mentions that 'it is difficult to find a review in all the first fifty years of the nineteenth century that does not mention and deplore the oppressive prevalence of portraits in the Royal Academy exhibitions'. p. 12.
71. Hall, *Retrospectives of A Long Life from 1815–1883*, pp. 194–5. Also, Mancoff, 'Samuel Carter Hall: Publisher as Promoter of the High Arts', pp. 11–21.
72. Roberts, 'Art Reviewing in the Early Nineteenth-Century Art Periodicals', p. 10, for these and other periodicals of the period.
73. *Art Journal*, 1 (1839), p. 102 as cited by Roberts, 'Art Reviewing in the Early Nineteenth-Century Art Periodicals', p. 10.
74. Hall, *Retrospectives of A Long Life from 1815–1883*, pp. 195 (quote), 197–8.
75. *Blackwood's Edinburgh Review*, the *Illustrated London News*, *Fraser's Magazine* or *Belgravia* for example.
76. Roberts, 'Exhibition and Review:', p. 83.
77. R. St J. Tyrwhitt, 'Skilled and Literary Art-Criticism', *Contemporary Review*, 11 (1869), p. 107.
78. E. Pennell, 'The Two Salons', *Fortnightly Review*, 53 (1893), p. 775.

79. G. P. Landow, 'There Began to Be a Great Talking about the Fine Arts', in J. L. Altholz (ed.), *The Mind and Art of Victorian England* (Minneapolis, MN: University of Minnesota Press, 1976), p. 130.
80. Hunt, *Pre-Raphaelitism and the Pre-Raphaelite Brotherhood*, vol. 1, p. 218. For other negative press coverage of the early works of the Pre-Raphaelite Brotherhood see *The Times* (7 May 1851), p. 8, and *Athenaeum* (7 June 1851), p. 609.
81. Roberts, 'Exhibition and Review', pp. 80–1.
82. D. Macleod, 'F. G. Stephens, Pre-Raphaelite Critic and Art Historian', *The Burlington Magazine*, 128 (June 1986), pp. 398–402.
83. On Hamerton, see H. S. Spatt, 'The Aesthetics of Editorship: Creating Taste in the Victorian Art World', ed. J. H. Wiener, *Innovators and Preachers* (London: Greenwood Press, 1985), p. 47; for Morris, p. 53; for Thomson; Fletcher and Helmreich, 'The Periodical and the Art Market', p. 325.
84. Hall, *Pre-Raphaelitism and the Pre-Raphaelite Brotherhood*, vol. 1, pp. 202–4, 208, 431.
85. Fletcher and Helmreich, 'The Periodical Press and the Art Market: Investigating the "Dealer-Critic System" in Victorian England', *Victorian Periodicals Review*, pp. 325–6.
86. C. Parsons and N. McWilliam, 'Le Paysan de Paris: Alfred Sensier and the Myth of Rural France', *Oxford Art Journal*, 6:2 (1983), pp. 37–58; Green, 'Dealing in Temperaments'; White and White, *Canvases and Careers*, pp. 94–7.
87. On Quilter, see Roberts, 'Exhibition and Review', p. 87; on Carr, see Spatt, 'The Aesthetics of Editorship', p. 44.
88. See above n. 48.
89. Maas, *Gambart*, pp. 106–7.
90. Ibid., p. 89.
91. Pennell, 'The Two Salons', p. 775.
92. Hunt, *Pre-Raphaelitism and the Pre-Raphaelite Brotherhood*, vol. 1, p. 343.
93. G. Burne-Jones, *Memorials of Edward-Burne-Jones* (London: The Macmillan Company, 1906), p. 127. Also correspondence between Ruskin and Shields reproduced in *The Life and Letters of Frederic Shields*, pp. 69, 71, 73, 87, 89, 167.
94. J. Ruskin, *Modern Painters* (Boston, MA: Dana Estes & Company, n. d.), vols 2 and 3, pp. 61–4, 83–4, 88, 130, 133–62, 175, 181, 83, 193–7, 214–16; vols 4 and 5, pp. 15–112. T. Hilton, *John Ruskin: The Early Years* (New Haven, CT: Yale University Press, 2000); and D. Birch, 'Father and Sons: Ruskin, John James Ruskin and Turner', *Nineteenth-Century Contexts*, 18:2 (1994), pp. 147–62.
95. Roberts, 'Exhibition and Review', p. 86.
96. Maas, *Gambart*, p. 69.
97. J. Christian, 'A Serious Talk: Ruskin's place in Burne-Jones Artistic Development', in L. Parris (ed.), *Pre-Raphaelite Papers* (London: Tate Gallery, 1984), pp. 184–205. S. Casteras (ed.), *John Ruskin and the Victorian Eye* (New York: H. N. Abrams, 1993) and Hunt, *Pre-Raphaelitism and the Pre-Raphaelite Brotherhood*, vol. 1, pp. 254–6, 415.
98. W. M. Rossetti (ed.), *Pre-Raphaelite Diaries and Letters* (London: Hurst and Blackett, 1900), letter no. 104.
99. Rossetti (ed.), *Pre-Raphaelite Diaries and Letters*, letter no. 174.
100. L. Austin, *The Practical Ruskin: Economics and Audience in the Late Work* (Baltimore, MD: Johns Hopkins University Press, 1991) and W. Henderson, *John Ruskin's Political Economy* (London: Routledge, 2000). Also J. T. Fain, *Ruskin and the Economists* (Nashville, TN: Vanderbilt University Press, 1956).

101. I. Street (ed.), *Ruskin's Principles of Art Criticism* (Chicago, IL: Herbert s. Stone & Company, 1901), pp. 422–3.
102. See his *Modern Painters*, 3, preface, reprinted in *Ruskin's Principles of Art Criticism*, pp. 55–6, also his 'Lectures on Art,' lecture III, p. 255. This topic is also addressed by Austin, *The Practical Ruskin*, ch. 3.
103. *Stones of Venice*, 3, chapter IV, reprinted, *Ruskin's Principles of Art Criticism*, p. 308.

8 The Formation of a Nexus: A Story of Christie's

1. Whitley, *Art in England*, p. 142, states that in 1808 Christie's was already 'easily the most important of the auctioneers of works of art'. Our data show that the firm was only slightly ahead of its competition by then, but public perception may have differed.
2. Ormrod, 'The Rise of the London Art Market', 1660–1760, p. 313; De Marchi, 'Auctioning Painting in Late Seventeenth-Century London', p. 122.
3. The other houses were Langford, Greenwood, Philips, Coxe, Stanley, Robins, Sotheby's and Foster.
4. Graves only lists studio sales of painters whose works have sold for £100 or more. At the time of this writing Jeremy Rex-Parkes, the former head archivist at Christie's, is researching these studio sales.
5. W. Roberts, *Memorials of Christie's: A Record of Art Sales from 1766–1896*, 2 vols (London: George Bell & Sons, 1897), vol. 1, p. 119.
6. Listed as *Dutch Fishing Boats, with the Sun rising-Group of figures bargaining for Fish, others unloading a vessel.*
7. G. M. Constantinides, M. Harris, R. M. Stulz, *Handbook of the Economics of Finance* (Amsterdam: Elsevier B.V., 2003), vol. 1, pp. 589–92.
8. Graves's data sorted by auction house and sale date.
9. Hall, *Retrospectives of A Long Life from 1815–1883*, pp. 197–8.
10. Whitley, *Art of England 1821–1837*; H. C. Marillier, *'Christie's' 1766–1925* (London: Constable & Company Ltd, Boston and New York: Houghton Mifflin Company, 1926); Roberts, *Memorials of Christie's.*
11. L. Schibeci, 'The London Auction Market and the Commodification of English Taste, 1766–1823' (PhD dissertation, Northwestern University, 1999).
12. Our records also list Skinner and Dyke, and Chapman and Annesley.
13. Christie opened his business around 1766, but his early auctions consisted almost exclusively of household goods. Roberts, *Memorials of Christie's*, pp. 8–11.
14. Other consignment of note included the estate of Joseph Salvador, the first Jewish director of the British East India Company; the estate of General Gansell; the former governor of Maryland, Thomas Bladen, the engraver Robert Strange, Lord Montfort and the Earl of Essex. Graves's data sorted by auction house and date of sale.
15. Marillier, *'Christie's'*, p. 18.
16. Farington, *Diaries*, vol. 1, p. 265. Records list a Charles Price as consignor of a large collection of a mixture of Italian and Dutch old masters sold on 13 February 1778. We are unable to determine if there was any connection between Chace Price and Charles Price.
17. The sum of £14,000 in 1799 translates into £750,000 using the retail price index or £11 million based on average earnings. Eh.net.
18. Cooper, *Under the Hammer*, p. 45.
19. Farington, *Diaries*, vol. 1, p. 227.

20. This was mentioned to Thomas Bayer by Dr Schibeci. See also Marillier, *'Christie's'*, p. 6, referring to Farington's diary entry of 2 August 1795 which mentions a conversation with the solicitor Mr. Drew 'on the subject of Christie not having yet settled for the sale of Sir Joshua's [Reynolds] pictures'.
21. Walter Agnew, the son of the dealer William Agnew, was a partner in Christie's from 1889 to 1915.
22. For this and other information on bidding at auctions see R. P. McAfee and J. McMillan, 'Auctions and Bidding', *Journal of Economic Literature*, 25, 2 (June 1987), pp. 699–739.
23. Sale of 3 March 1879 and 5 May 1879.

9 Commoditization and the Artist as a Producer: Product Differentiation and the Domestication of Pictures

1. *Autobiographical Recollections by the late Charles Robert Leslie*, p. xviii.
2. London Post office Directories for this period.
3. E. Waterhouse, *The Dictionary of British 18th Century Painters in Oils and Crayons* (Woodbridge, Suffolk: Antique Collectors' Club, Ltd., 1981); and Wood, *The Dictionary of Victorian Painters*.
4. Frith, *My Autobiography and Reminiscences*, vol. 1, p. 489; *Report of the Select Committee on Art Unions* (1845), quoted in P. Gillett, *The Victorian Painter's World* (New Brunswick, NJ: Rutgers University Press, 1990), p. 48.
5. Hunt, *Pre-Raphaelitism and the Pre-Raphaelite Brotherhood*, vol. 1, p. 95.
6. Frith, *My Autobiography and Reminiscences*, vol. 1, pp. 193, 222; Burne-Jones, *Memorials of Edward Burne-Jones*, vol. 2, p. 262; an informative discussion on potboilers and replicas can be found in Gillett, *The Victorian Painter's World*, pp. 46–9.
7. Millais, *Life and Letters of Sir John Everett Millais*), vol. 1, p. 360.
8. Hunt. *Pre-Raphaelitism and the Pre-Raphaelite Brotherhood*, vol. 1, p. 81.
9. Millais, *Life and Letters of Sir John Everett Millais*, vol. 1, p. 344.
10. Frith, *My Autobiography and Reminiscences*, vol. 1, pp. 131, 207, 235; also his *A Victorian Canvas*, pp. 107–8 and 192–3 on his loath of contemporary fashion. For quote, A. Noakes, *William Frith* (London: Jupiter, 1978), p. 49.
11. Frith, *My Autobiography and Reminiscences*, vol. 1, pp. 279, 294.
12. Noakes, *William Frith*, p. 40; and Frith, *A Victorian Canvas*, p. 56.
13. Frith, *Victorian Canvas*, p. 81.
14. A. Graves, *The Royal Academy of Arts* (London: George Bell and Sons, 1905), vol. 2, under Frith; also Noakes, *William Frith*, pp. 35–50.
15. Noakes, *William Frith*, pp. 51–2.
16. Frith, *A Victorian Canvas*, pp. 84–5.
17. Ibid., pp. 107–9.
18. Noakes, *William Frith*, p. 107. The painting is presently displayed in the lobby of the Windsor Court Hotel in New Orleans.
19. W. Arnstein, *Britain Yesterday and Today* (Boston, MA: Heath, 1996), ch. 11 and F. M. L. Thompson, *The Rise of Respectable Society* (London: Fontana Press, 1988), ch. 7.
20. *Art Journal*, 1 May 1858, pp. 165, 173.
21. Graves, *Auction Sales*, under Frith.
22. Frith, *Autobiography*, vol. 1, pp. 100–1, 157, 272.
23. Wood, *The Dictionary of Victorian Painters*, vol. 1, p. 269.

24. J. Maas, *Victorian Painters* (London: Barrie and Rockliff, 1969), pp. 171–3; C. Wood, *Victorian Painting* (Boston, New York, London: Little, Brown and Company, 1999), pp. 314–16.
25. Mary Clive, because of this artist's repetitive use of a specific female type, referred to these works as 'Dorothy' pictures. Clive, *The Days of Reckoning*, p. 47.
26. Graves, *Art Sales*, under Marcus Stone.
27. Clive, *The Days of Reckoning*, pp. 47–9.
28. V. Swanson, *The Biography and Catalogue Raisonne of the Paintings of Sir Lawrence Alma-Tadema* (London: Garton & Co., 1990), p. 38.
29. W. Gaunt, *The Aesthetic Adventure* (London: 1945), p. 52.
30. Graves, *Art Sales*, vol. 1, pp. 4–7.
31. Swanson, *The Biography and Catalogue Raisonne of the Paintings of Sir Lawrence Alma-Tadema*, specifically the catalogue of pictures.
32. Except in 1907. *Royal Academy Exhibitors 1905–1970* (Wakefield, Yorkshire: EP Publishing, 1973), p. 28.
33. Swanson, *The Biography and Catalogue Raisonne of the Paintings of Sir Lawrence Alma-Tadema*, p. 42 and n. 22.
34. Alma-Tadema letter to Vosmaer, 4 September and 26 December 1873, CJJG Vosmaer Collection, Leiden. Cited by Swanson, *The Biography and Catalogue Raisonne of the Paintings of Sir Lawrence Alma-Tadema*, p. 50.
35. H. Hosmer, *Letters and Memoirs*, ed. C. Carr (New York: Moffat, Yard and Co., 1912), pp. 339–440.
36. O. Doughty and J. R. Wahl (eds), *Dante Gabriel Rossetti. Letters*, vol. 1, p. 252, quoted in L. and R. Ormond, *Lord Leighton* (London: Yale University Press, 1975), pp. 30–1.
37. F. G. Stephens, *Athenaeum* (11 May 1878), p. 609.
38. *Art Journal* (June 1855), p. 169.
39. R. Barrington, *Life, Letters & Works of Frederic Leighton*, 2 vols (New York, Macmillan, 1906), vol. 1, pp. 233–4.
40. *Atheneaum* (10 May 1856), p. 591.
41. Leighton's correspondence with Colnaghi in the Victoria & Albert Museum, quoted by Ormond, *Lord Leighton*, p. 38.
42. Barrington, *Life, Letters & Works of Frederic Leighton*, vol. 1, pp. 287–8.
43. L. Ormond, in S. Jones and R. Ormond, *Frederic Lord Leighton: Eminent Victorian Artist* (Harry Abrams: New York, 1996), p. 109.
44. A. Smith, 'Nature Transformed: Leighton, the Nude and the Model', *Frederic Leighton: Antiquity Renaissance Modernity*, ed. T. Barringer and E. Prettejohn (New Haven, CT and London: Yale University Press, 1999), p. 19.
45. Barrington, *Life, Letters & Works of Frederic Leighton*, vol. 2, p. 45.
46. Ormond, *Frederic Leighton: Eminent Victorian Artist*, p. 110.
47. Barrington, *Life, Letters & Works of Frederic Leighton*, vol. 2, p. 39.
48. Ibid., vol 2, pp. 40–61.
49. *Athenaeum* (4 May 1861), p. 600; *The Times* (4 May 1861), p. 12; *Macmillan's Magazine* IV(1861), pp. 206–7; *Art Journal* (1861), pp. 162, 172; *Saturday Review*, 11 (25 May, 1861), p. 531; *Critic* (11 May, 1861), pp. 606–7 (25 May, 1861), p. 531.
50. Barrington, *Life, Letters & Works of Frederic Leighton*, vol. 2, pp. 62–3.
51. *Art Journal* (June 1861), p. 172.
52. *Saturday Review*, 2 (November 1861), p. 447.
53. Barrington, *Life, Letters & Works of Frederic Leighton*, vol. 2, p. 95.

54. Letter to Stephens of 30 April 1862, cited by Ormond, *Frederic Leighton: Eminent Victorian artist*, p. 49.
55. Barrington, *Life, Letters & Works of Frederic Leighton*, vol. 2, pp. 119–20.
56. W. M. Rossetti, *Fraser* (LXVII), p. 790.
57. *Athenaeum* (9 May1863), p. 622.
58. Barrington, *Life, Letters & Works of Frederic Leighton*, vol. 2, p. 120.
59. *The Art Journal* (1 June 1864), p. 157.
60. Barrington, *Life, Letters & Works of Frederic Leighton*, vol. 2, pp. 114– 123.
61. Barrington, *Life, Letters & Works of Frederic Leighton*, vol. 2, p. 123. See also a letter of July 1864 to Stephens in which Leighton mentioned that Gambart had bought 'several' pictures. Cited by Ormond, *Frederic Leighton: Eminent Victorian artist*, p. 50, n. 37.
62. *Pall Mall Budget* (3 July 1890), p. 849.
63. V. Lee in a letter to her mother, 2 July 1883, reprinted in *Vernon Lee's Letters* (London: private publication, 1937), p. 123, as cited by A. Stephenson, 'Leighton and the Shifting Repertoire of "Masculine" Artistic Identity in the Late Victorian Period', in T. Barringer and E. Prettejohn (eds), *Frederic Leighton: Antiquity Renaissance Modernity* (New Haven, CT and London: Yale University Press, 1999), p. 224.
64. Reported by his studio assistant Thomas Rooke in his diaries, Victoria and Albert Museum, London. Quoted by A. Staley, 'Post-Pre-Raphaeliteism' in *Victorian High Renaissance*, exhibition catalogue (Machester City Art Galleries; the Minneapolis Institute of Arts; the Brooklyn Museum, New York, 1978–9), p. 28.
65. *Saturday Review,* 2 (November 1861), p. 447.
66. L. Campbell, 'Decoration, Display, Disguise: Leighton House Reconsidered', in *Frederic Leighton: Antiquity Renaissance Modernity*, p. 267.
67. P. Barlow, 'Transparent Bodies, Opaque Identities: Personification, Narrative and Portraiture', in *Frederic Leighton: Aniquity Renaissance Modernity,* p. 193.
68. Ormond, *Frederic Leighton: Eminent Victorian Artist*, p. 119. In 2010 amounts, around £ 300,000 to £ 400,000, or upwards of £ 2,000,000 depending on the conversion method. EH. net.
69. Farington, *Diaries*, vol. 2, p. 86.
70. Burne-Jones, *Memorials of Edward Burne-Jones*, vol. 1, p. 101.
71. Frith, *Autobiography*, pp. 100–1, 157, 272.
72. Millais, *Life and Letter of Sir John Everett Millais*, vol. 1, pp. 34, 82, 346.
73. Hamerton, *Etchers and Etching*, p. 328.
74. Linnell papers as cited by Maas, *Gambart*, p. 58. The influence of dealers on the formal aspects of Linnell's landscapes is discussed in greater detail by E. R. Firestone, 'John Linnell and the picture merchants', *Connoisseur* (February 1973), pp. 124–31.
75. Hunt, *Pre-Raphaelitism and the Pre-Raphaelite Brotherhood*, vol. 1, pp. 73–4 and vol. 2, p. 136.
76. Agnew, *Agnew's*, pp. 61–7.
77. 7 May 1855, p. 10.
78. Redgrave, *A Century of Painters of the English School*, pp. 263–4.
79. S. A. Hart, *The Reminiscences of Solomon Alex. Hart, R.A*, ed. A. Brodie (London: Adam and Charles Black, 1882), pp. 16–18 for a description of some of the financial challenges involved in painting his R.A. diploma picture *Execution of Lady Jane Grey*.
80. Our findings are also echoed by L. S. King, *The Industrialization of Taste: Victorian England and the Art Union of London* (Ann Arbor, MI: UMI Research Press, 1985), p. 57. His analysis of subjects of Art Union prize paintings between 1847 and 1866 shows that

64 per cent were landscapes, 28 per cent genre, 1.2 per cent history and 7 per cent literary and biblical. Unfortunately, he grouped literary and biblical subjects together, whereas our analysis indicates that these two categories had different popularity degrees.

81. Frith, *My Autobiography and Reminiscences*, vol. 2, p. 238.

Chapter Ten: The End of the 'Golden Age'

1. Agnew, *Agnew's*, pp. 11, 65. For Gambart see Maas, *Gambart*, pp. 41, 106.
2. *Athenaeum* (20 August 1864), p. 250.
3. *The Times*, 3 November 1862.
4. Maas, Gambart, pp. 132, 134, involving engravings after Rosa Bonheur's *Horsefair* and Hunt's *Light of the World*. On the court case, pp. 159–62.
5. Agnew, *Agnew's*, p. 27; also Maas, *Gambart*, p. 209 for a similar comment.
6. Gillott papers as cited by Maas, *Gambart*, p. 131.
7. Frith, *My Autobiography and Reminiscences*, vol. 1, p. 334.
8. *Art Journal*, July 1872, pp. 194–5.
9. Reitlinger, *Economics of Taste*, vol. 1, p. 149.
10. *Art Journal*, June 1887, p. 210.
11. M. P. Tedeschi, 'How Prints Work: Reproductions, Originals, and their Markets in England, 1840 – 1900' (PhD dissertation, Northwestern University, 1994).
12. P. G. Hamerton, 'Modern Etching in France', *Fine Arts Quarterly Review*, 2 (1864), p. 96; H. Alken, *The Art and Practice of Etching* (London, 1849), p. 7.
13. M. Rajnai, 'The Norwich School of Etching', in C. Hartley and S. Ridyard (eds), *The Print in England 1790–1930* (Cambridge: Fitzwilliam Museum, 1985), pp. 18–32.
14. Tedeschi, 'How Prints Work', p. 184 and ns.41 and 42; pp. 200–1.
15. F. Keppel, 'Modern Disciples of Rembrandt', *Art Review*, 2 (September–November 1887), pp. 145–9. (Quote p. 145).
16. For example, the essay, 'Painters' Etchings, Part I', *The Art Union* (January 1848), p. 9.
17. F. Wedmore (ed.), *Rembrandt: His Life, His work and His Time* (London: Heinemann, 1894).
18. Hamerton, 'Modern Etching In France'.
19. Ibid., p. 69.
20. Hamerton, *Etching and Etchers*, pp. 28–9.
21. Ibid., p. 42.
22. F. Wedmore, 'My Few Things', *Art Journal* (January 1894), pp. 6–10.
23. Hamerton, quoted in *English Etching* (1888), p. 41.
24. M. Hardie, *Frederick Goulding: Master Printer of Copper Plates* (Sterling: Eneas Mackay, 1910), p. 83.
25. S. Haden, 'Mr. Seymour Haden on Etching', *Magazine of Art* 2 (1879), pp. 188–91, 221–4, 262–4.
26. T. Duret, 'Whistler and His Work', *Arts and Letters* 1 (February 1888), pp. 222–3.
27. H. Herkomer, cited in *The Athenaeum* (15 April 1893), p. 478.
28. 'Mr. Whistler's New Etchings: A Chat with the Master' *The Pall Mall Gazette* (4 March 1890), p. 2.
29. Hamerton, *Etching and Etchers*, p. xiii.
30. M. B. Huish, 'Etching in England', *Magazine of Art*, 1 (1878), p. 146.
31. Hamerton, *Etching and Etchers*, p. 70.
32. Hamerton, 'Mr. Seymour Haden's Etchings', quote, p. 590.

33. Haden, 'Mr. Seymour Haden on Etching', pp. 188–91; 221–4; 262–4; quote, p. 188.
34. Hamerton, *Etching and Etchers*, pp. 60–2.
35. Reynolds, *Discourse on Art*, p. 171.
36. *The Saturday Review* 2 (November 1861), p. 447.
37. F. Wedmore, *Etching in England* (London, George Bell and Sons, 1895), p. 46.
38. S. Haden, 'About Etching', *Fine Arts Quarterly Review* 1 (1866), pp. 145–60.
39. Tedeschi provides numerous other examples of promotional writing on original etching in chapter 3 of her dissertation.
40. Haden, 'Mr. Seymour Haden on Etching', p. 264.
41. *The Athenaeum* (2 February 1878), p. 163.
42. Pennell, 'The Two Salons', p. 775.
43. C. E. Halle, *Notes from a Painter's Life, including the Foundation of Two Galleries* (London: J. Murray, 1909), p. 179.
44. King, *The Industrialization of Taste*, p. 204.
45. O. Wilde, *The Picture of Dorian Gray*, ed. P. Ackroyd (Reprint, Harmondsworth, England: Penguin, 1985), p. 24.
46. S. Casteras, 'Burne-Jones and the Pre-Raphaelite Circle at the Palace of the Aesthetes', in S. Casteras and C. Denney (eds), *The Grosvenor Gallery: A Palace of Art in Victorian England* (New Haven, CT and London: Yale University Press, 1996), p. 86, n. 55.
47. Casteras, 'Burne-Jones and the Pre-Raphaelite Circle at the Palace of the Aesthetes', p. 86, n. 5.
48. C. Denney, 'The Grosvenor Gallery as Palace of Art: An Exhibition Model', in Casteras and Denney (eds), *The Grosvenor Gallery: A Palace of Art in Victorian England*, p. 23.
49. P. Gillett, 'Art Audiences at the Grosvenor', in S. Casteras and C. Denney (eds), *The Grosvenor Gallery: A Palace of Art in Victorian England* (New Haven and London: Yale University Press, 1996), pp. 39–58.
50. Wilde, *The Picture of Dorian Gray*, p. 24.
51. Denney, 'The Grosvenor Gallery as Palace of Art: An Exhibition Model', p. 19 and n. 39.
52. Ibid., p. 27.
53. 'The Palace of Art (New Version), Part I', *Punch*, 72 (7 July 1877), p. 9. The poem was a satirical version of a poem by Tennyson by the same title.
54. J. Franklin, *The Gentleman's Country House and Its Plan, 1835–1914* (London, Boston and Henley: Routledge and Kegan Paul, 1981), pp. 55–60.
55. M. Girouard, *The Victorian Country House* (New Haven, CT: Yale University Press, 1985), revised and enlarged edition, p. 36.
56. Middlesex County Secessions Records, County Licensing Committee, Hanover Square Division (St. Georges), Greater London Record Office, MA/C/L 1878/70.
57. Denney, 'The Grosvenor Gallery as Palace of Art: An Exhibition Model', p. 31.
58. Walter Crane, *An Artist's Reminiscences* (London: Methuen, 1907), p. 150.
59. M. H. Spielman, 'The Truth About the Grosvenor "Split" An Interview with Sir Coutts Lindsay', *Pall Mall Gazette*, 3 November, 1887, p. 2.
60. Spielman, 'The Truth About the Grosvenor "Split"', p. 2.
61. C. Halle and J. Comyns Carr, 'To the Editor of the Times', 1 November 1887, reprinted in *Correspondence with Sir Coutts Lindsay concerning the Resignation of Messrs. C.E Halle and J. Comyns Carr*. Victoria and Albert Museum Library (National Art Library), London, 1887.
62. *Mrs. J. Comyns Carr's Reminiscences*, ed. E. Adam, 2nd edn (London: Hutchinson, n.d.), p. 90.

63. J. Comyns Carr, 'La "Grosvenor Gallery" a Londres', L'Art, 9(1877), p. 265.
64. Halle, *Notes from a Painter's Life, including the Foundation of Two Galleries*, p. 158.
65. Halle to Sir Coutts Lindsay, 7 October 1887, *Correspondence with Sir Coutts Lindsay concerning the resignation of Messrs. C.E. Halle and J. Comyns Carr*, Victoria and Albert Museum Library (National Art Library), 1887.
66. Lindsay to Halle and Carr, 29 October 1887, *Correspondence with Sir Coutts Lindsay concerning the resignation of Messrs. C.E. Halle and J. Comyns Carr.*
67. Reitlinger, *Economics of Taste*, vol. 1, pp. 159–60.
68. Ibid., vol. 1, p. 164.
69. P. ten-Doesschate Chu, 'The Lucre of London: French Artists and Art Dealers in the British Capital, 1859–1914', *Monet's London: Artists' Reflections on the Thames* (Ghent: Snoeck Publishers, 2004), pp. 39–42.
70. For Rubens, see Christie's sale of 2 May 1856, lot 608; for Rembrandt, see Christie's sales of 15 March 1851, 31 July 1851, 26 March 1852, 24 June 1853, 24 March 1854, 2 May 1856, 6 June 1860.
71. On the dealer Duveen, see Behrman, *Duveen.*
72. Hunt, *Pre-Raphaelitism and the Pre-Raphaelite Brotherhood*, vol. 2, pp. 469–75.
73. 'The purpose of art is, in love of guileless beauty, to lead man to distinguish between that which, being clean in spirit, is productive of virtue, and that which is flaunting and meretricious and productive of ruin to a nation'. Hunt, *Pre-Raphaelitism and the Pre-Raphaelite Brotherhood*, vol. 2, p. 493.

11 Postscript: A Perpetual Innovative Whirl

1. D. Galenson, *The Careers of Modern Artists: Evidence from Auctions of Contemporary Paintings* (Cambridge, MA: National Bureau of Economic Research, 1997), p. 32. Galenson, however, neglects to recognize the gallery system as the responsible agent, but rather assigns accountability to the 'evolution of modern painting and a growth in the demand for contemporary American art ...' See Abstract.
2. We are referring to Edward Bernays' classic volume on Public Relations, *Crystallizing Public Opinion* (New York: Boni and Liveright, 1923).
3. This was brought to our attention by Suzanne Modica of Thea Westreich Art Advisory Services, New York.

WORKS CITED

Manuscript Sources

BL Add. MSS 47,792, fol. 14 verso.

British Museum, Add. MS 23724.

British Museum, Department of Manuscripts, 46140.

Houlditch, R., of Great Queen Street located in the manuscript collection of the Victoria and Albert Museum, London (MS 86.008–19).

Leathart papers, Victoria and Albert Museum, London.

Letter to Effie of 27 June 1861. Pierpont Morgan Library, New York. Accession number: MA1485D, record identification: 132647.

Middlesex County Secessions Records, County Licensing Committee, Hanover Square Division (St. Georges), Greater London Record Office, MA/C/L 1878/70.

Public Record Office, London, cust 3 register of imports and exports 1693–1774.

Periodicals

Art Journal.

Art Union.

Athenaeum.

Critic.

Daily Courant.

Englishwoman's Review.

Fraser.

Gazetteer and New Daily Advertiser.

General Evening Post.

Gentleman's Magazine.

Illustrated London News.

Literary Panorama.

Lloyd's Evening Post, and British Chronicle.

London Chronicle.

London Evening Post.

London Gazette.

Macmillan's Magazine.

Pall Mall Budget.

Pall Mall Gazette.

Public Advertiser.

Public Ledger.

Punch.

Saturday Review.

Spectator.

St James Chronicle.

Tatler.

The Times.

Whitehall Evening Post.

Published Sources

A Brief Historical and Descriptive account of the Royal Gardens, Vauxhall (London, 1822).

Adam, E. (ed.), *Mrs. J. Comyns Carr's Reminiscences*, ed. E. Adam, 2nd edn (London: Hutchinson, n.d.).

Agnew, G., *Agnew's 1817–1967* (London: The Bradbury Agnew Press, Ltd, 1967).

Akerlof, G., 'The Market for "Lemons": Quality Uncertainty and the Market Mechanisms', *An economic theorist's book of tales* (Cambridge University Press, 1970). pp. 7–22.

Alken, H., *The Art and Practice of Etching* (London, 1849).

Allen, R. J., *The Clubs of Augustan London* (Cambridge, MA: Harvard University Press, 1933).

Alma-Tadema letter to Vosmaer, 4 September and 26 December 1873, CJJG Vosmaer Collection, Leiden.

Altick, R. D., *The Shows of London* (Cambridge: Harvard University Press, 1978).

Amory, M. B., *John Singleton Copley, R.A.* (New York: Houghton, Mifflin and Co., 1982).

Anonymous, 'Our Royal Academical Lounge', *Fraser's Magazine*, 5 (July 1832), pp. 710–11.

Anonymous, *The Conduct of the Royal Academician with Members of the Incorporated Society of Artists of Great Britain* (London, 1771).

Armstrong-Totten, J., 'Expand the Audience, Increase the Profits: Motivations Behind the Private Contract Sale', in R. Panzanelli and M. Preti-Hamard (eds), *La Circulation des*

Oeuvres d'Art, 1789–1848 (Rennes: Presses Universitaire de Rennes Institut National d' Histoire de l' Art, Getty Research Institute, 2007), pp. 45–55.

—, 'The Rise and Fall of a British Connoisseur: the career of Michael Bryan (1757–1821), picture dealer *extraordinaire*', in Warren and Turpin (eds), *Auctions, Agents and Dealers. The Mechanisms of the Art Market 1660–1830* (Oxford: The Beazley Archive and Archaeopress in association with The Wallace Collection, 2008), pp.141–150.

Arnstein, W., *Britain Yesterday and Today* (Boston, MA: Heath, 1996).

Austin, L., *The Practical Ruskin: Economics and Audience in the Late Work* (Baltimore, MD: Johns Hopkins University Press, 1991).

Barlow, P., 'Transparent Bodies, Opaque Identities: Personification, Narrative and Portraiture', Barringer, Tim and Elizabeth Prettejohn (eds.) *Frederic Leighton: Aniquity Renaissance Modernity* (New Haven; London: Yale University Press, 1999), pp. 193–220.

Barrell, J., *The Political Theory of Painting from Reynolds to Hazlitt* (New Haven, CT and London: Yale University Press, 1986).

Barringer, T., *Men at Work* (New Haven and London: Yale University Press, 2005).

Barrington, R., *Life, Letters & Works of Frederic Leighton*, 2 vols (New York, Macmillan, 1906).

Barry, J., *Inquiry into the Real and Imaginary Obstructions to the Acquisition of the Arts* (New York: Garland Publishing, 1972).

Bass, J., 'Reconsidering Walter Benjamin', in G. Weisberg and L. Dixon (eds), *The Documented Image* (Syracuse: Syracuse University Press, 1987), pp. 337–47.

Bateman, J., *The Law of Auctions* (London, 1838).

Bayer, T. M., 'Degas and the English Connection 1872–1876', *Athanor*, XVI (1998), pp. 31–8.

Bayer, T. M., J. Page, Y. Raviv and Joshua Rosett, 'Age, Human Capital and the Quality of Work: New Evidence from Old Masters'. Abstract, http://ssrn.com/abstract=1364417.

Behrman, S. N., *Duveen* (New York: Random House, 1952).

Beljame, A., *Men of Letters and the English Public in the 18th Century* (London: K. Paul, Trench, Truber, 1948).

Benjamin, W., *Das Kunstwerk im Zeitalter seiner Reproduzierbarkeit* (Frankfurt: Surkamp Verlag, 1977).

Bennett, M., 'The Price of "Work": The Background to its First Exhibition, 1865', in L. Parris (ed.), *Pre-Raphaelite Papers* (London: Tate Gallery, 1985), pp. 143–52.

Bennett, S., *Thomas Stothard* (Columbia, MO: University of Missouri Press, 1988).

Bermingham, A., 'Landscape-O-Rama: The Exhibition Landscape at Somerset House and the Rise of Popular Landscape Entertainment', in D. Solkin (ed.), *Art on the Line* (London and New Haven, CT: Yale University Press, 2001), pp. 127–43.

Bindman, D.,'The Orleans Collection and its Impact on British Art', in R. Panzanelli and M. Preti-Hamard (eds), *La Circulation des Oeuvres d'Art 1789–1848* (Rennes: Presses

Universitaire de Rennes Institut National d' Histoire de l' Art, Getty Research Institute, 2007), pp. 57–66.

Birch, D., 'Father and Sons: Ruskin, John James Ruskin and Turner', *Nineteenth-Century Contexts*, 18:2 (1994), pp. 147–62.

Borsay, P., *The English Urban Renaissance, Culture and Society in the Provincial Town 1660–1770* (Oxford: Clarendon Press, 1989).

Bredius, A., *Künstler-Inventare; Urkunden zur Geschichte der Holländischen Kunst des XVIten, XVIIten und XVIIIten Jahrhunderts* (The Hague: M. Nijhoff, 1915–22), 7 volumes and index.

Brown, M., *Degas and the Business of Art: A Cotton Office in New Orleans* (University Park, Pa.: Pennsylvania State University Press, 1994).

Bruntjen, S. H. A, *John Boydell (1719–1804) A Study of Art Patronage and Publishing in Georgian London* (New York: Garland Publishing, Inc., 1985).

Buchanan, W., *Memoirs of Painting* (ed.), J. Greig, 2 vols (London: Ackermann, 1824).

Bulow, J., M. Huang; P. Klemperer, 'Toeholds and Takeovers', *Journal of Political Economy*, 107 (1999), pp. 427–54.

Burkart, M., 'Overbidding in Takeover Contests', *Journal of Finance*, 50 (1995), pp. 1491–1515.

Burne-Jones, G., *Memorials of Edward-Burne-Jones* (London: The Macmillan Company, 1906).

Burnett, J., 'Autobiography of John Burnett', *Art Journal* (August 1850).

Burton, A., 'Nineteenth Century Periodicals', T. Fawcett and C. Phillpot, (eds), *The Art Press: Two Centuries of Art Magazines* (London: The Art Book Company, 1976), pp. 3–10.

Butlin, M., 'An Eighteenth Century Scandal: Nathaniel Hone's "The Conjurer"', *Connoisseur*, 174(1970), pp. 1–9.

Calè, L., *Fuseli's Milton Gallery 'Turning Readers into Spectators* (Oxford: Clarendon Press, 2006).

Campbell, L., 'Decoration, Display, Disguise: Leighton House Reconsidered', in *Frederic Leighton: Antiquity Renaissance Modernity* (New Haven; London: Yale University Press, 1999), pp. 267–94.

—, 'The Art Market in the Southern Netherlands in the Fifteenth Century', *Burlington Magazine*, 118 (March 1976), pp. 188–98.

Campbell, R., *The London Tradesman* (London: T. Gardner, 1747).

Carr, C. J., 'La "Grosvenor Gallery" a Londres', *L'Art*, 9 (1877).

Cassady, R., *Auctions and Auctioneering* (Berkeley, CA: University of California Press, 1967).

Casteras, S. (ed.), *John Ruskin and the Victorian Eye* (New York: H.N. Abrams, 1993).

—, 'Burne-Jones and the Pre-Raphaelite Circle at the Palace of the Aesthetes', in S. Casteras and C. Denney (eds) *The Grosvenor Gallery: A Palace of Art in Victorian England* (New Haven and London: Yale University Press, 1996), pp. 75–92.

—, 'The 1857–58 Exhibition of English Art in America and Critical Responses to Pre-Raphaelitism', in L. Ferber and W. Gerdts (eds), *The New Path, Ruskin and the American Pre-Raphaelites* (New York: Schocken Books, Inc, 1985), pp. 109–33.

Catalogue of the dwelling House of the Rt. Hon. General (Wm.) Stuart (deceased) (14 April 1730), Bodleian Library Johnson collection d778.

Chong, A., 'The Market for Landscape Painting in Seventeenth-Century Holland', in Peter Sutton (ed.), *Masters of the Seventeenth Century Dutch Landscape Painting* (Boston, MA: Boston Museum of Fine Art, 1987), pp. 104–20.

Christian, J., 'A Serious Talk: Ruskin's place in Burne-Jones Artistic Development', in L. Parris (ed.), *Pre-Raphaelite Papers* (London: Tate Gallery, 1984), pp. 184–205.

Chu, P. ten-Doesschate, 'The Lucre of London: French Artists and Art Dealers in the British Capital, 1859–1914', *Monet's London: Artists' Reflections on the Thames* (Ghent: Snoeck Publishers, 2004), pp. 39–42.

Clive, M., *The Days of Reckoning* (London: Macmillan, 1964).

Collins, A. S., *Authorship in the Days of Johnson* (London: R. Holden and Co., Ltd, 1927).

Collins, W., *A Rogue's Life* (London: Richard Benley and Son, 1879).

Constantinides, G. M., M. Harris and Rene M. Stulz, *Handbook of the Economics of Finance* (Amsterdam: Elsevier B.V., 2003).

Cooper, A. A., third Earl of Shaftesbury, *Second Characters, or the Language of Forms*, ed. B. Rand (Cambridge: Harvard University Press, 1914).

—, *Characteristics of Men, Manners, Opinions, Times* (1711), ed. J. M. Robertson, 2 vols (Indianapolis, IN and New York: University of Indiana Press, 1964).

Cooper, J., *Under the Hammer* (London: Constable, 1977).

Copley, S., *Literature and the Social Order in Eighteenth-Century England* (London: Croom Helm, 1984).

Corbett, D. P., *The World in Paint* (University Park, PA: The Pennsylvania State University Press).

Correspondence with Sir Coutts Lindsay concerning the resignation of Messrs. C.E. Halle and J. Comyns Carr, Victoria and Albert Museum Library (National Art Library), 1887.

Cowan, B., 'Arenas of Connoisseurship: Auctioning Art in Later Stuart England'. Michael North and David Ormrod (eds), *Art Markets in Europe, 1400–1800* (Aldershot: Ashgate, 1998), pp. 153–166.

—, 'Art and Connoisseurship in the Auction Market of Later Seventeenth-Century London', in N. De Marchi and H. Van Miegroet (eds), *Mapping Markets for Paintings in Europe, 1450–1750* (Turnhout, Belgium: Brepols 2006), pp. 263–82.

Crafts, N., 'The Industrial Revolution', in F. Floud and D. McCloskey (eds), *The Economic History of Britain since 1700*, 2 vols (Cambridge: Cambridge University Press, 1981).

Crane, W., *An Artist's Reminiscences* (London: Methuen, 1907).

Cressy, D., 'Literacy in Context: Meaning and Measurement in early modern England', Brewer and Porter (eds), *Consumption and the World of Goods* (London: Routledge, 1993).

Cust, L., *The History of the Society of Dilettanti* (London: Seeley & Co., 1898).

Dallaway, J., *Anecdotes of the Arts in England* (London: 1800).

De Marchi, N., 'Auctioning Paintings in Late Seventeenth-century London: Rules, Segmentation and Prices in an Emergent Market', in V. A. Ginsburgh (ed.), *Economics of Art and Culture* (Amsterdam: Elsevier, 2004), pp. 97–128.

—, 'The Role of Dutch Auctions and Lotteries in Shaping the Art Market(s) of 17th Century Holland', *Journal of Economic Behavior and Organization*, 28 (1995), pp. 203–21.

De Marchi, N. and H. J. van Miegroet, 'The History of Art Markets', in V. Ginsburgh (ed.), *Handbook of the Economics of Art and Culture* (Amsterdam: Elsevier, 2006), vol. 1, pp. 69–122.

De Marchi, N. and H. J. Van Miegroet, 'Art, Value and Market Price in the Netherlands in the Seventeenth Century', *Art Bulletin* 76 (1994), pp. 451–64.

De Marchi, N., and H. J. Van Miegroet (eds), *Mapping Markets for Paintings in Europe, 1450–1750* (Turnhout, Belgium: Brepols Publishers n.v., 2006).

De Marchi, N., and H. J. Van Miegroet, 'Rules Versus Play in Early Modern Art Markets', *Louvain Economic Review*, 66 (2000), pp. 145–65.

Denney, C., 'The Grosvenor Gallery as Palace of Art: An Exhibition Model', in S. Casteras and C. Denney (eds), *The Grosvenor Gallery: A Palace of Art in Victorian England* (New Haven and London: Yale University Press, 1996), pp. 9–36.

Denvir, B., *The Eighteenth Century* (London and New York: Longman, 1983).

Dibdin, E. R., 'Liverpool Art and Artists in the Eighteenth Century', *Walpole Society* (Oxford: Oxford University, 1917–18).pp. 59–61.

Dickson, P. G. M., *The Financial Revolution in England* (London: Macmillan, 1967).

Dobai, J., *Kunstliteratur des Klassizismus und der Romantik in England*, 3 vols (Bern: Bentelli Verlag, 1974).

Doughty, O. and J. R. Wahl (eds), *Dante Gabriel Rossetti: Letters*, 3 vols (Oxford: Clarendon Press, 1965–7).

Dryden, J. (trans.), *De Arte Graphica: The Art of Painting*, 2nd edn (London: Bernard Lintott, 1716).

Duret, T., 'Whistler and His Work', *Arts and Letters*, 1 (February 1888), pp. 215–26.

Durkheim, E., and M. Mauss, *Primitive Classification*, trans. R. Needham (Chicago, IL: The University of Chicago Press, 1963).

Dyson, A., *From Pictures to Print: the Nineteenth Century Engraving Trade* (London: Farrand Press, 1984).

Earland, A, *John Opie and his Circle* (London: Hutchinson & Co., 1911).

Eisenberg, M., 'Watteau Paintings in England in the Early Eighteenth Century', *Burlington Magazine*, 107 (September 1975), pp. 576–82.

Eitner, L., *Géricault, his Life and Work* (London: Orbis Publishing, 1983).

Elliott, E. C., 'Reynolds and Hazlitt', *Journal of Aesthetics and Art Criticism*, 21 (1962), pp. 73–9.

Ellis, A., *The Penny Universities, A History of the Coffee-Houses* (London: Secker & Warburg, 1956).

Englefield, W. O., *History of the Painter-Stainer Company* (London: Chapman and Dodd, Ltd, 1923).

Evelyn, J., *Diary & Correspondence of John Evelyn, Frs.*, ed. Wi. Bray (London: G. Bell and Sons, 1883–87).

Fain, J. T., *Ruskin and the Economists* (Nashville: Vanderbilt University Press, 1956).

Farington, J., *The Farington Diary*, 2 vols (London: Hutchinson & Co., 1923).

Ferdinand, C. Y. 'Selling it to the Provinces: News and Commerce around eighteenth-Century Salisbury', Brewer, J. and R. Porter (eds), *Consumption and the World of Goods* (London: Routledge, 1993), pp. 393–411.

Firestone, E. R., 'John Linnell and the picture merchants', *The Connoisseur*, February (1973), pp. 124–31.

Fletcher, P. and A. Helmreich, 'The Periodical and the Art Market: Investigating the "Dealer-Critic System" in Victorian England', *Victorian Periodical Review*, vol 41, no. 4 (Winter 2008), pp. 323–44.

Fletcher, 'Creating the French Gallery: Ernest Gambart and the Rise of the Commercial Art Gallery in Mid-Victorian London', http://www.19thc-artworldwide.org/index.php?option=com_content&view=article&id=143:creating-the-french-gallery-ernest-gambart-and-the-rise-of-the-commercial-art-gallery-in-mid-victorian-london&catid=4-6:spring07article&Itemid=68.

Floerke, H., *Studien zur Niederlandischen Kunstgeschichte* (Munchen and Leipzig: Georg Muller, 1905).

Foss, M., *The Age of Patronage* (Ithaca, NY: Cornell University Press, 1971).

—, *Man of Wit to Man of Business: The Arts and Changing Patronage, 1660–1750* (Bristol: Bristol Classical Press, 1988).

Franklin, J., *The Gentleman's Country House and Its Plan, 1835–1914* (London, Boston and Henley: Routledge and Kegan Paul, 1981).

Frith, W. P., *A Victorian Canvas: The Memoirs of W.P. Frith, RA.*, ed. N. Wallis (London: Geoffrey Bles, 1957).

—, *My Autobiography and Reminiscences*, 2 vols (New York: Harper & Brothers, 1888).

Fry, R., *Art and Socialism, Vision and Design* (London: Phoenix, 1928).

Galenson, D., *The Careers of Modern Artists: Evidence from Auctions of Contemporary Paintings* (Cambridge, MA: National Bureau of Economic Research, 1997).

—, *Painting outside the Line* (Cambridge, MA: Harvard University Press, 2001).

Galenson, D., and R. Jensen, 'Careers and Canvases; the Rise of the Market for Modern Art in Nineteenth-Century France', *Current Issues in 19th-Century Art*, Van Gogh Studies 1 (2007), pp. 137–66.

Gaunt, W., *The Aesthetic Adventure* (London: 1945).

Gibson-Wood, C., 'Picture Consumption in London at the End of the Seventeenth Century', *Art Bulletin*, 84 (2002), pp. 491–500.

Gillett, P., 'Art Audiences at the Grosvenor', in S. Casteras and C. Denney (eds), *The Grosvenor Gallery: A Palace of Art in Victorian England* (New Haven and London: Yale University Press, 1996), pp. 39–58.

—, *The Victorian Painter's World* (New Brunswick, NJ: Rutgers University Press, 1990).

Girouard, M., *The Victorian Country House* (New Haven, CT: Yale University Press, 1985).

Godfrey, R., *Printmaking in Britain* (New York: New York University Press, 1978).

Goldthwaite, R., *Wealth and the Demand for Art in Italy, 1300–1600* (Baltimore, MD: The Johns Hopkins University Press, 1993).

Goldwater, R. and M. Treves (eds), *Artists on Art* (New York: Pantheon Books, 1945).

Goodwin, C., 'Art and Culture in the History of Economic Thought', *Handbook of the Economics of Art and Culture* (Amsterdam: Elsevier, 2006), vol. 1, pp. 25–68.

Gool, J. van, *De Nieuwe Schouburgh der Nederlantische Kunstschilders en Schilderessen*, 2 vols (The Hague: 1750).

Graves, A., *The Royal Academy of Arts*, 8 vols (London: George Bell and Sons, 1905).

—, *Art Sales from Early in the Eighteenth Century to Early in the Twentieth Century*, 3 vols (1918; New York: Burt Franklin, 1970).

Graves, W., *Sculptura-Historica-Technica; or the History and Art of Engraving* (London, 1747).

Green, N., 'Dealing in Temperaments: Economic Transformation of the Artistic Field in France during the Second Half of the Nineteenth Century', *Art History*, 10:1(March 1987), pp. 59–76.

Guerin, M.,ed., *Degas Letters* (Oxford: Cassirer, 1947).

Haden, S., 'Mr. Seymour Haden on Etching'. *The Magazine of Art* 2 (1879), pp. 188, 221, 262.

Hall, S. C., *Retrospective of A Long Life from 1815–1883* (New York: D. Appleton and Company, 1883).

Halle C., and C. Carr, 'To the Editor of the Times', 1 November 1887, reprinted in *Correspondence with Sir Coutts Lindsay concerning the Resignation of Messrs. C.E Halle and J. Comyns Carr*. Victoria and Albert Museum Library (National Art Library), London, 1887.

—, *Notes from a Painter's Life, including the Foundation of Two Galleries* (London: J. Murray, 1909).

Hamerton, P. G., 'Modern Etching In France', *The Fine Arts Quarterly Review* 2 (1864), pp. 69–97.

—, 'Mr. Seymour Haden's Etchings', *Scribner's Monthly* 20 (1880), pp. 586–600.

—, *Etching and Etchers* (London, Macmillan and Co., Ltd, 1868).

—, 'Modern Etching in France', *The Fine Arts Quarterly Review* 2 (1864) pp. 69–110.

Hamerton, P. G., *Thoughts about Art* (Boston, MA: Roberts Brothers, 1871).

Hansard, *Parliamentary Debates*, 1 (1803–4).

Hardie, M., *Frederick Goulding: Master Printer of Copper Plates* (Sterling: Eneas Mackay, 1910).

Harris, M., *London Newspapers in the Age of Walpole* (London: Associated University Presses, 1987).

Hart, S. A., *The Reminiscences of Solomon Alex. Hart, R.A*, ed. A. Brodie (London: Adam and Charles Black, 1882)

Haskell, F., *The Ephemeral Museum: Old Master Paintings and the Rise of the Art Exhibition* (New Haven, CT: Yale University Press, 2000).

—, *Patrons and Painters* (New Haven, CT and London: Yale University Press, 1980).

Hazlitt, W., *Criticism on Art and Sketches of the Picture Galleries of England* (London: J. Templeman, 1843; 2nd edn, 1846).

—, *Complete Works*, ed. P. P. Howe, 21 volumes, after the edition of A. P. Waller and A. Glover (London and Toronto: J. M. Dent & Sons, Ltd, 1930–34).

Henderson, W., *John Ruskin's Political Economy* (London: Routledge, 2000).

Hermann, F., *The English as Collectors* (New York: W. W. Norton & Co., 1972)

Hilles, F. W., *Literary Career of Sir Joshua Reynolds* (New York: The Macmillan Co., Cambridge, England: The University Press, 1936).

Hilton, T., *John Ruskin: The Early Years* (New Haven, CT: Yale University Press, 2000).

Hogarth, W., *The Analysis of Beauty with the Rejected Passages from the Manuscript Drafts and Autobiographical Notes*, ed. J. Burke (Oxford: Clarendon Press, 1955).

Holme, C., *The Royal Academy from Reynolds to Millais* (London, New York: The Studio, 1904).

Holt, E. G., *Triumph of Art for the Public* (Washington, DC: Decatur House Press, 1980).

Holt, *From the Classicists to the Impressionists* (New Haven and London: Yale University Press, 1986).

Hosmer, H., *Letters and Memoirs*, ed. C. Carr (New York: Moffat, Yard and Co., 1912).

Hudson, D., and K. W. Luckhurst, *The Royal Society of Arts, 1754–1954* (London: Murray, 1954).

Huish, M. B. , *The Year's Art 1891: A Concise Epitome of all Matters Relating to the Arts of Painting, Sculpture, And Architecture which have occurred During the year 1890 together with Information respecting the Events of the Year 1891* (London: J.S. Virtue & Co., Ltd, 1891).

Huish, M. B., 'Etching in England', *Magazine of Art* 1(1878), pp. 146–8.

Hunt, H., *Pre-Raphaelitism and the Pre-Raphaelite Brotherhood*, 2 vols (New York; London: Macmillan Co., 1905–6).

Hutchison, S., *The History of the Royal Academy 1768–1968* (London: Robert Royce, Ltd, 1968).

Ireland J., and J. Nichols, *Hogarth's Work* (Edinburgh and London: Oliphant, Anderson & Ferrier, 1874).

—, *Hogarth Illustrated*, 3 vols (1791–8; London: J. & J. Boydell, 1805).

Irwin, D. and F., *Scottish Painters at Home and Abroad 1700–1900* (London: Faber, 1975).

Jansen, R., *Marketing Modernism in Fin-de-Siècle Europe* (Princeton, NJ: Princeton University Press, 1994).

Johnson, L., 'The Raft of Medusa in Great Britain', *Burlington Magazine*, XCVI (August 1954), pp. 249–54;

Junius, F., *The Painting of the Ancients* (London: 1638).

Keppel, F., 'Modern Disciples of Rembrandt', *The Art Review,* 2 (September-November 1887), pp. 145–9.

Keynes, G. (ed.), *The Complete Writings of William Blake* (London, New York: Oxford University Press, 1972).

King, L. S., *The Industrialization of Taste: Victorian England and the Art Union of London* (Ann Arbor, MI: UMI Research Press, 1985).

Knowles, J. (ed.) *The Life and Writing of Henry Fuseli*, 3 vols (London: Templeman, 1831).

Koch, G. F., *Die Kunstausstellung* (Berlin: Walter de Gruyter & Co., 1967).

Kopytoff, I., 'The Cultural Biography of Things: Commoditization as Process', in A. Appadurai (ed.), *The Social Life of Things: Commodities in Cultural Perspective* (Cambridge, MA: Yale University Press, 1986), pp. 64–91.

Lamb, W. R. M., *The Royal Academy* (London: A. Maclehose & Co., 1935).

Landow, G. P., 'There Began to Be a Great Talking about the Fine Arts', ed. J. L. Altholz, *The Mind and Art of Victorian England* (Minneapolis, MN: University of Minnesota Press, 1976), pp. 124–45.

Law Geo.III cap 50, of September 1777 and 19 Geo. III cap 56 in 1779.

Lewis, L., *Connoisseurs and Secret Agents in 18th Century Rome* (London: Chatto & Windus, 1961).

Lillywhite, B., *London Coffee Houses* (London: G. Allen and Unwin, 1963).

Lipking, L., *The Ordering of the Arts in Eighteenth-Century England* (Princeton, NJ: Princeton University Press, 1970).

Lippincott, L., *Selling Art in Georgian London* (New Haven, CT: Yale University Press, 1983).

Lodge, S., 'Géricault in England', *Burlington Magazine*, CVII (December 1965), pp. 616–27.

Luckhurst, K., *The Story of Exhibitions* (London, New York: Studio Publications, 1951).

Maas, J., *Gambart* (London: Barrie & Jenkins, 1975).

—, 'S.C.Hall and *The Art Journal*', *Connoisseur* 191 (March 1976), pp. 206–9.

—, *Victorian Painters* (London: Barrie and Rockliff, 1969).

Macleod, D. S., 'F.G. Stephens, Pre-Raphaelite Critic and Art Historian', *Burlington Magazine*, 128 (June 1986), pp. 398–402.

—, *Art and the Victorian Middle Class* (Cambridge: Cambridge University Press, 1996).

Mancoff, D., 'Samuel Carter Hall: Publisher as Promoter of the High Arts', *Victorian periodical Review*, 24:1 (Spring 1991), pp. 11–21.

Mander, K. van, *Dutch and Flemish Painters* (New York: MacFarlane, Warde, MacFarlane, 1936).

Mandeville, B., *The Fable of the Bees: or Private Vices, Publick Benefits*, ed. F. B. Kaye, 2 vols (Oxford: Clarendon Press, 1924).

Manwaring, E. W., *Italian Landscape in Eighteenth-century England* (London: F. Cass, 1965).

Marillier, H. C., *'Christie's'1766–1925*(London: Constable & Company Ltd, Boston and New York: Houghton Mifflin Company, 1926).

Mason, W., 'The Art of Painting', *The Works of William Mason, M.A.*, 3 vols (London: 1811).

Mathias, P., *The First Industrial Nation*, 2nd edn (New York: Methuen, 1983).

—, *The Transformation of England* (London: Methuen, 1979).

McAfee, R. P., and J. McMillan, 'Auctions and Bidding', *Journal of Economic Literature*, 25, 2 (June 1987), pp. 699–739.

McKendrick, N., J. Brewer and J. H. Plumb, *The Birth of a Consumer Society* (London: Europa Publications Limited, 1982).

Memoirs and Recollections of the Late Abraham Rainbach (London, 1843).

Millais, J. G., *Life and Letters of Sir John Everett Millais*, 2 vols (New York: Frederick A. Stokes Company, 1899).

Mills, E. (ed.), *The Life and Letters of Frederic Shields* (London: Longmans, Green and Co., 1912).

Mitchell, C., 'Benjamin West's "Death of General Wolf" and the popular History Piece', *Journal of the Warburg and Courtauld Institute*, 7 (1944), pp. 20–3;

Montias, J. M., 'Art Dealers in the Seventeenth-Century Netherlands', *Simiolus* 18:4, pp. 244–56.

—, 'Cost and Value in Seventeenth-Century Dutch Art', *Art History*, 10 (December 1987), pp. 455–66.

—, 'Works of Art Competing with Other Goods in Seventeenth-Century Dutch Inventories', in De Marchi and Miegroet (eds), *Mapping Markets for Paintings in Europe, 1450–1750* (Turnhout, Belgium: Brepols Publishers n.v., 2006), pp. 55–64.

—, *Artists and Artisans in Delft: a Socio-Economic Study of the seventeenth Century* (New York: Princeton University Press, 1983).

—, 'Flemish and Dutch Trade in Works of Art in the 16th and 17th Centuries', *Institution for Social and Policy Studies* (Cambridge: Yale University Press, 1985), working paper no. 1022;

Myrone, M., in D. Solkin (ed.), *Art on the Line* (New Haven and London: Yale University Press, 2001), pp. 77–92.

Neal, L., *The Rise of Financial Capitalism* (Cambridge: Cambridge University Press, 1990).

Nichols, R. H. and F. A. Wray, *The History of the Foundling Hospital* (London: Oxford University Press, 1935).

Noakes, A., *William Frith* (London: Jupiter, 1978).

Noon, P., 'Colour and Effect, Anglo-French Painting in London and Paris', *Crossing the Channel, British and French Painting in the Age of Romanticism* (London: Tate Publishing, 2003), pp. 12–27.

North, R., *The Lives of the Norths*, ed. A. Jessop, 3 vols (London: G. Bell and Sons, 1890).

Ogden, H. V. S. and M. S., *English Taste in Landscape in the 17th Century* (Ann Arbor, MI: University of Michigan Press, 1955).

Okley, J., *St. James Chronicle* (2 April 1761).

Ormond, L., in S. Jones and R. Ormond, *Frederic Lord Leighton: Eminent Victorian Artist* (Harry Abrams, New York: 1996), pp. 13–20.

Ormrod, D., 'The Art Trade and its Urban Context: England and the Netherlands compared, 1550–1750', in J. Warren and A. Turpin (eds), *Auctions, Agents and Dealers* (Oxford: The Beazley Archive and Archaeopress, 2008), pp 11–19.

—, 'The Origins of the London Art Market 1660–1730', in M. North and D. Ormrod (eds), *Art Markets in Europe 1400–1800* (Aldershot, Great Britain: Ashgate Publishing, 1998), pp. 167–86.

—, 'The Rise of the London Art Market, 1660–1760', *Economica e arte, secc. XIII-XVIII* (March 2000), pp. 305–21.

Parson, C., and N. McWilliam, 'Le Paysan de Paris: Alfred Sensier and the Myth of Rural France', *Oxford Art Journal*, 6 (no. 2, 1983), pp. 37–58;

Pasquin, A., *Memoirs of the Royal Academicians; being an Attempt to Improve the National Taste* (London, 1796).

Paulson, R., *Hogarth*, 3 vols (New Brunswick, NJ: Rutgers University Press, 1991).

—, *Hogarth: His Life, Art, and Times*, 2 vols (New Haven, CT and London: Yale University Press, 1971).

Pears, I., 'Patronage and Learning in the Virtuoso Republic: John Talman in Italy 1709–12', *Oxford Art Journal*, 5:1 (1982), pp. 24–30.

—, *The Discovery of Painting* (New Haven & London: Yale University Press, 1988).

Pennell, E., 'The Two Salons', *Fortnightly Review*, LIII (June 1893), pp. 774–82.

Pevsner, N., *Academies of Art, Past and Present* (Cambridge: Cambridge University Press, 1940).

Plant, M., *The English Book Trade* (New York: P. P. Bowker, 1939).

Plumb, J. H., 'The Public, Literature and the Arts in the Eighteenth Century', in P. Fritz and D. Williams (eds), *The Triumph of Culture: Eighteenth Century Perspectives* (Toronto: A. M. Hakkert, Ltd, 1972), pp. 27–48.

Pointon, M. (ed.), *Pre-Raphaelites Reviewed* (Manchester and New York: Manchester University Press, 1988).

Pye, J., *Patronage of British Art, A Historical Sketch* (London: Longman, Brown, Green and Longmans, 1845).

Raimbach, M.T.S., *Memoirs and Recollections of Abraham Raimbach* (London, 1845).

Raines, R., 'Watteaus and "Watteaus" in England before 1760', *Gazette des Beaux Arts*, 89 (Feb. 1977), pp. 51–64.

Rajnai, M., 'The Norwich School of Etching', in C. Hartley and S. Ridyard (eds), *The Print in England 1790–1930* (Cambridge: Fitzwilliam Museum, 1985), pp. 18–32.

Raven, J., 'The Book Trades', in I. Rivers (ed.), *Books and Their Readers in Eighteenth-century England: new Essays* (London and New York: Leister University Press, 2001), pp. 1–34.

Redford, G., *Art Sales: A History of Sales of Pictures & Other Works of Art* (London: 1888).

Redgrave, R., *A Century of Painters of the English School* (London: Sampson Low, Marston & Company, Ltd, 1890).

Reff, T., 'Some unpublished letters of Degas', *Art Bulletin*, 50:1(March 1968), pp. 87–94.

Reist, I., 'The Fate of the Palais Royal Collection: 1791–1800', R. Panzanelli and M. Preti-Hamard (eds), *La Circulation des Oeuvres d'Art 1789–1848* (Rennes: Presses Universitaire de Rennes, 2007), pp 27–44.

Reitlinger, G., *The Economics of Taste, The Rise and Fall of Picture Prices 1760–1960*, 2 vols (New York: Hacker Art Books, 1982).

Reynolds, Sir J., *Discourses on Art*, ed. R. R. Wark (New Haven, CT and London: Yale University Press, 1959).

Richardson, J., *Essays on the whole Art of Criticism as it relates to Painting* (London: 1719).

Rivers, I. (ed.), *Books and Their Readers in Eighteenth-Century England* (New York: St Martin's Press, 1982).

Roberts, H. E., 'Exhibition and Review: the Periodical Press and the Victorian Art Exhibition System', in J. Shattock and M. Wolff (eds), *The Victorian Periodical Press: Samplings and Soundings* (Toronto: University of Toronto Press, 1982), pp. 79–107.

—, 'Art Reviewing in the Early Nineteenth-Century Art Periodicals', *Victorian Periodicals Newsletter*, 19 (March 1973), pp. 9–20.

Roberts, W., *Memorials of Christie's: A Record of Art Sales from 1766–1896*, 2 vols (London: George Bell & Sons, 1897).

Romein, E. and G. Korevaar, 'Dutch Guilds and the Threat of Public Sales', in De Marchi and Miegroet (eds), *Mapping Markets for Paintings in Europe, 1450–1750* (Turnhout: Brepols, 2006), pp. 165–88.

Rosenthal, M., 'Turner Fires a Gun', in D. Solkin (ed.), *Art on the Line* (London and New Haven, Yale University Press, 2001), pp. 145–55.

Rossetti, D. G., *Letters*, ed. O. Doughty and J. R. Wahls (Oxford: Clarendon Press, 1965–67).

Rossetti, W. M. (ed.), *Pre-Raphaelite Diaries and Letters* (London: Hurst and Blackett, 1900).

Rouquet, J.A., *The State of the Arts in England* (London: J. Nourse, 1755).

The Letters of Peter Paul Rubens, trans. R. S. Magurn (Cambridge, MA: Yale University Press, 1955).

Ruskin, J., *Modern Painters*, 5 vols (Boston, MA: Dana Estes & Company, n. d.).

Sandby, W. *The History of the Royal Academy of Arts from its Foundation in 1768 to the Present Time* (London: Longman, Green, Longman, Roberts, & Green, 1862).

Schibeci, L., 'The London Auction Market and the Commodification of English Taste, 1766–1823' (PhD dissertation, Northwestern University, 1999).

Schiff, G., *Johann Heinrich Fuesslis Milton Galerie* (Zurich: Fretz & Wasmuth, 1963).

Schumpeter, J., *Capitalism, Socialism and Democracy*, 3rd edn (New York: Harper, 1950).

Scott, W. B., *Autobiographical Notes* (New York: Harper, 1892).

Sekora, J., *Luxury: The Concept in Western Thought, Eden to Smollett* (Baltimore, MD: Johns Hopkins University Press, 1977).

Sherburn, G., *The Early Career of Alexander Pope* (Oxford: Clarendon Press, 1934).

Simpson, F., 'Dutch Paintings in England before 1760', *Burlington Magazine*, 95 (February 1953), pp. 39–42.

Singh, R., 'Takeover bidding with Toeholds: The case of the owner's curse', *Review of -Financial Studies*, 11(1998), pp. 679–709.

Smiles, S., *Memoir and Correspondence of the late John Murray*, 2 vols (London: Murray, 1891).

Smith, A., 'Nature Transformed: Leighton, the Nude and the Model', *Frederic Leighton: Antiquity Renaissance Modernity*, ed. T. Barringer and E. Prettejohn (New Haven, CT and London: Yale University Press, 1999), pp. 19–48.

—, *An Inquiry into The Nature and Causes of the Wealth of Nations* (Edinburgh: A. and B. Black, 1872).

Smith, J. T., *Nollekens and His Times*, ed. W. Whitten, 2 vols (London and New York: 1917).

Solkin, D. H. (ed.), *Art on the Line: The Royal Academy Exhibitions at Sumerset House 1780–1836* (New Haven and London: Yale University Press, 2001).

—, *Painting for Money* (New Haven and London: Yale University Press, 1993).

Spatt, H. S., 'The Aesthetics of Editorship: Creating Taste in the Victorian Art World', J. H. Wiener (ed.), *Innovators and Preachers* (London: Greenwood Press, 1985).

Spielman, M. H., 'The Truth About the Grosvenor "Split" An Interview with Sir Coutts Lindsay', *Pall Mall Gazette*,3 November, 1887.

Stabel, P., 'Selling Paintings in Late Medieval Bruges: Marketing Customs and Guild Regulations Compared', in De Marchi and Miegroet (eds), *Mapping Markets for Paintings in Europe, 1450–1750* (Turnhout: Brepols, 2006), pp. 89–103.

Staley, A., 'Post-Pre-Raphaeliteism', *Victorian High Renaissance*, exhibition catalogue (Manchester City Art Galleries; the Minneapolis Institute of Arts; the Brooklyn Museum, New York, 1978–9), pp. 21–31.

Steegmann, J., *The Role of Taste from George I to George IV* (London: MacMillan and Co. Ltd, 1936)

Stephenson, A., 'Leighton and the Shifting Repertoire of "Masculine" Artistic Identity in the Late Victorian Period', in T. Barringer and E. Prettejohn (eds), *Frederic Leighton: Antiquity Renaissance Modernity* (Yale University Press, New Haven & London: 1999), pp. 221–46.

Stephens, F. G., *The Athenaeum* (11 May 1878).

Steuart, J., *Principles of Political Oeconomy*, 2 vols (London: A. Millar and Cadell, 1767; reprinted New York: Augustus M. Kelley).

Strange, R., *Memoirs*, 2 vols (London: E. and C. Dilly, 1775).

Street, I. (ed.), *Ruskin's Principles of Art Criticism* (Chicago, IL: Herbert s. Stone & Company, 1901).

Surtees, V., *Dante Gabriel Rossetti: A Catalogue Raisonne*, 2 vols (Oxford: Clarendon Press, 1971).

Swanson, V., *The Biography and Catalogue Raisonne of the Paintings of Sir Lawrence Alma-Tadema* (London: Garton & Co., 1990).

Taylor, T. (ed.), *Autobiographical Recollections by the late Charles Robert Leslie* (Boston, MA: Ticknor and Fields, 1860).

Tedeschi, M. P., 'How Prints Work: Reproductions, Originals, and their Markets in England, 1840–1900' (PhD dissertation, Northwestern University, 1994).

The Life and Letters of Frederic Shields, ed. E. Mills. (London: Longmans, Green and Co., 1912).

Thompson, F. M. L., *The Rise of Respectable Society* (London: Fontana Press, 1988).

Trawick, L. M., 'Hazlitt, Reynolds, and the Ideal', *Studies in Romanticism*, 4 (1965).

Treble, R., *Great Victorian Pictures* (London: Arts Council, 1978).

Trolander, P., and Z. Tenger, *Sociable Criticism in England 1625–1725* (Newark, DE: University of Delaware Press, 2007).

Turnbull, G., *Treatise on Ancient Painting* (London: A. Millar, 1740).

Tyrwhitt, R. St. J., 'Skilled and Literary Art-Criticism', *Contemporary Review*, 11 (1869), pp. 101–18.

Vermeylen, F., *Painting for the Market: Commercialization of Art in Antwerp's Golden Age* (Turnhout, Belgium: Brepols, n.v., 2003).

Vernon Lee's Letters (London: private publication, 1937).

Vertue, G., *Notebooks* (for 1729), 6 vols, *The Walpole Society*, 22 (1934).

Walpole, H., *Anecdotes of Painting in England*, 3 vols (London: Henry G. Bohn, 1849).

Ward, C., *The Life of John Dryden* (Chapel Hill, NC: University of North Carolina, 1961).

Warren, J. and A. Turpin (eds), *Auctions, Agents and Dealers* (Oxford and London: The Beazley Archive and Archaeopress in association with The Wallace Collection, 2008)

Waterhouse, E., *Dictionary of British 18th Century Painters in Oils and Crayons* (Woodbridge, Suffolk: Antique Collectors' Club, Ltd, 1981).

—, E., *Painting in England 1530–1790* (London and Baltimore, MD: Penguin Books, Ltd, 1953).

Wedmore, F. (ed.), *Rembrandt: His Life, His work and His Time* (London: Heinemann, 1894).

—, 'My Few Things', *The Art Journal* 46 (January 1894), pp. 6–10.

—, *Etching in England* (London, George Bell and Sons, 1895).

Weinreb B., and C. Hibbert (eds), *London Encyclopedia* (New York: St Martin's Press, 1983).

White, C. and H. White, *Canvases and Careers: Institutional Changes in the French Painting World* (Chicago, IL: University of Chicago Press, 1965).

Whitley, W. T., *Art in England*, 2 vols (New York: Hacker Art Books, 1973).

—, *Artists and Their Friends in England 1700–1790*, 2 vols (London & Boston, MA: The Medici Society, 1938).

Wilde, O., *The Picture of Dorian Gray*, ed. P. Ackroyd (Harmondsworth, England: Penguin, 1985).

Wiles, R. M., 'Provincial Culture in Early Georgian England', Fritz and William (eds), *The Triumph of Culture: Eighteenth Century Perspectives* (Toronto: A. M. Hakkert Ltd, 1972), pp. 49–68.

Williams, R., *Culture and Society 1780–1950* (New York: Columbia University Press, 1983).

Wilson, J. C., 'The Participation of Painters in the Bruges' "Pandt" Market, 1512–1550', *Burlington Magazine*, 125 (August 1983), pp. 476–9.

Wind, E., 'The Revolution of History Painting', *Journal of the Warburg and Courtauld Institute*, II (1938/9), pp. 116–27.

Winstanley, Thomas, *Observations on the Arts* (Liverpool: W. Wales, 1828).

Wittkower, R., 'The Artist', in J. Clifford (ed.), *Man versus Society in Eighteenth-Century Britain* (Cambridge: Cambridge University Press 1968), pp. 70–84.

Wolfthal, D., *The Beginning of Netherlandish Canvas Painting: 1400–1530* (Cambridge: Cambridge University Press, 1989).

Wood, C., *Dictionary of Victorian Painters* (Woodbridge, Suffolk: The Antique Collectors' Club, 1995).

—, *Victorian Painting* (Boston, New York, London: Little, Brown and Company, 1999).

Wood, P., 'Commodity', R. S. Nelson and R. Shiff (eds), *Critical Terms for Art History* (Chicago, IL: University of Chicago Press, 1966), pp. 257–80.

Wrigley, E. A., 'Urban Growth and Agricultural Change: England and the Continent in the Early Modern Period', *Journal of Interdisciplinary History*, 15, pp. 683–728.

Wroth, W., F.S.A., *The London Pleasure Gardens of the Eighteenth Century* (London: MacMillan and Co., Ltd, 1896), pp. 287–326.

Yeldham, C., *Women Artist in Nineteenth-Century France and England* (New York: Garland: 1984).

INDEX

www.ingramcontent.com/pod-product-compliance
Ingram Content Group UK Ltd.
Pitfield, Milton Keynes, MK11 3LW, UK
UKHW010957180926
475701UK00004B/423
* 9 7 8 1 1 3 8 6 6 1 3 0 1 *